The Lynching of Emmett Till

The American South Series

Edward L. Ayers, Editor

The LYNCHING of EMMETT TILL

A Documentary Narrative

Edited by Christopher Metress

University of Virginia Press

Charlottesville and London

The University of Virginia Press
© 2002 by the Rector and Visitors of the University of Virginia
All rights reserved
Printed in the United States of America on acid-free paper
First published 2002

9 8 7 6 5 4 3 2 1

Library of Congress Cataloging-in-Publication Data
The Lynching of Emmett Till : a documentary narrative / edited by
  Christopher Metress.
      p.   cm. — (the American South series)
  Includes bibliographical references and index.
  ISBN 0-8139-2121-X (alk. paper) — ISBN 0-8139-2122-8 (pbk. : alk. paper)
      1. Till, Emmett, 1941–1955. 2. Mississippi—Race relations—Sources.
  3. Lynching—Mississippi—History—20th century—Sources. 4. African
  Americans—Crimes against—Mississippi—History—20th century—
  Sources. 5. Racism—Mississippi—History—20th century—Sources.
  6. Trials (Murder)—Mississippi. 7. Milam, J. W. —Trials, litigation, etc.
  I. Metress, Christopher. II. Series.
    F350.N4 L96 2002
    305.8′00975—dc21

                                                        2002002337

Contents

2 The Trial

3 Post-Trial Reactions and Assessments

4 Searching for the Truth

Acknowledgments

A book six years in the making owes a debt of gratitude to more people than it is possible to name here. The following list represents the most visible recipients of my gratitude.

I must first thank a long line of Samford University undergraduates who helped to prepare this manuscript: Caroline Woolridge, Anna Ogle, Adam Plant, Lisa Wethman, Cathlena Martin, John Harkey, Dana Dews, and Joi Tribble. A special thanks must go to Jay Woods, my first research assistant, whose ability to track down references and addresses helped to get this project underway and, I hope, prepared him for a pretty good run at law school. I also owe my deepest thanks to the two Staceys—Stacey Roberson and Stacey Cowan—students who developed an unmatched passion for this project. Their enthusiasm sometimes surpassed mine, often shaming me into working all the harder just to keep up with them. Nearly half the material included in this book was either researched or prepared by them. I cannot imagine having worked without the assistance of my two "private eyes."

In addition, I must thank Jim Netherton, Joe Lewis, Roderick Davis, and the Samford University Committee on Academic Affairs for approving a faculty development grant that allowed me to travel to collections and offset the costs of preparing this book. I also received additional funding from the James O. and Alice F. Cole Foundation, and I would like to thank Fred Ashe of Birmingham-Southern College for helping me to secure this grant. To the staff of the Davis Library at Samford (Sandy Fox, Bob Sharp, Brooke Becker, Olivia Woods, Elizabeth Wells, and all the others), I appreciate your support throughout the project. Above all, I must give special thanks to Cheryl Cecil in Interlibrary Loan. Without Cheryl's tireless energy, boundless good cheer, and endless patience, this book would have been impossible to complete. She never tired of filling my request for materials, even when I kept ordering the same microfilms over and over again because I hadn't researched them correctly the first time. No amount of thanks can be enough. I promise the next project won't be so demanding.

A grant from the National Endowment for the Humanities allowed me to attend a Summer Seminar at the DuBois Institute for African American Studies in the fall of 1995. Several participants, in particular Glenn Eskew, John Dittmer, and Bill Moore, encouraged me to expand the scope of my project and recommended texts and contacts. Fortunately, my proposal came into the able hands of Boyd Zenner at the University of Virginia Press. Boyd not only embraced the idea but also suggested ways to make this anthology more inclusive and attractive, and its final form owes much to her vision. For sticking with me over the last four years as my concentration waxed and waned—and for knowing when to push gently and not so gently during many an eleventh hour—I extend my deepest gratitude.

Because so much of this project rests on finding copyright holders and securing permission rights, I could not have completed this anthology without the expertise of many people, among them Alan Wald, Bridget Bower, Elva Griffith, Deborah Rouse, Allida Black, and Anne Lipscomb Webster. For helping me to evaluate, select, and secure many of the photo images for this work, I extend my deepest appreciation to Claude Jones of the *Memphis Commercial Appeal.* I also must thank those permission holders who waived their usual fees in support of this project, especially the *Chicago Defender,* the *Daily Worker,* the *Delta Democrat-Times,* the *Memphis Commercial Appeal,* the *Cleveland Call and Post,* and the *Washington Afro-American,* as well as Lewis Nordan, Bob Dylan, June Akers Seese, Sam Cornish, Julius Thompson, Lesley Himes, and Barbara Epstein. A special note of thanks must go to Martha Hunt Huie, one of the first to throw her support behind this anthology. Now that this book is finished, I look forward to working on some of the other projects we have discussed.

Finally, several friends and colleagues read this manuscript in progress. I thank Amanda Moberg, a former student, for taking a break from her legal studies to give me a general reader's response to the first part of this work. To Adam Meyer, Steven Epley, and Michael Kreyling, I appreciate your helpful comments and input. And a final thanks to Patrick and Josie Metress, the first for offering valuable rewrites and ongoing encouragement, the second for reminding me repeatedly that "thinking about it" is not always enough.

On August 24, 1955, Emmett Till, a fourteen-year-old black boy from Chicago, entered a rural grocery store in the small hamlet of Money, Mississippi. Because the young boy had been bragging about his friendships with white people up north, his southern cousins had dared him to go into the grocery and say something to the white woman working the register. Emmett accepted their challenge; moments later he was at the counter, set on purchasing two cents worth of bubble gum. What he did or said next will never be known for certain, but whatever passed between these two strangers from two very different worlds set off a chain reaction that would forever change the way we talk about race in America.

The Lynching of Emmett Till

Introduction
The Shifting Grounds of History and Memory

When I first conceived of this anthology, I had in mind a structure completely different from the one now framed in the table of contents. My intent was to begin with a lengthy introduction that would establish the context within which Emmett Till's murder took place. It is August 1955. Fifteen months have passed since the Supreme Court decision in *Brown v. Board of Education,* and the nascent stirrings of massive resistance are rumbling across the South. For a year now, Citizens' Councils have been meeting throughout Mississippi, and just a few months before young Till arrives in the small hamlet of Money, the Reverend George W. Lee, an NAACP activist from nearby Belzoni, is shot dead in his car for seeking to register local blacks for an upcoming election. The coroner's report lists the cause of death as a car accident—despite the presence of shotgun pellets throughout the automobile—and Lee's murderers escape prosecution. On the other hand, nearly a decade has passed since African American soldiers returned home from World War II. Although not mobilized in the way they would be later in the decade, civil rights groups, many led by these former soldiers, are beginning to strengthen their grassroots organizations in cities and towns throughout the nation, and especially in the South. One such group, the Montgomery Improvement Association in Alabama, is poised to launch the first great mass protest of the civil rights movement, and it will get its chance in late November when a quiet seamstress refuses to give up her seat to a white man in a Montgomery city bus. In a larger context, America is firmly entrenched in the Cold War. American democracy and Soviet communism are the two competing ideologies in a world that seems up for political grabs. The Red Scare is a hard reality for many Americans, and communism—whether in the guise of a Soviet spy, a leftist politician, or an agitating NAACP lawyer—is to be opposed at every turn. For other Americans, however, the internal enemies of democracy are on the political right:

1

segregationists whose acts of violent racism give aid and comfort to a political and military enemy trying to persuade the nations of the Third World (and their colored populations) that democracy is an illusion and communism the only true promise of brotherhood and equality.

After establishing this context—so the original plan went—I would then move on to Emmett Till himself. I would begin with some background about his life in Chicago and why he decided to spend two weeks of his summer visiting his extended family in the Mississippi Delta. I would then relate what happened on August 24, 1955, when young Emmett entered the Bryant Grocery in Money, giving the facts where I could and noting those facts that were in question, all the while drawing judgments on the veracity of competing accounts and interpretations. This done, I could then move on to the story of the trial, telling about who testified on what day, what they testified to and, in the end, who appeared to be speaking the truth. Here, the introduction would cover how it took a day and a half to seat the jury; how the judge recessed the trial on the second day so the prosecution could seek out missing witnesses who had only recently come to its attention; how on that very same day Mrs. Mamie Till Bradley and Democratic congressman Charles Diggs of Michigan arrived at the trial and caused a sensation; how on day three Mose Wright, Emmett's uncle, defied three hundred years of tradition and testified against a white man in court; how the next day Carolyn Bryant, recipient of the alleged "wolf-whistle," gave her testimony, but only after the jury had been removed by the judge because what she had to say was not deemed relevant to the case; and, finally, how on day five of the trial the jury took just sixty-seven minutes to reach a verdict of not guilty, and only that long because, as one jury member put it, they had taken time to have a cola before returning to the courtroom.

My introduction done, the anthology would begin. First, there would be responses to the verdict, both pro and con. After this, a selection of works by investigative journalists who attempted to get at the truth of the case, highlighted by the first reprinting in more than forty years of William Bradford Huie's infamous articles from *Look* magazine. Next, there was the heart of the anthology: a generous sampling of memoirs and literary representations that would reflect how the Till lynching had worked its way into what I was calling, at the time, the "American imagination" (the working title of the collection was "Emmett Till and the American Imagination: An Anthology").

The purpose behind this structure was a modest one. Emmett Till, it has often been claimed, was the spark that set off the civil rights movement. When the producers of the documentary *Eyes on the Prize* had to select an event to mark the beginning of the movement, they chose not Rosa Parks's protest but, tellingly, Emmett Till's murder. A host of other sources—interviews, autobiographies, oral histories, poems, and novels—bear testament to the assertion that Till's lynching was a primal event for many Americans, a moment when the veil was rent and the full extent of the nation's racial problems exposed for all to see. In particular, many young African Americans were profoundly changed by the lynching, and future activists such as Anne Moody, Eldridge Cleaver, and Cleveland Sellers marked Till's murder as a turning point in their lives. According to the Democratic congressman from Georgia and civil rights veteran John Lewis, Till's lynching "galvanized the country. A lot of us young black students in the South later on, we weren't sitting in just for ourselves—we were sitting in for Emmett Till. We went on Freedom Rides for Emmett Till." By all accounts, the trial of Till's murderers was a media frenzy—the O. J. Simpson trial of its day, if you will. More than one hundred press representatives attended the trial—including reporters from foreign wire services—and all three networks had footage flown in daily from the tiny town of Sumner. Murray Kempton, John Popham, Dan Wakefield, John Herbers, James Hicks, John Chancellor, and a young David Halberstam were just a few of the reporters in attendance. More than forty years after the trial, in a cover story on twentieth-century crimes that defined their respective decades, *U.S. News and World Report* chose the Till murder to represent the 1950s. It was, as Halberstam was to recall later, "the first great media event of the civil rights movement."

Its impact notwithstanding, only one comprehensive study of the case was available for general readers (Stephen J. Whitfield's 1988 *A Death in the Delta: The Story of Emmett Till*), and certainly no one had produced an anthology that traced the full extent of the lynching's influence on the American imagination. My purpose, then, was threefold: provide an introduction giving a full historical account of the murder and trial; collect, for the first time in one place, many of the significant cultural and literary texts about the case; and, finally, via the historical introduction and selected readings, keep alive for a new generation of readers the pivotal importance of Emmett Till's lynching and its enduring presence in our collective memory.

As I went deeper into my research, however, a new story began to emerge, one not so much centered on a particular moment in history as concerned about the relationship between memory and history. It was this story, along with the story of Emmett Till, that began to pull my anthology in a different direction and, eventually, demanded that I scratch my original concept and put something else in its place. I had imagined, as it were, that I would put my voice first as a kind of aid to my readers because, I assumed, only after they understood the details of the case and the context surrounding it would they be able to appreciate the anthology itself. I found myself, inevitably, distilling information, sifting and sorting facts, distinguishing between false testimonies and true declarations. I was—I kept telling myself—merely doing the work of a good historian.

The assumption I was working under—but did not recognize until late in the process—was that I was writing my introduction because I thought I needed a "history" to preface what for the most part was an anthology of "memory." That history, of course, would not answer all questions about the case. Too much of what happened in 1955 will remain forever unknown. What, exactly, did Emmett Till say in the grocery store to Carolyn Bryant? Who, if not Carolyn, told Roy Bryant about the incident? How many men showed up that night at Mose Wright's cabin (and was it only men)? Why, when it appears at first that they did not intend to harm him, did Bryant and Milam end up torturing and killing Till? Did others help them? If so, were there black men involved in the murder? What role did they play and why? My introduction could not hope to answer these questions fully, but nonetheless it would still serve as a sort of polestar for my readers so that—when needed—they might catch their historical bearings as they sampled their way through the anthology. Otherwise, history—what had really happened—and memory—what others recall had happened, and perhaps falsely—might get confused as readers tried to sort out truth from fiction in this particular case.

Let me give an example. In the opening stanza to "The Death of Emmett Till," Bob Dylan claims that he will sing of a "boy's dreadful tragedy I can still remember well / The color of his skin was black and his name was Emmett Till." After recounting the details of Till's murder—some of which he doesn't seem to remember too well—Dylan summarizes the trial:

> And then to stop the United States of yelling for a trial,
> Two brothers they confessed that they had killed poor Emmett Till.
> But on the jury there were men who helped the brothers commit this awful crime,
> And so this trial was a mockery, but nobody seemed to mind.

This account of the trial contains several "misrememberings" that can only be classified as errors. Yes, Bryant and Milam confessed to the crime, but they did so *after* the trial was over, not before. And there is absolutely no evidence that any of the jury members helped "the brothers" (actually half-brothers) commit the crime. Was the trial of mockery of justice? Perhaps so. But not for the reasons that Dylan suggests.

My intended introduction would have given the rudimentary facts about the case and allowed readers to perceive these errors for what they truly were. Otherwise, without the right background, history might fall prey to Dylan's false memory. And there were plenty of false memories out there—and not just in the lyrics of a young protest singer with perhaps more ideology than insight. In "Afterimages," Audre Lorde, a poet with a well-deserved reputation for brutal honesty and self-examination, painfully mines her own memories of how in "Jackson, Mississippi," Emmett Till whistled at a "white girl [who] passed him in the street" and as a result was murdered and tossed into "the midnight waters of the Pearl [River]." Moreover, she recalls seeing photos of Till in which she spies a "gash across the dead boy's loins," remembering how his murderers "ripped his eyes out his sex his tongue / and flung him to the Pearl weighed with stone." Finally, these same murderers later that night

[...] took their aroused honor
back to Jackson
and celebrated in a whorehouse
the double ritual of white manhood
confirmed.

The errors here are numerous. Till was not murdered in Jackson; after he was murdered, he was thrown into the Tallahatchie River, not the Pearl; he wasn't whistling at a woman on the street; there was never any evidence he had been castrated (though this detail has appeared in other recollections of the event); and, finally, there was never any suggestion that either Bryant or Milam capped off their evening by celebrating in a whorehouse.

While poets and songwriters often employ "poetic license," how is one to know that such writers are exercising that license unless one knows the liberties that are being taken in the first place? My introduction, so I assumed, would give my readers the proper knowledge to make such judgments, and to evaluate not just poets and songwriters, but others writing in genres that allowed a lot less room for license. For instance, in a 1987 memoir entitled "Memories of the Mississippi Delta" published in the *Michigan Quarterly Review,* Endesha Ida Mae Holland opens her essay by proclaiming:

The region of the country where I was born and raised, the Mississippi Delta, is a testament to African American inferiority. My town is famous for the infamous "wolf-whistle." In the mid-1950s, a young boy, Emmett Till, was standing on the corner with a couple of his friends. A White woman passed and claimed that young Till had whistled at her. Later that night, a mob of White men took the Black Chicago youth back to the river. They put a millstone around his neck, they cut his penis off and stuck it in his mouth and then lowered him into his watery grave. That's the town I'm from.

Again, errors abound here as memory seems to fail in the service of truth. Till was not standing on a corner when the alleged offense occurred; a mob never went after him; he was abducted three days after his indiscretion, not "later that night"; and, finally, he was never castrated. With each passing example of this conflict between true history and specious memory, the need for a strong and clear introduction seemed to grow.

I then came across two passages that changed my mind. The first was from Bob Blauner's superb collection of interviews entitled *Black Lives, White Lives: Three Decades of Race Relations in America* (1989). One of the book's interviewees is Howard Spence, a Mississippi native who, after living for many years in Chicago, returned home following World War II and became active in the grassroots movement for civil rights. As an NAACP field secretary, Spence played a pivotal role in investigating the Till case for Medgar Evers, who was at the time secretary of the Mississippi NAACP. In his recollection of those days, Spence is guilty of several misrememberings (for instance, he recalls Till as being taken out of Lennox, not Money). But then he offers a detail I had not come across in sixteen months of research, a memory so unbelievable on the surface that it distinguished itself from all other memories. According to Spence, "they [it is not clear whether he means whites or blacks] began to search the rivers; they began to search from place to place; they got everybody together. And as a result he [Till] was found in the Tallahatchie River. When they brought him to Greenwood, what we had formerly thought was a bullet hole—it was explained to us that it was a bit that had been drilled through the child's head. This is a fact—I'm only talking facts."

Here was a "fact" like no fact I had encountered before in my research. The claim was so outrageous I simply wrote it off as having no basis in reality. This was not another memory about castration that once again managed, somehow, without any evidence, to work its way into a part of the collective memory. This was an altogether different claim and, as it was unsubstantiated by either evidence or rumor, I merely made a note of it and placed it in my "Mistakes" file.

And then a few months later I was working through back issues of the *Washington Afro-American,* one of the half-dozen or so black papers that devoted extensive coverage to the case. I was almost finished when I came across an "open letter" dated November 19, 1955, from James Hicks to Attorney General Herbert Brownell and FBI Director J. Edgar Hoover. In this letter (included in this volume) Hicks, who covered the Till trial for the National News Association, was telling these two government officials how to find new evidence about the murder, evidence that would allow the federal government to claim jurisdiction and open up a new prosecution of Milam and Bryant. After giving a series of door-to-door directions, Hicks pleads with Brownell and Hoover to send agents to talk with Leroy "Too Tight" Collins, a black man whom Hicks claims witnessed the murder. Because Collins may be in hiding and hard to find, Hicks suggests that government agents ask the cotton pickers at Reid's Café what "Too Tight" has said about the murder: "Listen to them tell how Too Tight boasts that the hole in the Till boy's head was not a bullet hole, but a hole drilled in his head with a brace and bit by one of the white men."

I could not at first remember where I had heard this "fact" before, but a quick check of my "Mistakes" file led me back to Spence. It's not that all of sudden I now believed him. Instead, Spence's memory of the event came to have a different status for me. And it was here that Till's story became a story about the relationship between memory and history, and the structure of this documentary anthology had to change.

Why, I asked myself, did I dismiss Spence's memory outright the first time I read about it? The answer seemed simple: the memory had no support. Did Spence think the memory was true? Of course he did. According to him, he was "only talking facts." But his facts didn't jibe with anything I had read about the case. Were these facts part of his memory? Certainly. But they weren't part of "history." However, discovering Hicks's letter changed, for me at least, the standing of Spence's memory. It now matched with something else I had read, and because it did it now was possible, just possible, that it might be true. At the least, I had to consider the possibility. "Too Tight" Collins told his story to the cotton pickers in Reid's Café in 1955. Spence's interview was given in 1968. As an NAACP investigator, Spence certainly could have heard the story firsthand from one of the cotton pickers and remembered it correctly after all these years. Spence may have even been in the café that evening. Collins, however, never testified in court. When the trial date arrived, he could not be found. Later, when he was found, he refused to cooperate. Other witnesses did come forward to testify. For instance, an eighteen-year-old black boy, Willie Reed, testified in court that he saw four white men and three black men driving in Milam's pickup the morning of the murder, and he watched as that pickup entered a barn on a piece of property owned by Milam's brother Leslie. Later, Reed heard muffled cries coming from within the barn and then saw Milam walk out of the barn wearing a pistol. If Spence had offered any of these details in his recollection—and not said anything about a drill hole—I would have been more likely to judge his memories as closer to the truth, as more "historical." I could have taken his memories, compared them to news accounts of the trial, seen that his recollection was confirmed by Reed's testimony, and then concluded that Spence was remembering "history" and not merely following the vagaries of an eccentric and susceptible "memory." However, if Hicks was right, Collins did actually testify. Not before a jury of white men in a court of law—that is true—but certainly among a jury of his peers in a local café. Hicks's letter, then, was akin to a reporter's summary of the trial—evidence of events that had taken place. Spence's memory suddenly seemed more historical than when it was first encountered in my research.

I then went on to consider the following scenario. What if Collins had testified at the official trial? As readers of this anthology will soon learn, if Collins had testified to everything he knew about the case, Emmett Till's death would not be remembered in the same way. The specific point of concern here, of course, is the story of the drill hole in the boy's head. Had Collins testified to this extraordinary fact, Spence's 1968 account would surely not have been the first recollection of it. Collins's story would have immediately seared itself into the collective memory and been repeated over and over again down through the years. One can imagine it taking on the status of *Jet* magazine's horrifying photo of Till's battered corpse lying in state during the young boy's funeral in Chicago. A brutal and senseless murder would have become, in our recollections, an even more appalling crime.

Whether Collins's story is true or not is important—nothing that is true is unimportant—but it is not central to the point I am making. Had his story been widely circulated during the trial or immediately afterwards, it would have undoubtedly influenced our collective memory of the murder. Whether true or false, it would have appeared in memoirs and oral histories, poems and songs, plays and novels. Recall how Till's lynching is portrayed in Lorde's poem and Holland's memoir. Both accounts "remember" that Till was castrated. Somewhere along the line, this image entered into the collective memory and stuck. It was never mentioned at the trial. No major piece of investigative journalism after the trial proposes such an idea. Nonetheless, the story was circulated in the community. In a 1995 memoir, Dr. Walter Trumbull, founder of the Harlem Boy's Choir, remembers as much. "As the story goes," Trumbull writes, "the fourteen-year-old boy came down from Chicago to visit his relatives in Money, Mississippi, and supposedly whistled at a white woman in August 1955. He was shot in the head and thrown in the river with a cotton gin fan tied around his neck. In some versions of the story, he was found with his cut-off penis stuffed in his mouth." Here is a detail that is reaffirmed again and again in "some versions of the story." Thus, in one sense, the story is "true" if we ask ourselves whether or not it has a place in the collective memory of Till's murder. And yet, however much it may be part of that collective memory, it is not "true" in the historical sense. A thoughtful and discerning historical introduction would make this clear and thereby delineate the necessary distinction between history and memory.

Since Collins's story was never entered into any official, or even unofficial, version of events (except, of course, in Hicks's letter), it was not—like the castration stories—part of the material I had to weigh in my assessment of what really happened to Emmett Till. In choosing not to testify—and with very good reason, one can imagine—Collins chose not to put the drill hole story into circulation. Thus, when I first read about it forty years later in Spence's interview, the story looked absurd, a false memory that could be easily dismissed as untrue. But when I discovered information that corroborated the story, Spence's recollection had to be reevaluated. Perhaps it was true, and thereby closer to history than to memory. And yet, the only reason I was reevaluating Spence's memory was because I had come across another memory of the drill hole story (in Hicks's letter). But wasn't Hicks merely recounting the memories of the men in Reid's Café, who were in turn bearing witness to another man's memory (Collins)? One memory standing alone looked absurd. But add to that another memory and it looked less absurd. Toss in a few more memories and it might begin to look like history.

Here, finally, was what I had to admit. Prepared to write an introduction that would give my readers a history of the case before launching them into my collection of memories, I was working under the misguided assumption that it was best to have an account of what had truly happened before one got all entangled in memories of what people remembered about what had happened, memories which—although they would underscore the continuing impact of Till's murder on the American imagination—could distort rather than illuminate the truth. In writing this introductory history, I soon realized, I would be betraying the process of how we determine what history is and how it comes to have meaning for us, especially in the case of Emmett Till. I also realized I was falling prey to the temptation to think of memory as different from history. "Memory" is unstable, prone to the vagaries of self-interest, susceptible to error with the passage of time and the shifting popular perceptions of historical events. "History," on the other hand, is more objective, a detached assessment that, while still prone to error, subjects itself to more demanding rules of evidence. There is, of course, some truth to this, but to insist on such a fierce distinction between memory and history is to overlook the more intimate relationship between the two perspectives. In trying to determine what happened in the Till case—what the young boy might have said to Carolyn Bryant, who might have told Roy Bryant about the alleged offense, how many men might have been involved in Till's murder—I had memory as my main source of evidence. Some of these memories came in the form of court testimonies, others in news articles, still others in post-trial interviews, exposés, and confessions. Yes, many of these memories looked awfully suspicious, but they looked suspicious only when juxtaposed with other memories. Memory, then, seemed to be both a threat to and a foundation for the very history I was trying to write. And it would be out of those memories—unstable, self-interested, and susceptible to error—that I would try to build the historical record—stable, disinterested, and a guard against error. Memory, I was forced to conclude, does not come after history. It is, instead, the very stuff of history, the narrative material out of which history emerges.

To shape my anthology around a structure that placed history first and memory second seemed to betray this realization. Worse yet, it concealed the fact that any historical understanding of what happened to Emmett Till was a result of wrestling with many different memories. It seemed important, then, to rethink the beginning of the collection to illustrate, rather than to conceal, this point. As a consequence of this new perspective, the historical introduction has been dropped in favor of something quite different. In place of this introduction— where I had planned to make the necessary distinctions for my readers—I decided to step back, let the primary texts speak for themselves and, as much as possible, allow the competing versions of memory to be presented to readers for their own evaluation. In the opening chapter, I have had to interject myself just a bit into the field of primary texts (newspaper accounts and editorials) simply for reasons of clarity. The first chapter seeks to tell the story of the discovery of Till's murder and the weeks leading up to the indictments of Milam and Bryant. To make this narrative flow smoothly, I have had to provide transitional comments between the selected texts. Although I tried to avoid editorializing in these passages (and I hope to be forgiven for pointing out occasional details I don't want readers to miss), I realize there is no way for me to step back fully from the process and let the texts speak completely for themselves. The fact that I am choosing the selections testifies to my presence in this chapter—and in the whole anthology, for that matter. Still, I have tried to resist the impulse to "do history" here, if by doing history we mean sifting and evaluating sources for accuracy. Instead, I want to use the primary texts to recreate a narrative that places before the reader the experiences of those who were living through the events and seeking, at the same time, to understand them.

In the second chapter, which tells the story of the trial, I am able to step back more fully. Again, I am present in the selection of the texts and in the brief introductory comments that preface the selections, but I have not tried to determine what readers should think about the testimonies given at the trial and the nature of the proceedings. I have, wherever possible, given competing accounts of the testimony and juxtaposed rival evaluations of the proceedings. My original intention would have taken me in a different direction. Now, instead of doing the work for the reader, I encourage the reader to think about what is true and not true in the historical record. Whose testimony (or memory) is most reliable? Where do some testimonies (or memories) break down? Do they break down because of internal contradictions or only in relation to other testimonies (or memories) that challenge them? Unfortunately, no transcript of the trial exists, and so we will never know fully or exactly what was said in court. This absence has its own advantages, however, because it recreates for us the experience of most people who were trying to understand the truth about what happened in Money. Only 280 or so people had access to the trial each day. Everyone else had to arrive at his or her own conclusions by reading the papers (there were, of course, radio and television reports, but no record of either medium exists as a matter of public record). Unfortunately, it is not possible to give a complete representation of all the news accounts of the trial. Permission costs for reproducing some of the accounts are prohibitive, and space limitations restrict the scope of representation. Still, I have tried, as best I could, to offer a fair and representative sampling of how this trial was covered in a variety of news outlets (northern and southern, white and black, conservative and liberal).

So, instead of beginning this book *with* a history, I have anthologized, to a greater extent than I had originally intended, the materials *of* history. Some readers may find this frustrating when facts get repeated, then undermined, then repeated again, and all without any substantial judgment being passed on them. Moreover, patently obvious distortions of the truth, as well as distasteful prejudices, are given voice but are not censured. In doing this, I am not seeking to frustrate or antagonize. Rather, I am trying to provide a sample of the materials we have for determining not only what happened to Emmett Till but also what his legacy means. There is, of course, no unanimity on either front here, but that is because the available materials do not allow for a consensus on the facts, and they most certainly do not allow for a consensus on the larger meaning of the Till's lynching.

What the opening chapters now allow for—and what my original structure precluded—is a more intimate look at the relationship between history and memory. History emerges from and flows through memory. Memory helps to shape history but then is reshaped by the history that evolves out of many competing memories. I hope this will be one of the experiences my anthology recreates for the reader, and not just in the opening chapters. Instead of reading a Gwendolyn Brooks poem, an Eldridge Cleaver essay, or a John Edgar Wideman memoir in relation to a historical introduction where judgments have already been passed on the facts of the case, I hope that readers will be able to place these works in relation to a 1955 editorial in the *Jackson Daily News,* a transcription of court testimony from the *Daily Worker,* or a letter to the editor of the *Chicago Defender.*

Conceived as an anthology of "history *and* memory," this collection now strives to be something more. Is it a "history *of* memory"? Perhaps, but only if by history we no longer mean an evaluation of material but instead a sort of chronological ordering of memories. The phrase is provocative, but does not suffice. If we turn the terms around, could we call this collection a "memory of history"? Perhaps, but the exact meaning of this phrase escapes me. In the end, I have settled on the word "narrative"—a phenomenon common to both history and memory—to define what I set out to accomplish in this collection. As a "documentary narrative," this collection endeavors to be both an accumulation of narratives about the lynching of Emmett Till *and* a documentary that in itself strives to tell a larger story. On the one hand, this collection gathers together narratives (news articles, editorials, poems, songs, interviews, essays, and memoirs) about one of the most important events in American history. As such, it explores not only the impact of the lynching during its day but also the enduring presence of the crime in the cultural and literary imagination of this country. On the other hand, this documentary tells a larger narrative, one not so much about Emmett Till as about ourselves. It is a tale about how we come to know what we know, and how we accept that knowledge as the truth; how we evaluate what we believe we know, and how we strive in response to know more; how we seek to remember what we know, and how soon we may forget it. It is also a tale about how ideas and images and remembrances enter into the collective memory and pass out again; how that ever-shifting collective memory moves among us and within us to form what we know and believe. Finally, it is a tale about the power of narrative itself—about how we possess the strength to shape our stories, but they, in turn, possess as well the strength to reshape us.

A note concerning the texts in this anthology. I have faithfully transcribed the documents collected here, except for the following changes: obvious typographical errors (such as "than" for "that") have been silently corrected; when clarity demands it, punctuation has been adjusted and noted with the addition of square brackets; other emendations in square brackets have occasionally been inserted to promote clarity; the correct spelling of a proper name has been added in square brackets the first time a document misspells it, but not thereafter. Any omissions on my part have been indicated by the notation [. . .]; all other ellipses are in the original documents.

Chapter 1 *Discovery and Indictment*

J. W. Milam and Roy Bryant abducted Emmett Till from the home of his uncle, Mose Wright, at 2:00 A.M. Sunday morning, August 28. When Till did not return within a few hours, Elizabeth Wright, Mose's wife, called her cousin Crosby Smith, who then reported the abduction to Leflore County sheriff George Smith in Greenwood. On Monday, less than forty-eight hours after the abduction, Sheriff Smith arrested Milam and Bryant on kidnapping charges.

Although the *Jackson Daily News* reported on Monday that Bryant was being held in connection with the kidnapping of a "negro youth" from Chicago, it was not until charges were pressed that the story broke in several Mississippi papers. The Greenville *Delta Democrat-Times,* edited by Hodding Carter, a left-of-center moderate who often championed unpopular causes in defense of racial progress in the South, pulled a brief report off the United Press wire and ran it on the front page.

Two White Men Charged with Kidnaping Negro
Delta Democrat-Times, 30 August 1955

Greenwood, Miss. (UP) — Two white men charged with kidnaping a 15-year-old Chicago Negro because they claimed he insulted the wife of one of the men claimed today they released the missing boy unharmed.

Sheriff George Smith said Roy Bryant, a storekeeper in nearby Money community, and his half-brother, J. W. Nilan [Milam], were held on kidnap charges in the mysterious disappearance of Emmett Till of Chicago. They were arrested yesterday.

Smith said Till's whereabouts was the "$64 question."

Smith said he planned to question Bryant's wife, allegedly insulted by Till in Bryant's small store Saturday. He said there was "nothing new" to indicate where the boy might be.

It was possible that relatives of Till were hiding him out of fear for the youth's safety, Smith said, or had sent him back to Chicago. He said he "couldn't say" if the boy had been harmed.

The Bryants were said to have become offended when young Till waved to the woman and said "goodbye" when he left the store.

Witnesses said Mrs. Bryant identified the boy as "the one." The group then drove away with him. Smith said Bryant and Mila[m] claimed that later they found out he was not "the one" who allegedly insulted Mrs. Bryant, and that Till then was released.

Several Negro youths, all under 16, were reported to have been with Till in the store and were said to have forced him to leave the store for being "rowdy."

Another local paper, the *Jackson Advocate,* a small-circulation African American weekly, ran a more detailed story a few days later. The *Advocate's* story was filed early Wednesday morning, only a few hours before Till's body was found in the Tallahatchie River by Robert Hodges, a seventeen-year-old white boy. Note that the *Advocate* reports three white men present at the Wright cabin on Sunday morning. Although Milam and Bryant later confessed to the crime and insisted they were the only two men involved in the abduction and murder, other eyewitness accounts—especially those reported in the African American press—contradicted their testimony. This *Advocate* article marks the first suggestion that more individuals were involved in the abduction than either Milam or Bryant let on.

Parents and Relatives Keep Silent in Case of Boy Charged with Ugly Remarks to Storekeeper[']s Wife
Jackson Advocate, 3 September 1955

Greenwood, Miss. Aug. 31 — The parents and relatives of a 14-year-old Negro boy, abducted by three white men from the home of his uncle at nearby Money early this week, after he had been accused of making "ugly remarks" to the wife of a white storekeeper, were continuing their silence in regard to the incident as far as could be learned here early Wednesday.

The youth, Emmitt [Emmett] Louis Till, of 6427 St. Lawrence Street, in Chicago, Illinois was taken from the home of his Uncle Mose Wright with whom he was spending a summer vacation. A car containing three white men went to the Wright home Monday, where two of them entered the house and came out with the boy. When the uncle asked where they were taking him, according to reports, the reply was, nowhere if he is not the right one.

Shortly after the abduction Sheriff George W. Smith arrested storekeeper Roy Bryant, and later arrested J. W. Milam, his half-brother, both of whom are reportedly being held pending finding of the boy.

According to reports the boy, in company with two other teenage youths[,] waved and said "goodbye" to the storekeepers wife when they left the store after making some purchases last Saturday.

The sheriff is reported as having expressed the fear that the boy had been subjected to foul play by his abductors.

However, there was also the strong possibility that relatives were hiding the boy for fear of his safety, or had sent him back to Chicago, the home of his parents.

When Till's body was discovered on August 31, a story of disappearance became a tale of murder, and throughout the nation the story exploded into the headlines. The *Chicago Daily Tribune* reported, "Find Kidnaped Chicago Boy's Body in River." New York's *Daily Worker* announced, "Negro Youth, 15, Kidnaped, Slain in Mississippi." In New Orleans, the *Times-Picayune* exclaimed, "Kidnaped Boy's Body Found," while in Atlanta the *Constitution* noted, "Negro, 14, Called Insulter, is Pulled from River Dead." Just over the Mississippi line, the *Memphis Commercial Appeal* printed one of the most extensive articles on the discovery. Over the next three months, few other papers would cover the Till incident as thoroughly.

Muddy River Gives up Body of Brutally Slain Negro Boy
Memphis Commercial Appeal, 1 September 1955

Greenwood, Miss. Aug 31 — The body of a 14-year-old Negro boy was found in the muddy Tallahatchie River Wednesday and officers said two white men will be charged with his death.

A fisherman found the body of Emmett L. Till, who reportedly made "insulting remarks" to the wife of a Money, Miss., storekeeper. The body was weighted down with a heavy gin fan. He had been battered about the head and had a bullet wound above his right ear.

Sheriff H. C. Strider of Tallahatchie County said two men, jailed here on kidnap charges in the case since Monday, will be charged with murder Thursday.

Jurisdiction in the case will apparently be given to Tallahatchie County since the body was found in that county about 25 miles north of Greenwood. Talla-hatchie County is directly north of Leflore County.

Held in Leflore County jail here are Roy Bryant, 29, whose wife was report-edly insulted by the youth, and his half-brother, J. W. Milam, about 40.

Orders were issued Wednesday night to arrest an unidentified third person for investigation in the case.

Sheriff Strider said the men would probably be kept in the jail here until the grand jury convenes Monday in Tallahatchie County.

However, Dist. Atty Stanny Sanders of Indianola said a more intensive inves-tigation will be made to determine jurisdiction. He said the Negro's body was unclothed when it was found and he was known to be wearing shoes and white pants when he was abducted.

If the clothing can be found, its location would give an indication of where the slaying took place, Mr. Sanders said.

Sheriff Strider said he believed the boy was dumped into the river "about two days ago." He said Till's body was found "a good 10 miles" in Tallahatchie County, indicating the body was dumped into the river in that county since "it couldn't have floated up the river."

Says Boy Wasn't Hurt

Earlier, Bryant told officers he took Till from the home of Till's uncle, Mose Wright, early Sunday. Bryant said, however, Till was released unharmed when it was found he wasn't the boy who insulted Mrs. Bryant, Leflore County Sher-iff George Smith said.

Sheriff Smith and his deputies had been searching the Tallahatchie River, which flows by Money, since Monday.

The boy['s] uncle made the identification Wednesday, officers said.

Sheriff Strider said the body was found 12 miles north of Money by 17-year-old Floyd [Robert] Hodges who was running a trotline. "He went into the river in a motorboat and saw Till's feet and legs sticking up.

"He came back and called me. We went down and found the body hung in a drift," the sheriff said.

Officers reported the body had been weighted down with a cotton gin fan weighing about 125 pounds which was tied with barbed wire.

Officers said the youth had apparently been brutally beaten before he was shot. One officer said the beating was the "worst I've seen" in eight years of law enforcement.

Mamie Bradley, mother of the victim, said in Chicago she would seek legal aid to help convict the slayers of her son. His body will be returned to Chicago.

"The state of Mississippi will have to pay for this," she said. "I don't understand it. No matter what the boy did it wasn't worth killing him. I would expect that down there if the boy did something wrong he might come back to me beaten up. But they didn't even give me that," she sobbed.

Had Feared Foul Play

Sheriff Smith had said earlier he feared "foul play in the case."

The sheriff quoted Wright as saying two white men and a woman came to his home Sunday morning in an auto and took the youth away.

Wright said he asked the men where they were taking his nephew and was told, "Nowhere, if he's not the right one."

In Washington, the Justice Department said it was taking no official interest in the case. A spokesman said the slaying "appears to be a matter for local authorities. The Justice Department is not interested in such cases unless some civil right factor is involved."

Regret is Voiced

A statement issued by the head of Mississippi's pro-segregation Citizens Councils called the youth's death "regrettable."

Robert Patterson, executive secretary of the Citizens Councils, said at Winona the slaying could not be attributed in any way to activities of pro-segregation groups.

"This is a very regrettable incident," Mr. Patterson declared. "One of the primary reasons for our organization is to prevent acts of violence. We are doing our best in spite of constant agitation and inflammatory statements by the National Association for the Advancement of Colored People and outside agitators."

Gov. Hugh White said in Jackson he had not been officially notified of the recovery of the boy's body. He declined to comment on the case otherwise.

NAACP Fires Blast

In New York, Roy Wilkins, executive secretary of the NAACP, termed the slaying a "lynching" and charged that "it would appear that the State of Mississippi has decided to maintain white supremacy by murdering children."

Tuskegee Institute in Alabama said it had not received a report on the death and therefore had not classified it as [a] "lynching" or placed it in any other category.

Wilkins also leveled criticism at Governor White, saying "We have protested to Governor White, but judging by past actions of the state Chief Executive, little action can be expected."

While the discovery of Till's body made the story front-page news in papers from Boston to Los Angeles, it was in Mississippi and Chicago that the story became daily news and quickly developed into a tale of North versus South. The regional dynamics of the murder were intensified by an official statement from NAACP executive secretary Roy Wilkins (the statement alluded to in the *Commercial Appeal* article above). According to Wilkins, "It would appear from this lynching that the state of Mississippi has decided to maintain white supremacy by murdering children. The killers of the boy felt free to lynch him because there is in the entire state no restraining influence of decency, not in the state capital, among the daily newspapers, the clergy nor any segment of the so-called better citizens."

The *Jackson Daily News,* a conservative daily published in Mississippi's state capital, was swift to respond. The following five-part editorial not only prefigures the regional animosities that would develop from the case, but it also gives an early example of how Till's murder would be, for the next few months at least, both front-page and editorial-page news.

Designed to Inflame
Jackson Daily News, 2 September 1955

I

On August 16 of 1954, a New York City Negro factory worker, Willard Menter, awakened from a drunken stupor on a park bench in Brooklyn near the East River. The pain that awakened him was caused by lighted cigarettes being pressed against the naked sole of his foot.

When he roused himself enough to comprehend that there were four dark figures standing over him, he started to run. The four figures halted him, beat him mercilessly and then walked him to the East River, where he was pushed in, senseless. His body was found some time later.

A passer by had seen something of what took place and alerted Brooklyn Police, who, an hour later, arrested four youths for the murder of the Negro worker. The four confessed to not only that killing but also to the brutal slaying of steeplejack Reinhold Ulrickson. More, they admitted horsewhipping several girls and sadistically burning the legs of another man.

Everyone agreed that the murder of Menter was a frightful crime and everyone rallied to deplore the fact that the teen-aged boys who committed the crime had no cause for their action. The boys were subsequently sentenced to long terms in the New York State penitentiary.

No one called the killings anything other than useless, senseless acts of savagery. No one believed they were lynchings. NAACP Executive President Roy Wilkins admitted Thursday that his organization did not classify the murder as lynching but said he did not know why. The National Association for the Advancement of Colored People didn't turn a hand about Willard Menter's death. The courts of New York took care of that matter.

II

Tuskegee Institute, which seems to have the official task of classifying lynchings, says that a lynching is a race killing in which three or more persons take part. Tuskegee Institute did not classify the New York murder as a lynching in spite of the fact that the four boys who murdered the Negro man were all white.

III

Last Sunday, a teen-aged Negro boy, Emmitt [Emmett] Louis Till, was kidnapped and murdered by what the Leflore County sheriff says witnesses say were two white men and a white woman. The boy was a visitor to the little Mississippi community of Money. He is said to have given a "wolf whistle" at the wife of storekeeper Roy Bryant. The boy was a polio victim and seems to have had a speech impediment which might have caused the whistle. He was also said to have been "feeble minded."

His body was found in the Tallahatchie River, weighted with a gin fan, a bullet behind one ear and his face badly torn by what must have been a savage beating.

At once, Sheriff George Smith, of Leflore County, arrested the storekeeper, Roy Bryant, and his half brother, J. W. Milam. Both men were said by the sheriff to have been identified as being in the automobile which drove the Negro boy from the home of his uncle, whom he was visiting.

Sheriff Smith said the two men denied killing the boy and had instead released him at once.

Sheriff Smith took exactly the same action as the Brooklyn Police Department after being notified of the crime. He did his sworn duty, as any law enforcement officer is expected to do.

IV

Gov. Hugh White has ordered district attorneys from two counties to investigate the crime. The governor said Mississippi "will not tolerate" such actions. He is right.

Every responsible citizen in the state of Mississippi agrees that the murder was a brutal, senseless crime and just incidentally, one which merits not one iota of sympathy for the killers. The people of Mississippi deplored this evil act just as much as the people of New York State deplored the terrible crime of the teenagers.

Citizens Council officials have deplored the act. Robert Patterson, executive secretary, said a "primary reason" for the existence of his organization was to "prevent violence."

The kidnap-killing must have been the act of a depraved mind, or minds. The people of Money, where the crime took place, were shocked and appalled. Everyone is in solid agreement that it was a stupid, horrible crime. Intelligent Mississippians can only suppose it came about in the sick mind of men who should be removed from society by due course of law.

V

In New York City, NAACP's executive secretary, R[o]y Wilkins, callously called the killing a lynching. He said that "it would appear from this lynching that the State of Mississippi has decided to maintain white supremacy by murdering children. The killers of the boy felt free to lynch him because there is in the entire state no restraining influence of decency, not in the state capital, among the daily newspapers, the clergy nor any segment of the so-called better citizens."

Just how he terms the murder a lynching when NAACP and Tuskegee Institute declined to label the New York City murder as a lynching is not made clear. What does come clear, by implication, is that anytime a Negro is murdered by whites in Mississippi, it will be considered a lynching by the NAACP. That is because the NAACP is trying its best to inflame the nation against the South in general and Mississippi in particular. It serves only to arouse hatred and fear.

Perhaps NAACP will try to hide behind the wording of a proposed Federal anti-lynching bill which declares that lynching must be an ["]act under pretext of services to justice, race or tradition." But there is no more evidence in this case to show racial hatred on the part of those who murdered the boy than there was to show racial hatred for the New York factory worker in the minds of the sadistic quartet of teen-agers.

Mississippi law officers are doing all they can to bring the guilty parties to justice. There is nothing but contempt in the hearts of all right-minded Mississippians for those who committed this evil crime.

But the kidnap-murder was not a lynching and when NAACP so says, it proves its cynical purpose of inflaming the Negro people of this state against the whites. Its reckless allegations must not go unchallenged.

A few days after publishing this editorial, the *Jackson Daily News* ran the first of many columns by Tom Ethridge on the Till case. Ethridge's "Mississippi Notebook" ran twice a week and was often reprinted in the *Citizens' Council,* the official newspaper of the Citizens' Councils of America.

Mississippi Notebook: Our State a Target for Hate Campaign
Tom Ethridge, *Jackson Daily News,* 4 September 1955

The kidnapping and murder of 15-year old Emmett Till, [a] Chicago Negro boy visiting near Greenwood, has shocked and outraged law-abiding citizens of Mississippi and America. Two white men charged with this brutal crime are now in jail and a speedy trial within the month seems definitely assured.

With typical zeal, the National Association for the Advancement of Colored People is making the most of this tragic and incredible episode. Tailor-made for NAACP purposes, the Till crime is now being used as a springboard for an organized hate campaign aimed at the entire population of this state.

This sickening and needless atrocity comes at a time when leaders of both races are striving desperately to promote harmony, good will and understanding in a delicate situation. This sensational case furnishes the NAACP with a trump card, to be played with all the skill and cunning characteristic of that well-financed, efficiently organized pressure group.

To read the inflamatory statements from Negro leaders of the North, one would suppose that young Emmett Till was the victim of a gigantic conspiracy involving every white person in our state. In fact, the anguished mother is quoted by Chicago news dispatches as saying, "The whole state of Mississippi is going to pay for this."

If our nation adopts the theory that the entire people of an entire state are to be punished for the crimes of individuals, then Chicago itself will be in for a bad time. While few if any sane persons condone the brutal murder of Emmett Till in Mississippi, this is by no means the first atrocity committed in the United States. Illinois certainly has no spotless record. In fact, that state has more crime than any in the land, with the possible exception of New York.

Yet NAACP Executive Secretary Roy Wilkins has said in New York, "the killers of the boy felt free to lynch him because there is in the entire state no re-straining influence, not in the state capital, among the daily newspapers, the clergy nor any segment of the so-called better citizens." (In other words, all two million Mississippians sanction murder. And observe how quickly an open-and-shut case of murder has become a "lynching.")

Even for a hysterical parent, the victim's mother has made some patently ridiculous statements, if Chicago press dispatches are correct. "Such things are an every-day occurrence in Mississippi," she said, "but the state of Illinois doesn't allow these things to happen."

Evidently Mrs. Till doesn't read Chicago newspapers. She needs to talk to the sorrowing loved ones of hundreds who are murdered in her own Windy City each year. If she wants to meet someone who shares her sad experience, perhaps she will talk to the mother of little 17-year old Joanne Pushis. This helpless white child was waylaid on the streets of Chicago the other night. Like Mrs. Till's boy, this Detroit child was visiting another state.

She was seized by a negro giant—a drunken soldier—who had patiently lain in wait for his innocent victim. Little Joanne was savagely beaten, raped and mur-dered. Oddly enough, her stricken parents did not blame the entire Negro popu-lation of Chicago. No NAACP official mounted a soapbox to denounce the clergy, press and citizenry of Illinois. Negro newspapers now screaming for vengeance in Mississippi took little Joane's murder quite calmly, almost with a yawn.

In fact, the anti-white *Chicago Defender* shed maudlin tears over the plight of her bestial killer simply because he was a Negro. Its sob-sister account conveyed the impression that any girl venturing on the streets unaccompanied should ex-pect to be murdered. It was inferred that she gave her consent to be ravished, beaten and slain. Chicago stories did not identify her killer as a Negro, playing down the racial angle. Not so, here in Mississippi.

A clear-out case of murder, the kidnap-slaying of young Emmett Till has already been branded as a "lynching" by militant Negro zealots, whose definition of a "lynching" seems to include any killing wherein the victim is colored and the killer is white.

Conversely, this definition does not apply when colored thugs murder a white victim. If so, such all-too-common crimes would force Tuskegee Institute to add several statisticians to keep track of "lynchings."

Headline-hungry NAACP leaders have said, "Mississippi has decided to maintain white supremacy by murdering children." This is unfair and untrue.

By the same warped logic, the Joanne Pushis slaying justifies the assertion that Negroes have decided to assert their equality by raping and murdering white women.

We are nauseated and disgusted at what happened near Greenwood. Like every other responsible, law-abiding Mississippian, we are anxious to see justice done, fully and quickly. At the same time, we bitterly resent violent and inflamatory rantings or rabble-rousers seeking to blame our entire people for last Sunday's happenings.

Certainly it is a reflection on society when crimes are committed in Mississippi. It is also a reflection on society when brutal crimes occur in Chicago. If we all are to blame for the killing of young Till, as his mother infers, then she is equally to blame for the fiendish murder of little Joanne Pushis in Chicago. Such shallow reasoning is, of course, contrary to justice and common sense.

The state of Illinois will try Joanne's killer by its own orderly and established procedures. Likewise, the State of Mississippi will try Emmett Till's slayers without regard to outside interference.

Justice will be done in this case—in a Mississippi court, by a Mississippi judge and jury. It will be done not on account of NAACP pressure, but in spite of it.

Several states away, the moderate *Atlanta Constitution* expressed less uncertainty about the NAACP than it did about the justice system of fellow southerners in the Magnolia State. In the following editorial, the *Constitution* shows that there was no monolithic "southern position" on the case. Moreover, the *Constitution* became one of the first papers to express concern for the international ramifications of the "Till incident." Such a concern reminds us that Till's murder took place not only within the context of the nascent civil rights movement here in America (Rosa Parks's refusal to give up her seat on a Montgomery bus was only two months away) but it also occurred at a time when the nation was facing the threats and challenges of a global cold war.

A Lynch-Murder Aids Enemies of the South
Atlanta Constitution, 2 September 1955

The body of a 14-year-old Negro boy has been taken from a river near Greenwood, Miss. He had been shot. The weighted body then had been thrown into the river.

Once again the South has been rubber-stamped with a lynch-murder. The victim was a helpless child. His offense reportedly was that some days before his kidnapping and disappearance he had "wolf-whistled" when a lady passed by. If such were the case, juvenile courts or regular legal procedures were in effect to cover any offense.

The brutal murder is grist in the mill of those who picture all the South as a region of violence. It assists the Communist propagandists. It conveys us into the hands of our enemies. Unless the officials of Mississippi vigorously follow up this murder and bring the guilty to justice, all of us will be smeared by it.

In this critical period in the South's effort to adjust itself to the rest of the nation, we cannot continue to trample out the vintage where the grapes of wrath are stored without paying the price in the years ahead.

In Till's hometown, the most active paper in support of his cause was the *Chicago Defender,* one of the most influential African-American weeklies in the country. Not so certain that Mississippi officials would vigorously follow up on the murder and bring the guilty to justice, the *Defender* called for federal intervention into the case, an intervention that would never materialize.

Blood on Their Hands
Chicago Defender, 10 September 1955

The lynching of 14-year-old Emmett Louis "Bo" Till of Chicago in Mississippi last week is an outrage to all decent American citizens, white, and colored, and dramatically points out to the world the ugliest aspects of life in our Democracy.

The Chicago youth vacationing in Mississippi was kidnapped from the home of relatives and brutally lynched after he was accused of whistling at the wife of a storekeeper in Money, Miss.

The blood of "Bo" Till is on the hands of the five candidates for governor of Mississippi who campaigned on an anti-Negro platform in the recent elections. They charged the atmosphere of the state for acts of violence.

We accuse these racist rabble-rousers with contributing directly to the murder of "Bo" Till and the lynching of American reputation for decency and respect for law and order in the eyes of the entire world.

No country that tolerates the barbarous hate-killing of a child within its midst deserves nor can it expect the respect of the civilized world. There can be no compromise this time. Your child can be the next victim of the white supremacists.

It is up to the administration in Washington to begin action once and for all to end the crime of lynching that has degraded our nation. Full justice must be meted out to the two men now being held for this dastardly crime. A federal anti-lynching law must be passed and in addition, it should be made a federal offense to interfere with or attack any religious or racial group in elections. Republicans and Democrats alike have been too quick to appease and forgive bigotry and its consequent acts of violence.

Unless the Administration acts at once to stop this wanton and ruthless taking of lives, the blood of "Bo" Till, Rev. George Lee, Lamar Smith and the long line of martyrs in the fight for first class citizenship for the Negro in America will be on its hands and "all the perfumes of Arabia will not wash it away."

The *Defender*'s call for federal intervention in the Till case was echoed by the *Daily Worker,* the New York–based newspaper of the Communist Party, U.S.A. The *Daily Worker* devoted extensive coverage to the case and, as its later coverage would bear out, it saw in Till's murder not only a chance to right racial wrongs in America but also an opportunity to address larger issues of economic injustice.

End the Racist Conspiracy!
Daily Worker, 8 September 1955

The mutilated body of 14-year-old Emmett Louis Till has been laid to rest in Chicago. But the racist conspiracy which set the stage for his murder, and those of two other Negroes, is still abroad in Mississippi and elsewhere. New Klan-like groups are still being formed. White-collared and well-tailored members of these groups are continuing to fan racial passions. And many state officials are using their official position for the same purpose.

This was plain to be seen in the Mississippi primary election prior to the Till lynching. Two Negroes were murdered. Law and order broke down in a number of counties. Calls for protection to Gov. Hugh White and to the U.S. Department of Justice went unanswered. Protected by this wall of silence and inaction, the lynchers struck down young Till.

These organized merchants of hate have declared the U.S. Supreme Court to be "subversive," and are in open rebellion against fedc,ally constituted authority.

Their reckless use of force and violence to maintain white supremacy endangers the peace and order of the nation, and threatens to make lynching the mainstay of the "southern way of life."

As the CIO United Packinghouse Workers leader, Charles Hayes, declared, "No one can any longer remain silent, and especially the labor movement." In this crisis of racism voices of the people will have to ring out with the demands:

1. Full prosecution and punishment for the murderers of Till.

2. Prosecution by the Department of Justice, under federal law, of officials who have conspired to deprive Negroes of their federally-guaranteed rights.

3. An Executive Order directing the FBI to protect Negroes everywhere in the exercise of their right to vote and other federally-guaranteed rights.

4. Aid from U.S. District Attorneys and from the U.S. Attorney General's office in prosecuting suits against violators of the Supreme Court's desegregation decrees.

5. Presidential condemnation of officials and private groups who persist in using intimidation, terror and murder as weapons to support defiance of federal law.

6. Pledges of support from U.S. Senators and Representatives for anti-lynching, anti-poll tax, FEPC legislation and for amendments bringing all bills into line with the national policy of desegregation.

In the eyes of many if not most Mississippians, the opinions of the African American press and the Communist *Daily Worker* represented the kind of "outside agitation" that jeopardized a just investigation. Nowhere was this more clearly expressed than in an editorial from the *Greenwood Morning Star,* the daily paper of record in the Mississippi town where the grand jury was meeting to review charges of kidnapping and murder against Milam and Bryant.

Meddling in Local Case Creates Problems
Greenwood Morning Star, 6 September 1955

The meddling of outside agitators in the Till murder case has created a number of ugly problems, and there is a growing resentment against those who seek to use the affair to create strife and ill feeling.

The Till case started out as a routine crime affair which the Leflore County officers were handling in the same manner they would a crime of one white against another or involving only negroes. They prosecuted the investigation of the case with commendable vigor and were making excellent progress when the mayor of Chicago, the NAACP and other outsiders tried to create a false impression by labeling it as an act of race hatred which whites in Miss. might condone.

Justice in the Till case appeared certain of being carried out by the court had the outsiders not interfered. Now there are rumors that the whole thing was a plant by the NAACP and sympathy is swinging to the side of the accused.

A dangerous situation has been created by the threats of certain persons that Northern negroes are coming to Miss. to interfere with the case. The National Guard patroling the courthouse and streets is mute evidence of the jittery situation which exists, and which might erupt into a holocost [sic] which would claim the lives of innocent persons.

Greenwood has had a lot of unwarranted and unfavorable publicity which all our good citizens, both white and colored[,] regret very much.

This is a time for cool heads and calm action. There is no actual danger of an invasion of armed outsiders. All the reports of such have been explored and found to be utterly fantastic. We have checked the sale of firearms and shells the past few days and find that there has been a scare which is not only regrettable but dangerous. There are plenty of officers to take care of all situations and there is absolutely no danger or need for civilians to arm themselves. In fact, there is much greater danger from the possibility of gunshot accidents with weapons in the hands of those who are not experienced in their use than there is from race trouble.

The negro leaders of Leflore County are cooperative and anxious to clear the whole matter without trouble. They realize the problems which exist and are cooperating with the authorities in trying to keep agitators from causing trouble.

We sum up the whole thing by giving the warning that the agitation is inspired by Communists or by persons who have become unwitting victims of the Communist plan to stir up trouble where possible. The way to combat the situation is to handle this situation with cool heads and firm hands.

In the midst of all this editorializing, Emmett Till's mother, Mrs. Mamie Till Bradley, had a son to bury. When Till's body returned to Chicago, she insisted that the sealed casket be opened so that, in her famous words, "everyone can see what they did to my boy." For three days, Till's body lay in state as tens of thousands of Chicagoans viewed his battered and bloated corpse. The viewing and funeral were covered extensively in the African American press and were interpreted by many southerners as another unjust agitation on the part of the NAACP. For northern blacks, however, the funeral served as an opportunity to expose southern injustice to an entire nation.

Not surprisingly, the *Chicago Defender* gave Till's three-day funeral its most extensive coverage. Here is how the *Defender*'s Mattie Smith Colin reported the arrival of Till's body from Mississippi.

Mother's Tears Greet Son Who Died a Martyr

Mattie Smith Colin, *Chicago Defender,* 10 September 1955

"Oh, God. Oh, God. My only boy," Mrs. Mamie Bradley wailed as five men lifted a soiled paper wrapped bundle from a huge brown wooden mid-victorian box at the Illinois Central Station in Chicago Friday and put it into a waiting hearse.

The bundle was the bruised and bullet-ridden body of little 14-year old Emmett Louis Till of Chicago, who had been lynched down in Money[,] Miss.

Limp with grief and seated in a wheel chair among a huge throng of spectators, Mrs. Bradley cried out:

"Lord you gave your only son to remedy a condition, but who knows, but what the death of my only son might bring an end to lynching."

As Bishop Louis Ford and Rev. Isaac Roberts prayed and rolled the wheel chair, Mrs. Bradley screamed, "Let me pray," and assisted by the ministers dropped to her knees, crying, "Lord take my soul, show me what you want me to do and make me able to do it."

A morbid silence engulfed the station. Veteran newspapermen and photographers, whose daily schedules include murders and fatal accidents, were grimfaced as they watched the procedure and then went about their work.

Dr. T. R. M. Howard of Mound Bayou, Miss., while boarding a plane at Midway Airport here Wednesday said when queried about this case, "There is going to be hell to pay in Mississippi."

[...]

Could it be possible that one of the poorest economic states in the Union, who should thank Negroes for their agricultural contribution for the meager wealth that it has[,] is still fighting the civil war?

Could it be possible that Mississippi resents the Federal Government to the extent that when there was a meeting of the "minds" (47th annual Governors' conference in Chicago, Aug. 9–12 of this year), their leader, Gov. Hugh Lawson White[,] was conspicuous by absence?

Could it be possible that in Mississippi's blind frenzy to continue to humiliate Negroes, they cannot observe their lack of public health education, in which the so-called poor white trash suffers along with the Negroes?

Could it be possible that they are in a dream world, thinking that "Cotton" is still KING, and therefore cannot see the forest for the trees?

Or is it as Mrs. Bradley hysterically shouted, about the untimely death of little Emmett, "Darling you have not died in vain[;] your life has been sacrificed for something."

In the same issue, the *Defender* ran another story intended to give more background on the murder and the victim.

Mother Waits in Vain for Her "Bo"
Mattie Smith Colin and Robert Elliott, *Chicago Defender,* 10 September 1955

Mrs. Mamie E. Bradley sobbed softly in the home of her mother, Mrs. Alma Spearman, at 1628 W. 14th place in Chicago.

"I have to keep hoping that he is still alive. I can't give up hope."

She was talking about her son, 14-year-old Emmett Louis Till, the day before he was found dead in the Tallahatchie River near Money, Miss. That according to Roy Bryant, Bo Till made "ugly remarks" to Bryant's wife that day in the Bryant store in Money, Miss.

While the search for him went on hundreds of miles away, his mother sat in the home of his grandmother and talked about "Bo" Till.

"He has his faults," she said, "like most boys, but he is very mannerable. People like for their children to associate with him. Bo was liked by everybody."

She showed the reporter a letter received from Bo's aunt, Mrs. Elizabeth Wright, of Greenwood, Miss. The letter is dated Aug. 27 three days after Bo's incautious whistle and the day before he was spirited away.

Mrs. Wright wrote: He is certainly a nice kid, just as obedient as you would want to see.

But Sheriff George Smith says that according to Bryant, Bo Till made "ugly remarks" to Bryant's wife that day in the Bryant store in Money, Miss.

According to Wheeler Parker, 16, of Argo, Ill., Bo's cousin and Mrs. Wright's grandson, Bo had gone into the store at the urging of one of several companions to "look at the pretty lady" behind the counter and to buy some bubble gum.

Parker had accompanied Bo to Mississippi two weeks before. After Bo disappeared, Parker's grandfather, Moses Wright, spirited him out of town and put him on a train for Chicago.

Parker said he was in the next room when three men came for Bo that Sunday morning. He didn't see the men, he said, but he heard one threaten to "blow your head off" when Till failed to say "sir" while answering their questions.

He said there were three men and a woman at the house that morning. The woman stayed in the car, but identified Bo as "the one" when the men took him out to her.

According to Parker's description of the incident at the store, Bo went in at the urging of an older boy. He said "goodby" to the woman when he came out, and when she followed him, Bo whistled at her.

Parker said the woman then rushed back to the store and one of the boys said "she's going to get a pistol." The boys and a girl fled then, Parker said.

Parker, a student at Argo Community high school, identified the youths who accompanied him and Bo to the store at Money as Thelton Parker, 19; Roosevelt Crawford, 15; Maurice Wright, 16; Simeon Wright, 12 and Ruth Mae Crawford, 18. All are residents of Money.

Just how many Chicagoans viewed Emmett Till's body is uncertain. In the *Washington Afro-American,* a banner headline proclaimed "10,000 View Dixie Lynch Victim's Body." The *New York Amsterdam News* reported "50,000 Line Chicago Streets to Look at Lynch Victim." The *Pittsburgh Courier* suggested an even more impressive figure as a four-inch headline exclaimed, "100,000 View Battered Body of Lynch Victim." Reporting on the front page of the September 5 issue of the *Daily Worker,* Carl Hirsch conveyed the local and national outrage the funeral helped both to express and to generate.

50,000 Mourn at Bier of Lynched Negro Child
Carl Hirsch, *Daily Worker,* 10 September 1955

Chicago, Sept 4 — The almost inexpressible indignation of the people over the Mississippi lynching of 14-year-old Emmett Louis Till has overflowed Chicago like a tidal wave. In the Negro community of South Side, a mass outpouring of endless thousands flowed into the area where the body was on display, and funeral services were held.

Over 50,000 persons came on Friday night to view the pitifully mutilated body of the youngster laid out in the funeral chapel at 4141 Cottage Grove. They poured four abreast through the chapel, until 2 A.M. when the doors were finally closed. Strong young men were weeping openly without shame; some were shaken with uncontrollable cries of grief; others fainted as they saw the mute evidence of the unspeakable barbarity of the white supremacist lynchers.

Within the conflicting emotions of the throng, a mute, speechless anger stood above the wracking grief. Near midnight, the mother, Mrs. Mamie E. Bradley, pushed her way quietly outside and spoke to the sea of mourners in the darkness. She urged them to come and see for themselves the terrible evidence of the lynching—all that was left of her son "Bo," to steel themselves for the crusade to bring the killers to justice and to end such barbarism forever.

"For Other Boys"

"This is not just for Emmett, because my boy can't be helped now," Mrs. Bradley said, "but to make it safe for other boys. Unless an example is made of the lynchers of Emmett, it won't be safe for a Negro to walk the streets anywhere in America. I intend to fight this case all the way to the Supreme Court, until we get a death verdict for all four lynchers."

"I'm not bitter against all white people. Many good white people will help me, I know, but I do want these lynchers of my boy punished. And it's the Federal government's job to punish Mississippi for its refusal to protect colored people. I want to go to the Mississippi trial; I want other people to go with me to see this thing through. I'm willing to go anywhere, to speak anywhere, to get justice."

The child's mutilated body will lie in state until Tuesday morning.

Mrs. Bradley and church officials postponed the burial in order to enable all people who so desire to view the body.

A statement, "Punish the Child Lynchers," by Claude Lightfoot, chairman of the Communist Party of Illinois, was distributed to the crowd outside the funeral chapel. Onlookers helped to distribute the 600 copies in a few minutes. "What can we do?" was the question on everyone's lips.

Rescued Body

The State of Mississippi tried to bury the evidence of its barbarism in the two-foot, nameless grave in a Money church-yard. But the irresistible anger of the nation penetrated even there, and no resistance was made when Crosby Smith, the boy's uncle, came to claim the body at the burial ground in his cotton-farm pickup truck. "They were getting ready to spill the body into that two-foot hole," he said. "He hadn't even been embalmed."

So Emmett Till's body came home in a Mississippi pinewood casket. The boy's teeth were knocked out, the right side of his face was bludgeoned in, and there was a bullet hole in the right temple. The body was found in the Tallahatchie River, weighted down with a giant cotton pully and barbed wire, three days after he was kidnapped from his uncle's home by three white men. He was accused of "whistling" at the wife of a white storekeeper, Roy Bryant. Bryant and his half-brother, J. W. Milam, have been arrested.

Earlier, when the crime was first uncovered, Governor Hugh White of Mississippi remarked that the public outcry over the lynching was much ado about nothing. Local police still claim they are unable to find any tangible "evidence" or to locate Mrs. Bryant, who is alleged to have identified Emmett as the one who "insulted" her.

Throughout the week the Chicago press has headlined the events as the Mississippi child lynching. A *Sun-Times* editorial declared: "A revolting crime against humanity has been committed in Mississippi in the name of white supremacy. . . . The senseless killing of Emmett Till is a shameful blot not only on Mississippi but on America. Until justice has been done by publishing [sic] his murderers to the full extent of the law, no American with a conscience can have peace of mind.

"If, as is often the case, an all-white jury should be lenient toward the lynchers, decent Americans will demand federal anti-lynching legislation. . . . If the states cannot cope with these criminals, the Federal government must."

Mayor Richard J. Daley has wired President Eisenhower demanding federal action against the lynchers. "We join with all decent citizens in urging swift prosecution of those who are guilty of this act," the mayor told the President. "I strongly urge that all facilities of the Federal government be immediately utilized so that the ends of justice can be served."

Governor William C. Stratton instructed his Attorney General to urge the Mississippi state authorities to make a "complete investigation."

The people's organizations in Chicago, including a number of unions and the NAACP, are channelizing the indignation of their members into action. The Chicago District of the CIO United Packinghouse Workers invited Emmett Till's mother, Mrs. Bradley, to speak at a mass meeting at the union center, to help launch a plan of action for their membership.

Gerald B. Bullock, regional director of the NAACP, declared that "the atmosphere in Mississippi . . . reeks with race hatred and defiance of all law based
on democratic principles." He blamed the lynching of the Chicago child to the
"reign of terror" directed against the movement of Negro people to exercise their
democratic rights, and called for federal action.

The Washington Park forum has announced plans for an open-air mass
protest rally as soon as arrangements can be made with the Chicago park district.

This is just the beginning. The unspeakable lynching of a Chicago child, the
son of a World War II soldier killed in action, promises to touch off the most powerful movement against racism, jimcrow and lynch-law that this city has ever seen.

Meanwhile, back in Mississippi, on Tuesday, September 6—the same day
that Emmett Till was finally laid to rest in Burr Oak Cemetery—a Mississippi grand jury convened and, in one day, indicted Bryant and Milam on
murder and kidnapping charges. Just as the Chicago press had run feature
stories to elicit sympathy for Mamie Bradley, the Mississippi press had run
similar stories in support of Bryant and Milam.

"Were Never Into Meanness" Says Accused Men's Mother
Memphis Commercial Appeal, 2 September 1955

Sharkey, Miss., Sept. 1. A graying, worried mother bit her lips Thursday in this
community's lone store as she talked about two of her sons who faced charges in
the slaying of Emmett Till, a Negro youth.

"They were never into any meanness," said Mrs. Eula Lee Bryant, adding, "I
raised them and I'll stand by them."

She stopped her work in the store to show family photographs of her eight
sons and three daughters. In the collection were pictures of Roy Bryant of Money,
Miss., and his half-brother, J. W. Milam of Minter, Miss. They wore uniforms.

"Roy, who's 22, spent three years in the paratroops," Mrs. Bryant said. "J. W.
was a lieutenant in the Army. He served in Germany during World War II. He's 36."

Won Purple Heart

Mrs. Bryant said Milam entered service as a private, where he won a Purple Heart
and other honors.

"He got his commission the hard way," she added.

Mrs. Milam and her two small sons were with Mrs. Bryant in her country store, about five miles north of Glendora in Tallahatchie County.

"He's an ideal father," Mrs. Milam said. "The children worship him. And all the Negroes at Glendora (where he owned a store until it was destroyed by fire last year) liked him like a father. They always came to him for help."

Bryant and Milam each have two young sons, all under 4 years of age. The Milam children were playing in the store.

Roy Bryant has a twin brother in Memphis, Raymond Bryant of 1433 Willett.

Mrs. Bryant said her sons were born in Charleston, Miss., and attended the Baptist Church there as youths. They also lived at Tutwiler, Miss., at one time.

"You could never tell they were half-brothers," she said, "unless they told you."

Has Battle Scar

She said the family liked to get together almost every weekend for supper and fellowship. Mrs. Bryant said the boys were always liked wherever they lived.

Mrs. Milam said her husband bears a big scar on his left chest and back from war wounds.

"They had to take out 27 pieces of shrapnel," she said.

Milam is a big man. He stands six feet, two inches and weighs about 220 pounds. Bryant is about six feet.

Mrs. Bryant said seven of the eight boys have been in military service. Recalling happier hours, she said all of them liked to hunt and fish.

An apartment is maintained in the back of the store. Mrs. Bryant said she had operated it for more than two years.

In nearby Glendora, many citizens spoke highly of the boys.

"I've never heard anything against them," said Elmer Kimball, a gin operator. "I haven't known them too long but they've all been nice to me."

In a curious turn of events, on the day when Emmett Till's body first lay in state in Chicago—and two days before the grand jury was to convene in Greenwood—Sheriff Strider offered an interpretation of the murder that, no matter how outrageous on the surface, would eventually play an important role in the acquittal of Till's murderers.

Charleston Sheriff Says Body in River Wasn't Young Till
Memphis Commercial Appeal, 4 September 1955

Sheriff H. C. Strider said yesterday he doesn't believe the body pulled from the Tallahatchie River in Mississippi was that of a Negro boy who was whisked from his uncle's home accused of whistling at a white woman.

"The body we took from the river looked more like that of a grown man instead of a young boy," the Tallahatchie County Sheriff said in Charleston, Miss. "It was also more decomposed than it should have been after that short stay in the water."

The body, thought to be that of 14-year-old Emmett Till, was taken from the river Wednesday. It was tied with barbed wire to a heavy gin wheel.

Uncle "Wasn't Sure"

"Even the boy's uncle wasn't sure the body was that of Emmett Till," the sheriff said.

However, in Chicago young Till's cousin, Ray F. Mooty, said: "The family is convinced the body is Emmett." He said Sheriff Strider's comments appeared to be an attempt to "cover up."

The boy's mother, Mamie Bradley, said, "Yes, I'm positive" when asked if the body was that of her son. Then she added, "I'm positive until something is proven different."

Mooty said if a question as to the identity of the body arose, the family would turn the body over to the authorities for positive identification by them.

Sheriff George Smith of adjoining Leflore County said last night that Sheriff Strider's deductions were "news to me."

Deputies Took Ring

"I thought the body had been positively identified," Sheriff Smith said. "One of my deputies took the ring and carried it to the boy's home where I understand it was identified as Till's ring. That's all I know about the identification."

Sheriff Strider said the victim looked at least 18 years old and probably had been in the water four or five days. He said there was a large silver ring on the boy's middle finger of his right hand.

"Mose said he couldn't identify the ring and would have to talk to his boys to see if they could identify it," Sheriff Strider said. He was speaking of Mose Wright, Till's uncle with whom he had been staying.

Sheriff Strider said he believes Till is still alive.

On the eve of the grand jury hearing, Sheriff Strider continued to make news, this time with his claims that Bryant and Milam, housed in the Greenwood jail, were in danger of being victimized by mob violence. The *Jackson Daily News* printed the following story, very much intended to draw out specific sympathies.

Grand Jury Gets Case: Troops Posted in Delta as Mob Violence Feared in Aftermath to Slaying
Jackson Daily News, 5 September 1955

Greenwood, Miss. (AP) — Two white prisoners were under guard against threatened mob violence today as a grand jury prepared to study their connection with the fatal shooting of a Negro youth from Chicago.

Sheriff George Smith of Leflore County said he had received calls threatening action against Roy Bryant, 24, of Money, and his half-brother J. W. Milam, 36, [of] Glendora.

They are charged with kidnaping Emmett Till[,] a 14-year-old Negro boy from Chicago, after Till whistled at Mrs. Bryant in her husband's country store. They claimed they freed the boy later.

Sheriff H. C. Strider of Tallahatchie County, where a body identified as that of Till was found in a river, said members of the Bryant family and other persons had their cars forced off the road over the weekend by automobiles bearing Illinois license plates.

Strider said he had received letters threatening Bryant and Milam. He said one also threatened the life of James H. Bryant, a brother of the jailed man, who is stationed in the Navy in New York. The Navy was notified, Strider said.

Strider said most of the letters, which he described as "filthy and vicious," were postmarked in Chicago. He said he asked the FBI to investigate.

The Tallahatchie County Grand Jury meets today. Dist. Atty. Gerald Chatham said he would present the case either today or tomorrow. If indicted for murder, Bryant and Milam would be taken to Tallahatchie County for arraignment.

Among the anonymous threats was one that 1,000 Negroes were bound for Greenwood from Chicago. However, there were no reports to verify any such caravan.

Referring to cars being forced from the roads, Strider said, "Those folks seem to think they are coming down here and take over—I don't think they are."

Sheriff Smith said he had various telephone calls telling him Negroes from both Chicago and south Mississippi would come to Greenwood to tear up the jail and take the two men.

Smith ordered out National Guardsmen and deputies to join the city police in patrolling the courthouse area.

He said the group was out to "suppress any possible disturbance that might occur as a result of rumors that have been circulating."

Smith said he had authority from Gov. Hugh White to call out members of the National Guard.

White has called the case a murder and denied charges by the National Assn. for the Advancement of Colored People that it was a lynching.

Strider has said the body may not be that of Till.

"The whole thing looks like a deal made up by the NAACP," he said.

A few miles to the west in Greenville, Hodding Carter was holding no brief with Strider's wild deductions. In a scathing editorial denouncing both the NAACP and Strider, Carter carved out a unique position among Mississippi—and southern—editors, a position assured to agitate both northern liberals and southern conservatives.

Lynching Post-Facto
Delta Democrat-Times, 6 September 1955

It is becoming sickeningly obvious that two groups of people are seeking an acquittal for the two men charged with kidnaping and of brutally murdering afflicted 14-year-old Emmett Till, a Negro youth accused of "wolf whistling" at a white woman.

Those two groups are the NAACP[,] which is seeking another excuse to apply the torch of world-wide scorn to Mississippi, and the friends of the two white men. Among the latter apparently can be counted Sheriff H. C. Strider.

All the macabre exhibitionism, the wild statements and hysterical overtones at the Chicago funeral of the Till child seemed too well staged not to have been premeditated with the express purpose of (1) inflaming hatreds and (2) trying to set off a reaction in reverse in Mississippi, where there had previously been honest indignation.

Were the promoters of these demonstrations successful, they could make prospective Mississippi jurors so angry at these blanket indictments of our whole society that it would seem a confirmation to convict any member of it, no matter how anti-social he or she might be. Then the purpose would have been accomplished and Mississippi could go down in further ignominy as a snakepit where justice cannot prevail for each race alike. That would suit the NAACP fine—that's what they have been saying all along about us—and that would provide them with the best possible proof.

Working hand in hand with this devious intent, however unwittingly, are some officials who are handling the case. Upon their shoulders may rest the honor of Mississippi's courts.

Whoever heard of a sheriff offering on the flimsiest construction of fact, the perfect piece of evidence for the defense? Without a corpus delecti, there can be no murder conviction—of anyone. We would not say, for we do not know, who specifically is guilty of this murder. But we would say that the information that the body found was that of Emmett Till was accurate enough.

It is a neat twist that the same sheriff who says the body recovered was not that of Till, has tried to locate the murder within his county by the discovery of blood on a bridge there.

Sheriff Strider bases his supposition mainly on the fact that the body, after being shot, beaten and soaked in the muddy river for several days, did not resemble a picture taken some while ago, which appeared in a Jackson newspaper and that it appeared to have been in the river a longer time. This defies the fact that the body was identified by relatives, was accepted by the boy's mother. It defies also the evidence of the ring.

Had such a murder been planned to replace another body for Till's, the ring, engraved 1943 LT (for the boy's father, Louis Till)[,] someone would have had to have been killed before the boy was abducted, the ring stolen from young Till; and placed on the dead person's finger. Without the prior knowledge that Roy Bryant and his half-brother would kidnap young Till, as they admittedly did, such a conspiracy defies even the most fantastic reality.

Fortunately the officials of Leflore County are acting a bit more sensibly about the whole matter. And kidnaping is a capital offense in Mississippi, just as is murder.

They are calling this a lynching in some places outside of Mississippi. Well, it wasn't. But it may well become a lynching post-facto, if the courts in Mississippi are unable to accomplish justice in this matter.

And if this happens, we will deserve the criticism we get.

On September 6 the grand jury returned two indictments against Bryant and Milam for kidnapping and murder. The *Jackson Daily News*, so obviously in sympathy with the two defendants, did not, however, miss the chance to praise the grand jury and thus score political points in its long-standing feud with the NAACP. Here is the paper's lead editorial in response to the indictments.

Bad News for NAACP
Jackson Daily News, 8 September 1955

The National Association for the Advancement of Colored People took a blow Tuesday when a Tallahatchie County Grand Jury returned an indictment against two men accused of kidnapping and murdering Emmett Till, the 14-year-old Negro boy. NAACP didn't expect an indictment, even as the radical organization of Northern do-gooders and Negroes didn't anticipate the characteristic Southern reaction of shock toward the violence of the crime.

NAACP obviously didn't want the reaction which made that organization and its leaders liars. They said the South condoned such actions. It was plain that the South does not.

NAACP was disturbed by the arrest of the two men accused of the crime. It would have suited NAACP propaganda purposes better had no arrests been made. Then the Mississippi law enforcement officers would have conformed to the distorted portrait NAACP agitators painted of them for the equally distorted Chicago and New York press.

NAACP has taken a stunning blow from this action in Mississippi by Mississippians. Mississippians have proven beyond a doubt that the NAACP characterization of them is a lie. The Negro of Mississippi knows this to be a fact, even though the Northern press may not bother to tell its readers the true facts of the case.

> *Daily News* columnist and Citizens' Council favorite Tom Ethridge was even more aggressive in his anti-NAACP rhetoric, which depended in large part upon his unabashed appeal to racist stereotypes.

Mississippi Notebook: Our People Have Behaved Mighty Well
Tom Ethridge, *Jackson Daily News,* 11 September 1955

Justice and reason seem certain to prevail in the explosive Emmett Till kidnap-slaying which has disturbed Americans of all races and focused the national spotlight on Mississippi. Despite frantic efforts of paid agitators seeking to incite racial friction, white and colored citizens of our state have behaved admirably in a tense situation.

The two accused men have been arrested and indicted with all due speed. The case will be tried through established procedures by a Mississippi judge and jury. Although this development is gratifying to all thinking persons, it must be a bitter cup for outside agitators who apparently hoped that events would take a far different turn.

NAACP Secretary Roy Wilkins and his associates, seeking to exploit the unfortunate Till affair, have dug deeply into their bag of tricks. In a sense, they have reverted to ancient tribal instincts. They have unsuccessfully tried to replace American concepts of justice with those of the African Congo in centuries past.

Since the horrifying details of the Till crime first came to light, NAACP Secretary Roy Wilkins has harped on a curiously un-American theory. He has argued that the guilt and responsibility rests not merely with Emmett Till's killers but with the entire state of Mississippi as well. His hysterical outbursts blame our entire clergy, press and citizenry.

In African jungles long ago, cunning witch doctors preached a similar doctrine. The Congo witch doctor was happiest when inciting his emotional followers to anger. Trouble was his business and he thrived on it. He loved the limelight and lost no opportunity to strut, talk big and throw his weight around.

When a fellow tribesmen was slain by rivals, the witch doctor immediately sprang into action. He ordered the victim's mangled body displayed for all to see. As infuriated tribesmen filed by, the dead one's family sobbed and moaned. Meanwhile the witch doctor screamed, raved and ranted. In the language of Churchill—this was his finest hour.

"We must avenge our murdered brother," the witch doctor would shriek. "Behold his torn body, the work of fiends and demons! We must punish the entire tribe of those who did this dreadful thing. Every man, woman and child must pay. All are bad and all are guilty!"

That was years ago, in darkest Africa. Yet our nation has just heard almost identical utterances in the violent statement of NAACP's Roy Wilkins speaking in New York City. True he did not urge bloodshed, but he must have been aware that it might easily result from his angry outburst.

The nation was shocked at the fury of a senseless Mississippi crime. It was further shocked by the carefully staged Congo circus at a Chicago funeral home, where a youngster's last rites were used as an occasion to collect funds for promoting further racial strife and perhaps to fatten the wallets of agitators.

For a brief time it appeared as if Witch Doctor Wilkins and his associates might be entirely successful in employing jungle techniques to incite mass hatreds, and perhaps violence. They had all the cards necessary, but failed, possibly because they do not really understand their people. Like other Americans the great majority of Negroes apparently want no part of Congo concepts.

Thousands of respectable Negro citizens who viewed Till's remains were understandably disturbed and indignant. Yet to their eternal credit they kept their heads and refrained from rash actions which would only have complicated an already deplorable situation. If the ill-considered Chicago demonstration was intended to touch off more violence, it failed in its purpose.

Analyzing possible motives, it is conceivable that the funeral frenzy was deliberately contrived to further aggravate the situation in Mississippi. Had federal intervention been necessary to preserve order here, nothing on earth could please Roy Wilkins more. He has torn his shirt trying to bring about such intervention.

Federal troops and martial law would have another black eye for Mississippi and a big feather in the NAACP cap. Such a situation might have given that organization the "foot in the door" it has so desperately wanted. Federal intervention might have made it easier to overthrow established customs in a state that is a formidable stumbling block to the unrelenting NAACP drive for integration.

While our leaders were urging sanity and justice in the brutal Till affair, NAACP Secretary Roy Wilkins seemed to be doing just the opposite. His inflamatory statements only added fuel to flames which could have gotten out of hand had our people of both races been less sensible.

Two wrongs never make a right. The overwhelming majority of all races and creeds in America recognize this fact. That is why law-[a]biding people have refused to be stampeded into rash actions by headline-hungry hate mongers and latter-day witch doctors.

That is why the State of Mississippi has moved swiftly to insure justice. That is why the U. S. Government has refused to interfere, as agitators hotly demand. That is why not one single act of violence between white and colored citizens has resulted from the tragic Till case.

And last but not least, that is why the American concept of justice and fair play will never hold innocent persons responsible for crimes committed by a few.

Ethridge's fellow Mississippian, William Faulkner, was not so confident that his people would behave so well. In an open letter published in newspapers throughout the nation, Faulkner, writing from Rome, called attention to the "sorry and tragic error committed in my native Mississippi by two white adults on an afflicted Negro." Placing the lynching within the context of the Cold War and rising Third World nationalism, Faulkner asked, "When will we learn that the white man can no longer afford, he simply does not dare, to commit acts which the other three-fourths of the human race can challenge him for, not because the acts are themselves criminal, but simply because the challengers and accusers of the acts are not white in pigment?" For Faulkner, the issue was the survival of American democracy in a world of conflicting political ideologies. As a nation, Faulkner urged, we must "present to the world one homogeneous and unbroken front," and the trial of Till's murderers would give Mississippi, and America, a chance to "find out now whether we are to survive or not." Concluding in the tones of a modern-day Jeremiah, Faulkner implored his native state to choose justice over provincialism, "Because if we in America have reached that point in our desperate culture when we must murder children, no matter for what reason or what color, we don't deserve to survive, and probably won't."

In an editorial entitled "Mississippi Barbarism," *Crisis* magazine, an official publication of the NAACP, applauded Faulkner while expressing indignation toward the rest of the state: "Mississippi whines that she is misunderstood, that she is slandered, traduced, and maligned, that there are good people in the State who condemn the lynching-crime of Money. But where are they? Excepting the novelist William Faulkner, no responsible citizen has spoken out in rage and indignation. There is no use for Mississippi to tell the country that the State condemns the Till murder if at the same time no responsible, highly-placed Mississippian denounces the crime and his State's preachers of violence and hate." Following *Crisis*'s warning that "the white minds of Mississippi are poisoned with every imaginable lie and slander about Negroes and the NAACP," the national African American press cautiously reported the indictments of Milam and Bryant. Instead of praising the indictments, black newspapers were more likely to focus on Mississippi's long record of legally sanctioned racial injustice. With the trial scheduled to begin in less than two weeks, the task at hand was to keep the spotlight and pressure on Mississippi. Indictments now secured, the question before much of the American public—and certainly all of black America—was the same one that found its way onto the cover of the September 24 issue of *Jet* magazine: "Will Mississippi 'Whitewash' the Emmett Till Slaying"?

By the end of the month, everyone would have an answer to this question.

Chapter 2 *The Trial*

The trial of J. W. Milam and Roy Bryant lasted from Monday, September 19, to Friday, September 23. More than seventy reporters and thirty photographers attended, turning the tiny town of Sumner into one of the most talked-about places in America. As David Halberstam, who covered the Mississippi beat as a young correspondent, recalled, "The murder of Emmett Till and the trial of the two men accused of murdering him became the first great media event of the civil rights movement."

What follows is the story of that trial as it was told in a handful of newspapers. The three southern papers devoting the most attention to the case were the *Memphis Commercial Appeal,* the *Jackson Daily News,* and the *Jackson State Times,* and selections from each of these dailies—as well as from a few other Mississippi papers—help to recreate the southern perspective on the trial, which was defensive but by no means monolithic. Outside of the South, the white-owned papers most thorough in their coverage were the *Chicago Daily Tribune,* the *New York Post,* the *New York Times,* and the New York–based *Daily Worker.* Among these papers, only the *Daily Worker* and the *New York Post* are sampled in this anthology; reprinting pieces from the *Times* and the *Daily Tribune* proved prohibitively expensive.

More space is given in this chapter to white newspapers (both southern and national) than to black newspapers simply because, with the exception of the *Atlanta Daily World* (which did not send a correspondent to Mississippi), all the major African American newspapers were weeklies and thus produced only one issue during the short span of the trial. Extensive coverage from the *Chicago Defender* is included here, as are pieces from the *Washington Afro-American,* the *Baltimore Afro-American,* and the *Cleveland Call and Post.* Those intimate with the history of trial will notice the absence of James Boyack's work from the *Pittsburgh Courier* (and, for that matter, any work from the *Courier*); once again, prohibitive costs have prevented the republication of this material.

Trial coverage is divided into separate days, each one headed by an introductory note kept brief in order to let the reports speak for themselves. Because no trial transcript exists (Mississippi law did not require transcripts to
be preserved if the case was not appealed), I have given priority to articles
that relate "direct testimony" from the trial. It must be noted, however, that
all the "direct testimony" related in these articles depended upon the quick
pen of the reporter and not upon any reference to an official transcript. As a
result, we have no perfectly reliable version of what was said in court. In
order to make this clear, I occasionally juxtapose articles giving conflicting
accounts of the testimony. Included alongside these testimonies are feature
articles and editorials about the trial that illustrate the range of responses to
the events in Sumner.

DAY ONE: MONDAY, SEPTEMBER 19

Monday was devoted to jury selection. More than one hundred and twenty
veniremen—all white and all male—were called for possible duty. By the
end of the day, ten members of the jury had been selected, the following two
slated to be chosen at the start of the next day's proceedings.

Jury Selection Reveals Death Demand Unlikely

John Herbers [UP Correspondent], *Jackson State Times*, 19 September 1995

Sumner, Miss (UP) — Two half brothers went on trial today in a tense-packed
courtroom for the wolf whistle slaying of a 14-year-old Chicago Negro.

Selection of a 12-man jury began promptly. The line of questioning put to
prospects disclosed that the state probably will not ask for the death penalty.
Prosecutors failed to ask veniremen whether or not they believed in capital punishment, a usual procedure in cases where execution is demanded.

Tense As Trial Opens

Co-defendants Roy Bryant, 24, and J. W. Milam, 36, came into court in a jovial
attitude but their faces tensed as the trial got underway before a packed throng.

Negro reporters were segregated behind a railing that separates the trial prin-
cipals from spectators.

All spectators were searched by 270-pound Sheriff H. C. Strider and his deputies. The sheriff said he has received many threatening letters and could "take no chances."

Ordering Negro reporters to operate from a table separate from white newsmen, the sheriff said that "we haven't mixed so far down here and we don't intend to."

Dist. Atty. Gerald Chatham refuses to say whether or not he would decide during the trial to ask that Bryant and Milam be sent to the state gas chamber for the slaying of young Emmett Till, allegedly because he whistled at Bryant's young wife in a grocery store.

The pretty brunette wives of Bryant and Milam and their young children were allowed to sit with the defendants. The children are Roy Bryant Jr., 3; Lamar Bryant, 2; Bill Milam, 4, and Harvey Milam, 2.

One of the first prospective jurors dismissed was A. N. Brower[,] who said he contributed $1 to the expenses of the defense.

Racial Prejudice Questioned

Prospects also were asked if they had "any prejudices because the defendants are white and the deceased was colored."

"Because of the wide publicity in this case," Chatham told the jury, "the prosecution will take special pains to see that fair and impartial men are selected to try the case on law and evidence and on nothing else."

"The burden is on the state to prove beyond a reasonable doubt that the defendants are guilty but that does not mean that you must know that they did it because if you knew they did it, you would be witnesses and not jurors."

From the first panel of 12 veniremen only one, power company employee Robert Smith, said he had formed an opinion as to the guilt or innocence of the defendants.

Chatham told him not to say why he had a fixed opinion and soft-spoken Circuit Judge Curtis M. Swango broke in and dismissed Smith.

Milam and Bryant were indicted for murder in young Till's death. Conviction on murder charges without recommendation of mercy from the jury means automatic death in the gas chamber in Mississippi. But the prosecution, when it feels it cannot win so severe a conviction because of lack of evidence, may go into court and ask for a lesser penalty than death.

The prosecution usually states its demands in briefing the jury on the case after the actual trial gets under way.

About 50 Negro spectators were in the rear and spilled over into the second floor hallway outside the two-story courthouse.

Circuit Judge Curtis M. Swango, graying and with a soft-spoken voice, delayed the opening of court 15 minutes while photographers took pictures. He said no photographs would be allowed while court was in session.

Empaneling of the 12-man jury got under way at 9:25 AM (CST).

Defense attorney C. Sidney Carlton said Milam and Bryant were "in very good spirits."

Anxious for Justice

Dist. Atty. Gerald Chatham was assisted in the prosecution by former FBI Agent Robert B. Smith, appointed by Gov. Hugh White because "the people of Mississippi are anxious that justice be done."

Carlton said Milam and Bryant were confident of acquittal on charges of a murder that brought cries of indignation from many parts of the world, directed both at them and the state of Mississippi.

Attorneys said the two were anxious to get the trial over with and were ready to face trial on additional charges of kidnapping. The kidnapping charge could bring a maximum of 10 years in prison under Mississippi law. Conviction of murder could mean a life sentence if mercy is recommended and death in the gas chamber if mercy is not recommended.

Milam and Bryant admitted routing the boy from bed at the home of an uncle he was visiting at the tiny community of Money, Miss., last Aug. 28 and taking him away at gunpoint. But they claimed they released Till unharmed.

Group of Teenagers

Sheriff George Smith of Leflore County, in which Money is located, quoted the defendants as saying they thought Till was one of the group of teen-agers who had insulted Bryant's attractive 24-year-old wife at the Bryant's rural store by directing a wolf call and an "insulting good-bye" at her.

The half-brothers said they drove Till to Mrs. Bryant but let him go when she said he was not "the one."

Wright reported the incident and a widespread search for the boy ended three days later when his battered body was found in the Tallahatchie River, weighted down by a heavy cotton gin fan. There was a bullet hole behind the left ear.

Jim Crow Press at Till Trial

L. Alex Wilson, *Chicago Defender,* 24 September 1955

Sumner, Miss — When court adjourned Monday afternoon no jury had been selected to hear the case for and against two men charged with the kidnapping and
murder of Emmett Till, 14-year-old Chicagoan.

But a number of things, many of them precedent making and unusual, had occurred.

Difficulty in selection of the jury can be attributed to several factors:

1. —They had contributed to a defense fund for J. W. Milam and Roy Bryant,
half brothers charged with the crime.

2. —They were related to attorneys involved in the case or to the defendants.

3. —They had formed definite opinions about the case.

4. —They lived in the area where the crime was committed.

The day opened hot and humid, the heat eventually climbing to an almost unbearable 95 degrees that drove every one including Sheriff H. Z. [H. C.] Strider
to abandon a white sports coat he was wearing when he briefed the press prior
to opening of the court.

At Briefing

This correspondent was the only Negro reporter present when the briefing occurred. Strider explained to the more than 100 newsmen present that he had provided seats for 22 white newsmen inside the rail where they could easily hear the
proceedings.

The Negro press, he explained, was to be limited to four seats directly behind
the rail where the public is seated.

"We don't mix down here," he explained, "and don't intend to start now."

Strider was advised by this writer that the Negro newsmen might not be able
to hear proceedings well from their positions. He said[,] "Whenever you are unable to hear just let me know. We'll have order in this court."

Sheriff Strider then told the newsmen they would have to go back downstairs
and come up the front and into the courtroom and submit to search.

Reporters Frisked

The reporters were lightly frisked and photographers had to allow deputies to
rummage through their camera cases.

"I have received over 150 threatening letters and I don't intend to be shot. If there is any shooting, we would rather be doing it." Here he made reference to himself and to his deputies.

Judge Curtis Swango welcomed the press to the court after calling for order and allowed time before opening for photographers to make pictures. Here a precedent was established when a Negro photographer, J. J. Mason, representing Defender publications, climbed on chairs like other lensmen to get his "shots."

Then the judge laid down the rules for the press and others in the courtroom. No pictures were to be made during the transaction of the business of the court; no sketches; no recordings or broadcasts.

He stated that smoking would be allowed and suggested that the men take off their coats for comfort.

Negro spectators numbering approximately 40 were seated and stood in the left rear of the courtroom. Outside the courtroom in the corridor a crowd was jammed beneath the door.

The alleged slayers of Emmett L. Till, J. W. Milam and Roy Bryant, were brought into the court accompanied by their wives.

The wives and children arrived at the Sumner courthouse in a green 1955 Chevrolet with a Memphis-Shelby County license No. 294-297.

During the court session the children played about in the courtroom while both Milam and Bryant sat quietly and without handcuffs. Both of the wives appeared to be slightly worried and not once during the session was a smile noted on either face.

Defendants Somber

Throughout the morning session both men maintained somber expressions. Milam appeared to be nervous, smoking incessantly and shifting about restlessly in his seat.

While almost the whole panel of 120 veniremen was being exhausted [sic] for one reason or another, six whites armed with shot guns were reportedly patrolling the area near Money, Miss., where the crime occurred. The purpose, it is believed, was to find out why so much Negro traffic had been going through the area.

Prosecution attorneys, Gerald Chatham and Roy Smith III, made clear in their challenges to members selected for trial jury that they would press for a fair and impartial trial.

Challenge Veniremen

During the vigorous challenges three men were disqualified for contributing to a defense fund to aid the defendant; six were tossed out for holding fixed opinions of the case and one was ordered to stand aside because he was the brother to one who had contributed to the defense fund. Another was disqualified because he was a distant relative of the defense attorney.

Earlier, Atty. Chatham said in his talk to the prospective jurors, "the State of Mississippi will take every step to see that an impartial and fair trial is held in this case."

When Atty. Smith took over the questioning he asked[,] "Would you be moved by any consideration, race, or anything else in helping to see that a fair trial is held?"

This line of questioning was responsible for eliminating most of the first panel selected for jury service.

What appears to be a lead to a sensational development in the Emmett L. Till slaying is now being investigated. This writer is unable to comment further at this time.

Negro Newsmen

Among the members of the Negro press present were: James Hicks of the *Afro American Newspaper* and NNPA; Simeon Booker, Clotye Murdock and David Jackson of *Ebony;* Mrs. Nannie Mitchell Turner, publisher of the *St. Louis Argus;* L. Alex Wilson, (Defender Publications) and Ernest Withers of the same paper.

Among members of the white press present were Clark Porteus [Porteous] of *Memphis Press-Scimitar;* John Popham of *New York Times;* Jim Kilgallen, of INS; Paul Burton, of INS; Murray Kempton of *New York Post;* William Desmond, *New York Daily News,* and John Gunter of the *Memphis Commercial Appeal.*

Wives Serious, Children Romp as Trial Begins

James Gunter, *Memphis Commercial Appeal,* 20 September 1955

Sumner, Miss., Sept. 19. — The four handsome sons of Roy Bryant and J. W. Milam squirmed, squealed, climbed, ran, cried, laughed, chewed gum, ate candy, drank liquids and played cowboy in the courtroom Monday as their fathers went on trial for murder.

The defendants made a dramatic entrance with their attractive wives and children at 10:25 A.M., setting off a buzz of interest and lightning-like flashes from the combined action of 30 cameramen.

Mrs. Carolyn Bryant, a 21-year-old brunet who is expected to be a key witness, was dressed in a simple, dark-gray dress with a high neckline. She leaned close to her 24-year-old husband and fidgeted her fingers, never speaking.

Expression Stern

Mrs. Juanita Milam, 27-year-old wife of the other defendant, wore gray in a lighter shade with white trim at the neck and sleeves. Her long hair was bound in a bun at the back of her neck. Her facial expression remained stern throughout the proceedings.

The boys were scrubbed and neatly dressed in their Sunday best, including suspenders and neckties, at the beginning of the tiresome session. They sat quietly on their parents' laps for a few minutes.

Bryant held his two sons, Lamar Bryant, 2, and Roy Bryant Jr., 3, and Milam clutched his boys, Harvey Milam, 2, and Bill Milam, 4, for a while.

When the children grew restless, their mothers held them. But finally, the boys broke away and explored the courtroom.

Families Together

The families sat together in front of Judge Curtis M. Swango near their five attorneys. Relatives in the first row of the spectators area passed them drinking water from time to time and ran errands in efforts to keep the boys happy.

Once, Bill Milam picked up a toy pistol and fired an imaginary shot at Roy Bryant Jr.

Bill, the oldest child present, clambered over the rail and stamped down the aisle making little boy noises. He ran his hand along the courtroom railing pickets, apparently deriving great satisfaction from the machine-gun clack-clack he produced.

The 2-year-olds whimpered and wriggled. Bryant spoke sharply to them and cautioned them to be still.

A spectator passed the boys chewing gum. Mrs. Bryant rocked from side to side in attempts to calm her youngest. Bill Milam by then had climbed to the top of the rail where he stood precariously and shouted a greeting to his cousins.

Candy Supplied

The mothers and their husbands smoked many cigarets.

A relative brought the boys a bag of candy suckers. This appeased them briefly.

Lamar Bryant finished his candy and played peek-a-boo with onlookers through the rail pickets.

By afternoon the boys had shed their shirts.

J. J. Breland, senior defense attorney who has practiced law in Sumner 40 years, has experienced more than one sensational trial.

He engineered the defense more than 15 years ago when Dr. Sarah Ruth Dean went on trial in Greenwood, Miss., for the widely-publicized poison-murder of Dr. Preston Kennedy.

Dr. Dean was convicted but was pardoned by Gov. Mike Connor before she went to prison. She is still practicing medicine in the state.

Four Aid Defense

Every other Sumner attorney is serving with Mr. Breland in the defense of Milam and Bryant. They are C. Sidney Carlton, J. W. Kellum, John Whitten and Harvey Henderson.

On the opposite side of the table sit the prosecuting lawyers, led by Gerald Chatham of Hernando, district attorney for 14 years. Mr. Chatham, who has high blood pressure, said most of the work in the case will be handled by Robert Smith, suave 41-year-old ex-Marine and former FBI agent. The third prosecutor is Hamilton Caldwell, Tallahatchie County attorney.

During the noon recess, a rumor spread through the crowd in the courthouse lobby that Bryant, an Army paratrooper after the Korean War, had served under a Negro corporal in his outfit. Bryant later said this was false. He said he was a sergeant and had a Negro corporal under him.

Milam said he has been a good friend of the Negroes he has known. He said five years ago he plunged into the Tallahatchie River, from which the body of Emmett Till was pulled, and saved the life of a drowning 7-year-old Negro girl.

Milam said he also lent his car to Gilbert Henderson of Glendora, a Negro, to take his child, stricken with polio, to a doctor. Four years ago, Milam rushed Jack Mammon of Glendora, a Negro, to a hospital when Mammon's jugular vein was slashed, he said.

The townspeople of Sumner have never seen anything like it here—the crowds, the out-of-state newsmen and the excitement of a big trial—not even on Saturdays or when merchants conduct a drawing to give away an automobile.

Citizens estimated as many as 1,000 outsiders came, more than come on the biggest trade days.

Bernard Henderson, a banker, said he had never seen such doings here in 32 years.

Business Brisk

Businessmen did a rush trade and no one seemed to feel there was danger of an outbreak of violence as a result of a murder trial with racial overtones.

Crowds unable to get inside the small upstairs courtroom stood under large oaks outside the 45-year-old brown brick courthouse or loafed in the halls.

Inside the courtroom, spectators lined the green plastered walls or sat in tall windows equipped with dilapidated pull shades, in addition to filling the 108 available seats.

Not more than 15 women, white and Negro, entered the courtroom. All the rest were men. Negroes sat segregated in a rear corner.

Combined body and sun heat in the high-ceilinged room brought on much hat fanning. Judge Swango said it was permissible to remove coats and smoke.

A porter was kept busy passing a pitcher of ice water to trial officials. Downstairs, a cold drink stand had its biggest day in history.

The Baby Sitter
Murray Kempton, *New York Post*, 20 September 1955

Sumner, Miss., Sept. 20 — J. W. Milam sat with his son, William, prattling on his knee yesterday and watched with hard, incurious eyes while the better element in the State of Mississippi scrounged to find 12 men who would bravely and truly try to judge him for the murder of a Negro boy just for whistling at his sister-in-law.

Sumner began as best it could yesterday to try J. W. Milam and his half brother, Roy Bryant, for killing 14-year-old Emmett Till.

The Bryant family came to watch and turned the courtroom into a nursery school with little boys tottering around and bleating and every now and again lifting their water pistols and pointing at a deputy sheriff and going "boom-boom" while the state went through the business of picking a jury to try their father for murder.

Both state and the defense agreed on 10 members for the all-male, all-white jury. Two more must be selected today.

Then the prosecution will reveal its case, which it says is so circumstantial it will not ask for the death penalty.

Meanwhile, in the nursery-courtroom:

J. W. Milam let little Billy wriggle on his lap and little Billy would yip and J. W. would bow his head and shoosh little Billy.

Little Billy would still yip and the prosecuting attorney would continue trying to pick a jury and J. W. would take his hamlike hand and adjust little Billy's celluloid bowtie and no one present doubted that J. W. loved little boys, especially if they were white ones and of the family.

There were the delicate hands and pipestem legs of the little boy and then you had to remember that the State of Mississippi believed that on the night of Aug. 28 J. W. Milam went to the house of a field-hand named Moses Wright and dragged another little boy out of bed and said, "You from Chicago?" And the boy said, "Yes," and J. W. said "Don't you say yes to me or I'll knock hell out of you."

*   *   *

They are trying J. W. Milam and Roy Bryant in a courtroom which compounds every mistake that interior decoration has made in the last 30 years. It is vastly deep with dirty, pale lime-green walls and circular fans and a special air-conditioning system and a judge who drinks cokes in court and lets us all smoke.

The Judge brings an odd blend of gentility and informality to the entire proceedings, while jurors are nodding and bowing their heads to the fiction that they have no opinion and that none of them will change the script. J. W. and his kids don't "send" that jury: it knows that he is a peckerwood and not to be trusted and still it will vote to let him go.

The Bryants and the Milams all came to the matinee, swelling and bulging out of the seats with assurance. There was Carolyn Bryant, who alone knows what touched the fuse, her lower jaw scarred by lipstick, her cheeks cadaverous and her eyes smoky. She sat there and soothed a puckish vagrant child while the better element went on searching for a fair and impartial jury.

Every time a stranger looked at J. W. Milam and wanted to hate him, there was always a little boy in the line of vision. That is the horror. For here was the man sitting in that place who was loved by his children and deserved their love and who is charged with killing a boy because he was black and didn't know his place. J. W. Milam is a violent man of bad reputation.

The defense danced around his name yesterday because even though it knows its client will walk free sometime late this week, it is not proud of him.

*   *   *

He seemed to own and overwean this courtroom. He is a defendant but by-standers shuffle up and wish him luck. The colored spectators who seek his healing touch say, "Yes sir, Mr. Milam." He shook off his kids yesterday afternoon and stood up all by himself at adjournment and asked: "Where are our goddamned guards: we've got to get out of here."

In his huge shadow the judge and the prosecuting attorneys were doing what they should to get the fairest jury they could find, but J. W. Milam was sure he was a power larger than them all.

Carolyn Bryant walked out, pushing one of the little boys in front of her, and there was a sudden sense that someone would be writing the script and it may be that the Milams and the Bryants might not own this court. Sidney Carlton, the most vocal of the defense attorneys, watched her go and said that no one could understand what Emmett Till had done to her.

And so we seem to have reached the point where Carolyn Bryant will have to do the violated dove bit. Otherwise, J. W. Milam, who likes little boys, might get found guilty of taking one out and kicking the back of his head in just for being a Negro in a strange country.

DAY TWO: TUESDAY, SEPTEMBER 20

The day began with the selection of the final two jurymen. After this, District Attorney Chatham requested a recess because the state had just learned of the existence of other possible witnesses to the kidnapping and murder (see chapter 4 for James Hicks's account of how these witnesses were discovered and persuaded to testify). The defense objected to the delay, but Judge Swango granted the prosecution a recess. The trial was adjourned with no witnesses being called. In the day's other big news, Mrs. Mamie Till Bradley and Congressmen Charles C. Diggs made their first appearance at the trial.

Lynched Boy's Mother Sees Jurymen Picked
Rob F. Hall, *Daily Worker*, 21 September 1955

Sumner, Miss., Sept 20 — A young Negro mother returned today to her native Mississippi county to fight to avenge the life of her 14-year-old son, kidnaped and murdered 20 miles from this courthouse.

Judge Curtis M. Swango was at the bench and the 10 jurors already chosen were in the box when Mrs. Mamie Bradley, 33, accompanied by two men relatives, walked quietly but purposefully through the center aisle of the court-room thronged by relatives, friends and neighbors of Roy Bryant and J. W. Milam, the two white men charged with the murder of Emmett Louis Till, her child. Mrs. Bradley and her companions took seats near the card table to the left front of the courtroom. At the card table were the reporters and photographers. But before she reached the table a hum of voices had identified her, and photographers leaped over chairs and stood on [the] table to get pictures of her.

In a quiet voice she answered the questions of newsmen. She was born at Webb, near here, 33 years ago, and left at the age of two when her parents moved to Chicago.

Emmett's father, Louis Till, was killed in action overseas in World War II.

The press report that she had received more than 2,000 letters was correct, but only 30 of them contained threats.

She is a demure woman whose attractiveness was set off by a small black hat with a veil folded back, a black dress with a white collar. In the more than 99-degree heat of the courtroom, she fanned herself with a black silk fan with a red design.

Father and Cousin

The two men with her she identified as her father, John Anderson Carthan, of Detroit, and her cousin, Rayfield Mooty, president of Local 3911, CIO Steel-workers, of Chicago, and a steelworker in the Reynolds Plant. She herself is a civil service employee with the Chicago Procurement Division of the U.S. Air Force.

Later, when the jury was finally selected, she came to the front of the court as a clerk called names of the state's witnesses. Standing beside her were seven white witnesses who are expected to help identify the body which was dragged from the Tallahatchie River, and two of Mrs. Bradley's relatives, her uncle, Mose Wright, 64-year-old sharecropper, and his grandson, Simmy Wright, who appeared to be about nine or 10 years old.

The final selection of the jury was a long and arduous process and was not completed until 11 o'clock of the second day of the trial. Last night 10 had been selected but it was necessary to call nine today before two additional jurors could be agreed upon.

Six were dismissed by Judge Swango because they had contributed to the defense fund for Bryant and Milam or acknowledged a fixed opinion of the case. The seventh was thrown off when the state used its 12th and last peremptory challenge. To secure a 13th or alternate juror, it was necessary to call four names.

In its final composition, the jury consists of two carpenters, one retired insurance man and nine farmers. The alternate is also a carpenter.

The defense had little fault to find with the prospective jurors, excusing only two, and J. J. Breland was quoted as saying they wouldn't have challenged them except through ignorance of their background. They were young men and Breland said the defense didn't want any younger men on the jury.

A highlight of the morning session was the arrival of Rep. Charles C. Diggs, Jr., (D-Mich) with Basil Brown, prominent Negro attorney, and James Del Rio, businessman, all of Detroit. They too took their seats near the segregated press table, and during a brief court intermission were photographed by news cameramen.

Local people were obviously surprised when white newsmen shook hands with Rep. Diggs and addressed him as "Mr. Congressman."

Gerald Chatham, district attorney, made a remark today to a prospective juror which contradicts his reported previous statement that he would not ask for the death penalty. Quizzing the veniremen he asked whether he would hesitate, if convinced of the defendants' guilt, to cast a vote that would mean life imprisonment or the gas chamber for them.

The prosecution used its 12th peremptory challenge to rid the jury of A. C. Thomas, whose brother, Dave, is town marshall of nearby Tutwiler. Earlier challenges had removed relatives of other local and county law enforcement officers. The prosecution apparently has little faith in the capacity of such persons to render fair and impartial verdicts in this case.

Jokes, Threats Are Blended at Tension-Packed Sumner

James Gunter, *Memphis Commercial Appeal,* 21 September 21 1955

Sumner, Miss., Sept. 20. — "For truth dies not . . . and by the low tents of the deathless dead they lift the cause that never yet has failed."

When Virginia F. Boyle signed her name in 1913 to this inscription for a Confederate memorial at the Courthouse here she had no inkling of what is happening now.

A proud Southerner, her only thought must have been to honor Tallahatchie County's fallen men in a bitter war less than 50 years before.

Tuesday, descendants of those deathless dead crowded around the stone monument and alternately joked and grimaced as they discussed the murder proceedings inside a courtroom. They would have been inside, also, had they found room in the sweltering flesh-pack to stand.

The death of a 14-year-old Negro boy and the trial of two white men had sharpened the form of old battle lines.

A reporter could not ignore the signs of tension.

Sheriff H. C. Strider showed an airmail letter postmarked Chicago and received at the Courthouse Tuesday. It enclosed photo clippings of the defendants and the dark-eyed woman who said she was insulted by the Negro youth before he died.

Holes were burned and punched in the paper figures. Large wounds were represented by a red substance which appeared to be nail polish.

"If the judge don't find them guilty, look for this to happen to all whites in Money, Miss.," the scrawling read. The letter was not signed.

Unprintable remarks were written, too.

The sheriff said he had received about 150 similar communications, "some worse than that."

The sheriff told his 20 deputies at the Courthouse to maintain a watchful eye following an unpublicized incident Monday. He said two Negro men turned around at the door when they saw that those who entered were being searched for weapons.

They were seen to place a pistol in an automobile outside, but the new Pontiac with Illinois license plate was gone when deputies got downstairs, he said.

The mother of the dead Negro boy caused a sensation when she walked into the courtroom flanked by her father and advisors. Reporters and photographers joined around her so thickly that those on the outside of the circle could not see her.

Attention received by the fashionably dressed Negro woman swept an expression of almost painful dislike across the faces of the local spectators.

A United States Representative with dark skin, Charles C. Diggs, Jr., a Democrat from Michigan's 13th District in the heart of Detroit, entered the courtroom. Judge Curtis Swango conferred with Sheriff Strider and the sheriff went back to escort the Negro representative to a table for the Negro press.

The Negro lawmaker said he was here as a private citizen. After a day which included no testimony, he said he had formed no opinion of the trial and would have no observations until it is over.

Two relatives stood like bodyguards on either side of Mamie Bradley at first. Later they relaxed and sat down. The small woman wore a dark dress with white trim and a black hat with veil. Large blue drops hung from her ears and she fluttered a black fan constantly.

Judge Swango announced that two photographers had broken his rule against picture-taking during court sessions. He warned that penalties would be imposed in future violation.

The *Sumner Sentinel,* [a] weekly newspaper operated here by William M. Simpson, opened its quarters to visiting newspapermen.

Some of the nation's top reporters wrote their stories in the "back shop" where they had room to place typewriters on tables. Mr. Simpson entertained many of the reporters at his home. The newspaper's front office was crammed with news covering equipment—cameras, typewriters, a teletype and a machine for transmitting photographs by telephone wire.

Only one bachelor was seated on the jury, members of which range in age from 28 to 74. One juror wore a necktie and the others all wore sport shirts or dress shirts open at the collar.

Grandstand Play Again
Jackson Daily News, 21 September 21

The mother of a Negro boy who was murdered in Mississippi has finally decided to come down to Sumner to testify in the state's trial of two men for the murder and kidnapping of her son. She has done so only after many announcements from the National Association for the Advancement of Colored People stated that it would be "too dangerous" and that she must have "guaranteed protection."

Nothing could be more foolish.

The mother of that boy will probably be safer in Mississippi than she has ever been in gang-infested Chicago, where she lives. In Chicago, murder is so commonplace—or so it seems—that the daily press there rarely sees fit to carry front page stories about killings.

It is well that the mother has been more intelligent than her many, many self-appointed spokesmen. She has agreed to come to testify in the trial, as she should, and she may be certain that she will be adequately protected.

The NAACP is merely grandstanding again and playing fast and loose with

the truth when it suggests violence to her. It isn't so. She'll be safer here than in
her own backyard.

Roman Circus
Jackson Daily News, 22 September 1955

The trial of two men in Sumner for the kidnap-murder of 14-year-old Emmett
Till has turned into a Roman circus. If justice is done, it will have been done despite the steady flow of slanted and reckless copy which has come from the trial
scene.

The appearance Tuesday morning of New York's [sic] Negro Congressman
Charles Diggs, flanked by two attorneys, indicates the political ore to be mined
from this judicial molehill by cynical vote seekers. Diggs has about as much business being at the trial as he has being in Congress, where he has not distinguished
himself for unbiased thinking.

Congressman Diggs, as well as many of the representatives of Negro publications, is interested only in the sensation he can create at the trial scene. Nothing
would better suit his purpose than be mistreated in some way.

One hopes that the good people of Sumner are able to stomach this blatant
display of bad taste and phony sympathy[,] for if they react as they have just cause
to do, it will make banner copy throughout the North. Sumner citizens will be
called upon to maintain a stoic calm during this trial[,] for any other course
would best suit the NAACP and its dubious allies.

Meantime, Judge Curtis Swango, Jr., is to be warmly commended for his
scrupulously correct conduct in the face of what must be a difficult situation.
Openly hostile outsiders are pre-judging the judge and jury.

While an open trial was the only possible way for this trial to be conducted,
it is plainly a trying situation for all the court officials and must be intensely re-
pulsive for the jurors, who are most certainly going to deliver a verdict according
to the dictates of their own consciences.

Judge Swango Is Good Promoter for South
Harry Marsh, *Delta Democrat-Times*, 21 September 1955

Sumner—Circuit Judge Curtis M. Swango is providing the South with the best
public relations it had since the invention of the Southern Accent first enchanted
northern ears.

Judge Swango[,] as presiding officer at the trial of Roy Bryant and J. W. Milam for the murder of Emmett Till[,] has a heavy weight of responsibility on his shoulders. They are well able to bear it.

The dignified magistrate has an authoritative voice and a husky gavel and doesn't hesitate to use either. But most of all he has displayed great patience and fairness in the two days required to select a jury in the hot, crowded courtroom.

Sign Commendation

Tues. afternoon reporters covering the case signed a commendation of all court officials for their conduct of the trial, but from their comments it was easy to see that Swango had captured their admiration more than others.

The commendation was signed moments after Judge Swango recessed court until 9 a. m. Wednesday and told the packed audience that at the next day's session he would be forced to exclude all persons standing in the courtroom who were not there on official business.

"This is your courtroom[;] it belongs to Tallahatchie County for the use of citizens, but we must keep these aisles clear; if a fire were to break out here it would be a great tragedy," he told the audience motioning to the packed groups of people crowded into the center aisle, along the rail of the courtroom, at the rear entrance and around the jury and press table.

Crowded Courtroom

Monday and all morning Tuesday, spectators crowded the second story courtroom which has a seating capacity of 250. Monday morning crowds in the anteroom of the main entrance climbed the stairs leading to the attic to see into the courtroom and kicked out a window.

At noon and during Monday afternoon and Tuesday morning, before the jury could leave the courtroom, bailiffs had to clear the aisles.

Tuesday afternoon, with the jury complete and testimony in the sensational case expected to start[,] almost 400 people jammed into the room. Judge Swango ordered the recess until 9 A.M. Wednesday and warned that no standing would be available.

Then he turned to the jury, "Since we're furthest from the door let's you and I sit here for a while until the courtroom clears[,]" he said.

The judge's consideration of reporters and photographers was equally considerate and firm. Monday he warned photographers not to take pictures during the time court business was underway. Tues. he was informed that pictures had been made during the session. He issued a warning that if pictures were made during court business thereafter, suitable action would be taken. Other photographers took the offender aside for warnings of their own.

Make Comparison

The chaotic courtroom conditions Tuesday afternoon prompted some of the veteran newsmen on hand to make comparisons with the recent Sheppard murder trial in Cleveland, Ohio.

"The courtroom at the Shep[p]ard trial was just about one-fourth as large as this one—we were sitting on the floor and writing on our knees," commented gray-headed Paul Holmes of the *Chicago Tribune*.

He said the congestion of press people at the Sheppard trial was much worse than it is at Sumner, where almost all the reporters are seated around four big tables—three for whites inside the rail, and one for Negroes just outside the rail.

Many photographers are also able to find chairs. Others sit on the floor, lean against the wall or wait outside.

Worse Congestion

But spectator congestion is much worse here than at the S[h]eppard trial. It seems that almost everyone in western Tallahatchie County is anxious to see the proceedings. When Judge Swango excused the special 120-man venire at noon today, telling them they could go home if they wished, not a person moved from his place.

But Judge Swango's job will become harder, beginning today. Testimony of a highly volatile nature will begin, and tempers which have been on an even keel up to now are likely to wither under the terrific September heat and the trial tension.

Heart of Darkness

Murray Kempton, *New York Post*, 21 September 1955

Sumner, Miss., Sept. 21 — A gentleman of quality drafted to salvage the honor of the State of Mississippi last night oversaw a desperate search across the dark jungles of the Delta for four Negro field hands he hopes could testify that they were there when two poor whites administered the death penalty to 14-year-old Emmett Louis Till for the capital crime of whistling at a white woman.

The head of the search party was District Attorney Gerald Chatham, a tired, grave man whom fate has called to prosecute J. W. Milam and Roy Bryant for snatching young Till from his great-uncle's home and beating him to death somewhere down the road.

He has to reach the conscience of a lily-white jury, overwhelmingly constituted of farmers, all of whom have sworn bare-faced, against all their traditions, that it will not affect their verdict that the accused are white men like themselves and the victim a Negro boy from Chicago.

Last night, against his own traditions, Gerald Chatham, as proof he really cares, turned to the scorned, buried Negro community and asked it to bring him a proof so copper-riveted that even this jury might be forced to believe it and return a guilty verdict.

The theory on which he is proceeding is one which up to now has only been whispered among Delta Negroes. They believe that a Negro called "Two-Tyke" led Milam and Bryant to the cabin of 64-year-old Moses Wright, where they seized the boy two hours after midnight and took him out and killed him, and that "Two-Tyke" and a second Negro, out of fear, stood by and watched him die.

* * *

Yesterday, Gerald Chatham went looking for Leroy Collins and Henry Logan [Loggins] as unwilling body-servants to Milam and Bryant at the murder scene. He also searched, reportedly with success, for two other fieldhands who are said to have heard young Till scream and run to see him die.

If and when they are brought to witness, Gerald Chatham will do something no Mississippi District Attorney has ever dared to try: Go for the capital conviction of two white men on the word of four black ones.

Last night Gerald Chatham claimed to be sure that he could put Logan and Collins on the witness stand today and have them tell the State of Mississippi that Milam and Bryant had not only killed a little boy for whistling but had commandeered two Negroes to come along and clean up the mess afterwards.

Gerald Chatham played this wild card yesterday afternoon after he had finished picking the shabby best of possible juries and the defense was exuding its satisfaction and its assurance of a two-day trial and a two-minute acquittal.

The miasma of steaming flesh was rising from the spectators, and behind him there was a sea of waving fans. It was the kind of heat which excuses murder; J. W. Milam sat with his child on his knee and the sweat from his arm-pits running in pools down his yellow shirt and observed that it was hard not to feel mean.

* * *

Sumner put up for two days with the invasion of spectacles that were not just unfamiliar but shocking to its sense of fitness. Its citizens had sat on its courthouse steps and watched Negro and white reporters exchanging notes, and there was more incredulity than menace in their comments. The few local Negroes who were not out in the fields watched from the base of the Confederate monument, which is the only seat available to them, and were obviously as unbelieving as the peckerwoods there.

But it was not a mood of detached curiosity that could survive the heat; and yesterday afternoon, white Sumner, unlike J. W. Milam, was having a hard time not to feel mean. After lunch, the Negro reporters came into court and Sheriff G. W. Trider [H. C. Strider], who looks like Sidney Greenstreet, stared at them and said, "Hello, niggers."

The courtroom was so crowded that Moses Wright, the chief known prosecution witness, had to stand up all morning. Still it was a place made almost pleasant by the pervading presence of Judge Curtis Swango, a quiet man firmly and graciously committed to a fair trial whatever the verdict, and there was a conviction that while he sat there the State of Mississippi would do its honest best to run an honest race and that the burden would rest on the jury alone.

*   *   *

Then Gerald Chatham stood up to begin his case. He would like more time; he had just learned of the possible existence of four major witnesses and he would need the whole afternoon to run them down. Defense Attorney C. L. Breeden [J. J. Breland] jumped up and said the state was stalling and should proceed to trial at once. And Judge Swango came back with cold courtesy to say that it seemed like a reasonable request to him.

And then last night, Gerald Chatham went hunting through the cotton fields for four Negroes with a strange story to tell. He and Swango really care; they are the conscience of Mississippi; the prosecution's case is a mess and it seems impossible that Emmett Till can ever win a judicial vengeance; but, whatever their reasons, they are not men who will have it said of them that they did not well and truly try.

Somehow, J. W. Milam looked smaller in the afternoon than he had in the morning; he played gently with his little boys but he hated everyone else. By now the kids are bored and J. W. has a hard time keeping them amused. Yesterday little Harvey diverted himself by putting a rope around his little brother's neck and tugging it for sport.

The prosecution opened by calling its first witness, Mose Wright. After this, they called more than a dozen witnesses, among them Chester A. Miller, black undertaker in Greenwood; Sheriff George Smith of Leflore County; Robert Hodges, the seventeen-year-old white boy who discovered the body; B. L. Mims, a landowner who lived near where the body was discovered; and John Ed Cothran, Leflore County deputy sheriff.

He Went All the Way
Murray Kempton, *New York Post*, 22 September 1955

Sumner, Miss., Sept. 22 — Moses Wright, making a formation no white man in this county really believed he would dare to make, stood on his tiptoes to the full limit of his 64 years and his 5 feet 3 inches yesterday, pointed his black, workworn finger straight at the huge and stormy head of J. W. Milam and swore that this was the man who dragged 14-year-old Emmett Louis Till out of his cottonfield cabin the night the boy was murdered.

"There he is," said Moses Wright. He was a black pigmy standing up to a white ox. J. W. Milam leaned forward, crooking a cigaret in a hand that seemed as large as Moses Wright's whole chest, and his eyes were coals of hatred.

Moses Wright took all their blast straight in his face, and then, for good measure, turned and pointed that still unshaking finger at Roy Bryant, the man he says joined Milam on the night-ride to seize young Till for the crime of whistling suggestively at Bryant's wife in a store three miles away and three nights before.

*   *   *

"And there's Mr. Bryant," said Moses Wright and sat down hard against the chair-back with a lurch which told better than anything else the cost in strength to him of the thing he had done. He was a field Negro who had dared try to send two white men to the gas chamber for murdering a Negro.

He sat in a court where District Attorney Gerald Chatham, who is on his side, steadily addressed him as Uncle Mose and conversed with him a kind of pidgin cotton-picker's dialect, saying "axed" for "asked" as Moses Wright did and talking about the "undertaker man."

Once Chatham called him "Old Man Mose," but this was the kindly, contemptuous tolerance of the genteel; after 21 minutes of this, Moses Wright was turned over to Defense Counsel Sidney Carlton and now the manner was that of an overseer with a field-hand.

*   *   *

Sidney Carlton roared at Moses Wright as though he were the defendant, and every time Carlton raised his voice like the lash of a whip, J. W. Milam would permit himself a cold smile.

And then Moses Wright did the bravest thing a Delta Negro can do; he stopped saying "sir." Every time Carlton came back to the attack, Moses Wright pushed himself back against his chair and said "that's right" and the absence of the "sir" was almost like a spit in the eye.

When he had come to the end of the hardest half hour in the hardest life possible for a human being in these United States, Moses Wright's story was shaken; yet, he still clutched its foundations. Against Carlton's voice and Milam's eyes and the incredulity of an all white jury he sat alone and refused to bow.

*   *   *

If it had not been for him, we would not have had this trial. It will be a miracle if he wins his case, yet it is a kind of miracle that all on account of Moses Wright, the State of Mississippi is earnestly striving here in this courtroom to convict two white men for murdering a Negro boy so obscure that they do not appear to have even known his name.

He testified yesterday that as Milam left his house with Emmett Till on the night of Aug. 28, he asked Moses Wright whether he knew anyone on the raiding party. "No sir I said. I don't know nobody."

Then Milam asked him how old he was, and Moses Wright said 64 and Milam said, "If you knew any of us, you won't live to be 65."

And, after the darkened car drove off with his great nephew, Moses Wright drove his hysterical wife over to Sumner and put her on the train to Chicago, from which she has written him every day since to cut and run and get out of town. The next day, all by himself, Moses Wright drove into nearby Greenwood and told his story in the sheriff's office.

*   *   *

It was a pathetic errand; it seems a sort of marvel that any thing was done at all. Sheriff George Smith drove out to Money around 2 P.M. that afternoon and found Roy Bryant sleeping behind his store. They were good friends and they talked as friends about this little boy whose name Smith himself had not bothered to find out.

Smith reported that Roy had said that he had gone down the road and taken the little boy out of "preacher's" cabin, and brought him back to the store and, when his wife said it wasn't the right boy, told him to go home.

Sheriff Smith didn't even take Bryant's statement down. When he testified to it yesterday, the defense interposed the straight-faced objection that this was after all the conversation of two friends and that the state shouldn't embarrass the sheriff by making him repeat it in court. Yet, just the same, Sheriff Smith arrested Roy Bryant for kidnapping that night.

* * *

When the body supposed to be Emmett Till's was found in the river, a deputy sheriff drove Moses Wright up to identify it. There was no inquest. Night before last, the prosecution fished up a picture of the body which had been in the Greenwood police files since the night it was brought in, but there was no sign the sheriff knew anything about it, and its discovery was announced as a coup for the state. But, with that apathy and incompetence, Moses Wright almost alone has brought the kidnappers of his nephew to trial.

The country in which he toiled and which he is now resigned to leaving will never be the same for what he has done. Today the state will put on the stand three other field Negroes to tell how they saw Milam and Bryant near the murder scene. They came in scared: one disappeared while the sheriff's deputies were looking for him. They, like Moses Wright, are reluctant heroes; unlike him, they have to be dragged to the test.

They will be belted and flayed as he was yesterday, but they will walk out with the memory of having been human beings for just a little while. Whatever the result, there is a kind of majesty in the spectacle of the State of Mississippi honestly trying to convict two white men on the word of four Negroes.

And we owe that sight to Moses Wright, who was condemned to bow all his life, and had enough left to raise his head and look the enemy in those terrible eyes when he was 64.

Uncle of Till's Identifies Pair of Men Who Abducted Chicago Negro

Sam Johnson [AP Correspondent], *Greenwood Commonwealth*, 21 September 1955

Sumner, Miss. Sept 21 (AP) — Mose Wright pointed a knobby finger at J. W. Milam today and said "There he is"—identifying him as one man who abducted the sharecropper's nephew in the early morning hours Aug. 28.

Then the 64-year-old farmer pointed out 24-year-old Roy Bryant, Milam's half brother, as the second man who roused the Wright family from bed at 2 A.M. and took Emmett Louis Till away.

Bryant and Milam are accused of murdering the Chicago negro boy because he allegedly whistled at Mrs. Bryant. Dis. Atty. Gerald Chatham called Wright as the state's first witness.

Testimony began shortly after Chatham said he had six new witnesses who would place the defendants "with the negro boy several hours after he was taken from Mose Wright's shack." He also said the witnesses would place the accused men in the area where Till's body was pulled from the Tallahatchie River.

Chatham said the witnesses have "absolutely newly discovered evidence" but did not elaborate further.

Wright pushed his way firmly through the crowded courtroom and sat down in the big witness chair. The back of the chair reached almost to the top of his head. Chatham asked the neatly dressed farmer to describe the events of Aug. 28.

"About two o'clock . . . someone was at the door. They said, 'Preacher, preacher.'"

"'This is Mr. Bryant,'" Wright said the voice told him. "I got up and opened the door.

"Mr. Milam was standing at the door with a pistol in his right hand and a flashlight in the other," Wright declared.

Wright started to continue, but Chatham interrupted: "Uncle Mose, do you see Mr. Milam in the courtroom?"

The little negro rose from the big chair and pointed at the defendant. "There he is," he said.

Wright then pointed out Bryant as the man who stood in the darkness of the front porch with Milam. The district attorney did not identify the new witnesses.

Wright answered questions without hesitation in a loud voice. Now and then he pounded his right fist on the table before him.

At first, the witness said he couldn't recognize Bryant as the man he saw standing before his screen door with Milam just before the boy was abducted. But after vigorous defense objections, Wright finally said Bryant[,] sitting in the court-room[,] was the same man who identified himself on the front porch as Bryant.

He said Milam carried the pistol and added:

"He asked me if I had two boys out of Chicago."

The visiting boys were Till, 14, his nephew, and 16-year-old Wheeler Parker, Wright's grandson. They had been vacationing there a week.

Wright said one man told him: "I wants that boy who done that talk at Money."

He said Milam told him after seizing Till, "If that's not the right boy, we are going to bring him back and put him in the bed."

Till and young Parker had been sharing the same bed in the six-room cot-tonfield shack.

As the men left the house, said Wright, one of them warned him not to cause any trouble or "you'll never live to be 65." Wright said his wife left her bed at the height of the commotion, and one of the men ordered her "to get back in that bed and I want to hear those springs."

"My wife said," Wright testified, "'Listen,' she said, 'we'll pay you whatever you want to charge, we'll pay you if you release him.'"

Wright said the men didn't answer.

The witness said he watched from a screened porch as the men took the boy to a car parked on a gravel road about 50 feet from the porch. Its headlights were off. He said he heard one man ask—apparently of someone in the car—"Is this the boy?"

"Someone said 'yes,'["] said Wright.

"Was that a man's voice or a woman's?["] He was asked.

"It seemed a little lighter than a man's," Wright replied.

Wright then told of watching the car drive away toward Money, its lights still off.

He said he never saw the Till boy alive again.

He said he was an onlooker when the body was taken from the river.

"Who was it?" asked Chatham, referring to the body.

"Emm[e]tt Till," Wright answered.

The witness, speaking firmly, said he watched authorities remove from the boy a ring like the one young Till wore—an initialed signet ring originally worn by his father.

Defense Attorney Sidney Carlton quickly moved to cut down Wright's iden-tification of Milam and Bryant in cross-examination.

Wright admitted the only light in the darkened house came from the flashlight held by the man he identified as Milam.

Then, after a series of rapid questions, Carlton asked the elderly negro:

Q: Didn't you ever tell defense lawyers that the only reason you thought it was Mr. Milam was because he (the man at the door) was big and bald.

Wright paused.

A. That's right.

The sharecropper said he had never seen Milam or Bryant before Till's abduction.

Q: Was there ever any light turned on in the house?

A: No sir.

Q: Did you ever see (the flashlight) light shine on his (Bryant's) face that night.

A: No sir.

But Wright still insisted he could identify the men.

The defense hammered hard at Wright's identification. He is reportedly the only eyewitness—unless the district attorney's surprise witnesses as yet unidentified saw something.

The state called Sheriff George Smith of Leflore County. The jury was sent out of the room and Smith described a conversation he had with Bryant on the day Till was abducted.

Smith said Bryant told him "he went down there to his (Wright's house) and brought him (Till) up there to his (Bryant's) store and he wasn't the right one and (Bryant) turned him loose."

Judge Curtis Swango Jr. ruled out this testimony, stating the state must first prove Till was murdered.

"The only proof is that Emmett Till is dead," the judge said. "There's no evidence of any criminal agency."

Chester Miller, Greenwood undertaker, took the stand for the second time and described Till's body.

"The whole top of the head was crushed in. A piece of the skull fell out in the boat," he said.

After being pulled from the river, Till's body was placed in a boat, where Miller found it on his arrival with an ambulance.

"I saw a hole in his skull, about one inch above the right ear," he said. Miller could not say what caused the hole or other wounds.

Sheriff H. C. Strider of Tallahatchie County has said a bullet caused the hole above Till's ear. [. . .]

Slain Boy's Uncle Identifies Bryant, Milam on Stand

Ralph Hutto, *Jackson State Times,* 21 September 1955

Mose Wright, first witness for the state as the Emmett Till case opened Wednesday morning, and uncle of the slain 14-year-old boy, identified the two murder defendants as the men who kidnaped his nephew.

But he admitted on cross-examination he had never seen the faces of Roy Bryant and J. W. Milam in the light.

Wright was questioned at length by both state and defense counsel concerning events which led to the murder of Till.

As court convened at 9:16 A.M. Dist. Atty. Gerald Chatham began questioning Wright. Here are excerpts from his testimony:

(Chatham questioning)

Q: Emmett and the other boys had been to Greenwood that night [August 28] and came in about 1 A.M. Is that correct?

A: Yes sir.

Q: Which room did Emmett Till go to bed in?

A: The east front room.

Q: Who was in bed with him?

A: Simmy, my youngest son.

Q: Did any person call after that?

A: Somebody came to the house about 2 o'clock.

Q: What did they do?

A: Somebody out on the doorstep yelled, "Preacher, preacher, this is Mr. Bryant. I want to talk to you and the boy."

Q: What did you do?

A: I got up and opened the door. Mr. Milam was standing in the door. He had a pistol in one hand and a flashlight in the other.

(At this point, Chatham asked Wright to point out the man in court who was [the] defendant, and Wright did so)

Q: What did Milam say when you let him in?

A: He asked me if we had two boys from Chicago.

Q: Who was there from Chicago?

A: Wheeler Parker and Emmett Till had been visiting us a week that very day.

Q: What did he say then?

A: Mr. Milam said he wanted the boy who'd done the talking at Money.

Q: Did you recognize Mr. Bryant?

A: He said [who] he was, but his face was in the shadows.

Q: What did you do when you went to the room?

A: Mr. Milam told me if it was not the right boy he would bring him back and put him in bed.

Q: What happened then?

A: Mr. Milam told him to get up. When he started out, he asked me if I knew him. I said, "No." He asked me how old I was and I told him 64. He said if I ever recognized him I would never live to be 65.

Q: When he started out, did he say anything to your wife?

A: He said, "Get back in bed. I want to hear them springs squeak."

Q: What did she do?

A: She got back in bed.

Q: He had a pistol in his hand at all times, did he not?

A: Yes.

Q: Did you make any efforts to try and get him not to take the boy?

A: Yes. We said, "We'll pay you whatever you want to charge, if you just release him."

Q: After they left, what did you do?

A: I came to the screen door. I could see the road very clearly. There was a car parked towards Money.

Q: Did you hear them ask anything?

A: Yes. One of them asked "if this is the boy," and a voice from the car answered, "Yes." It was a lighter voice than the men.

Q: Did you watch them leave?

A: Yes. I stood on the porch about 20 minutes after they left.

Q: Have you seen Emmett Till alive since that night?

A: No.

Q: When was the next time you saw Emmett?

A: He was in a boat where they had taken him out of the river.

Q: Was he living or dead?

A: He was dead.

Q: Could you tell whose body it was?

A: It was Emmett Till.

Q: Did you notice a deputy sheriff taking the ring off his finger?

A: Yes.

Q: What did you do with the body?

A: Chester Miller, an undertaker, took him back to Greenwood.

(The defense then objected to state attempts to show that Till's body was first sent to Money for burial and then brought back to Tutwiler to be shipped to Chicago on the grounds that Wright had not seen the body shipped. Circuit Judge Curtis M. Swango sustained that objection and the line of questioning about disposition of the body was discontinued.)

Q: What did Miller do with the ring?

A: He put it on the seat on the ambulance.

Q: Did you ever get it?

A: Yes sir. I asked for it and he gave it to me.

(Wright then identified a ring handed to him by Chatham as the one taken from Till's body.)

Q: What did you do with the ring after he gave it to you?

A: I took it home and later gave it to deputy sheriff J. E. Cochran [Cothran] of Leflore County.

(At 9:48 A.M. defense attorney Sidney Carlton, Sumner, began his cross examination of Wright.)

Q: When these two men entered your house, did you ever turn on your light?

A: No sir.

Q: The man who entered first was carrying a flashlight, was he not? Did he ever shine it in his own face or the face of the man with him?

A: No.

Q: You went in the house side by side?

A: Yes.

Q: The flashlight was always in front, wasn't it?

A: Yes.

Q: The other man walked behind you, didn't he?

A: Yes.

Q: Was there any other men present besides the two you mentioned earlier?

A: Yes. There was a man standing out on the place with his head down, as if he was trying to hide it.

Q: I believe you told us before the trial began that this was a colored man?

A: He acted like it.

Q: How did you know who they were looking for when they came to your house?

Heard Talk

A: I had heard that the boy had done some talk around Money Thursday and Friday.

(At this point, the defense asked if Mose had punished Emmett Till for "the talk" he had done at Money, but the state objected to that line of questioning. Judge Swango sustained the objection and the line of questions was discontinued.)

Q: Don't you remember talking with five defense attorneys and telling us that the only reason that you believed it to be Milam is that he is a big man and has a bald head?

A: No sir. I don't remember that.

Q: Isn't it true that the first time you saw these two was in this courtroom?

A: No sir.

Q: In your house, all that you saw was a bald-headed man. Isn't that right?

A: Yes sir.

Q: Isn't it a fact that you saw Milam's pictures in the newspaper before you came to this trial?

A: I don't remember whether I did or not.

Q: How did Emmett talk?

A: He talked in a kind of stammer.

Q: Was he a pretty good-sized boy?

A: He looked like a grown man. He was about five feet four inches and weighed about 150 pounds.

Q: How close to the boat were you when you first knew it was Emmett?

A: I don't remember.

Q: When you first came up, he was lying on his face and all you saw was his head and back, isn't that true?

A: Yes.

Q: When they turned the body over, it was the first time you knew it was Emmett, is that correct?

A: Yes sir, that's right.

(Wright admitted to Carlton that he had never seen the ring before it was taken from the body, but said it had Emmett's father's initials on it. He said he had heard Emmett say that the ring was too big and he had to put tape on it to make it fit. Wright said that when the body was discovered, the ring fit tightly and there was no tape on it.)

Q: Didn't you tell the defense the only reason you could tell that the body was Emmett's was that it was smooth-faced and had no whiskers?

A: I did not make that statement.

Q: Where were you the Wednesday night before when the incident at Money took place?

A: I was at church. The boys went out and had taken my car.

Q: When the men came to the door, you knew what boy they wanted to see, didn't you?

A: Yes sir. They said they wanted the boy who did the talking at Money.

Q: You knew who that was?

A: Yes.

Q: Would you have identified him as Emmett if he had not been missing?

A: Yes, because I had evidence: the ring.

Mother, "Surprise Witness" Give Dramatic Testimony: Mamie Bradley Says Corpse Was That of Her Slain Son [part 2]
Ralph Hutto, *Jackson State Times,* 22 September 1955

The following is the second part of Hutto's article, which gives the most detailed account of what the state witnesses who followed Mose Wright had to say. The first part of the article—covering parts of Thursday's testimony—is reprinted in the section covering "Day Four" of the trial.

Here are excerpts from Wednesday afternoon's testimony:

(First witness called was Robert Hodges, teenage fisherman of Phillip [Philipp] who found the body)

(Special prosecutor asked questions for the state)

Q. Did you see anything unusual[?]

A. I saw two knees sticking out of the water.

Q. Where was this[?]

A. About a mile from my house on the left side of the river the Tallahatchie County side. The body was hung on a snag.

Q. What did you do[?]

A. I ran my lines and then reported what had happened to my father. He told our landlord[,] who called Sheriff H. C. Strider of Tallahatchie County.

Hodges said after Deputy Sheriff Garland Melton arrived they took two boats and went down the river, finding the body in the same place. Melton tied a rope around the legs and pulled the body loose from the snag. They towed the body to a bank of the river, where they found it had been weighted with a heavy gin fan tied to the body with barbed wire around the neck.

Q. Did you observe the wound[?]

A. He was beaten pretty bad on the back of his head and had a gash on the side of his head.

The defense objected to any conclusion about what caused the hole and Judge Swango ruled the testimony could be taken only on the condition of the body.

Hodges said Negro undertaker Chester Miller, a morning witness, took charge of the body and removed a silver ring from one finger.

Another witness to the discovery of the body, B. L. Mims, Phillip [Philipp], said he was in the boat with deputy Melton when the body was pulled from the river. His testimony was substantially the same as that of Hodges.

Next to testify was Sheriff Smith of Leflore County.

Dist. Atty. Gerald Chatham asked Smith if he talked to Bryant Sunday afternoon, Aug 28.

A: Yes, sir, we talked in my car about 2 P.M., outside his store at Money.

[The next question is missing from the original article.]

A: He said they took him from Mose Wright's house but let him go when Mrs. Bryant did not identify him as the one who made remarks to her.

Q: Where did they turn him loose[?]

A: Outside the store.

Q: Did Bryant give you an explanation for the fact he was sleeping at 2 P.M.[?]

A: He said that he went to the home of some of his people and played cards the rest of the night.

Cross-Examination

At this point, Chatham turned the witness over to defense attorney J. J. Breland for cross-examination.

Q: You and Bryant were good friends, weren't you[?]

A: Yes, sir.

Q: You trusted him and he trusted you[?]

A: Yes, sir.

Q: In the last election when you ran for representative he supported you, didn't he[?]

A: Well. I hope he supported me.

Q: When you talked to him you requested he come to your car so you could confer privately?

A: Yes, sir.

Q: You asked deputy sheriff Cothran to leave the car while you talked with Bryant?

A: Yes, sir.

Q: You did so to talk confidentially[?]

A: I asked him about his troubles and he came out to talk.

Q: What you said was just between you two, wasn't it[?]

A: That's right.

Q: Did you tell him you came to arrest him[?]

A: Not at the time.

Q: You had no warrant[?]

A: No.

Q: You didn't tell him you were investigating for the sheriff's office. You went as a friend didn't you[?]

A: I went up as a friend.

Q: And of course you didn't tell him any statement he made might be used against him[?]

A: He didn't make any statement. We were just talking. No, I didn't tell him that.

Q: Did you arrest him that afternoon[?]

A: Yes, I told him he was under arrest and he asked if he could put on some clean clothes. I allowed him to do so before taking him in.

The defense relinquished the witness and Prosecutor Chatham asked him several additional questions.

Q: How long had you known Bryant[?]

A: Oh, about two years.

Q: When he talked to you, he knew you were sheriff of Leflore County[?]

A: Yes.

Q: How far is it from the store to Mose Wright's home[?]

A: About three miles.

Q: Did he ever give an explanation why he didn't take Till back home after he let him go[?]

A: He said he figured the boy knew the way.

Overrules Objections

Breland moved that the Smith testimony about the Bryant statement be excluded because it was not given freely and voluntarily, was obtained under improper circumstances, and without the defendant being advised of his rights. He further objected on the ground that the state had not proved the corpus delecti: had not proved that Till died by illegal means. Judge Swango overruled all objections and deputy sheriff Cothran was called to the stand.

He was questioned first by special prosecutor Smith.

Q: What was he doing when you got there?

A: He was asleep.

Q: What did he tell you about the boy?

[The answer to this question is missing from the original article.]

Q: Did you have the occasion to talk with Milam after his arrest?

A: I did, on Monday, the day after he was arrested.

Q: Who was present?

A: Just Milam and myself at the Tallahatchie County jail.

Q: Did you promise to reward him for his statement?

A: He didn't make a statement. We just talked.

Q: In your conversation, though, he did make a statement, didn't he?

A: Yes.

Q: What did he say?

A: He said he turned the boy loose at Bryant's store.

Q: Did he say why he went to Mose Wright's house to get the boy in the first place?

A: No, sir.

Q: Did he explain why he didn't take Till back home?

A: No, sir.

Examined Body

Cothran told the jury of examining the body, saying that when he saw it the head was "caved in" and that Till had a small wound about an inch above his right ear.

Cross-examination by C. Sidney Carlton of the defense raised the possibility the injuries to the back of Till's head might have been caused by the 70-pound gin fan used to weight down his body in the river. He also suggested that a snag might have caused the hole above the ear. Cothran admitted the injuries could have been caused in that manner.

Q: You testified he was not mutilated?

A: That's right.

Q: His privates weren't mutilated?

A: Not that I could see.

Q: When you removed a ring from his finger, did the finger or fingernails come off?

A: I didn't notice.

Q: Wasn't the skin slipping badly?

A: I didn't notice.

Q: What was the condition of his tongue?

A: It was swelling out of his mouth.

Q: Was his body swollen?

A: It was in pretty bad shape.

Q: How old would you estimate the person found to be?

A: I wouldn't estimate it.

That concluded Tuesday [Wednesday] afternoon's testimony after the state introduced as evidence the gin fan weight and barbed wire used to attach it to the body.

DAY FOUR: THURSDAY, SEPTEMBER 22

This was the most important day of the trial. The first witness called was Chick Nelson, mayor of Tutwiler, who testified that his funeral home had picked up Till's corpse in Greenwood and, after preparations, shipped it to Chicago. He was followed by Mamie Bradley, who testified that the body in the river was indeed her son's. After her testimony, the prosecution called its "surprise witness," Willie Reed, who told the court that he saw Milam on the day of the alleged murder exiting a barn wherein he, Reed, could hear screams. After calling other witnesses to corroborate Reed's story, the State rested its case just before 2:00 P.M. Soon afterwards the defense asked for a directed verdict of not guilty. Judge Swango denied the request and the defense began its case by calling Carolyn Bryant to the stand. Judge Swango allowed Mrs. Bryant's testimony but removed the jury from the courtroom. She was followed on the stand by Mrs. Juanita Milam, and then Sheriff Strider, who once again repeated his contention that the body in the river was not Till's. The defense called several more witnesses as it prepared to rest its case the next day.

Mother, "Surprise Witness" Give Dramatic Testimony: Mamie Bradley Says Corpse Was That of Her Slain Son [part 1]
Ralph Hutto, *Jackson State Times*, 22 September 1955

Sumner — A witness who testifies he saw Negro Emmett Till alive in Sunflower County the day he was kidnapped and the mother of the slain boy were main witnesses Thursday morning in the trial of two white men for the murder of 14-year-old Till.

Willie Reed, young Negro plantation hand, said he saw a boy who appeared to be Till being driven to a barn on the plantation run by Leslie Milam, brother of J. W. Milam, one of the murder defendants.

He also said he saw Milam come from the barn.

Mamie Bradley, Till's mother, positively identified the body she saw at a Chicago funeral home as that of her son.

The first witness of the morning was C. M. "Chic" Nelson, manager of a Tutwiler Funeral Home, who testified that he sent Till's body to the A. A. Rainer Funeral Home in Chicago for services and burial.

Mamie Bradley took the stand at 10:03 A.M., and was questioned by special prosecutor Robert Smith. Here are excerpts of her testimony:

Did your son leave Chicago to visit Mississippi the latter part of August?

To Spend Two Weeks

A: Yes, sir, he left Chicago Aug. 20 and was supposed to spend two weeks in Mississippi.

Q: Was his body later sent to Chicago?

A: Yes, sir.

Q: Where did you first see the body?

A: I saw it at the A. A. Rainer funeral home in a casket and later after it had been placed on a slab. I positively identified the body I saw in the casket as my son.

Q: How did you know that?

A: I looked at his face carefully. I looked at him all over thoroughly. I was able to see that it was my boy without a shadow of a doubt.

Q: His father, Louis, was killed overseas in the armed forces, was he not?

A: Yes, sir.

Q: Were his father's personal effects sent to you after his death?

A: Yes, sir.

Q: Was there a ring in those personal effects?

A: Yes, sir.

Q: Did you give your son the ring which was returned?

Identifies Ring

(At this point Smith handed her a ring and Mamie Bradley identified it as the one she had given to her son.)

Q: You did give this ring to your son?

A: Yes, but his hand was too small to wear it at the time. However, since he was 12 years old, he has worn the ring on occasions, using Scotch tape or a string to keep it from coming off. When he left Chicago, he was looking for some cuff links in his jewelry box and found the ring and put it on his finger to show me that it fit and he didn't have to wear a tape anymore.

Q: And you say definitely that he left Chicago with the ring in his possession?

A: Yes, sir.

(The state then had her identify a picture of Till's body and passed it around to members of the jury. Tears came into her eyes as the photo was passed around. She took off her glasses, blinking rapidly and wiping tears away with her bare hands.)

Cross-Examined

(The witness was turned over to the defense and attorney J. J. Breland cross-examined her.)

(The state objected strenuously to introduction of a photograph of Till's body run in a Chicago newspaper and Judge Swango excused the jury from the court while the controversy was debated. Judge Swango ruled the defense could enter one photograph of Till before he died, which was submitted by his mother, and also the clipped photograph at the funeral.)

(While the jury was still out, Breland asked Mamie Bradley if she discussed the trip with her son and if she cautioned him how to behave.)

A: Yes, sir.

Q: You have been quoted in the press as saying, "I told him several times to kneel in the street and beg forgiveness." Did you make that statement?

A: I said something like that. I told him he was coming South and that he would have to adapt himself to the customs. I told him to be careful how and to whom he spoke, to say "yes, sir" and "no, sir" at all times, humble himself if necessary by going on his knees whether he thought it was wrong or right. I told him to be careful how he walked the streets.

Q: Did you caution him not to insult white women?

A: I did not mention women when I referred to white people in general. Naturally coming from Chicago he wouldn't know how to act.

Q: Had he ever done anything to cause trouble before?

A: No, sir, he never caused trouble at any time.

Reed to Stand

(The witness was excused from the stand at 10:55 A.M., whereupon Willie Reed, a hand on the Sheridan plantation near Drew, was called for questioning by Smith.)

Q: Do you know Mr. Leslie Milam?

A: Yes, sir. His place is just down the road.

Q: Do you know J. W. Milam?

A: Yes, sir. (He pointed Milam out in the courtroom.)

Q: Going back to Sunday, Aug. 28, did you ever see J. W. Milam that day?

A: I saw him coming to a well at the Leslie Milam place.

Q: What time did you leave home that morning?

A: I left about six or seven, going to the store.

Q: Was it necessary to pass by the Leslie Milam place?

A: Yes, sir.

Q: Was there a shed, barn or any other building on the place?

A: Yes, sir, there was a barn there.

Q: As you came up did you see anything?

Sees Truck

A: Yes, sir, I saw a truck pass by with a white top and a green body. It was a 1955 Chevrolet.

Q: Who was in the truck?

A: I saw four white men in the cab and three colored men in the back. One was sitting on the bottom and the others sat on the side of the body.

Q: How close did you get to the truck?

A: About from here to the door (he pointed to the courtroom door about 50 feet away).

Q: Did you see Mr. J. W. Milam in the cab?

A: I didn't pay any attention at that time.

Q: I show you this picture which was placed in the evidence of the testimony of Mamie Bradley, and ask you if it resembles the person you saw sitting on the floor of the back end of the truck.

A: It looks like the picture of the boy I saw in the back of the truck.

Q: Did you walk up the road?

A: Yes, sir, and I saw the truck sitting in front of the barn.

Truck Empty

Q: As you passed the barn, was there anyone in the truck[?]

A: No, sir.

Q: Later in the morning did you see J. W. Milam?

A: He came out of the barn and went over to the well to get a drink of water.

Q: Did you see anything unusual about him?

A: He had on a gun.

Q: What did he do?

A: He went to the well and got a drink of water and then went back to the barn.

[. . .]

Mother Insulted on Witness Stand

Washington Afro American, 24 September 1955

Sumner, Miss. — In a dramatic highlight of the lynchburg trial case, Mrs. Mamie Bradley took the witness stand Thursday and tenderly, but without tears, identified the ring taken from her murdered son's hand when his body was dragged from the Tallahatchie River, Aug. 31.

The pretty, pert mother stepped to the witness stand as the prosecution's first witness on the fourth day of the trial.

She was immediately asked about the ring because all day Wednesday the defense had hammered at six prosecution witnesses in an attempt to prove that the body taken from the river was not that of Emmett Till.

The ring, taken from the boy's finger by an undertaker, Chester Miller, was turned over to the sheriff and not sent to Chicago with the body.

Robert B. Smith, white prosecutor specially assigned to the case by Gov. Hugh White, began questioning his own witness, Mrs. Bradley, by referring to her as "Mamie" instead of Mrs. Bradley.

After Mrs. Bradley told how she had identified her son's crushed body through careful study of what was left of his face, Prosecutor Smith handed her the ring.

She tenderly identified it as belonging to her dead soldier husband, Louis Till, and said that her son was wearing it when he left Chicago.

The defense immediately jumped to cross-examination and defense counsel J. J. Breeland [Breland] of Sumner began by making the unusual request that he be allowed to remain seated while cross-examining her. The permission was granted, but Breeland soon got to his feet to question her.

He began by asking her if she had been born in Mississippi.

She replied that she was born in Webb, a town about three miles from Sumner, but that she had left here when she was two years old.

Addressing her all the while as "Mamie," Breeland then began an attempt to question her about the newspapers she reads.

When he asked her if she is a subscriber to the Chicago weekly, the prosecution sternly objected.

Prosecutor Smith pleaded with the court not to allow the defense to follow this line of questioning. He did not say so, but he apparently had the tense racial situation in mind here.

Judge Swango ordered the jury to leave the courtroom while he listened to what the defense had to offer before he ruled on the objection.

When the jury left[,] Breeland revealed that he planned to question Mrs. Bradley on a number of clippings and articles from the colored press.

Judge Swango finally ruled that he would not permit her to be questioned about news articles or photographs with the exception of one photograph which the defense presented.

Breeland then asked her if, when her son left Chicago, she had cautioned him on how to act around white[s] in the South.

She answered that she had cautioned him on how to act and speak when he came here.

At this point Judge Swango then ruled that all such questions from the defense were objectionable and said he sustained the objections of the prosecution.

He then ordered the jury brought in again after warning Breeland that, that kind of questioning was definitely out.

The Future
Murray Kempton, *New York Post,* 23 September 1955

Sumner, Miss., Sept. 23 — The special prosecutor representing the State of Mississippi stood up yesterday morning and called "Mamie Bradley."

The mother of Emmett Louis Till, who is an affront to Sumner's white populace and a stranger to its black one, walked the long, narrow, crammed pathway from the back of the room to the witness box and sat herself down and pulled her skirt over her knee.

She put on her glasses and looked at Special Prosecutor Robert Smith; she wore a black bolero and a printed dress with a small black hat and a piece of a veil and she was very different from the cotton patch cropper who is the ordinary Negro witness in a Mississippi courtroom.

Still, Robert Smith had to call her "Mamie" and she accepted it with grace, because she knows that Robert Smith wants to avenge her dead son as much as she does, and there are customs where she is now.

She lives, she said, in Chicago and she had a son known as Emmett Till, whom she saw alive last when he left home to "visit my uncle, Moses Wright." She had seen him next early this month when the body came back to Chicago. "I positively identified the body I saw on the slab in Chicago as being my son, Emmett Louis Till."

She turned to that white jury and tried to reach them.

"I looked at the ears, the forehead, the nose, the lips, the chin"—she ran through the catalog very slowly and precisely—"I knew definitely that was my boy, beyond the shadow of a doubt." She was trying to bridge the gap between herself and that jury, and she knew that containment was the only way.

Robert Smith showed her a police picture of the body brought out of the Tallahatchie River. She had never seen that particular picture before, and she looked at it and bowed her head and said, "Yes, Sir." Smith turned to put the picture on the table; in the interval of silence she took off her glasses and wiped her eyes, almost furtively, as though it would destroy the line she was desperately casting to the jury to show emotion.

Then Robert Smith showed her the ring that had been taken off a finger of the body in the river. She said it had been her first husband's and had been given to Emmett and he had put it on the day he left Chicago for Mississippi and shown her that he was large enough to wear it and she had said, "Gee, you're getting to be a big boy now."

Then Smith sat down, and G. L. Breeland [Breland] moved in for the defense. He began quietly asking where she had been born and how long she had lived in Chicago, and whether she had discussed its difference from Mississippi with Emmett when she sent him on vacation to Mose Wright's, and she said yes.

Breeland's every implication was trying to reach the jury, too, and it was easy for him to be casual about it. How much insurance has she had on Emmett's life? She answered $400.

"Have you collected on the policies?"

She sat, with his innuendo all over the courtroom, and answered very quietly: "I've been waiting for the death certificate."

"What newspapers do you subscribe to in Chicago," Breeland asked: "Do you read the *Chicago Defender*?" He was flourishing the Negro press before the jury: Judge Curtis Swango stopped him there and told the jury to get out of the room so he could judge whether this line of questioning was pertinent or merely diversionary inflammation.

*   *   *

With the jury out, Breeland began again on the difference between Chicago and Mississippi. Had she talked to Emmett about the way he should act down here. Had she said that he should get down on his knees in the street before any white man.

"I can give you a liberal transcription of what I said," Mrs. Bradley answered at last. "I told him to be very careful how he spoke and to say 'yes, sir' and 'no, mam,' and not to hesitate to humble yourself if you had to get down on your knees."

Breeland went on asking her if she didn't live in the Black Belt of Chicago and how Emmett, being from Chicago, could know the customs of Mississippi. When he had finished, Judge Swango cut in, a sudden sharpness in his habitual courtesy, and said:

"Every question you have asked will be excluded; and there'll be no reference to it."

Just this once in Mississippi, they'd try a murder case and not Chicago; and, having made that guarantee, Curtis Swango told the bailiffs to invite the jury back to court.

*   *   *

And that was all for Mrs. Mamie Bradley; the defense would not be permitted to use her to wave the bloody shirt and whisper the farthest implication. The defense had to let her go, and she thanked the judge and left with all her dignity.

As the Till trial went on, she sat outside the court all by herself reading her paper; the ordinary Negroes of Tallahatchie County huddled in their appointed place around the base of the Confederate monument, not quite able to communicate with her; and she alone among them seemed to have faith that justice would be done and the future would be different. She alone seemed to understand the implications of this week to Sumner, whatever its final verdict.

She is a civil service worker who makes $3,600 a year and will rise to $4,500 before long. She and Emmett lived in a two-family house in what was very definitely not the teeming slums of South Chicago. "We are," she said, "what you might call the lower middle class." And Emmett had had lower middle class ambitions; he had dreamed of being a professional baseball player and learning a skilled mechanic's trade; what Negro here could hope for that?

*   *   *

Still Emmett Till was pulled out of a river a few miles from here, and there is no assurance that his mother [can] expect to collect even the $400 insurance. But even so, too, as she talked about the books she reads, there was the sense that there will be Negroes like her in the county in our lifetime.

Upstairs, Curtis Swango fought to give her a fair trial, and there was the sense that there will be law enforcement officers like him even in Tallahatchie County in our lifetime.

All that makes the headlines—the murder, the deputies, the inevitable acquittal—is a dying present; Curtis Swango and Mamie Bradley are the future; just the sound of their voices, speaking with dignity and without fear, is a death verdict for the beast that sits and swaggers all around them.

Youth Puts Milam in Till Death Barn

James L. Hicks, *Washington Afro-American,* 24 September 1955

Sumner, Miss. — Willie Reed, 18-year-old farm hand, testified Thursday that he saw J. W. Milam enter a barn in Sunflower County, Aug. 28 and seconds later heard human screams coming from the barn.

Reed was the first of a parade of surprise colored witnesses rounded up by Mississippi law officers acting on information given them by Dr. T. [R. M.] Howard and reporters here covering this trial.

Five other witnesses provided by Dr. Howard are present and ready to testify in the new and sensational development which is expected to show that J. W. Milam and Roy Bryant killed Emmett Till in barn on a plantation 10 miles from Mound Bayou that is managed by Milam.

The parade of colored witnesses began the day before when, in what will stand out as one of the most dramatic moments of the trial, the 64-year-old Rev. Moses Wright, Emmett Till's uncle, took the witness stand.

He told of the two white men coming to his house—one with gun in hand—and demanding "the boy who made the big talk."

There was stark drama in the courtroom when the prosecuting attorney asked the Rev. Mr. Wright if one of the men with gun in hand at his door had been J. W. Milam, one of the defendants.

When the aging minister answered "yes," the attorney asked the Rev. Mr. Wright to stand up.

"Now, Uncle Mose," he said, "Do you see J. W. Milam in this room? If so point him out."

With his thin body racked with emotion, but his face a deadly calm, the Rev. Mr. Wright arose, pointed a bony finger at a white man and declared:

"There he is."

Uncle Mose, as he was called by prosecuting attorney Gerald Chatham, was on the stand for 30 minutes, during which time he gave detailed information as to how the white men had come to his home in the middle of the night and taken the boy.

Other colored persons to testify included Mrs. Mandy Bradley, no relation to the boy's mother, Ed Reed, father of Willie Reed.

After these witnesses testified, the state rested its murder case against Roy Bryant and J. W. Milam Thursday at 1:55, having presented five witnesses Thursday and seven on Wednesday.

The two prosecutors felt they had proved that the two white men killed 14-year-old Emmett Till in a barn Aug. 28.

Gerald Chatham and Robert Smith, prosecutors, told reporters during recess they are "confident" they have made a good case, but would not venture a guess on the jury verdict.

The defense is expected to try to show that the body taken from the river was not that of Emmet[t] Till.

Ending of the state argument left several witnesses still to be heard from and reporters who had aided officials in rounding them up were surprised that they were not called.

One such witness was Frank Young, who was brought to the Sheriff's office in the roundup Tuesday night and was said to have important evidence in the case.

At noon the prosecution told the *Afro* that Young has disappeared completely.

Another witness not called was Walter Billups, who was present Wednesday and photographed, but not called today to testify. Both are colored.

Some of the colored witnesses who testified were immediately released to go to the fields and pick cotton.

This brought great concern to Congressman Diggs and others at the colored press table who saw them leave in a car driven by a white man.

The farm managed by Milam is in Sunflower County. If the prosecution can definitely fix this as the murder site, the trial here will come to an end and a new one will begin again.

Judge Sends Jury out of Courtroom during Testimony of Defendant Roy Bryant's Wife
Jackson State Times, 23 September 1955

Sumner, Miss. — The state completed its case in the Emmett Till murder trial Thursday afternoon, and defense attorneys questioned most of their important witnesses.

Early in the afternoon two more so-called "mystery witnesses" told of an incident at a Sunflower County barn the day Emmett Till was kidnapped.

Ed Reed, grandfather of Willie Reed who was on the stand just before noon, said he passed by the barn about 8 A.M. Sunday, August 28, and saw Leslie Milam and "another man I didn't know."

Mandy Bradley, who said she lived on the Leslie Milam place, testified she lived within sight of Leslie Milam's home. She said Willie Reed came to her house early that morning and mentioned something unusual. She told special prosecutor Robert Smith she saw four white men "coming in and out of the barn" and that a truck was outside.

Q: Did you recognize any of them?

Saw Bald Man

A: All I did was see them coming in and out. I just saw a tall man with a bald head.

She did not identify J. W. Milam, one of the defendants, as the man she saw though he fits that description. Mandy said that before the truck left it backed up under the shed, then drove off.

With Mandy's testimony the state rested its case at 1:57 P.M. and after a recess the defense moved that the jury be directed to return a verdict of not guilty. Judge Swango overruled the motion.

Mrs. Roy Bryant, whose encounter with Emmett Till in her husband's store set off the chain of events which led to the murder trial, was called to the stand as first defense witness.

But when she began to tell of the incident with Till in the store Wednesday night, Aug. 24, the state objected to using the story as evidence.

C. Sidney Carlton, defense attorney, protested that the testimony of Mose Wright, Till's uncle, that the men who took him away "wanted to see the boy who did the talking at Money" raised the inferences the defendants "believe they are entitled to explain."

Special prosecutor Smith said: "Our proof started Sunday at 2 A.M. when the boy was taken from Mose Wright's house. We have offered no proof of anything that happened prior to that time. Mrs. Bryant has not been brought up in any way. We have not mentioned her name. The Supreme Court has ruled many times that whatever happened prior to time of a crime has no bearing on the case."

Swango ruled: "The court is of the opinion that such testimony would be admissible only if there was some question of who was the aggressor at the time of the crime, or over acts of the deceased at the time of the crime."

The judge allowed the defense to record Mrs. Bryant's testimony with the jury out of the room. Carlton did the questioning.

Q: Who was in the store with you[?]

A: I was alone.

Mrs. Milam There

Q: Was there anyone in the living quarters of the store[?]

A: Mrs. J. W. Milam was there with her children and my children.

Q: Did any incident take place that made an impression on you?

A: About 8 o'clock a Negro man came in the store and went to the candy case. I walked up to the candy counter and asked what he wanted. I gave him the merchandise and held out my hand for the money.

Q: Did he give you the money?

A: No.

Q: What did he do?

A: He caught my hand in a strong grip and said "How about a date baby."

Q: What did you do then?

A: I turned around and started to the back of the store, but he caught me at the cash register.

Q: How did he catch you?

Hands on Waist

A: He put both hands on my waist from the side.

Q: What did he say?

A: He said, "What's the matter baby, can't you take it?"

Q: Did he say anything else?

A: He told me, "You needn't be afraid."

Q: Did he use words that you don't use?

A: Yes.

Q: It was unprintable, wasn't it?

A: Yes. He said that and added "with white women before."

Q: What happened then?

Dragged Away

A: Another Negro came in and dragged him out of the store by his arm.

Q: Did he say anything further?

A: He said goodbye.

Q: Did anything further happen?

A: He said goodbye.

Q: What happened then?

A: I called Mrs. Milam, and then went out to the car and got a pistol from under the front seat. He was still standing on the porch, and he whistled. (Carlton whistled) Q. Was it like that?

A: Yes.

Q: Have you ever seen that man before or since?

A: No.

Q: What size man was he?

A: He was about 5 feet, six inches tall, and weighed about 150 pounds.

No Speech Defect

Q: Did he have a walking or speech defect, did you have trouble understanding him?

A: No.

The jury was returned and Mrs. Bryant was dismissed with no testimony about the incident on the record.

Mrs. J. W. Milam was brought to the stand and she gave brief information on her family and husband.

The third defense witness was H. C. Strider, Tallahatchie County sheriff, who testified that in his opinion the body had been in the river "about ten days, if not 15." He said he could not tell if the body was white or Negro, except by kinky hair. The odor was strong, Strider said.

He was asked by state attorneys if wounds might not cause a body to decompose more quickly. Strider said he thought the rate of decomposition depended on temperature. He told the jury he probed the round wound over Till's right ear, and could not find any place where it entered the skull.

Physician Testifies

Dr. L. B. Odkin, Greenwood physician, next testified that he was called to view the body pulled from Tallahatchie River.

Carlton asked him the state of the body.

A: I would say it was in an advanced state of decomposition.

Q: Could his brother or mother identify him?

A: I doubt it.

Q: What in your opinion was the length of time between the time of death and finding the body?

A: About 8 to 10 days.

He told Robert Smith on cross examination that the wound over the right ear had entered the skull, but emphasized that he made no pathological examination. He admitted that a fat person or one with a beaten body decomposes more rapidly than others, but he said that did not change his opinion about the length of death.

Following Dr. Ogden's testimony, Smith recalled Strider to ask him if any efforts were still being made to find the identity of the body. Strider said the investigation was continuing, but no progress had been made.

Embalmed Body

Last witness of the day was H. D. Malone, embalmer who has worked for the Negro and white funeral homes in Tutwiler for the last two years. He said he had embalmed the body taken from the river, and described it as "not recognizable."

Malone said the body was swollen and bloated, the skin was slipping, the fingernails were loose in the right hand, the tongue was protruding, the eyes were bulging out, and hair came out easy.

Carlton asked: "How long did it appear to be since his death?"

A: The signs indicated to me he had been dead about 10 days or longer.

He said rigor mortis usually lasts 12 to 48 hours after a death and decomposition usually does not begin until then, and that decomposition probably would be retarded if the body was in a cooler atmosphere such as water.

He also admitted to state attorneys that bodies decompose quicker if they are beaten, or fat.

The court then adjourned until 9:30 A.M. Friday with Defense Attorney J. J. Breland putting Malone on notice that he might be called back to the stand.

Mrs. Bryant Tells How Northern Negro Grabbed Her, "Wolf-Whistled" in Store

Jackson Daily News, 23 September 1955

Following is the testimony of Mrs. Roy Bryant, black-haired, brown-eyed, shapely and slender 21-year-old wife of one of the defendants in the Till murder trial at Sumner. Mrs. Bryant testified with downcast eyes as she talked about something which seemed to offend her delicacy.

Defense Attorney Sidney Carlton questioned. She said she was five feet two inches tall, weighed 101 pounds.

"Do you have any children?"

"Yes."

"How many children do you have, Mrs. Bryant?"

"Two."

"What are their names?"

"Roy Bryant Jr., and Thomas Lamar Bryant."

"What are their ages?"

"Roy Jr. is three; Thomas Lamar is two."

"When were you married Mrs. Bryant?"

"April 25, 1951."

"Did your husband serve in the Armed Forces?"

Mrs. Bryant testified that her husband entered the Army in 1942.

"How long was Mr. Bryant in service?"

"Three years."

At this point Carlton asked:

"Who was in the store with you?"

Special prosecutor Robert Smith jumped up to object to the question. "Judge, Mrs. Bryant has not been mentioned in this case. . . . Whatever happened down there Wednesday is no justification for murder."

Defense Attorney Breland, at this time, said "Incidents may be separated by days or even weeks but if they are connected up they are admissible."

At this point the jury left the room and the defense requested that Mrs. Bryant's testimony be heard "for the record."

Carlton then asked "On Wednesday night, Aug. 24, who was in the store with you?"

"I was alone," answered Mrs. Bryant.

"Was anyone in the living quarters of the store?"

"Mrs. Milam and her two children."

"Did anything unusual occur?"

"Yes[,]" said the former high school beauty, almost inaudibly, as she looked at the floor.

She was attired in a simple, but becoming, black simply tailored dress trimmed with a white neckline.

"This Negro man came into the store and walked up to the candy case.["]

"Who was with you in the store when he came in?"

"No one."

"What did you do?"

"I walked up to the candy counter."

Mrs. Bryant, who was voted most beautiful girl at both Indianola and Leland High School during her school days, said that she didn't remember the merchandise the "Negro man" purchased.

"What did you do then[?]" Carlton asked.

"I held out my hand for his money."

"Did he give you the money?"

"No."

"What did he do?"

"He grabbed my hand."

"When he grabbed your hand, was it a strong grip?"

Mrs. Bryant testified that the "Negro man" grabbed her hand forcibly and that she had difficulty wrenching her hand free.

"What did this Negro man say?"

"He said 'How about a date, baby?'"

Mrs. Bryant said she then turned and walked to the back of the store. She said the "Negro man" followed her.

Carlton asked her "what happened then."

"He caught me at the cash register. He put both hands on my waist."

"Did he say anything?"

"Yes." Mrs. Bryant again looked downward and her voice was almost inaudible.

"He said, 'What's the matter, baby, can't you take it. You needn't be afraid of me.'"

"Did he then use a word that you don't use?"

Mrs. Bryant then testified that the "Negro man" used "unprintable" words and concluded with: "I've been with white women before."

Mrs. Bryant said[,] "This other Negro then came in and caught his arm and took him out.["]

"Were there any Negroes or white men in the store when this incident happened?"

"No."

"Were there any persons on the outside of the store?"

"There were some Negroes outside."

"How many?"

"About eight or nine."

"What did you do?"

Mrs. Bryant testified she went outside to the car to get a gun.

"Did you see him again?"

"Yes."

"Did he say or do anything?"

"He whistled."

"How did he whistle?"

"How did he whistle?"

Mrs. Bryant looked up at Carlton, her eyes asking a question.

Carlton then said:

"Did he whistle like this?"

Carlton then puckered his lips and made the noise known nationally, and perhaps, universally, as a "wolf whistle."

Mrs. Bryant said when she got the gun and turned to go back to the store that the Negro man "was getting" in a car and that he drove away with other Negroes.

"How tall was this Negro man?"

"About five feet six inches tall."

"How much would you estimate he weighed?"

"Around 150 pounds."

Carlton asked Mrs. Bryant if the Negro man limped or had any other difficulty walking. Mrs. Bryant said he did not.

"Did he have a speech impediment?"

"No."

"How did you feel when this happened?"

"I was just scared to death."

"Do you know most of the Negroes around Money?"

"Yes."

Money is a small, rural community of Leflore County deep in the cotton-rich Mississippi Delta.

"Was this Negro man one of those?"

"No."

"Did he talk with a Southern or Northern brogue?"

"Northern."

"Did you have any white men around to protect you?"

"No."

Mrs. Bryant then stated that her husband had gone to Brownsville, Tex. to "take a load of shrimp."

She said that Mrs. Milam was visiting in the Bryant home and store so "I wouldn't be alone."

After this statement, Defense Attorney Carlton said:

"I move that this testimony is competent."

Judge Swango said that the court had already moved.

Then Mrs. Bryant was excused. She left the stand and took her side by her husband, one of the two defendants.

Woman in Lynching Case Weaves Fantastic Story
Washington Afro-American, 24 September 1955

Sumner, Miss. — Mrs. Roy Bryant, the white woman whom 14-year-old Emmett Till allegedly whistled at, thereby causing his brutal lynching, began Thursday afternoon testifying as to what occurred in her Money, Miss. Store on the night of Aug. 24.

The testimony of the 21-year-old woman stunned the court when she never once mentioned the alleged wolf whistle.

Instead she charged that the Chicago youth grabbed her around the hips, asked her for a date and told her that he had "been with white women before."

Mrs. Bryant, speaking in a typical Southern accent, took the stand following the noon recess.

A slight brunette, she charged that young Till used obscene remarks when addressing her but refused to quote the exact words. She left the impression that to use such words would defile her.

Mrs. Bryant said that on August 24, a colored man entered her store in Money. She said that she asked him what he wanted and she got it for him. She never testified, however, just what purchase the colored man wanted.

The wife of one of the men charged with young Till's death, Mrs. Bryant said that when she put her hand out for the money for the purchase, the colored man grabbed her arm and said, "How about a date, Baby."

The woman testified that she struggled loose and turned from the colored man but he chased her around the counter and caught her at the cash register.

She said he placed his arms around her hips and then quoted the man as asking: "What's the matter, baby? Can't you take it?"

It was at this time Mrs. Bryant was asked to use some of the exact language used by the man but she declined. She even refused to repeat one obscene word used.

"You needn't be afraid of me[,]" Mrs. Bryant quoted the colored man as saying later. She said that he then told her: "I've been with white women before."

It was then, according to Mrs. Bryant[,] that another colored fellow entered the store and caught her alleged attacker by the arm and led him out.

She said the first colored man made another obscene remark on the outside where some other colored men were standing and she then went to her car and got her pistol.

Sheriff Strider's Testimony Raises Doubt Body in River Was Till Youth
Jackson Daily News, 23 September 1955

The defense called Tallahatchie Sheriff H. C. Strider to the stand.

Thirty-six year old Defense Attorney John W. Whitten, one of the five defense attorneys, questioned a witness for the first time since the sensational trial began.

Whitten is a first cousin of Mississippi Congressman Jamie Whitten.

"Did you have occasion on Aug. 31, when a body was taken from the Tallahatchie River, to examine the body down there?"

"I did," Sheriff Strider said.

Sheriff Strider said he arrived about 9:15 A.M. and that the body was in a boat and had not yet been placed in the river banks.

"Did you examine the body?"

"The best I could."

"What was the condition of the body?"

"It was in mighty bad shape. The skin was slipping on the entire body."

Sheriff Strider said the skull was crushed, there was a penetration above the right ear and that there was three gashes on the head. He testified that he took a small stick, about the size of a pencil, and probed the hole above the right ear. He said he could find no evidence of a penetration on the left side.

Strider testified that the tongue extended from the mouth about three inches and that the left eyeball "was out enough to call it out."

"Was there an odor?"

"It was so bad, we couldn't examine the body until the undertaker got there."

Sheriff Strider, a big gray-haired man who weighs about 275 pounds[,] said that the undertaker used a "deodorant bomb" but still the odor persisted. Sheriff Strider said that the undertaker then used about a quart of another deoderizing fluid before the odor subsided.

Whitten then asked Sheriff Strider if he had lived near the Tallahatchie River and if he was familiar with the temperature of the water at different seasons of the year and the depth of the river generally. Strider replied that he had lived near the Tallahatchie River for many years.

"What would be the temperature during August, would you say?" Whitten asked.

"I would say around 70 degrees."

Whitten then asked Sheriff Strider to estimate the depth of the river.

In the vicinity where the body was recovered, "25 to 30 feet," said Strider.

Whitten then asked Strider if he had been present at other times when bodies were taken from the river in his capacity as sheriff.

Attorneys from the State then objected and Strider was not allowed to answer. Then, Whitten asked:

"Have you ever taken a body out of the river that has been in there six days."

"Yes."

"What is your opinion about how long this particular body has been in the river?"

"I would say at least 10 days, if not 15."

Whitten then asked Strider if the body taken from the Tallahatchie River was recognizable.

Sheriff Strider said that the body was bloated beyond recognition and that he was unable to determine whether the body was that of a white man or a Negro.

Strider said the body's only Negro characteristic was "kinky hair." "But I've seen a lot of white men with kinky hair," he said.

"If one of my sons had been missing, I couldn't have told it was him. All I could tell it was a human being," Strider continued.

Whitten then showed Strider a photograph of the body, which was taken after it arrived in Chicago. The body was on a slab when the picture was taken.

"I hand you here a photograph and I ask you if this picture represents a true likeness of the body that you saw."

"It doesn't," the Sheriff said.

"I ask you if this picture shows the skin has slipped off."

"No."

Strider said that the body in the picture was darker than the body he saw at the river bank.

"At the time I saw the body, he was as white as I am!"

The defense then turned Strider over to questioning by special prosecutor Smith.

Smith asked Strider if the Sheriff had signed a death certificate and said it was Emmett Till.

Strider said that a death certificate had not been issued out [and] that he did not identify the body as that of Emmett Till.

Strider said he went to the river with Mose Wright, uncle of the boy. He said he asked Mose "Is this the boy?"

"What did Mose say?"

"Mose said, 'I think it is, but I don't know for sure.'"

DAY FIVE: FRIDAY, SEPTEMBER 23

After the defense rested its case early in the morning, the final day of the trial was taken up with closing arguments. Each of the five defense attorneys had his say, as well as both prosecuting attorneys. Just what order these lawyers went in is hard to determine from the news accounts, but the most important and oft-quoted closing arguments were made by John Whitten (for the defense) and Gerald Chatham (for the prosecution). While accounts vary slightly, the jury appears to have taken just sixty-seven minutes to pass its "not guilty" verdict.

Jury Hears Defense and Prosecution Arguments as Testimony Ends in Kidnap-Slaying Case

Sam Johnson [AP Correspondent], *Greenwood Commonwealth*, 23 September 1955

This story has three leads, each one written closer to Johnson's deadline. It appears the last lead was filed just after the case went to the jury. Had Johnson been able to wait a little more than an hour, he could have written another lead, this one announcing the jury's "not guilty" verdict.

Sumner, Miss., Sept 23 (AP) — A country jury began deliberating at 2:36 (CST) today on the fate of two white men accused of murdering a negro boy.

The 13th alternate juror was dismissed after final arguments and 12 shirt-sleeved men, mostly farmers, entered a small room and began considering the case against Roy Bryant, 24, and his 36-year-old half brother J. W. Milam.

Sumner, Miss. Sept 23 (AP) — A defense attorney told a country jury today there are groups which would throw a corpse into a river in the hope it would be identified as Emmett Louis Till.

John Whitten made the statement in final arguments in the trial of two white men accused of murdering Till, a 14-year-old Chicago negro youth.

"There are people in the United States who want to destroy the way of life of Southern people," said Whitten.

He said the state did not prove the body could have been Till and the defense proved it could not be. Defense witnesses testified the body had been in the river at least eight days, while Till was missing only three days before the body was found in the Tallahatchie River.

"There are people," said Whitten, ". . . who will go as far as necessary to commit any crime known to man to widen the gap between the white and colored people of the United States."

"They would not be above putting a rotting, stinking body in the river in the hope it would identified as Emmett Till."

Sumner, Miss., Sept. 23 (AP) — Defense attorney J. W. Kellum told a country jury today "your forefathers will turn over in their graves" if the jurors convicted two white men of murdering a 14-year-old Chicago negro boy.

But Dist. Atty. Gerald Chatham shouted "The killing of Emmett Till . . . was a cowardly act," and pleaded for conviction.

Roy Bryant, 24, and his half-brother John W. Milam, 36, are charged with murdering Emmett Louis Till in a widely publicized wolf-whistle slaying.

The case appeared likely to reach a jury composed principally of Mississippi Delta farmers during this afternoon.

Circuit Judge Curtis Swango Jr. recessed the trial for lunch halfway through closing arguments by the defense.

Kellum—one of five local attorneys defending Bryant and Milam—told the all-white, all-male jury it would be admitting freedom was lost forever, if it convicted the two defendants.

Defense attorney Sidney Carlton demanded, "Where is the motive?"

Testimony by Bryant's wife about a negro man who molested and whistled at her did not implicate Till, Carlton said, adding:

"If he (Mose Wright) had known Emmett Till had done something down there, he'd have gotten out and whipped him himself," Carlton said.

Wright is the sharecropper uncle young Till was visiting at the time he was abducted—and slain. "Down there" referred to Bryant's country store in which Mrs. Bryant testified the incident with an unknown negro with "a Northern brogue" happened.

Carlton asked how Wright could testify Milam carried a pistol during the abduction when the only light came from a flashlight shining in Wright's face. Wright testified about the kidnaping during early hours Aug. 28.

"Had any of you gone to Mose Wright's house with evil intent," asked Carlton, "would you have given your name? There's nothing reasonable about the state's theory."

He went on: "If that's identification, if that places these men at that scene, then none of us are safe." He shouted the words.

Sweating profusely in the heat of a Mississippi Delta courtroom, Chatham loudly said: "The first words that entered this case were literally dripping with the blood of Emmett Till."

He charged 24-year-old Roy Bryant and his 36-year-old half brother, John W. Milam, gave the Chicago boy "a court-martial with the death penalty imposed."

The first words in the kidnap-slaying, said Chatham, were "I want the boy from Chicago who did the talking at Money." [. . .]

Called Lynch-Murder, "Morally, Legally" Wrong
Cleveland Call and Post, 1 October 1955

Sumner, Miss. — In one of the most passionate pleas ever made by a white man in the south on behalf of a Negro, District Attorney Gerald Chatham Friday begged an all white jury to forget about race and condemn what is "morally and legally wrong" and convict Roy Bryant and J. W. Milam for the murder of Emmett Till.

The powerfully built District Attorney, serving his last year as prosecutor[,] made the plea as he and special prosecutor Roy B. Smith ended their arguments and sent the case to the jury. It was one of the most dramatic highlights in the drama studded trial as Mr. Chatman [Chatham] began his argument.

All-White Jury

For here was a southern born white man facing an all white jury and asking that jury to render a verdict which could hang two white men for killing a Negro. No white man has ever been given a death penalty in Mississippi for killing a Negro. It was a challenging and difficult moment in the career of Mr. Chatham, but in the interest of fair reporting it must be said that he rose to the challenge with all the ability at his command and he is a man of commanding ability.

In a loud booming voice which could be heard outside on the streets below the courtroom, Chatham told the jury and the 175 whites and 23 colored people that he is "not concerned with the pressure and agitation which the trial has produced, either within or outside the state of Mississippi. But I am concerned[,]" he said ["]with what is morally and legally wrong." Then with a direct reference to Mrs. Mamie Bradley, mother of the dead Emmett Till[,] he looked at the courtroom and the jury and said, "The next time it may be you who will be sitting here crying."

You May Be Next

Concluding his argument Chatham said: "I say to you, unless you judge this case on its merits it will endanger the precepts and examples which we hold dear here in the south."

By every courtroom standard the Mississippi born DA made a great plea for the dead colored youth. At times one got the feeling that he was in a Baptist church and that Chatham was the Baptist preacher.

For his numerous moments of brilliant oratory he brought tears to the eyes not only of those seated at the colored press tables but to some of the white listeners as well.

One of the key arguments that the defense had made was that the body found in the river had not been that of Emmett Till. They had presented a doctor, a sheriff and two undertakers whose testimony attempted to show that it could not have been Till's body.

"That Old Shep"

Against this testimony Chatham had relied heavily on the identification of the youth by his own mother. Recalling her testimony to the jury he told of the case of his own son who had a dog named "Shep."

He said one day his own son had come to him after his dog had been [killed and said to] him, "Dad, I've found old Shep."

The prosecutor said his young son then took him by the hand and led him to a hollow ravine behind the barn and pointed to the badly decomposed body of his dog.

"That dog's body was rotting and the meat was falling off its bone," the prosecutor said, "but my little boy pointed to it and said, 'That's old Shep, Pa. That's old Shep.'"

Dramatically tying this illustration in with Mrs. Bradley's identification of her son, Chatham in a pleading voice to the jury said, "My boy didn't need no undertaker or a sheriff to identify his dog. And we don't need them here to identify Emmett Till. All we need is someone who loved him and cared for him."

"If there was one ear left, one hairline, one part of his nose, any part of Emmett Till's body, then I say to you that Mamie Bradley was God's given witness to identify him."

The aroused DA then turned to damaging testimony offered by a defense witness, a white Doctor who had testified that the body could have been there at least ten days while Till had only been missing for three days.

Doctor Color Blind

On the stand the Doctor had stated that the body was so badly decomposed he could not tell whether it was colored or white. Addressing himself to this argument, Chatham said[,] "Everyone who had testified has stated that this was the body of a colored boy. When the sheriff was first told of the body his informer said, 'There is a little nigger boy in the river.' Everybody who saw the body said, 'a nigger boy in the river.'

"But now we have this doctor come up here with all his degrees and titles and tell us that he could not tell whether it was a white boy or a colored boy.

"[I] Tell you the people of this state are wasting their money sending a man to school and educating him to be a doctor when he is not able to tell a white man from a Negro.

"I want to say this about the doctor—if he can't tell black from white, I don't want him writing any prescriptions for me."

Chatham did not miss any strong points in his plea for conviction of the two white men. He constantly reminded the jury that he was a son of the South and he pointed out that the jury knew as southerners that even if the Till boy had done something wrong all the white men had to do was take a "razor strap, place him over a barrel and give him a good whipping."

Just a Boy

"That's the way I deal with my boy," he said. "You deal with a child as if he is a child—not as if he is a man."

"But did they do this[?]" he asked. "No they did not. Willie Reed (a colored witness) told you how he saw Emmett Till that Sunday morning on the Milam place and he told you how he later saw J. W. Milam with the pistol in his hand [and] that Uncle Mose saw him also [with a pistol]. If Willie Reed had been lying the five lawyers for the defense would have had fifty people up here to say he was not qualified to speak.

"But did they do this? They did not. They couldn't do it because Willie Reed was telling the truth. But the next time anyone saw that little boy his feet was sticking up out of the river and he was dead."

Chatham called the boy's death a cowardly act and the "unnecessary killing of a human being."

After he finished Mrs. Mamie Bradley[,] who was seated next to me at the press table[,] said: "He could not have done any better."

Defendants Receive Handshakes, Kisses

James L. Kilgallen, *Memphis Commercial Appeal*, 24 September 1955

Sumner, Miss., Sept. 23 — Young Roy Bryant and his older half-brother, J. W. Milam, were swiftly acquitted by an all-white male jury Friday afternoon of the charge of having murdered Emmett Louis Till, 14-year-old Chicago Negro boy.

The jury was out just an hour and seven minutes.

A murmur swept the crowded and sweltering courtroom as juror J. A. Shaw announced the verdict, but there was no demonstration.

Their Hands Shaken

Mr. Bryant, 24, and Mr. Milam, 36—accused of murdering young Till because he had whistled at and made improper advances to Bryant's pretty wife—looked happily at each other when the verdict was announced. Several persons nearby shook their hands.

The jury[,] comprised of predominantly cotton country farmers, retired at 2:36 P.M. and announced at 3:43 that it was ready with its verdict. In sending the jury out to deliberate[,] Judge Curtis M. Swango had instructed that the verdict, when returned, be in writing.

While the jury was deliberating[,] the large crowd in the courtroom—apparently anticipating a fairly quick verdict—remained in their seats.

At 3:43 P.M. the bailiffs guarding the door to the jury room were informed that the jury was ready to report. The jurors were brought immediately into the courtroom.

Judge Swango rapped his gavel to cut down the murmur that had arisen and he warned that there was to be no demonstration when the verdict was announced. He also said that photographers were not to take pictures.

Instructed To Stand

The jury, looking very solemn, walked to the box to the right of the judge's bench and prepared to sit down. The judge instructed them to stand and asked if they had reached a verdict.

"We have," said Juror Shaw, of Webb, Miss. All of the jurors were now standing.

"What is your verdict?" inquired the court.

"Not guilty," said Mr. Shaw in a firm voice.

A buzz of conversation started but immediately stopped when the judge looked sternly at the spectators.

So that the proceedings would be orderly in every sense the judge reminded the jurors that he previously had instructed them to write their verdict on a white piece of paper. He provided them with a new blank and asked them to go back into the grand jury room which the jury used—and follow out the court order.

Returned to Box

This they did. They returned to the jury box and Mr. Shaw said:

"We the jurors find the defendants not guilty."

The charge of kidnaping in connection with the alleged murder of the Till boy was nolle prossed insofar as Tallahatchie County is concerned. This was done upon the motion of Dist. Atty. Gerald Chatham.

The kidnaping of the boy occurred in Leflore County whereas the body was found in the river near the town of Philipp in Tallahatchie County.

The defendants were turned over to Leflore County officials for possible prosecution of the kidnaping charge that has been lodged against them.

Sheriff George Smith of Leflore County said the kidnaping count will be taken to the grand jury the first week in November.

The two defendants were all smiles as they received congratulations in the courtroom from men and women friends. Both men, who smoked cigarets in the courtroom during the trial, lit up cigars after the verdict was announced.

Kissed Their Wives

For the benefit of the battery of photographers, Mr. Bryant and Mr. Milam kissed their attractive young wives[,] who had been sitting with them while they were awaiting the verdict.

Mr. Bryant's wife smiled radiantly. She had appeared as a witness and testified that young Till had "wolf-whistled" at her and otherwise insulted her when he came to the Bryant General Store in Money, Miss., about 8 on the night of Aug. 24.

Carolyn Bryant is 21, black-haired, slim and pretty.

Mr. Milam's attractive 27-year-old wife, Juanita, had tears in her eyes as she watched her husband accepting congratulations from his friends.

Meanwhile, the greatest excitement prevailed in the small town of Sumner, population 700.

The Courthouse itself was a scene of great commotion.

Discussing Decision

Not only was there great activity in the courtroom after the verdict but crowds of people streamed down to the first floor and stood around discussing the jury's decision.

Reporters giving their stories to their offices were surrounded by townsfolk listening to what was being dictated.

On the first floor a refreshment stand was doing land-office business in the sale of sandwiches and soft drinks.

While the jury was deliberating a heavy rain was falling in Sumner but strangely enough just as the verdict was announced the sun came out brightly.

Legal Processes Continue

Two Mississippi men accused of killing a Negro from Chicago have been cleared by a jury at Sumner.

As this trial opened, and at its close, it seemed to us that evidence necessary for convicting on a murder charge was lacking. We believe that if the jury hearing this circumstantial evidence had agreed on conviction, the decision would have been reversed by any appeals court in the land, including Mississippi, Illinois, and New York.

The processes of the law have been followed in full in spite of agitation, inflammation of the public and efforts to make this trial more than a legal proceeding under long-established safeguards of the courts.

These same men are accused and are in custody for kidnaping the same Negro. The evidence of kidnaping will be heard on its own strength in another court of another county.

Until that jury has reached its decision, criticism of Mississippi justice from any source will be premature and its origin is subject to question.

2 Face Trial as "Whistle" Kidnapers—Due to Post Bond and Go Home
Murray Kempton, *New York Post*, 25 September 1955

Sumner, Miss., Sept 24 — The fresh cigars burning in their mouths and their clan all around them, J. W. Milam and Roy Bryant yesterday leaned back in their chairs and heard a 67-minute jury of their peers acquit them for the murder of 14-year-old Emmett Louis Till, who whistled at a white woman and whose punishment as of today is total, unavenged obliteration.

The only sound in the courtroom when the inevitable verdict came were the long gasps of two spectators, one white and one Negro.

Even after Judge Curtis Swango thanked the jury and adjourned court, there was no general sound from the departing audience except a low murmur which sounded as though everyone except J. W. Milam was a little embarrassed. He was beyond embarrassment, clutching the soft parts of his wife, Juanita's, flesh for the benefit of photographers and tipping his chair back, totally expansive.

Later he'll probably be back in Glendora, Miss., resting before he goes back to work or his old habit of bootlegging: and Roy Bryant will reopen his store at Money and old Moses Wright, from whose house the Till boy was snatched last Aug. 28, is back at his cabin 3 miles down the road: and Emmett Till's mother, Mamie Bradley, is on her way back to Chicago, her son so completely destroyed that she cannot even collect his insurance policy.

After their acquittal last night, Milam and Bryant were turned over to Leflore County authorities and taken to the Greenwood, Miss., jail charged with kidnapping Emmett Till. Sometime today, it was expected they will waive a hearing on the kidnap charge and County Judge Pollard will set bail. After they post bonds, they'll be free to go home to their families.

Then they'll be undisturbed until November when the State of Mississippi will seek indictments against them.

No one can say the state didn't give the murder jury its chance to do the right thing. The jury entered its splintery, fly-specked chamber in mid-afternoon, having seen the line clearly and chosen the dark side.

The line was drawn for the defense at the end by John W. Whitten Jr., a young man with glasses and an empty face who could not have anything but contempt for his audience but who knew what it wanted.

Whitten told the jury that the disappearance of Emmett Till was really easy to explain. J. W. Milam and Roy Bryant might, for purposes of argument, have abducted Emmett Till in the night.

But, if they did, they turned him loose three miles down the road at the Bryant store in Money and told him to walk home alone. Moses Wright had left his cabin, and driven down the road to Money and met Emmett coming home, and taken him to meet a friend from the National Assn. For the Advancement of Colored People, and the friend had persuaded Moses Wright to plant his nephew's ring on a "rotten, stinking corpse," which, when fished out of the river, would be identified by simple people as that of Emmett Till.

"There are people in the United States," Whitten told the jury, "who want to defy the customs of the South . . . and would commit perhaps any crime known to man in order to widen the gap. These people are not all in Gary and Chicago; they are in Jackson and Vicksburg; and, if Mose Wright knows one he didn't have to go far to find him. And they include some of the most astute students of psychology known anywhere. They include doctors and undertakers and they have ready access to a corpse which could meet their purpose."

The genteel Mr. Whitten was fingering Moses Wright out there in his cabin; his excuse presumably is that he was doing his job. And so he asked for an acquittal and expressed his confidence that "every last Anglo-Saxon one of you has the courage to do it."

The line for the state—a last ditch bastion of conscience—was drawn by Robert B. Smith 3d[,] the special prosecutor who had the last word:

"Gentlemen, we're on the defensive. Only so long as we can preserve the rights of everybody—white or black—we can keep our way of life. Once we get to the point where we deprive any of our people of their rights, we are all in danger. Emmett Till down here in Mississippi was a citizen of the United States; he was entitled to his life and his liberty."

Robert Smith lives just 50 miles away from here; he was a stranger to this jury. He was staking his case on Negro witnesses and staked it proudly.

"Old Mose Wright is a good old country Negro and you know he's not going to tell anybody a lie."

And he reminded them that Willie Reed, an 18-year-old Negro field hand, had testified that he saw the Till boy and J. W. Milam in the same place the morning after the kidnaping.

He looked at the jury in his desperation and he said the bravest thing a Mississippi prosecutor could say about a semi-literate Negro to a white jury.

"I don't know but what Willie Reed has more nerve than I have."

He trailed off there and the jury retired. In the interval he talked about the inevitable and said he hadn't hoped to win it. It is a proud thing for a man to say that he has taken his chances without real hope, and Robert Smith could take his place with Moses Wright.

After eight minutes, the jury sent for cokes; the hour that followed seemed very short. J. W. Milam finished his paper and lolled in his chair; and the Bryant family passed around the glossy prints of their newspictures.

Only Roy Bryant seemed a little short of assurance; at one point he asked Sidney Carlton, of defense counsel, "how long do you think it'll be" and Carlton answered, "25 to 45 minutes."

Then the jury knocked at the door and Bryant and Milam lit their cigars.

The defense opened the trial's final morning by calling to the stand nine witness, three for J. W. Milam and four for Roy Bryant, who testified according to ancient custom of the Mississippi criminal courts, that the reputation of the defendants "as to peace or violence" was "good."

On cross examination of the first such character witness, District Attorney Chatham attempted to introduce evidence that J. W. Milam had been arrested and had pleaded guilty to bootlegging at least five times. Then was an objection sustained by the court.

Then the defense, having called neither defendant, rested, and Gerald Chatham arose to begin the summation for the State of Mississippi. He told the jury that he had been a District Attorney for 15 years and that he was retiring soon and thanked them for their courtesy.

Milam went on with his paper; Bryant's cigar was almost out; Gerald Chatham was fighting to send them to the gas chamber. To win that fight he had to make that jury believe that the testimony of a Negro mother was worth more than the word of three white witnesses who had testified with loud assurances that the body taken from the Tallahatchie River last Aug. 31 could not be that of Emmett Till.

"If you found an unidentifiable body," he reminded the jury, "you wouldn't go to an undertaker who didn't know the child[,] you'd go to his mother. Here she told a forthright story and she identified the body as the body of her son. She suffered that child as a babe in her breast. If there was one ear, she would have known it. Mamie Bradley was God's given witness."

Then Chatham's voice ran down from indignation to a kind of weary sincerity that he, as your District Attorney, was [not] "concerned with pressure from any source. I am concerned with what is morally and legally wrong."

Someday, he said, every member of this jury may be in court and want fairness. "If you acquit, you will endanger the precepts and traditions we hold dear and sacred in the south." He stopped, a tired man who is not very well; he had fought what is likely to be his last murder case, and, lose or win, he could never be prouder of any of the others.

Then up rose Sidney Carlton for the defense to point out the holes in the state's case. Sometimes, he said, of course Mamie Bradley, a mother, believes what she wants to believe.

"The undisputed scientific facts are against her." If you vote to acquit, "may you feel," said Sidney Carlton, "in the words of Charles Dickens that 'tis a far, far better thing you do now than you have ever done."

Then J. W. Kellum rose for the second defense summary and told those jurors slouched in their sports shirts that they were "a peerage of democracy" and "absolutely the custodians of American civilization."

"I want you to tell me where under God's shining sun is the land of the free and the home of the brave if you don't turn these boys loose; your forefathers will absolutely turn over in their graves."

Kellum reminded the jury that Special Prosecutor Robert Smith—"a gentleman I don't know; the state has sent him here"—would have the final argument in rebuttal and that it was a powerful weapon.

And then said J. W. Kellum as his final word to the peerage:

"I want you to think of the future. When your summons comes to cross the Great Divide, and, as you enter your father's house—a home not made by hand but eternal in the heavens, you can look back to where your father's feet have trod and see your good record written in the sands of time. And, when you go down to your lonely silent tomb to a sleep that knows no dreams, I want you to hold in the palm of your hand a record of service to God and your fellow man.

"And the only way you can do that is to turn these boys loose."

Attendant Mississippi historians reported that the above peroration is stolen from the late Paul Johnson, who used to use it in his habitually losing campaigns for governor of the state. It is a blend of William Cullen Bryant and Robert Ingersoll.

The defense was summing up with a quote from a former editor of the *New York Post,* a great atheist, and a Mississippi politician who used to get the lesser-evil ballots of most of the 22,000 of the state's 999,000 Negroes who are permitted to vote.

The defense had all the rhetoric and all the tradition and all the town gossip behind it—everything in fact but conscience.

Mose Wright was outside the courtroom when the delicate young Mr. Whitten hung the whole plot on him; but somehow, he must have heard. Just after Whitten finished Moses Wright was observed in the sherriff's office, collecting his witness fee, and preparing to leave. He didn't have to wait for the end of what he had started. Someone asked him whether he really intended to leave Mississippi and Mose Wright answered:

"I don't know. I got this country so scrounged down in me that I just don't know."

Then he walked out of the courtroom, a tiny old man in his galluses, and down the road across the bridge all alone and leaving Sumner rotting behind him.

Mississippi Jungle Law Frees Slayers of Child
James L. Hicks, *Cleveland Call and Post,* 1 October 1955

Sumner, Miss. — An all-white male jury of sharecroppers demonstrated here Friday that the constitutional guarantees of "Life, Liberty, and the Pursuit of Happiness" do not apply to Negro citizens of their state.

The mockery of the sacred constitutional guarantees was made by the 12 sharecroppers in 65 short minutes of deliberation in the outmoded, antiquated Sumner, Mississippi courtroom where they returned a verdict of "not guilty" against two white men charged with the August 28 killing of 14-year-old Emmett (Bobo) Till.

Mississippi thus stands in the eyes of the nation today as a place where judgement and fair play have flown to the four winds, and where men have either lost their reason or refuse to recognize it when they are faced by it.

For if ever there was reasoning and logic, based on stark, cold facts, it was laid before the people of Mississippi during the five days of this historical trial which ended here Friday.

This reporter, a skeptic of Mississippi's white man's justice, had been amazed all week as the orderly procedure of law slowly, but surely, spun a web of conviction around the two white men who stood accused of a horrible and senseless crime.

I had come here almost with a preconceived idea that I would jeer a mockery of justice from the first day of the trial. But, as the state spun its web around the two men in five days, I stayed up late and long each night, waiting and getting ready to cheer a state which I felt was coming over to the side of decency and fair play when the rest of the world was saying that it couldn't be done.

And up to the very moment that the jury of white sharecroppers came out of the jury room to announce their verdict, I was inwardly cheering and rooting for the people of Mississippi as loud and as long as I root for the Brooklyn Dodgers.

For in the five days conduct of the trial, Mississippi just didn't follow the script written for her by the rest of the world.

Judge Was Impartial

Instead of a mock court of law, the little courtroom at Sumner began to stand out as a h[a]llowed place of justice.

No prosecutors anywhere in the United States could have worked harder or longer for a conviction than did District Attorney Gerald Chatman and Special Prosecutor Robert B. Smith, both native white sons of their state.

And no judge, whether on the Supreme Court bench or the rickety rocking chair of the bench at Sumner, could have been more painstaking and eminently fair in the conduct of the trial than Judge Curtis M. Swango of Saris, Miss.

And it must be stated that never in the history of this reporter's long years of court reporting has he seen a weaker and more inflammatory case based on pure fantasy as was presented by the battery of five white lawyers who defended the two white men.

Able Prosecution

Contrary to expectations the lawyers for the prosecution proved able and aggressive. Notwithstanding the pre-trial charges of "fix" the judge in the case was a paragon of jurisprudence. And, in spite of charges of intimidations, Negro witnesses paraded to the witness stand to point accusing fingers at the accused to make a solid and strong case for the state.

Add all this to the fact that the defense had the weakest of cases, and you have the picture as the case went to the jury.

It was a time of great decision for the State of Mississippi, and this reporter, based on the facts before him, was rooting for it to win.

But now I know what seasoned southern writers mean when they laughed at me whenever I said, during the trial, that I felt the men would be convicted.

Blind Prejudice

Now I know, as they knew before me, that the hidden factor in the backwardness of this state is the blind spot of racial prejudice in the eyes of its sharecropper people, which prevents them from seeing and thinking straight when they look upon a black face.

Now I know that the masses of people in Mississippi are still not ready for the enlightened democracy in the world of free men which its statesmen speak of so freely in the forums of the world.

In the past five days I saw the good and decent people in this state, both white and black[,] weighed on the scales of justice and found wanting.

I did not know then, but I know now, what tips the balance of the scales against them.

The scales are unbalanced because[,] in the hinterlands of the state from which they picked the jury such as were had at Sumner, there is a horde of people living in a darkness that few enlightened American can visualize.

There is still the law of the jungle and the jungle is still far darker and many times greater than the small island of light in the state.

MISSISSIPPI IS SIMPLY NOT READY.

Today the jungles of Mississippi are laughing their mockery of Justice—but the rest of the 47 states will be crying for Mississippi.

Chapter 3 *Post-Trial Reactions and Assessments*

The verdict at Sumner generated a storm of controversy. The national and African American press attacked the decision, assailing Mississippi justice and warning that the verdict would hurt the interests of democracy at home and abroad. In a banner headline, the *Pittsburgh Courier* proclaimed September 23, 1955, as "Black Friday," a direct challenge to the Mississippi-based Citizens' Councils of America, whose founding text, Tom Brady's *Black Monday,* was penned in response to the *Brown v. Board of Education* decision a year before. While the southern press did not speak with one voice, the consensus in Dixie was that Mississippi followed the rule of law and prosecuted Milam and Bryant with due and fair vigilance; the acquittal reflected the weakness of the evidence, not the prejudice of the court, the prosecution, or the jury. Even those southern papers critical of the happenings in Sumner were quick to temper that criticism and deflect a general condemnation of Mississippi. Writing from his editorial office in Greenville, Hodding Carter urged just such a position: "it was not the jury that was derelict in its duty, despite the logical conclusions it might have made concerning whose body was most likely found in the Tallahatchie River, and who most likely put it there, but rather must the criticism fall upon the law officials who attempted in such small measure to seek out evidence and to locate witnesses to firmly establish whoever was or was not guilty."

Culled from a wide variety of sources—editorials, magazine features, press releases, and letters to the editor—the following selections sample the fiery response to the verdict. These responses have been organized chronologically except for the letters to the editor, which are placed at the end of the chapter. Included as a means of revealing how "everyday Americans" responded to the verdict, these letters recover voices long excluded from assessments of this event.

Fair Trial Was Credit to Mississippi
Greenwood (Miss.) Morning Star, 23 September 1955

Those who were expecting anything but a fair and impartial trial, in which both the State and Defense did their best to produce the facts in evidence, were disappointed with the manner in which the Milam-Bryant case was handled.

James L. Kilgallen, dean of American crime reporters[,] told *The Morning Star* editor yesterday for the second time that Miss. had certainly conducted the whole affair in a way which reflects only credit upon the state. He said, "I have never seen any people who have gone out of their way to see that this trial has been given both sides in this case. I have enjoyed my visit here in Miss. immensely, and hope to be able to come back again and again on more pleasant matters."

This was one of those cases where the radicals and NAACP sympathizers were hoping that Miss. would give them occasion to lambaste our state because of its being a segregation stronghold. They were alert to every possibility and played every angle. Sometimes they wore your patience thin, but Miss. people rose to the occasion and proved to the world that this is a place where justice in the courts is given to all races, religions, and classes.

The top newsmen at the trial were unanimous in their opinions that the trial was fair and impartial. Your editor talked to men whom all three press services, the United Press, the Associated Press and the International News[,] had covering the trial and they were agreed on this point.

Miss. has been raised in the opinion of many who are in position to be competent critics in this matter of justice.

Acquittal
Delta Democrat-Times, 23 September 1955

One of the cautions of our system of laws is that evidence must clearly show guilt "beyond a shadow of a doubt," else the accused go free. This is a sensible safeguard meant to shield the innocent from the accusing finger of circumstance.

So, in the Till murder trial, it was not the jury that was derelict in its duty, despite the logical conclusions it might have made concerning whose body was most likely found in the Tallahatchie River, and who most likely put it there, but rather must the criticism fall upon the law officials who attempted in such small measure to seek out evidence and to locate witnesses to firmly establish whoever was or was not guilty. As it is[,] no one except the guilty parties themselves, whoever they may be, will ever likely know what actually happened and who actually was responsible.

It is incredible, in fact, that the prosecution should have begun testimony with as flimsy a case as was in evidence; evidence that was made stronger only by the voluntary information that came from frightened witnesses who seized a spark of courage to speak out at the last moment.

Spectators at the Till trial, from wherever they came, must have been impressed with the decorum of our courts under such strained conditions, the fairness of the judge and the sincerity of at least most of the officials involved. But they must also have been shocked at the quality of the investigation that preceded this most publicized trial in Mississippi history, and shocked that the very man who was designated to lead an investigation into an obvious case of brutal murder, was busy most of the time inventing diverting fantasies as to how the whole thing could have been arranged by someone else.

We must, at the same time, give due condemnation to the NAACP spokesmen for their part in the case. For without their blanket accusations of decent people, their studied needling of the citizens who had to decide a matter of local justice, and their indifference to truth in favor of propaganda-making, those local officials, put on the defensive from the outset, might otherwise have made an honest effort to do more than what resulted in an effective cover-up.

Effective, that is, from a legal point of view. For this whole unhappy affair, exposed as it was to the inquisitive eyes of the world, has been anything but covered up in reality. And Mississippi must now suffer for it for at least another generation.

We can only hope now that the evidence about these two men on charges of kidnaping will be more adequately presented.

The Verdict at Sumner
Jackson Daily News, 25 September 1955

The cold fact concerning the acquittal in Tallahatchie county of the two alleged slayers of a Negro youth from Chicago is that the prosecution failed to prove its case.

The law book says guilt must be proven "beyond a reasonable doubt." There was plenty of "reasonable doubt" in the Bryant-Milam case, even though many may think it was a case of the old Scotch verdict, "guilty, but not proven."

Guilt must be proven. It cannot be assumed. Practically all the evidence against the defendants was circumstantial evidence.

There was no lack of vigor in the prosecution. Gerald Chatham, a very able district attorney, handled the case to the best of his ability and had competent assistants. Judge Curtis Swango presided with admirable fairness.

The NAACP cannot truthfully contend that a Mississippi court was guilty of "an atrocious miscarriage of justice," as its loud-mouthed leaders are shouting.

The case for the prosecution was not helped the least bit when an impudent, South-hating Negro Congressman from Detroit named Diggs journeyed all the way from his home city, accompanied by three lawyers, and squatted themselves in the court room at Sumner as "spectators." They took no part in the case but the NAACP atmosphere they brought with them surely must have had an adverse effect on the state's case. Mississippi's courts do not like covert attempts at intimidation. Diggs and Mamie Bradley, mother of the dead Negro, went from Sumner to Mound Bayou, where they were guests of Dr. T. R. M. Howard, arrogant leader of the NAACP in Mississippi.

It is best for all concerned that the Bryant-Milam case be forgotten as quickly as possible. It has received far more publicity than it should have been given.

Letter to the Editor
Chester Himes, *New York Post,* 25 September 1955

You are a Negro in New York. You read of the Mississippi lynching and the trial in impotent fury. One moment you would like to beat the lynchers to a bloody pulp. That makes you as bad as they. The next minute, you wish you could find the one thing to say that would rally national indignation into the action which would stop this forever.

Then you realize it has already been said in practically every way, beginning with "Thou Shalt Not Kill." Murray Kempton is saying it again daily, as well as can be said.

The real horror comes when your dead brain must face the fact that we as a nation don't want it to stop. If we wanted to, we would. So let us all share the guilt, those in New York as well as those in Sumner, Miss.

So let us take the burden of all this guilt from these two pitiful crackers. They are but the guns we hired.

The Shame of Our Nation
Daily Worker, 26 September 1955

Good people everywhere—in America and throughout the world—feel a deep sense of horror over the outcome of the murder trial in Mississippi.

The unspeakable kidnaping and lynching of a Negro child has now been capped with a "white supremacy" verdict that makes the blood run cold.

We cannot share in the reasoning of those who say: "That's Mississippi—what can you expect?"

We join with the Negro people and with millions of white people who expected something different. We expected—or had a right to expect—that the Federal Government would intervene in this brutish violation of the Civil Rights Statute. We expected—or had a right to expect—that the highest political leaders in the country, the Administration and GOP political leaders, and presidential aspirants of the Democrat Party, would at the very least speak out in condemnation of the child-lynching.

It is true that the press gave this trial a coverage that was unusual. It is true that the Governor of Mississippi appointed a special prosecutor who did, in fact, bring out the necessary evidence. All this only testifies to the almost universal sense of outrage over the murder of Emmett Till and, especially, to the wrath expressed by the Negro people.

But the conduct of the trial cannot hide the fact that white supremacy is the official doctrine of the state of Mississippi, beginning with the governor himself, and the Dixiecrat Senator Eastland. It is this barbarous doctrine which was responsible first for the murder and then for the verdict.

The fact that the prosecutor procured the evidence cannot be used as an alibi for the federal government to shun its responsibility. On the contrary, the gap between the evidence and the verdict only prove a thousand times over that no Negro, whether alive or brutally dead, can get justice in a Mississippi court.

We know our readers join with us in paying our deepest respects to the mother, Mrs. Mamie Bradley, who felt in the racist fury inflicted upon the body of her child, not only a great personal grief but an injury to an entire people. Our respects to those heroes of the Negro people, Mr. Moses Wright, uncle of the boy Emmett, Mrs. Mary [Mandy] Bradley, Mr. Willie Reed, and Mr. Add Reed, who stood up in court and in defiance of a white supremacist code fearlessly gave their testimony.

We cannot pass by here one note that unfortunately creeps in to some of the expressions of outrage over the verdict. This is that the verdict "gives comfort to the Communist world." To most people throughout the world, the matter rightly appears otherwise: that the white supremacist verdict gives comfort to those who support, condone and fatten on the white supremacy system!

The murder trial is to be followed by a kidnaping trial in a nearby county. But what has just taken place in Sumner, Mississippi, can lead to only one conclusion. The federal government—particularly Attorney General Herbert Brownell's Department of Justice—must step in without any further delay. The Federal Civil Rights Statute gives the Attorney General not only the right but the inescapable duty to intervene. Protection must be guaranteed the Negroes who are defying death in order to testify. Above all, the case of Emmett Till cannot be closed until justice is done and the full penalty enacted for cold-blooded, deliberate murder.

The State of Mississippi Still Carries the Burden
Atlanta Constitution, 26 September 1955

In Sumner, Miss., a 14-year-old Negro boy afflicted physically (and some suggested mentally) by polio, was killed.

Reportedly his lynching, or murder (a matter of semantics), resulted from his "wolf whistle" or "insulting remarks" directed at the wife of a community storekeeper.

Apparently there was no immediate reaction. Some three days afterwards he was taken from the home of his uncle and killed.

The two men charged with this killing have now been acquitted.

The sheriff testified they had admitted abducting the boy. But there was no witness to the death.

The prosecution conducted a vigorous case. It was obvious Mississippi was stirred. The lynching, or murder, was brutal. A boy had been killed for an act for which a boy of another color would have been whipped or reprimanded. The state's prosecutors honestly and valiantly sought a conviction.

The jury, summoned by due process, declared the defendants not guilty. That's that. But some person, or persons, are guilty.

The burden remains with Mississippi and with the conscience of the people in the county or counties involved.

Someone killed a 14-year-old boy. He would not have been killed were it not for his color.

What will Mississippi and Sumner do about it so the Communists of Russia and of China may not say that in our country the law means one thing for one person and another thing for another[?]

This crime, unhappily, is known the world around. Unfortunately the verdict will not conclude the case.

Someone, or some persons, are guilty. That's an uncomfortable fact.

The burden still rests on Mississippi.

Justice in Sumner
Dan Wakefield, *The Nation,* 1 October 1955

The crowds are gone and this Delta town is back to its silent, solid life that is based on cotton and the proposition that a whole race of men was created to pick it. Citizens who drink from the "Whites Only" fountain in the courthouse breathe much easier now that the two fair-skinned half brothers, ages twenty-four and thirty-six, have been acquitted of the murder of the fourteen-year-old Negro boy. The streets are quiet, Chicago is once more a mythical name, and everyone here "knows his place."

When the people first heard that there was national, even worldwide publicity coming to Sumner and the murder trial they wondered why the incident had caused such a stir. At the lunch recess on the first day of the trial a county health-office worker who had stopped by to watch the excitement asked a visiting reporter where he was from, and shook his head when the answer was New York City.

"New York, Chicago, everywhere," he said. "I never heard of making such a mountain of a molehill."

The feeling that it all was a plot against the South was the most accepted explanation, and when Roy Bryant and J. W. Milam ambled into court September 19 they were armed not only with their wives, baby boys, and cigars, but the challenge of Delta whites to the interference of the outside world. The issue for the local public was not that a visiting Negro boy named Emmett Louis Till had been dragged from his bed and identified later as a body that was pulled from the Tallahatchie River with a seventy-pound cotton-gin fan tied around its neck with barbed wire—that issue was lost when people learned that the world was clamoring to have something done about it. The question of "nigger-killing" was coupled with the threat to the racial traditions of the South, and storekeepers set out jars on their counters for contributions to aid the defense of the accused murderers.

Donations to the fund disqualified several prospective jurors, as prosecutors Gerald Chatham, district attorney, and Robert B. Smith, special assistant attorney general appointed to the case, probed carefully at every candidate for a day and a half before accepting the jury. Judge Curtis Swango, a tall, quietly commanding man, combined order with a maximum of freedom in the court, and when he had Cokes brought in for the jury it seemed as appropriate courtroom procedure as pounding the gavel.

While the jury selections went on inside, the crowds outside the building grew— and were automatically segregated. Aging, shaggy-cheeked Anglo-Saxons with crumpled straw hats lined a long wooden bench. Negroes gathered across the way at the base of the Confederate statue inscribed to "the cause that never failed." The Negro numbers increased, but not with the Negroes of Sumner. A red-necked deputy whose pearl-handled pistol showed beneath the tail of his sportshirt explained that the "dressed-up" Negroes were strangers. "Ninety-five per cent of them's not ours," he said. "Ours is out picking cotton and tending to their own business."

Moses Wright, a Negro locally known as a good man who tends to his business, was the state's first witness. He pressed his back against the witness chair and spoke out loud and clear as he told about the night two white men came to his house and asked for "the boy from Chicago—the one that did the talking at Money"; and how the big, balding man came in with a pistol and a flashlight and left with Emmett Till. Mose fumbled several times under cross-examination but he never lost his straightforward attitude or lowered his head. He still of course was "old man Mose" and "Uncle Mose" to both defense and prosecution, but none of that detracted from the dignity of how he told his story.

The rest of the week he was seen around the courthouse lawn with his pink-banded hat tilted back on his head, his blue pants pulled up high on a clean white shirt by yellow-and-brown suspenders. He walked through the Negro section of the lawn with his hands in his pockets and his chin held up with the air of a man who has done what there was to do and could never be touched by doubt that he should have done anything less than that.

When Mose Wright's niece, Mrs. Mamie Bradley, took the stand it was obvious as soon as she answered a question that she didn't fit the minstrel-show stereotype that most of Mississippi's white folks cherish. Nevertheless, the lawyers of both sides were careful to always address her as "Mamie," which was probably wise for the favor of the jury, since a Clarksdale, Mississippi, radio station referred to her as "Mrs. Bradley" on a news broadcast and spent the next hour answering calls of protest.

J. J. "Si" Breland, dean of the defense attorneys, questioned her while he remained in his seat, occasionally slicing his hands through the air in the quick, rigid motions he moved with throughout the trial. She answered intelligently, steadily, slightly turning her head to one side as she listened to questions, replying with a slow, distinct emphasis. "Beyond the shadow of a doubt," she said, "that was my boy's body."

At lunchtime recess the crowds around the soft-drink and sandwich concession debated her identification of her son, and many were relieved in the afternoon session when Tallahatchie County Sheriff H. C. Strider squeezed his 270 pounds in the witness chair and said the only thing he could tell about the body that had come from the river was that it was human.

Sheriff Strider, who owns 1,500 acres of cotton land, farms it with thirty-five Negro families, has the grocery store and filling station on it, and operates a cotton-dusting concern with three airplanes, is split in his commitments in a way that might qualify him as the Charles E. Wilson of Tallahatchie County. What's good for his feudal plantation is good for the county, and his dual role as a law-enforcement officer and witness for the defense evidently didn't seem contradictory to him. His commitments were clear enough that prosecution lawyers once sent the two state policemen to search a county jail for one Leroy "Too-Tight" Collins, a key witness for the prosecution who was missing (and never found).

There were still missing witnesses, dark, whispered rumors of fleeing men who saw the crime committed, when Gerald Chatham tugged the sleeves of his shirt and walked over to the jury Friday morning to make the summation of the case for the prosecution. Both he and Smith, who is a former F. B. I. man, had followed every lead and sent state policemen driving through the countryside in search of the Mississippi witnesses, but only two of the four who were named—Willie Reed and Mandy Bradley—were found. The time had come for Chatham to work with what he had.

In a matter of minutes from the time he started talking the atmosphere in the court was charged with tension as he raised his arm toward the ceiling and shouted that "the first words offered in testimony here were dripping with the blood of Emmett Till." The green plaster walls of the room had grown darker from the clouds of the rain that was coming outside, as Chatham went on with the tones, the gestures, the conviction of an evangelist, asserting that "the guilty flee where no man pursueth," and retelling the story of the boy's abduction in the dark of night.

J. W. Milam, the bald, strapping man who leaned forward in his seat during most of the sessions with his mouth twisted in the start of a smile, was looking at a newspaper. Roy Bryant lit a cigar. With his eyebrows raised and his head tilted back he might have been a star college fullback smoking in front of the coach during season and asking with his eyes "So what?"

When Chatham was finished, C. Sidney Carlton, the able attorney for the defense whose large, fleshy face was unusually close to where the cameras were clicking, poured a paper cup of water from the green pitcher on the judge's desk, and opened his summation. He spoke well, as usual, but after Chatham's oratory he was doomed to anti-climax. There had been a brief rain and the sun was out with more heat than ever. Defense attorney J. W. Kellum, speaking briefly after Carlton before the noon recess, had the odds of discomfort against his chances of stirring the jury, but he did his best with the warning that the jurors' forefathers would turn in their graves at a guilty verdict and then he asked what was undoubtedly the question of the week. If Roy and J. W. are convicted of murder, he said, "where under the shining sun is the land of the free and the home of the brave?"

The question was a fitting prelude to the harangue of John Whitten, the defense's last speaker. The clean-shaven pale young man in a neatly pressed suit and white shirt that defied perspiration announced his faith that "every last Anglo-Saxon one of you men in this jury has the courage to set these men free."

Mr. Whitten went on to declare he had an answer for the state's most convincing evidence—the ring of Emmett Till that was found on the body discovered in the Tallahatchie River. The body really wasn't Emmett Till, Whitten said, and the ring might have possibly been planted on it by the agents of a sinister group that is trying to destroy the social order of the South and "widen the gap which has appeared between the white and colored people in the United States."

He didn't name any group, but the fondly nurtured local rumor that the whole Till affair was a plot on the part of the N. A. A. C. P. made naming unnecessary.

It took the twelve jurors an hour and seven minutes to return the verdict that would evidently help close the gap between the white and colored races in the land of the free and the home of the brave. Tradition, honor, God, and country were preserved in a package deal with the lives of Roy Bryant and J. W. Milam.

Reporters climbed tables and chairs to get a glimpse of the acquitted defendants, and the newspaper, magazine, and television cameras were aimed at the smiles of their wives and families in a flashing, buzzing finale. Then the agenda of the outside world disappeared in a rush to make their deadlines and the stale, cluttered courtroom was finally empty of everything but mashed-out cigarettes, crushed paper cups, and a few of the canvas spectator chairs that the American Legion had sold across the street for two dollars each.

The trial week won't be forgotten here soon, and glimpses of the "foreign" Negroes who don't till cottonfields but hold positions as lawyers, doctors, and Congressmen have surely left a deep and uncomfortable mark on the whites of the Delta. But at least for the present, life is *good* again. Funds are being raised for separate-and-equal school facilities in Tallahatchie County and on Wednesdays at lunchtime four of the five defense attorneys join with the other Rotarians of Sumner in a club song about the glad day "When men are one."

Langston Hughes Wonders Why No Lynchings Probes
Langston Hughes, *Chicago Defender,* 1 October 1955

OH, WHAT SORROW!
OH, WHAT PITY!
OH, WHAT PAIN
THAT TEARS AND BLOOD
SHOULD MIX LIKE RAIN
AND TERROR COME AGAIN
TO MISSISSIPPI

Come again
Where has terror been?
In some other section
Of the nation,
Lying low, unpublicized?
Jaundiced eyes
Showing through the mask

OH, WHAT SORROW,
PITY, PAIN,
THAT TEARS AND BLOOD
AND TERROR, FETID HOT
YET CLAMMY COLD,
REMAIN.

*   *   *

This is a poem written in memory of the dead boy, Emmett Till, whose body was found shot through the head, beaten and bruised, in the Tallahatchie River, 120 miles south of Memphis.

Charlie Lang and Ernest Green were young Negro boys like Emmett Till, too only 14 years old when they were lynched in Mississippi on Oct. 12, 1942. Their adolescent bodies were hanged together from the Shubuta bridge over the Chic[k]asawhay River.

Mississippi leads all the states in the United States in lynchings. Since the year 1882 it has had 576 lynchings according to official count, and how many more there are that have never been recorded, nobody knows.

Certainly, I think Mississippi must lead the world in the lynching of children.

No Probe

I have never heard or read about any Congressional committee investigating lynching. But there have been almost 5,000 recorded since Tuskegee Institute began keeping a list of lynchings and publishing them in the *Negro Yearbook.*

Of course, Negroes who have been murdered, beaten to death by individual whites, or simply shot down by southern police are not included in Tuskegee's record.

The lawless killing of black men and women is an old Southern custom going back to slavery days. In Ben Botkin's graphic book of slave memories published by the University of Chicago Press, *Lay My Burden Down,* there is a quotation from a former slave who remembers:

"My papa was strong. He never had a licking in his life. But one day the master says, 'Si, you got to have a whipping.' And my papa says, 'I never had a whipping and you can't whip me.' And the master says, 'But I can kill you.' And he shot my papa down. My mama took him in the cabin and put him on a pallet. He died."

Nobody Wants to Die

Because nobody wants to die, thousands of Negroes stayed away from the polls at the last election in Mississippi—for fear of their lives if they tried to vote.

If such intimidation of citizens of the United States—to the point where they are afraid to exercise the democratic right of the ballot—is not un-American, I don't know what is. Yet, I have not as yet read or heard of the House Committee on Un-American Activities investigating such activities.

Again, if the long-time lynch customs of the South are not un-American, I don't know what is. Yet, I have never yet heard or read of the Senate Permanent Committee on Investigations conducting any sort of probe into lynchings.

In recent years Congressional committees have taken up a great deal of time, and used up a great deal of tax money, investigating the loyalty of various Negro citizens of color as Channing Tobias, Jackie Robinson, Josh White and pretty Hazel Scott have gone to Washington to testify as to their loyalty and faith in democratic institutions.

It would seem to me sort of nice if the white politicians in Washington would now repay those distinguished colored Americans who have sworn and double sworn their allegiance to democratic ideals, by investigating JUST A FEW of the white folks who hang 14 year old boys to bridges and throw them in rivers, and who frighten and intimidate colored voters away from the polls—not to speak of those who continue to segregate the public schools, uphold Jim Crow on the railroads, and bar not only Negro citizens of the United States but East Indian diplomats from getting a decent meal in a public restaurant.

Just one little small investigation of these things, using just a wee tinnychee bit of our mutual tax money, and showing just one lynched body on TV, or forcing just one Southern mobster to take refuge in the Fifth Amendment, seems to me long overdue.

Senator Eastland from Mississippi might well consider calling such an investigation now while public interest is high. It ought to be even easier to catch lynchers than it is Communists especially in Mississippi, where they have no respect for the legal age.

Imagine lynching children! It makes me sick at the stomach.

Have senators no stomachs?

The Till Case Verdict
Jackson Advocate, 1 October 1955

Up at Sumner last Friday, after consuming the better part of four days in the sifting and weighing of the evidence in testimony, after hearing the exposition of the law in the argument of the opposing lawyers, and the instructions of the judge as to the law applicable in the case, an all white jury returned a verdict of "not guilty" in the trial of two white men charged with murder in the death of Emmett Louis Till, the 14-year-old Negro boy in the now internationally famous "wolf whistle" incident.

There appears to be enough in the case to justify the verdict in the eyes of those who would apply the strict letter of the law in such cases.

In the forum of world opinion[,] however, judging from the world-wide reaction to the verdict there must be times when the strict letter and interpretation of the law must give way to the demands of the higher virtues of justice, morality, right and Christianity.

Negroes in Mississippi with a deep understanding of the traditions and mores out of which such incidents arise, who remained tranquil during the trial, will continue to remain tranquil, secured by the knowledge that they and their cause have been helped, rather than hurt, by the "not guilty" verdict in the case.

What You Can Do about the Disgrace in Sumner
Chicago Defender, 1 October 1955

How long must we wait for the Federal Government to act? Whenever a crisis arises involving our lives or our rights we look to Washington hopefully for help. It seldom comes.

For too long it has been the device, as it was in the Till case, for the President to refer such matters to the Department of Justice.

And usually, the Department of Justice seems more devoted to exploring its lawbooks for reasons why it can't offer protection of a Negro's life or rights.

In the current case, the Department of Justice hastily issued a statement declaring that it was making a thorough investigation to determine if young Till's civil rights had been violated.

The Department evidently concluded that the kidnapping and lynching of a Negro boy in Mississippi are not violations of his rights.

This sounds just like both the defense and prosecution as they concluded their arguments by urging the jury to "uphold our way of life."

The trial is over, and this miscarriage of justice must not be left unavenged. The Defender will continue its investigations, which helped uncover new witnesses in the case, to find other Negroes who actually witnessed the lynching, before they too are found in the Tallahatchie River.

At this point we can only conclude that the administration and the justice department have decided to uphold the way of life of Mississippi and the South. Not only have they been inactive on the Till case, but they have yet to take positive action in the kidnapping of Mutt Jones in Alabama, who was taken across the state line into Mississippi and brutally beaten. And as yet the recent lynchings of Rev. Lee and LaMarr Smith in Mississippi have gone unchallenged by our government.

The citizens councils, the interstate conspiracy to whip the Negro in line with economic reins, the open defiance to the Supreme Court's school decision—none of these seem to be violations of rights that concern the federal government.

And Congress isn't concerned either. There has never been a congressional investigation of lynching, or of any of the other abuses and humiliations suffered by Negroes. And the inactivity of Congress is all the more pointed when we consider that there are three Negroes in Congress, any one of whom could at least propose such.

The President has steadfastly considered any effort to protect the Negro in the United States from those who would ignore him as a citizen, as "extraneous."

The appointment of a Morrow, [a] Wilkins, a Davis or a Mahoney is significant and is rightfully applauded, but it means little to the millions of Mose Wrights throughout the South.

For the Mose Wrights are born with low ceilings over their heads. They're denied an education, they're denied a fair return for their labor; they're denied the right to participate in their government; they're denied a chance to walk in the sun and frequently denied the right to live until they're sixty-five, as Milam reminded Mose Wright.

In the midst of this frustration, it appears that the Negro in the South[,] as well as the North, has but one way to go. That is to the ballot box.

One of the most important factors accounting for the difference between the Negro in Chicago and the Negro in Money, Miss., is that the Negro in Chicago can and does vote.

And the Negro in Money can and must register and vote. And the federal government, starting with the White House that has been so negligent in the past in these matters, must be prodded into making it possible for the Negro to exercise this one right—the right to vote.

Yes, the Till trial is over, but the Till case cannot be closed until Negroes are voting in Tallahatchie and Leflore counties and throughout the South.

A Careful, Last Look
Jackson Daily News, 2 October 1955

I

Because of the absolutely fantastic Northern repercussions to the results of the Delta trial for murder of two white men and the jury's subsequent "not guilty" verdict, perhaps a long, last and careful look at the true facts of the case and the long-range problem is in order. This hindsight appraisal has been prompted by the deliberately inflamed mob demonstrations in several northern cities and by the callous disregard and perversion of the truth by a number of Negro organizations which have exploited the issue.

Since all the demonstrations were essentially the same in character, there is no need to describe them beyond indicating their cynical nature: They boasted as main speakers men who had seen the trial and expressed satisfaction with judicial processes in Mississippi or they offered the uninformed opinions of men who had [not] been witness to the trial. In the case of the former, the change of mind represented a convenient—or worse—lapse of memory. The speakers said one thing in Mississippi, where they were open to challenge by others who had seen the trial, and another where political expediency suggested denunciation of the trial's conduct and outcome. In the case where speakers were used who had not seen the trial, even they must admit that they depended upon hearsay, slanted news coverage and their own prejudices.

II

With no effort to cover up what seems to have been shoddy police work—and this newspaper still believes a Bureau of Investigation is in order—almost every observer of the trial came away with the profound sense of having seen a fair trial. There was not sufficient evidence to secure a conviction. Detroit's Congressman Diggs said in public print that the trial was a proper one. Almost every reporter present, even those representing openly hostile publications, believed justice had been done on the strength of the evidence presented. No one accused officials of the court, the jurors, or judge, of introducing any element of racial discrimination into the trial. That being an indisputable fact, it is at least curious that honest reporters, filing objective copy from Sumner, should have been so heavily edited as to have seemingly presented another trial to their readers when their publications went on the streets. It is more curious still that Congressman Diggs should have found so much fault with the trial in Detroit when he spoke of its fairness in Mississippi.

III

The implication of deliberate distortion of the facts is unavoidable and not even the loftiest-intentioned observer can make anything else of the conflicting statements. Our Northern brethren of the Fourth Estate are due for some serious soul-searching for their misrepresentations, although such self-examination seems unlikely. It is still considered good form to lie about popular issues when the purpose can be justified with a fuzzy web of doubtful sociological logic.

IV

Sincere and forward-looking Mississippians are accused by Northern critics of being apologists for a system. It seems impossible for these self-appointed, self-announced experts, from a region where the problem of race is academic, to understand their own predispositions. They give the impression of studiously avoiding any genuine understanding of the South and the issues involved not only in the Till case but also in Southern custom and how it got that way. There is nothing incompat[i]ble with being intellectually honest and feeling an earnest distrust and deep fear of organizations seeking to impose radical change in an area unwilling to undergo radical change. There are, moreover, good and valid reasons to resist imposed change and those who claim change must be enforced are defying the aggregate knowledge of man's history.

V

Summing up the reaction elsewhere to the now celebrated Till case, any sincere and thoughtful man should be shocked at the efforts of the so-called social-reformers to fan the flames of hatred between regions of the nation and between races represented here. It can serve no purpose beyond that of disunity, and it lends another lie to the Communist line of the Big Lie. Those who engage in this pseudo-socially justified technique of using hate as a weapon have given aid and comfort to the Communist world. They seem eager to prove the Communist conception of the United States.

It is time for articulate defenders for our free system of government to scrutinize the efforts of these South-haters and the results of their obvious propaganda directed against this region. It will be found that they have caused vast damage to themselves as well as to the South, for the South is a part of the United States, and it is the U. S. that is being maliciously libeled.

Double Murder in Mississippi
Christian Century, 5 October 1955

Not often does anything happen in public life which is as unqualifiedly shameful as the double tragedy of the murder of Emmett Louis Till and the death of Mississippi justice in the ensuing trial. The brutality of the crime against an adolescent boy shocked us first. The brevity of the trial and its incredible verdict piled shock upon shock. It is generally agreed that the conduct of the court was right and proper. The judge was fair and the prosecution diligent. What offends common humanity was the spirit of the defense, the atmosphere in the community, and the swift certainty of the jury's decision. Which is to say that the structure of justice was correct but that the context of justice was not, so that, as always happens in such situations, justice died with all its formalities in perfect order. The community and jurors were obedient to the enemies of justice and contemptuous of its friends. The "outside interference" which Mississippians deplored— letters demanding conviction on threat of retaliation—are standard operating procedure for communist agitators who want for their propaganda exactly the opposite of their demand. The gullible community fell for it hook, line and sinker, stampeding to give the communists what they were finagling for. And to publicists all over the world who are eager to explain the promise there is in liberal democracy, the community gave the back of its hand. The horror and indignation that are rolling in from what have been the friendliest foreign journals indicate that the townspeople have engineered a local tragedy into an international calamity. The incident has been an eye-opener to our friends—and to us. Progress toward racial justice is an illusion, at least in Mississippi. This one local verdict eclipses the massive decisions of the Supreme Court, the gains made at great costs and many other places. Bewildered, outraged, ashamed we all are; but most of all, Christians are sick: sick that such a crime should have happened in the first place; sick that such a judgement should have been handed down; sickest that in the back eddies of our nation slow, dark minds are taking satisfaction in the verdict.

Southern Style
Roi Ottley, *Chicago Defender,* 8 October 1955

Those white men who traveled South to observe and report the trial of two white men—J. W. Milam and Roy Bryant—for the atrocious murder of 14-year-old Emmett Louis Till, saw a crudely extraordinary performance.

The experience undoubtedly touched them indelibly. For few Northern white men quite believe that the Southern white man can be a[s] vicious, lawless and barbarous as frequent reports from the area have related.

After all, they have been brought up to believe in the magnolias and chivalry of the South. Hollywood has handled the South romantically; and writers, intrigued by the soft southern drawl, have helped to perpetrate the fraud.

Actually, few places in the world can be as savage and inhuman. Few people nowadays remember that back in the 1930's Adolph Hitler sent a mission to the U.S. to study the South's treatment of Negroes, so that he could more efficiently terrorize the Jews.

Cultured Brutality

The manner in which Moses Wright, grand uncle of young Till, was treated was a shocking invasion of human dignity. Now, Wright is 64 years old and, as he said, never in his life had he accused a white man of anything.

Yet General Chatham, the district attorney, steadily addressed him as "Uncle Mose" and conversed with him in a kind of pidgin English—saying "axed" for asked as Moses Wright did and talking about the "undertaker man."

His manner was kindly, magnolia-scented, but edged with contemptuous tolerance as he called him "Old Man Mose."

Now, General Chatham is what is known as "quality white folks" down South. This grave, tired man, whom fate had chosen to prosecute two poor whites, carried off the racial conspiracy neatly, when he interrogated prospective jurors and accepted their barefaced lie that they would give justice to a Negro Boy, murdered by two white men.

He failed, too, to procure adequate evidence with which to convict Mila[m] and Bryant. Almost as shocking as the crime was the inadequacy of the local law enforcement machinery.

Moreover, the prosecution attorneys were without funds for investigations, but District Attorney Chatham failed to so inform the judge.

The trial was in fact a terrible farce. For no one expected a guilty verdict to be brought in against the white defendants.

The fact is, afterwards the milling white crowds congratulated Bryant and Milam for being acquitted—which in fact was applause for their foul murder of a child.

Crudities Galore

The defense attorney, Sidney Carlton, using his voice like the lash of a whip, turned on Moses Wright as though he had committed the murder—when in fact, Wright's only "crime" was to truthfully testify against two white men.

He even had enough courage, when goaded, to stop saying "sir"—which, in the southern context, is tentamount to a spit in the eye.

Old Moses Wright did one of the bravest things a Negro in the Delta could do, and, in the process, probably spent the hardest hours in the hardest life for a human in the United States.

He was badgered and mocked, threatened and insulted. Yet he still clutched the truth—Bryant and Milam had kidnapped young Till.

If Wright was the victim of crude prejudice, so too were the Negro observers. Negro reporters and photographers were labeled "niggers," and seated at a Jim Crow table where indeed they had difficulty hearing the proceedings.

Nevertheless, what happened was an eye-opener to the parochial elements of Tallahatchie County.

When Congressman Charles C. Diggs, Democrat of Detroit, stood on the courthouse lawn before a battery of microphones and sound cameras and voiced views, the people of Tallahatchie inched toward the sight watching in complete amazement.

To be sure, this sort of thing shook the foundation of their primitive way of life. No less impressive to them were the Negro reporters and photographers as they stood on tables and chairs to catch the proceedings.

As one observer put it, "The phenomenon wrote its mark on the faces of the white spectators."

Press Release, Office of Honorable Adam Clayton Powell, Jr., 11 October 1955

> FOR RELEASE AFTER 12 NOON, TUESDAY, OCTOBER 11, 1955
> CONGRESSMAN POWELL SPEAKS AT LABOR RALLY HELD AT
> SEVENTH AVENUE AND 37TH STREET

Congressman Powell, speaking at a Labor Rally held at 12 noon, Tuesday October 11, 1955, put forth a 6 point program of action to combat the recent wave of lynch murders in Mississippi.

Excerpts from Congressman Powell's speech follow:

Having just come back fresh from Africa, Europe and England, I can objectively report that the lynch murder of Emmett Till in Mississippi was, in the eyes of Europe, a lynching of the Statue of Liberty.

No single incident has caused as much damage to the prestige of the United States on foreign shores as what has happened in Mississippi. That is a thing we must face: —unless something is done by the legal forces of the United States to rectify the wrong in Mississippi, then our leadership is not only going to be seriously damaged, but it is going to continue to slide down hill.

I believe that some things can be done. In the first place, I have talked to the top lawyers of the NAACP and with Executive Secretary Roy Wilkins and they assure me that[,] under the present law, it is as impossible for the Federal Government to do anything concerning murder within the State of Mississippi, as it would be for them to do something concerning a murder on 135 Street and 7th Avenue. But, nevertheless, there are specific things that can be done.

In the second place, I need you to support me in demanding that there shall be convened immediately a special session of Congress. Mr. Walter Lippman[n], writing in the *Herald Tribune* on Thursday, September 29th[,] indicated in his column that this is a time of emergency for the United States. He said that by no stretch of the imagination can we say that because of President Eisenhower's illness, the machinery of the Government isn't going to move on. He pointed out that there are certain very definite threats facing the United States, such as the coming disarmament conference in October, the sale of arms to Egypt, the Moroccan crisis, our votes in the United Nations; all of these require the advice of the top man of our nation. He indicated, therefore, in his column that we should, despite our affections and prayers for the President, move into the position someone, on a temporary basis, who will be *the* President of the United States. I agree with Mr. Lippman[n] and I say that the greatest danger facing us right now is the danger of adverse world opinion because of the Mississippi lynchings and, therefore, a session of Congress must be called: —the illness of Mr. Eisenhower must not be used as an excuse.

In the third place, word has come to me that most of the FBI Agents working on the Mississippi incident are from the deep South, if not from Mississippi itself. They are known in the community[;] they are known to the Sheriffs and the Sheriffs know them. They cannot, therefore, do a good job. Negro people do not like to talk to white people in the South—they are afraid, especially if that individual comes with a Southern accent. I am, therefore, recommending that the FBI immediately send into Mississippi a fresh team of Agents, most of them from the Northern cities. I also would like to know why the FBI has not employed Negro FBI Agents in larger numbers. They should be down there in Mississippi with the full weight and authority of the United States Government backing them up.

In the fourth place, I believe that a national boycott of anything that comes from Mississippi should be organized by both Negroes and whites, including all groups, such as churches, trade unions and fraternities. Such a list of products could be drawn up by the NAACP. I place at the service of the NAACP, my ability to use the Congressional Record. I will print in that Record any list furnished to me and under my frank will distribute that list all over the United States. In the meantime, the Negro people in Mississippi should immediately stop buying in the local stores and do as much purchasing as possible from Sears Roebuck and Montgomery Ward catalogues.

In the fifth place, a fund should be set up under the auspices of the NAACP, to which church and trade union groups with large sums in their treasury, should contribute to establish something on the style of the old Underground Railroad during the pre–Civil War days. This would be an operation that would take out of Mississippi and any other sensitive area of the South, men, women and young people who are witnesses to crimes and dare not testify because they know their lives are in danger and their economic future would be threatened. Wherever such an individual is found, he should be given every bit of protection, brought North and a job made available to him. In this respect, I would like to applaud my colleague, Congressman Diggs, for what he has done, including bringing North one of the star witnesses.

In the sixth place, when the next session of Congress opens in January 1957, I will present a resolution upon that day demanding that no one from the State of Mississippi shall be seated in the Congress, due to the fact that they have refused to allow the people of the State to vote: present members have already been seated for this session, and nothing can be done until a new Congress is elected. It is definitely spelled out in the Constitution that a man is elected to the Congress on the basis of the number of people in his district who are American citizens and have the right to vote.

It is clear that the recent wave of lynching in Mississippi during the past few months is a terror campaign, organized by the entrenched white leadership to keep Negroes from voting, and from gaining first class citizenship. That is why there have been three lynchings so far this year, and that is why there may be others. I expect to campaign on this basis in 1956, and I will urge that both National Parties support such a plank in their platform.

To Wit: NO REPRESENTATIVE IN THE CONGRESS OF THE UNITED STATES, FROM A STATE WHICH REFUSES TO PERMIT NEGRO CITIZENS TO FREELY EXERCISE THEIR FRANCHISE WITHOUT FEAR OF LYNCHING OR COERCION OF ANY KIND, SHOULD BE SEATED.

Finally, we need to realize that the vast majority of white people in America are shocked to their heart at what has happened in Mississippi, and they will work in cooperation with us. This is no hour, therefore, to meet murder with hatred. This is an hour to use our minds, our hearts and our pocketbooks to stop this evil which[,] in reality, is not hurting the Negro as much as it is destroying the United States of America.

THIS IS WORLD COMMUNISM'S FINEST HOUR
SHALL WE LET THEM WIN BECAUSE OF A BIGOTED FEW?

I Think the Till Jury Will Have Uneasy Conscience
Eleanor Roosevelt, *Memphis Press-Scimitar,* 11 October 1955

New York, Monday — In the current issue of *Life Magazine* there is an editorial on the Till case which is an appeal to the conscience of all our people. The editorial says, quite rightly, that human justice often falls short of being justice, but that divine justice sooner or later is meted out to all of us according to our just dues.

After reading this editorial I think the jury that allowed itself to be persuaded that no one had really found and identified the body—tho it was granted that a boy had disappeared but the body found might not be his—and therefore, the accused men could not be convicted or punished in any way, will find their consciences troubled.

It is true that there can still be a trial for kidnapping, and I hope there will be. I hope the effort will be made to get at the truth. I hope we are beginning to discard the old habit, as practiced in a part of our country, of making it very difficult to convict a white man of a crime against a colored man or woman.

I remember a train trip I made many years ago between Atlanta and Warm Springs, Ga. I was with my husband. At one point we were delayed for a long time, and later we heard that a white man had shot a colored man on the train. Both of us were upset, and we asked if the white man had been arrested.

"Oh, no," we were told, "but he might later come up for trial."

Months later I was driving my husband thru the county seat near Warm Springs when he pointed out to me a white man standing on the corner near the courthouse, and said with a wry smile, "There is the man who delayed us so long that day on the train. He is as free as he ever was, tho the colored man is dead."

I never forgot this incident, but now it has taken on added meaning. I know everywhere in this country we must prove that what we say about equality before the law for every American citizen is a reality and not a myth.

The colored peoples of the world, who far outnumber us, will watch the Till case with interest, and if justice in the United States is only for the white man and not for the colored, we will have again played into the hands of the Communists and strengthened their propaganda in Africa and Asia.

At the recent meeting in San Francisco commemorating the signing of the United Nations charter, a suggestion was made—I think by Israel—that a statue should be placed in San Francisco harbor to parallel in a way the Statue of Liberty, which everyone coming into New York harbor looks at with warm affection and gratitude. Now I have a letter from Arthur Robinson of Volcano, Cal., saying that this statue should be a statue of justice and placed on Alcatraz Island from which, he believes, the prison is shortly to be moved.

Mr. Robinson suggests that the money raised by groups like his own and those in San Francisco might well be supplemented by money coming from every other United Nations member state, and he wants to get the project going because he feels that it should "catch fire in the hearts and minds of free men everywhere." It might be a reminder to us as a nation that we stand as the symbol of democracy to the world and that equal justice is looked upon as one of the essential parts of democracy.

If every citizen of our country were conscious of this, there might be no more juries such as sat at the first trial of the Till case.

Whose Circus?
Delta Democrat-Times, 12 October 1955

Although it is impossible to answer even a small portion of the poisonous diatribe that the NAACP is now firing at Mississippi, the comment Monday in Knoxville, Tenn. by an official of the NAACP that the Till murder trial in Mississippi was held in "a circus tent," prompts reply.

The demeanor of the court at Sumner, Miss. retained dignity despite the strongest efforts on the part of the NAACP to make it otherwise. What occurred at the funeral in Chicago, and at various public meetings since, in which admitted Communists have played a large part, comprises the "circus tent" atmosphere to which this NAACP spokesman refers.

It is increasingly obvious that the NAACP is putting its trained seals on the road in this case in a manner most likely to forever obstruct any true justice. The world is the audience for the sad spectacle.

The only way to have prevented the Till affair from becoming a "circus" in the light that is referred to here, would have been for all NAACP mass meetings to have been banned, all NAACP representatives ousted from the courtroom and all Negro publications censored.

It is certain that one injustice set this off, but one cannot but be impressed by the delight [that] the Communists and the NAACP alike took in it. Together they have set forth a mushrooming counter injustice against innocent and guilty alike that is making it very difficult for decent people in Mississippi to act in the course of righting the original wrong.

Whose circus is it?

Memo from the American Jewish Committee on European Reaction to the Till Case, 7 October 1955

THE AMERICAN JEWISH COMMITTEE

386 Fourth Avenue

New York 16, NY

MEMORANDUM

October 7, 1955

To: National Office
From: Paris Office
Subject: European Reaction to the Emmett Till case in Sumner, Mississippi

Europe's reaction to the trial and verdict in Sumner, Miss., was swift, violent and universal. There was a total and unqualified condemnation of the court proceedings, of the weakness of the prosecution, the behavior of the jury and the judge, and at the verdict of acquittal.

Europe's condemnation came from all sections of public opinion, all political directions, and was expressed immediately and spontaneously. Surprisingly, on this occasion the Communists were less vociferous than many of the liberal and conservative elements. These protestations were expressed in hundreds of newspaper editorials, statements by public leaders in every country of Western Europe, and by men in the street.

The proceedings of the trial were reported prominently and at great length in the daily newspapers. Seldom has a trial at such distance been reported so extensively. The descriptive and detailed reports were accompanied by dramatic photos of the court sessions.

The first reaction was astonishment that such a trivial beginning should have such tragic results. A typical expression of this reaction was the short inscription under a series of pictures in the Parisian illustrated weekly, *Radar*. Under the headline "Lynched for having admired a white woman," this paper said:

It is impossible to believe, but, alas, like many other exceptional crimes, this one is authentic. At Sumner in the state of Mississippi, a young Negro, Emmett Till, 14 years old, whistled in admiration at the young white woman, Mrs. Bryant. In Europe, this is a homage which provokes a smile. Here it was the equivalent of a death sentence. The husband of Mrs. Bryant, and his half-brother, Milan [Milam], kidnapped Emmett and after ignoble tortures threw him into the river. The twelve jurors, all white, acquitted them. This shows that racial prejudice is still very strong in the U.S., primarily in the South. To such a point that in the course of the proceedings, Negro journalists were not permitted to sit near the white ones, while the accused joked with the audience. This verdict of letting loose two assassins can be explained but not justified by the atmosphere of racial hatred against Negroes which prevails in the entire South of the United States.

Another Parisian weekly, *Aux Ecoutes,* summed up the trial and its background in even stronger terms:

Never was there a more abominable travesty of the truth. The assassins presented themselves with weapons to the house from which the child was kidnapped. This violent act is recognized, for after being acquitted they will, it seems[,] be prosecuted for kidnapping. The mother of the child formally recognized her son. The odious personality whom the child admired by whistling, a sign of admiration in the United States, has invented words which he is supposed to have said, although at the beginning she only said that he whistled. Imagine a Negro who permits himself to admire a white woman, and what a woman. A cruel shrew, who calls two men to take revenge for the outrage, accepts the massacre and accompanies her two miserable men who kidnap the child. And this jury, which in spite of overwhelming proof acquits the two monsters, proving thereby that it consisted of men who are worth no more than the accused. And the judge who permits that the two criminals hold on their knees two children who are being taught to hate the Negroes. And this press which relegates Negro journalists to a place from where they cannot see anything. And this country where no wave of indignation emerged after the acquittal.

The most prominent Parisian afternoon paper characterized the trial more moderately (*Le Monde*):

It is true that the accusation was technically weak. Owing to the lack of material means and handicapped at the beginning by a solidarity of the whites, the prosecution did not present sufficient objective conclusions to bring about a condemnation. What is much more serious is the sloppiness and the speed with which the defendants were judged and acquitted without the police having pushed the interrogations far enough. What was ignoble was the impudence of the defense, which in its desire to prove that the case was produced in order to defile the customs of the south, doubted the testimony of the young mother Till. . . . The white order continues to reign in Mississippi.

The news about the verdict was featured by the entire press and the most frequent words in the headlines were "Scandalous," "Monstrous" and "Abominable."

The comments varied in tone and intensity. Some limited their condemnation to the section in the South where the trial took place; others blamed the entire South for its segregation policies and the atmosphere of racial hatred which could produce such a trial; many others, on the basis of the trial and the verdict, raised sharp doubts about the sincerity of the U.S. in proclaiming itself as the defender of human rights and of oppressed peoples throughout the world.

Some elements in all these comments deserve particular emphasis. One is that the effects of the Supreme Court decision on desegregation, which was widely reported and commented upon in Europe after it was rendered, were to a great extent annulled by the events in Mississippi. Many commentators pointed out that while the Supreme Court decision and the policies of the federal administration aim to abolish racial barriers, the facts of life as illustrated by the Mississippi trial tell another and more poignant story.

Said *Le Phare* of Brussels, Belgium:

The southern states have refused to take account of the Supreme Court decision and all those who supported it were the object of such pressures that they have changed their attitudes. Employees who applied the decision lost their positions, merchants have seen their clients disappear. The decree of the Supreme Court was an error because it arose from abstract and ideological principles incompatible with the social realities of the southern states.

Franc-Tireur, anti-Communist liberal daily of Paris, said:

It is disquieting to see that in spite of the American laws condemning anti-Negro racism, the vilest passions can triumph unpunished under cover of the law of a state. Thus, there is still in certain corners of a great democracy a racist dogma of state, as anti-Semitism was a state dogma under Hitler and the confession trials under Stalin. We, who have always rejected with the same horror enslavement and assassination of men, no matter under what pretext, only because of their thoughts, their opinions, their origin or their color, how can we not be shocked by this new evidence of the rage of the whites? Racism like Hitlerism is still spreading its poison over the world.

La Giustizia of Rome, the daily newspaper of the right-wing Socialist Party of Italy, the leader of which, Mr. Saragat, is Vice-Prime Minister, commented:

It is far from our intention to accuse the entire judiciary system of America, or to make generalized accusations about its people and their deep savagery. However, it is only too clear and evident that as long as such cases call world attention to the painful and at the same time ignoble scar of racism, still so alive in the U.S., we cannot but reserve judgment on North American civilization.

And so that our judgment may not seem excessively hard, it is opportune to report the opinion of a U.S. magistrate, Judge Channing Tobias, president of the NAACP. "The unworthy and shameful verdict," said Dr. Tobias, "and such actions, bring mortal wounds to American democracy." And we, sincere admirers of many aspects of the "American way of life," agree in this case with the U.S. judge.

Obviously, the Communist press used this trial to launch general attacks against the U.S. and its "hypocrisy" in the attempt to lead the free world in the struggle against oppression.
Said *Das Freies Volk* of Dusseldorf:

The life of a Negro in Mississippi is not worth a whistle.

This verdict is again a sign of American democracy. Knowing that in the U.S. every hysterical woman can send a Negro to the electric chair by claiming that she was insulted, it is not surprising that until now no white man was ever sentenced to death in Mississippi because he killed a Negro. Dulles and the other roving preachers of American democracy and freedom who babble about the "American way of life" and who want to make us their satellites, have thrown a heavy veil over such freedom and democracy.

L'Humanit[é], the Communist daily of Paris, ran a series of articles in the same vein, and did not omit to refer to the McGee and Rosenberg trials. It said:

The two brutes of Mississippi whose guilt was not questioned by any Yankee newspaper were acquitted on "benefit of doubt," but neither the innocent Rosenbergs nor Willie McGee benefited from such a doubt. The outcries of joy by the audience at Sumner when the verdict was announced will join in the borders. . . Not too many Frenchmen have the right to give lessons to Americans in this area. However, certain Americans have a tendency to give lessons to others before having swept before their own door.

Le Peuple, the socialist daily of Brussels, deplored the proceedings at Sumner also for the reason that this will serve as an excuse to the colonial powers who are now on the defensive and make it possible for them to say that even in the U.S., the leading democratic power in the world, there is racial discrimination.

The *Libre Artois* of Arras emphasized this point by referring to the verdict at Sumner as follows:

Is not this a particularly odious manifestation of the colonialism that numerous Americans are so prompt to denounce in others — often, alas, with justice, but sometimes with a total lack of humility?

It is interesting that this reproach to America for criticizing other nations on racial policies was expressed not only by French publications but by Belgian and Swiss. Said *Nation Belge* of Brussels:

One is astonished that in the U.S., where there was elaborated the new Charter of the Rights of Man, for all men regardless of their color, there can still take place such an event a century after publication of *Uncle Tom's Cabin.*

And the *Gazette de Lausanne:*

A new war of secession is exacerbating spirits and inciting provocations. The jury of Sumner has defied the White House and world opinion. . . Colonialism, if not colonization, cannot find its justification in a regime which is born of the same motives and the same interests.

And the *Liberté* of Fribourg, Switzerland:

One is entitled to express surprise that such a denial of justice be permitted in a state which does not cease to offer its councils of virtue to European nations and to plead in favor of emancipation and equality of rights for colored races.

In addition, many French writers, intellectuals and artists voiced their protests in statements to newspapers, particularly through the anti-Communist daily *Combat.* The Catholic philosopher Gabriel Marcel said: "It is a racist judgment." Gerard Bauer of the Goncourt Academy commented: "The sentence rendered is of such flagrant injustice that it is impossible not to feel it as a painful blow against human dignity." Georges Duhamel of the Academie Française said: "When a crime is a racial crime I consider it particularly abominable, because men are men no matter what the color of their skin."

And finally, a significant voice came from North Africa. *L'Action,* the official publication of the Neo-Destour, the leading nationalist party of Tunisia which is now in power, had this to say about the Sumner trial:

> It is not enough for the U.S. to present itself verbally as the champion of liberty and justice. It is not enough for them to complain about the fate of unfortunate countries that are "oppressed by the Communist regime." If these are their real preoccupations, then they should be accompanied by internal policies directed in the same sense. . . This verdict is a shameless scandal which stains the justice of the U.S. It is one of those inequities that history does not forgive.

These are only few examples of the unanimous and violent reaction of Europe to the Mississippi trial. They can be multiplied a hundredfold.

Selected Letters to the Editor
From the *Washington Afro-American*

These lines are about the little Till boy who was slaughtered "way down in the Egypt-land-of-our-USA," which is called Mississippi.

God raised up Moses to bring his children out of Egypt because they were cowed slaves.

Who killed the child, if those two men didn't?

They are the ones who took him away from home. They put him out in the road five miles from home. Now, the paper I was taking carried news items of the trial on the back pages until the verdict. Then the news was put on the front page. We all know what that means.

And another thing. I wonder if those two men and that woman ever read the Bible?

It teaches us that an injustice we do to others will fall on our children to the third and fourth generation.

Someone should take the boy's uncle, and all his relatives[,] out of Mississippi if they are not already dead. Oh my God help them.

How can our government stand by and let such a disgrace cast shadows of the entire nation? —(Mrs.) Annie Caldwell, New York [1 October 1955]

From the *Baltimore Afro-American*

Although the two white defendants were acquitted, their trial did serve a useful purpose.

It laid bare for the whole world to see the rotten situation in Mississippi.

It makes a hollow mockery out of the loud contentions of Southern officials that colored citizens are granted equal justice in America. —(Mrs.) Emma Anderson, Philadelphia [1 October 1955]

How can our representatives in the United Nations with a straight face point to brain-washing in China and slave labor in Russia, while we allow white supremacy to run rampant in Mississippi?

The Mississippi trial gave the Communists all the ammunition they needed to rebut American accusations of injustice leveled at the Iron Curtain countries.

But I am willing to bet that Chairman Eastland and his Senate Subcommittee on Internal Security will never bother to investigate this glaring example of subversive activity. —Ralph Huston, Baltimore [1 October 1955]

The lynching of Emmett Till was one of the most appalling and horrifying crimes in the annals of modern times.

The subsequent acquittal of the criminals is perhaps one of the greatest miscarriages of justice ever perpetrated by a backward state.

It is distressing to hear so many of our people say complacently, "Let the crime lie upon the white man's conscience—let the guilt be his."

This attitude is both shortsighted and cowardly. Until we realize that we will have to fight vigorously and sometimes die for justice, nothing will be done to change existing conditions.

Mass meetings, protests, telegrams to the White House should be intensified and bombardment of the conscience of white America continued.

We must be men, be militant and fight for justice at home the way we fought so courageously for democracy abroad.

What happened to young Till could happen to any American whose skin chances to be black.

Ignoring, evading, ducking and dodging the issue is shameful procedure. Fight for justice now, or the shame will not be Mississippi's, but ours. —Alice Sunday, New York [1 October 1955]

In company with a great many other average Americans, I am profoundly disturbed at the apparent indifference of the press to the two unanswered questions in the Emmett Till case:

1. If the body taken from the Tallahatchie River in Mississippi on Aug. 31, with a bullet hole in the head, trussed, a piece of heavy machinery tied around the neck, is not that of Emmett Till, where is Emmett now?

2. If the murdered body is not that of Emmett Till, whose is it?

Suppose that in the great state of Mississippi a white child had been abducted by two black-skinned men.

Suppose that during this time this white child had been dragged into a barn. Suppose that from the barn had been heard the sounds of blows, anguished cries of a young human being tortured with pain and deadly fear—cries, incidentally, that have the same heartbreaking sound whether they issue from a black body or a white one.

Suppose that was what happened. Do you suppose that the Mississippi jury would have to consult its Anglo-Saxon conscience for even as long as a full minute before rendering a verdict?

And do you suppose that verdict would have been an acquittal?

We know the answers to these two questions. But until we have the answers to the first two—who was murdered and where is young Emmett Till—this nation should not rest.

The shame of the State of Mississippi is the shame of us all. The use to which the Communists can and will put the Emmett Till case, as it now stands, will hurt us all.

Justice cries out: "Whose body is that body? Where is Emmett Till?" —John Rust, New York City [22 October 1955]

From the *Cleveland Call and Post*

How long will this nation continue to use the "Rope and Faggot"? When you read and hear of the brutalities committed by Dixie rebels, you sometimes wonder if this nation is civilized. To me, our federal government is guilty of tolerance and negligence.

If we are American citizens, granted the protection of our constitution, then martial law should be granted in the savage states of the southland.

When tyranny and lynch laws are used to castrate Negroes, it is high time our federal government does something about it or lose face with the nations of the world.

Here in America, especially in the deep south, the four freedoms mean to us "freedom from equality, freedom from justice, freedom from education and freedom from the right to expression." It is an amazing situation of viciousness and stupidity.

Emmett Till's father died while serving his country. His son was sacrificed on the cross of ignorance and those who had the intestinal fortitude to point out the vicious killers were hunted down like dogs and were forced to flee, leaving all their earthly belongings.

This Mississippi state of darkness, together with its hypocrites, shall feel the wrath of God. This is not new to us[;] for countless generations we have lived in fear and deep poverty. The rope and faggot have been our destiny.

Equality and justice for millions have been an idle dream, and the southern hospitality we hear so much of surely was not meant for us. Things like this can create hatred. It can tear at the vitals of American democracy.

Down through history from ancient dynasties, since the dawn of civilization, men have conquered and oppressed, steeped in stupidity and hate. They, like their ancient cities, crumbled in the dust of despair. Is America today traveling the same road? Only time shall tell. —Melvin E. Lee, Cleveland [22 October 1955]

From the *Memphis Commercial Appeal*

The sorry spectacle we witnessed at Sumner, Miss., is revolting to no little degree. The advantage taken by Negroes and the rabid press to make a Roman holiday out of a murder trial is an example of the conditions we are, and will be, facing because of the judicial and executive effort to bring about first, integration in our schools, and later in all activities of our lives.

The fact that no attention has been given to the fiendish assault of a white woman by five Negro men is proof, if any proof is needed, that there is a certain element that will stop at nothing to humiliate and discredit the South and any other section (and there are other sections) who are trying to preserve the integrity of the white race.

While this carnival is taking place the good people of Hoxie, Ark., are battling to preserve the status quo of their schools, and gradually the people, even of Tennessee, are belatedly arousing themselves as they realize that "it can happen here."

And while all this trouble and anxiety and confusion are gripping the nation, information comes to us that the two young grandchildren of Mr. Eisenhower are safely tucked away in an exclusive private school in Virginia, far removed from the turmoil going on all around them, and the President is calling on the authorities in nearby Washington to become a model of integration for the country to follow.

Oh! Consistency, thou art a jewel. —Willis P. Newman [25 September 1955]

In these troubled days of racial agitation it behooves all of us to keep informed. Newspapers and periodicals see to it that the information is available, but let us not overlook another valuable source—books. Too many people never see the inside of their public libraries.

If every citizen, including newspaper editors, would read the Harper's prize-winning, *Trial,* by Don M. Mankiewicz, I am sure the parallel between that case so graphically told and the Till case in Mississippi would immediately be apparent.

Could there be any doubt that this Mississippi murder—from the weeks or months before young Till made his visit to the South—was communist-inspired, directed and executed? The party member who worked on Till did not know exactly what the boy would do to stir up trouble, but he planted ideas which he knew would explode in some way that could be used by his party. The apparently feeble-minded Negro reacted exactly as his mentor knew he would. The Southern white men followed the psychological pattern which the communists could easily predict. And they were on hand, ready to pounce and conclude this incident to their advantage. Did not some communist agent or agents murder the young Negro after the white men turned him loose?

What if some poor devil is murdered—the communists now have another martyr to use for racial antagonism—and what a field day they have as the money rolls in! A collection table is set up right beside the casket as morbid thousands file by to view the body. The boy's mother is interviewed by the press—she appears on television, working up sympathy and dollars for "the cause." More publicity flares up as she "consents" to appear at the trial only with FBI protection. Oh, she is a gold-plated exhibit for them—the exact counterpart of the young Mexican's mother in *Trial.*

How does the NAACP know all about the murder in less than hours after it happens? They are ready with prepared statements, carefully worded in the most vilifying and inciting language which communist experts with years of experience can produce.

No intelligent American believes that the NAACP cares one minute for the advancement of the Negro race. Their only aim, and it is deadly and powerful, is racial antagonism, one part of the over-all "divide and conquer" program. Thus far they are succeeding very well indeed, aided by that egotistical band of politicians masquerading as the United States Supreme Court, misinformed "do-gooders," and the ignorance of the masses and "don't-cares."

Until these undercover communist workers are apprehended and the NAACP is stripped of its "front," the South will suffer more tragedies of this kind. It will happen again and again. —Mrs. H. D. Scherck [25 September 1955]

Everyone regrets the unfortunate series of events leading to the death of the 14-year-old Negro Till.

The same day that the newspapers carried the story about the kidnap-murder of young Till, they also had stories about four Negro men charged with rape, their victims white women.

Not one time has any pro-Negro agitator found anything wrong with the provocation that caused the disappearance of young Till. Their silence seems to endorse adultery, fornication, seduction and rape, and kindred crimes, and to make a hero-martyr out of Till in his effort to indulge himself.

However much we deplore such a crime as that alleged which caused young Till to disappear, let it be known that it will be a long time before Southern people will be silent and submissive in the face of agents who insult and try to hurt womanhood.

Any society for the advancement of Negroes can profitably exercise itself with the inculcation of morals and the strengthening of their social customs. —W. A. Tyson [25 September 1955]

Because of the unfortunate incident at Sumner, Miss., the whole state of Mississippi has had her inalienable rights trespassed upon by critical eyes world-wide. She has truly become public fish bowl No. 1. It was very obvious that the NAACP took every precaution to really place her in a tremendous "hot spot" and they were very clever in their publicity endeavors.

However, the point is this: What genuine good have they accomplished? Evidently, they are defeating their own purpose. The public exhibition of Emmett Till's body in Chicago certainly did not ease any antagonism that presently existed between the two races. Perhaps they are patterning their movements after Karl Marx and his ideas of power through force and violence. Too, they responded over Till's death as though he was an angelic lad without dishonorable intentions or actions.

Why don't those people take that proverbial chip off their shoulders and seek to teach a little restraint and good will? In fact, it appears the NAACP could stand a lot of teaching in Christianity. —Bobby Parkins, Milan, Tenn. [2 October 1955]

Recent happenings in Mississippi have led me to the conclusion that the fight for first class citizenship for the American Negro is being helped as much by Mississippians as by the NAACP. The difference, of course, being that the NAACP's fight is designed to give first class citizenship to all Americans. On the other hand, the State of Mississippi, in attempting to deny these rights, is in effect making possible that which they are attempting to resist.

For instance, incidents such as occurred at Money, Belzoni and Brookhaven will certainly make the American people become fully aware of the fact that the sovereign state to our south is incapable of self government. When an elected representative of the state exhorts its citizenry to forget about the law and do as you choose regardless of the law, then this amounts to the breakdown of one of our most cherished possessions—Law and Order.

Whatever else may be said about the American people, one does not have to be a genius to know that by and large Americans believe in fair play. They do not like to see people deliberately persecuted. In our sporting events, we will "boo" the fellow whom we believe to be unfair. It is indeed unfortunate that the people of Mississippi are being looked upon with disfavor by civilized people all over the world. —H. A. Gilliam, Memphis [2 October 1955]

A few words for people like myself, who live in Mississippi! I believe everyone is supposed to have been born equal to everyone else[;] however[,] this is not always true, as some of us are sadly lacking where the brain is supposed to be.

The colored race, as a whole, is not ready to integrate with the "whites" as they call us. You cannot step to the head of the class without first earning that place.

As for the unfortunate affair at Sumner (I lived there for five years) no man whether he be white, black or in-between, has any right to take hold of a woman without being invited.

It appears that every state outside of Mississippi would have the world believe we live something like during the days of the Inquisition in Spain with dark dungeons, torture chambers, burning of possessed souls, etc. —Mrs. A. B. Brantley, Lake Cormorant, Miss. [9 October 1955]

Two men were indicted for murder and tried recently at a small town in Mississippi.

The murder charge was based on circumstantial evidence. The corpus delicti was a Negro: as a result public opinion in this nation and in Western Europe was strongly against the defendants. They had three ingredients which to them were strong indicators that justice cannot live in the South: those three ingredients are white men, a dead Negro, and Mississippi.

As far as public opinion was concerned, the case was not against two men but against the whole State of Mississippi.

Our state was being tried by an impartial judge called public opinion with an impartial jury of nations (including our own) which were certain that nothing good could come out of said state.

Before Mississippi took the witness stand, the judge was certain that she was guilty of prejudice, railroading, bigotry.

The jury waited to see if Mississippi would judge her children fairly, if she could free herself from emotionalism that afflicts so many parents. They wished to give her the opportunity to free herself from the partiality for her white child and administer justice with a reasonable amount of objectivity. The jury was unbiased. They sought righteousness. The jury hoped to see Mississippi punish her white child: for it was a known fact that her black child was mistreated. Therefore said jury knew if the white child were punished that justice would be administered: hence they would find the state not guilty. Yet if the state dared to treat circumstantial evidence as it is treated in the rest of this country, the jury would find Mississippi guilty.

Perhaps this situation can best be clarified by precedent. In the days of our forefathers, witchcraft was prevalent. If the person accused of witchcraft floated when thrown in a pond that was a favorable omen that he was guilty and must be hanged by the neck: however, if he sank to the bottom of the pool and did not come up, he was surely innocent! —Bernard Massey, Jr., University, Miss. [9 October 1955]

Since the trial of Milam and Bryant on the charge of murdering Emmett Till, I have read many letters to the editor of the *Commercial Appeal*. None of them seems to have reached the heart of the matter.

Many years ago the white people of the South realized that the law offered no adequate protection for their women, and as always all over the world, when the law is unable to protect, the people provide their own protection for their families. For this reason it became an unwritten law that no Negro should approach a white woman, and if he did, the penalty was drastic. The Negro himself, by his conduct only, can provide the answer to whether or not such situation exists today.

There had not been a Negro killed in this state for many years under such circumstances as may have been characterized as a lynching. During this time it appeared that the whites of Mississippi were determined to give the black an opportunity to establish his place among civilized people, and in spite of an unprecedented number of murders and rapes of white people by the black, too numerous to set out here, and each more savage and ghastly than anything that occurred in the Till incident, the white people of this state have exercised remarkable patience and restraint.

The Till incident was nothing more than spontaneous combustion generated by such criminal attacks upon a long-suffering people, and the Negroes have no one but themselves to blame for what happened. Had Till observed the code and custom here, with which he was fully familiar, he would, without doubt, be picking cotton with his hosts in Sunflower County.

Every Negro in the United States knows he will not be permitted to make advances to white women in Mississippi, and when Till deliberately, with full knowledge of the seriousness of his act propositioned a white woman, he must have known he was setting in motion a chain of events calculated to inevitably lead to his death. He might just as well have pointed a loaded pistol at his head and pulled the trigger. That would have been called suicide.

A Negro who bears respect for established custom here is safer and happier here than he would be anywhere in the world. —"Observer," Greenville, Miss. [16 October 1955]

From the *Atlanta Constitution*

With what humility and shame we "supreme" whites should bow our heads and implore God's mercy when we think of our own share of responsibility for the outrageous murder and the jury's cowardly verdict in the now-notorious Mississippi lynching of the Till boy.

I agree with Tuskegee Institute that this was a lynching, nothing less.

As long as we remain silent and inactive before the corruption of justice, all of us are criminal. When we see anyone deprived of his rights as an equal citizen in these United States, and make no objection, our own rights, lives and liberty are in jeopardy. —Rev. Joe A. Rabun, Atlanta [9 October 1955]

The recent "wolf call" trial in Mississippi reminds me of a boxing match in which one of the participants has his hands tied behind him.

I wonder how the mother feels to have someone who has never seen her boy tell her she didn't know her own son. How can the jury account for the fact that the son has never shown up, and that no one else has been reported missing.

As long as things like this still happen I think we had better quit bragging to the rest of the world about the American way of life.

The defense counsel referred to the Anglo-Saxon blood in the jury. I happen to be Anglo-Saxon. And I don't like the insinuation that the Anglo-Saxon blood had anything to do with the verdict. If there ever was any Anglo-Saxon blood in that jury it has degenerated into something that has forgotten the meaning of decency and fair play. —Ernest Hinson, Alto [4 October 1955]

Bryant's store (at left) in Money, Mississippi. It was here on the porch of the grocery that Emmett Till accepted a challenge from his cousins and went inside the grocery to talk to the "pretty white woman" working the register. (© 1955 *Memphis Commercial Appeal.* Used by permission.)

Mose Wright stands outside the cabin where Milam and Bryant abducted Emmett Till three days days after the incident in Money. Immediately after the abduction, Wright sent his family north for protection while he, despite their pleas for him to join them, remained to testify. (© 1955 *Memphis Commercial Appeal.* Used by permission.)

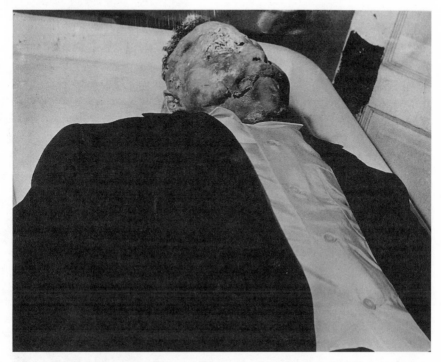

This photograph of Emmett Till as he lay in state in his casket ran in African American newspapers and magazines througout the nation and remains one of the most important images of the civil rights movement. (© 1955 *The Chicago Defender*. Used with permission from *The Chicago Defender*.)

On the day of Emmett
Till's funeral, crowds
overflow into the streets
outside of the Roberts
Temple Church of God
in Chicago. (© 1955 *The
Chicago Defender.* Used
with permission from
The Chicago Defender.)

Mamie Till Bradley (in black dress) watches her son's body lowered into its grave at Burr Oak Cemetery. (© 1955 *The Chicago Defender*. Used with permission from *The Chicago Defender*.)

Carolyn Bryant, the woman whom many African American newspapers dubbed "the cause of it all," poses for a picture outside of the law offices of J. J. Breland and John Whitten. Although at first no local attorney wanted the case, within a few short weeks all five lawyers in town offered their services pro bono. (© 1955 *Memphis Commercial Appeal.* Used by permission.)

Emmett Till's great uncle, Moses Wright (right), stands in a Delta cotton field. Despite threats against his life, he remains in Mississippi and testifies at the trial. (© 1955 *The Chicago Defender*. Used with permission from *The Chicago Defender*.)

Tallahatchie County Courtroom. Judge Curtis Swango presides over a hot and crowded courtroom. Because of the heat, the judge allowed the attorneys to remove their jackets. To accommodate the black reporters covering the trial, he set up a Jim Crow card table near the front of the courtroom (beneath the far right window). This is also where Emmett Till's mother was seated when she attended. (© 1955 *Memphis Commercial Appeal.* Used by permission.)

Tallahatchie County Sheriff H. C. Strider (standing, right) gives instructions to the jury. Because juries were selected from a list of male registered voters, and no blacks were registered to vote in Tallahatchie County in 1955, the jury was, inevitably, all white and all male. Ironically, Strider's testimony for the defense later in the trial would help to persuade the jury to acquit Bryant and Milam on all charges. (© 1955 *Memphis Commercial Appeal*. Used by permission.)

With children seated on their laps, defendants J. W. Milam (left) and Roy Bryant (right) listen to their attorneys question veniremen on the first day of the trial. By day's end, ten jurymen had been selected, with two more selected the next morning. (© 1955 *Memphis Commercial Appeal.* Used by permission.)

During a break in the trial, Mamie Till Bradley fields questions from both black and white reporters. Arriving on the second day of the trial along with congressman Charles Diggs of Michigan, Mrs. Bradley created a sensation and drew a crowd wherever she went. (© 1955 *Memphis Commercial Appeal.* Used by permission.)

The heavy cotton gin fan that was used to weight Emmett Till's body before it was dumped in the river. (© 1955 *Memphis Commercial Appeal*. Used by permission.)

This courtroom sketch by Franklin McMahon (published in *Life* magazine) depicts the high point of the trial. Asked to identify one of the men who came to his cabin at two in the morning searching for the "boy who'd done the talking," Mose Wright, in a dramatic gesture of defiance, stood up and, pointing directly at J. W. Milam, proclaimed, "Thar he." It was the first time in nearly a century that a black man had testified against a white man in a Mississippi court of law. (© Franklin McMahon/CORBIS. Used by permission.)

Chapter 4 *Searching for the Truth*

As the previous chapter bears out, many were dissatisfied with the verdict in Sumner. For them, the trial's importance was its demonstration that the process did not work, and they questioned whether, without federal intervention, blacks could get justice in Mississippi. For another set of dissenters, however, the trial raised a different set of questions involving the truths of the case. For instance, what really had happened that afternoon in the Bryant grocery? How did Milam and Bryant find out about the alleged transgression? Who else besides Milam and Bryant drove out to Mose Wright's cabin that night, and who were the other men spotted with Milam at the barn the next morning? Were there really black men in Milam's pickup that evening? If so, who were they and what had happened to them? Finally, how long did Emmett Till remain alive that night, and exactly when, where, why, and how did his murder take place? A handful of investigative reporters understood that the trial did not answer these questions fully and that the truth, more likely than not, had been obscured by the proceedings.

The selections in this chapter represent some of the conclusions and theories that were proposed in the days, weeks, and months immediately following the trial. Some of these theories, such as the one proposed by James L. Hicks, were based on tough, behind-the-scenes investigative journalism that took place during the trial; had it been aired in the courtroom, it could have changed the course of the proceedings. Other theories, such as the one suggested by the American Anti-Communist League, appear to have little basis in reality and were nothing more than accusations intended to inflame political animosities. Of all the accounts offered in this section, the one by William Bradford Huie in his infamous *Look* magazine article of January 1956 has most shaped our understanding of the events. For more than forty years, the article—reprinted within a few months in *Reader's Digest*—has remained the most influential account of what may have happened on the night Emmett Till was killed. Huie's version of events was given even greater currency when he was interviewed by the makers of *Eyes on the Prize*, who included a clip of Huie describing the details of the murder as he uncovered them in 1956. His account was not widely challenged until the publication of Stephen J. Whitfield's *Death in the Delta: The Story of Emmett Till* in 1986. While the full story of the tragedy will never be known, the theories and explanations put forth in this chapter can serve to flesh out—and in some cases to correct—the testimonies presented at the trial.

James L. Hicks's "Inside Story" of the Emmet Till Trial

James L. Hicks began his career as a reporter for the *Cleveland Call and Post* in 1935 and later moved on to the *Baltimore Afro-American.* As one of the premier investigative journalists of his generation, Hicks was also the Washington, D.C., bureau chief for the National Negro Press Association, which served more than one hundred newspapers. In 1955, he became executive director of the *New York Amsterdam News,* a position he would hold for the good part of twenty years. As the first black member of the State Department Correspondents Association and the first black reporter cleared to cover the United Nations, Hicks was truly a pioneer in the field. His coverage of the Till trial ran in dozens of African-American newspapers, and in the following piece of investigative journalism, which ran in four installments in October 1955, he tells about the role he played in discovering the existence of "missing witnesses" to the murder. Hicks's work in this area actually forced a trial recess on Tuesday, September 20, as the prosecution called for time to track down these newly discovered witnesses. In this series of articles—which ran in the *Baltimore Afro-American,* the *Cleveland Call and Post* and the *Atlanta Daily World*—Hicks argues that the forces of law in Mississippi conspired to prevent the full evidence of Milam and Bryant's guilt from surfacing at the trial. The version reprinted here draws its structure from the installments published in the *Cleveland Call and Post,* which presented the most condensed rendering of Hicks's article. Passages omitted from the *Cleveland Call and Post* articles, but included in some form or other in either the *Atlanta Daily World* or the *Baltimore Afro-American,* have been inserted throughout, enclosed in brackets.

Sheriff Kept Key Witness Hid in Jail During Trial

James L. Hicks, *Cleveland Call and Post*, 8 October 1955

New York, N.Y. — Here for the first time is the true story of what happened in the hectic five-day trial of two white men in Sumner, Mississippi, for the murder of 14-year-old Emmett Till of Chicago.

This story has never been written before. I did not write it in Mississippi for fear of bodily harm to myself, and to my colleagues.

No one else has written it because no one else in the capacity of a reporter lived as close to it as I did.

[Looking back on it now, I am ashamed that I did not throw caution to the winds and at least try to get out the story exactly as it was unfolding to me. I'm convinced, however, that if I had tried this, I would not be here in New York to write this.

[I should like also to add that not once in the stories that I did file from Sumner did I tell a lie. The offense, if I committed one, lies in the fact that the stories that I did file did not dig or go far enough into the truth. It just wasn't safe to do so.]

Here in the safety of New York I now charge (as I would have charged in Sumner, Mississippi) that:

Sheriff H. C. Strider frustrated the ends of justice by refusing to take an impartial person to the Charleston jail at Charleston, Miss., and permit them to check on his report that Leroy "Too Tight" Collins [was] not in the Charleston jail.

I further charge, and with the protection of proper law officials will go back to Mississippi and help prove, that Leroy Collins was in the Charleston jail on Friday at the very hour that the case went to the jury.

I charge further that Prosecutors Gerald Chatham and Robert B. Smith were told about this but that they decided that since the sheriff had given his word that Collins was not in the jail, they proceeded to close out the trial without this man whom everyone believes could have positively hung the crime on the two white men and seriously implicated at least one other white man.

I finally charge that if Leroy Collins is brought forward at this date and given all opportunity to talk where he is assured that he is not in any danger, he will be able to tell where Henry Lee Loggins is and that the two of them will prove to be the two colored men who were seen on the truck the night of the murder by Moses Wright and Willie Reed.

Knew Too Much

I believe that Henry Lee Loggins is dead and that he was disposed of because he knew too much about the case.

These are serious charges. But I welcome this opportunity to write down the evidence on which they are based.

This is the fantastic story as lived by this reporter:

Attended Funeral

On the Sunday before the opening of the trial I attended the funeral of "Kid" Townsend, a well[-]liked colored man who has lived in Sumner virtually all his life.

I had been told that a number of white people would attend the funeral and I felt that it would provide at least [a] good pre-trial story for my paper.

[I drove into the churchyard, got out with my notebook in my hand and went into the church[,] passing a number of colored people standing in the church-yard.

[Inside I found the church crowded with no seats and that white people were occupying the two rows on the left side of the church.

[The temperature was about 95 degrees and I decided to stand outside the church and listen to the services after I had been in the church about a half hour. This was easy to do because the church was the typical white-washed wooden structure and the minister who preached was shouting loud enough to be heard from outside.

[My notes, which I shall constantly refer to in this article, show that the preacher's name was the Rev. W. M. King, that there were 175 colored people in the church and 12 whites including five women, four men, and three white chil-dren.

[My notes also show that I recorded the sermon as being from "Fourth Chap-ter, Second Timothy," and beneath I have a quotation read by the minister which said, "I have fought the good fight. I have kept the faith. I have finished my course."]

I was leaning there against the fender of a parked car when a voice behind me said, "Are you down here for the trial?"

Up to this point I did not know a single colored person in Sumner and I had tried in the two days I'd been there [to keep] from spreading the word around that I was a reporter.

But as I turned to the voice I decided that it would get out anyway[,] so I turned to the man who addressed me and said, "Yes, I am down on the trial. I'm a reporter."

The man was colored and he said to me, "There's a lady behind this car who would like to talk with you. I think you'd be interested in what she has to say."

[I turned and looked but saw no one. At that moment the man said, "Go behind the car, but don't take out your notebook and write down nothing."

[Now at this point I should like to say to the reader, if this whole thing starts off reading like a cheap and fantastic Hollywood movie script, that is exactly what it is going to read like for the entire five days.

[But I can say also that every word of it is true and it is written exactly the way I lived it.]

I went back of that car and found a woman whom I shall not describe[,] for she told me in the beginning that she was actually endangering her life by talking to me about the trial.

Woman Gives Tip

The woman then told me that a young boy named "Too Tight" was in the truck the night of the murder and that he had suddenly disappeared and no one knew where he was.

She said she did not know "Too Tight's" real name but that she thought she could send me to a place to get all the information I wanted on him "if you aren't afraid to go."

I told her I was not afraid. Then standing and looking off in another direction she said to me[,] ["]Go to Glendora. That's about seven miles south of here. Be careful and don't let the people know what you are looking for. Don't talk to any white people.

"Go to a place called King's. It's the only colored dance hall in town. Hang around there and find the right people. They will tell you 'Too Tight's' name and what happened to him. But don't,["] she said, "get caught down there after dark."

Then she walked away from the car.

[As she walked away I looked at my watch. It was three o'clock. I reasoned that with any good luck I could drive down there in 20 minutes and spend an hour or so in town and still make it back to my hotel in Mound Bayou by dark.]

So I got in the car and headed immediately for Glendora.

The tavern called King's was easy to find. I just looked for a large group of colored people on a back street and there was King's.

King's Tavern

It was a typical hangout in a typical Mississippi town. The place was filthy and the cotton pickers who were enjoying their Sunday off crowded it to the doors.

At one end of the long hall was what served as a kitchen. Somewhere within the bowels of the place a jukebox was giving out with Rock and Roll blues and in the center of the floor couples were dancing attired in all kinds of clothing. Some of the young women up to 25 years old were dancing barefooted.

[I stood for a long time trying to "case" the place. I had not had a meal since my Mound Bayou breakfast that morning at seven and I was hungry. But I realized that I only had about a good hour to work in before dark and I wanted to get the most out of my time by circulating through the crowd instead of tying myself to an eating table.

[So I elected to spend my hour or so drinking beer and dancing to see what I could find. I walked over to the kitchen and foolishly asked for a "menu."

[That was a dead giveaway for a stranger and I realized it now. But at the time the words seemed to slip out of my mouth. It seemed that at the time I felt that if I had some reading matter in my hand I could stall a little bit until I made up my mind as to what approach to make.]

Spotted as Stranger

When I asked a girl waitress for a menu, a man behind the counter spoke up and said, "We don't have any menu. But we can fix you most anything you want." Then he asked the question I knew was coming.

"Where you from?"

You simply can't escape it in the South. They can spot a stranger a mile away.

I could tell by the authoritative way the man spoke that he must be the owner or manager of the joint, so I answered, "Oh, I'm from up the way a bit" and gradually I drew him into conversation.

After trying to convince him I was merely a drifting guy who had dropped in his place for a beer or two—and convincing myself that I hadn't convinced him of anything—I came at him right down the middle:

"Whatever happened to my boy 'Too Tight'," I said?

The man stopped as if I had hit him in the face. I looked over to my right and some men seated at a table playing "Georgia Skin" dropped their cards and turned to look at me at the mention of the name "Too Tight."

Looking for "Too Tight"

I knew then that I was on the trail of something big.

But I also knew that the man to whom I was talking would not talk to me in the hearing distance of the others[,] so I grabbed him by his arm and moved over in a direction away from the "Skinners" and nearer the kitchen all the while saying "Let's have a beer."

He said nothing until he got me a beer. Then he moved over to me and said, "What do you want with 'Too Tight'[?]"

I told him "Too Tight" was a friend of mine. That we used to gamble together and that I was in his town and decided to look him up.

He looked around and said, "'Too Tight' is in jail."

"In jail," I said. "What have they got Too Tight in jail for? He never bothered anybody."

The man looked at me and said, "See that chick over there," pointing to a girl seated near the wall. "She can tell you about 'Too Tight'."

While I drank my beer, I stood there trying to figure how to best approach the girl who had the key to what I was looking for. She was seated with a big husky guy and the last thing I wanted to do was to become involved with a man for "molesting" his girl friend.

But all around me I noticed that when the other men wanted to dance they didn't ask the women for a dance. They just walk up, grab the woman by the arm and start dancing.

I felt my time was running out and I decided to try the bold approach. So I walked over to where she was seated, grabbed her by the hand and said, "Let's dance."

She was up on her feet in a flash and I swirled her out in the middle of the floor into the crowd as fast as I could[,] hoping that the big guy at the table wasn't mad at me.

He's in Jail

She spoke first. And her questions were the usual. "Where are you from?" I told here that I was from up in Sumner and I was looking for my friend "Too Tight."

"Too Tight?" she said[.] "He's in jail."

I expressed surprised. "In jail for what[?]" I said. "I don't know," she answered. "They came for him Monday a week ago."

I let fly then with a barrage of questions[,] determined to get them all in before the dance was over and the big guy came to claim her. I asked her if she had been to see him in jail. She said no.

"You mean to tell me," I said[,] "that your boyfriend has been in jail a week and you haven't been to see him?"

She said[,] "'Too Tight' isn't my boy friend. He lived with us."

I asked her who was "Us" and she said[,] "Me and my husband."

["]Is that your husband over at the table?" I asked. "No," she answered. "He's in jail, too."

"What did they get him for?" I asked. "I don't know," she said. ["]Both of them worked for one of those white men who killed that boy from Chicago and they came and got both of them."

I then asked her what jail they were in and if she had been to see her husband. She said she had not—that she had been even afraid to talk about it to anyone.

I asked her what her name was. She told me. I then asked what her husband's name was. She said "Henry Lee Loggins."

Since the name she gave me did not have Loggins for a last name, I said to her, "I thought you said your name was so and so. Now you tell me your husband's name is Loggins."

"We're not married," she said. "We just lived together."

Then I asked her what to me was the $64 question in Glendora. "What," I said, "is Too Tight's real name? I've known him a long time but all I know is Too Tight."

Gives Mystery Name

She came right down the middle. "His real name is Leroy Collins[,]" she said.

She then told me that Too Tight lived with his grandfather on the Aklet farm near Glendora (about a mile and a half away) but that he stayed in town so much that he had just started living with her and her "husband."

I then tried to get real chummy with her. I complimented her on her dancing and her hair and I asked her if I could come back down to Glendora and take her out. Then for the first time I noticed that she was barefooted.

"We'll go to the jail first and see your husband," I said, "and then we can go out and have a few drinks."

She said that would be all right if I got back before ten o'clock that night. I told her then that I didn't mean that I was coming back that same night but that I had planned to come down and pick her up the next day.

Fears Beating

"I can't do that," she said. "I'll be picking cotton all during the day next week."

I told her that we couldn't get into the jail at night and that I'd pay her what she would make picking cotton if she would stay home from work the next day and go to the jail with me.

"I'd like to do it", she said[.] "But I'd get a beating."

I asked her who would beat her and she said that the white man for whom she worked came around and whipped everyone who didn't go out into the cotton fields and pick his cotton. "Even if they are sick, he whips them," she said.

I asked her to come with me while I ate something and she readily consented[,] completely ignoring the big guy at the table where she had been seated. I then found that the menu which was unwritten consisted of chitterlings or beef stew.

I ordered beef stew and sat down with her at a table. As hungry as I was, I couldn't go for the stew[,] so I pushed it away and told her I was about ready to leave. She then showed me where she lived and I promised to come back to Glendora some night. I never went back.

Things simply got too hot.

White Reporters Doublecrossed Probers Seeking Lost Witnesses
James L. Hicks, *Cleveland Call and Post*, 15 October 1955

I got into my rented car with Mississippi tags and headed back from Glendora in the direction of Sumner.

When I reached the little town of Webb about a mile and a half away and almost half way back to Sumner I noticed a dirt road which I reasoned if it were straight would cut across country and hit the highway leading back to Mound Bayou.

I stopped the car, consulted my map, reasoned that I was guessing right and headed down the dirt road to take the short cut.

If I had known then what I know now I would never have taken that dirt road.

Nothing happened to me on it but subsequent events proved what could have happened.

The road led me in back of the state penitentiary at Parchman, Mississippi and I heaved a sigh of relief when I finally came out of its unpaved dust and rejoined the main highway.

Tell Experience

When I arrived back in Mound Bayou, Simon [Simeon] Booker, Clotyde Murdock and photographer Jackson of the Johnson Publications out of Chicago were anxious to tell me of an experience they had had on their first day at Sumner.

They had gone to Money[,] which is below Glendora[,] and on their way back they too had seen the dirt road and reasoned as I did that it was a short cut.

But somehow as they went down the road they had become turned around and ended up going down a dead end road that led into the fields.

As they approached the dead end they encountered a truck load of white men all armed with shotguns and pistols, driving up the lonely road meeting them. They stopped, turned around and headed back. Upon questioning the presence of the guns they were told that the men were "deer hunting." However, on their arrival back in Mound Bayou they were told that deer hunting season had not yet started in Mississippi.

[I point this out without trying to get into my colleagues' story. I simply point all this out because it happened on the little dirt road which I had gone over a few minutes earlier.]

When I arrived back in Mound Bayou I told Dr. T. R. M. Howard[,] militant leader to the Delta[,] what I had found. I then learned that Dr. Howard had certain information which tied in beautifully with what I had.

He had been receiving reports for days that there had been two men on the truck with Emmett Till but he had not been able to establish who they were. He also had information on others such as Willie Reed and Mandy Bradley[,] whom he told me were willing to come forward and testify at the proper time.

Unearth Witnesses

Dr. Howard had given this information to other colored reporters but he had warned them not to publish a word about it until he could round up the witnesses and get them out of danger before stories broke in the press that they had valuable information which could lead to conviction. He impressed upon me and others that once a story got into the papers their lives would not be worth a nickel.

There then began some of the most trying days of my career as a reporter. I knew I was on something big and I wanted to break it with my papers right away.

The question was how to do so without tipping the white people of Mississippi off and thereby exposing myself and the innocent cotton pickers to bodily harm.

I argued that I should break the story. But Dr. Howard and my colleagues argued "How." They warned me that the wires out of Mound Bayou were not safe and they said it would be simply folly to put the story on Western Union and think that it would not get all over town.

All day Monday I worked through the trial almost in a daze, wrestling with whether I should plunge into my story of the two witnesses or hold off a little longer as Dr. Howard and others suggested.

[I filed copy on the testimony of the Rev. Moses Wright and Mrs. Mamie Bradley and let it go at that.]

Tuesday I continued to press for a release of the story. For by this time some of the white reporters had got wind of what we were working on and had asked me if I knew anything of a man named "Too Tight."

In one story I filed through Western Union on Tuesday I alluded strongly to important and new witnesses which might come up in the trial. I came as near as I could to telling my office that something big was about to break without putting any of the witnesses on the spot.

This was the fear which the others had and which I must admit made sense at the time. They knew that Sheriff Strider of Tallahatchie County was a witness for the defense, that he had said he doubted the body was that of Emmett Till and that he had shown hostility to colored people working on the case.

Fear Harm to Witnesses

They felt and I agreed that if Strider learned that we were going to produce some eye witnesses to the murder he would tip off the defense and others working with them and our witnesses would either be spirited away or come to bodily harm.

At first this sounded fantastic to me. To think that one could not trust the Sheriff. But when I looked at the hard cold facts that Strider had said the body was not Till's, that he was a witness against the state and that if "Too Tight" was in the Charleston jail Strider was the man who put him there, I agreed that it did not make sense to tip off Strider.

Then Ruby Hurley[,] NAACP field secretary[,] came to town and in a session in my hotel room which will live long in my memory I told Ruby what my problem was and told her that I could not see how I could sit on the story any longer no matter who was threatened by its publication.

Dr. Howard and my colleagues were all against my filing the story. They kept saying[,] "We don't want to get anybody killed. Wait."

Plan Shift

I put it up squarely to Ruby. She came through like a champion. She said that the evidence which we had was enough to stop the trial and shift it over to Sunflower County. Our witnesses were willing to testify that the crime was committed in Sunflower County instead of Tallahatchie County.

And she pointed out that if the case went to the jury in Tallahatchie County the two men would never have to stand trial again in another county because of double jeopardy. She said it was important that the evidence be made public right away before the case closed and went to the jury.

Ruby won the day on that point. But she stated that the story should be given the widest possible play on the dailies so that the public pressure could help to step in and stop the trial.

This meant that we had to call in white reporters since many of the weekly papers had already gone to the press. But who?

Simeon Booker, a Nieman fellow[,] suggested the name of Clark Porteous of the *Memphis Press Scimitar* who is also a Nieman fellow. I suggested that we add to it John Popham of the *New York Times* who was covering the story for the *Times*.

We agreed that we could call them in on it right away and that we'd have them ask the Sheriff where "Too Tight" was and to notify the Prosecutor and the District Attorney that we had new evidence to produce if they could offer the witnesses protection. We felt that these two men were men we could trust and we ruled out any other whites on the story either because no one in the group knew them well enough—or knew them too well to be trusted.

Makes Error

It was here that Dr. Howard committed what I will always feel was a tactical mistake. He was seated there in my room and suddenly he was going to Memphis to meet Congressman Diggs. Our agreement was sealed that we would notify Porteous and Popham and no one else.

Dr. Howard left. But a few minutes later we got word that Porteous and a "carload of reporters from Clarksdale" were coming down to hear the "story of the new witnesses."

Now we had agreed that no one but Porteous and Popham would be let in on the story but when Porteous arrived he came without Popham and instead had with him two white reporters of the Jackson, Mississippi *Daily News*[,] regarded by many as one of the most inflammatory papers in the state!

It now appears that Dr. Howard, who had been pledging to me secrecy all the time, had suddenly just thrown the whole story to the wolves. I was hurt and I said so. Ruby was shocked and she said so. We then began to wonder what would happen to our witnesses because through our underground with them we had informed them that nothing would appear in the press until they were off the plantation in safe hands.

Spills Beans

When the three white reporters showed up[,] Dr. Howard, who had not gone to Memphis[,] sat down with them in an insurance office in Mound Bayou. Without learning who they were or pledging them to any off the record secrecy he began to tell them every word of the evidence he had and that which we had produced.

Then after telling them all, he told them that they could not break the story until the next afternoon because he first wanted to get the witnesses off the plantation.

This is what he told them:

"Sunday night a Negro came to me with information that the killing of Till may have happened in Sunflower County. I have looked into this. I can produce at least five witnesses at the proper time who will testify that Till was not killed in Tallahatchie County but killed in Sunflower County about three and a half miles west of Drew in the headquarters shed of the Clint Sheridan Plantation[,] which is managed by Leslie Milam, brother of J. W. Milam, one of the defendants and half brother of Roy Bryant[,] the other defendant.

"Word had been brought to me that within the past eight hours efforts have been made to clean up blood stains on the floor of this shed. I am informed that if you reporters will go with the proper authorities in the morning, you will see some stains and where efforts have been made to remove them.

"I am informed that a 1955 green Chevrolet truck with a white top was seen on the place at 6 A.M. Sunday, August 28, the last time Till was seen alive. There were four white men in the cab and three Negro men in the back. Photos of Till have been identified. He was in the middle in the back.

"There are witnesses who heard the cries of a boy from the shed. They heard blows. They noted that the cries gradually decreased until they were heard no more.

"Later a tractor was moved from the shed. The truck was driven into the shed. The truck came out with a tarpaulin spread over the back. The Negroes who went into the shed were not seen at this time and have not been seen around the plantation since."

Jumps Gun

Porteous readily agreed to keeping the story off the papers until the next day but James Featherstone of the *Jackson Daily News* told Dr. Howard that he could not promise he would not print the story the next day. He said he had been called to come to Mound Bayou for a story, that he had not been told it was off the record and that he was going to print the story as quickly as he could get it in the papers.

This caused everyone in the room to almost faint because they knew what publication of the story would mean to the witnesses like Willie Reed and Mandy Bradley[,] who were at that moment still down on the plantation.

It took everyone in the room begging and pleading with Featherstone not to break the story. He finally agreed on the condition that on the following night when the witnesses were produced in Mound Bayou that no other white reporter be let in on the meeting except the three who were then there.

Dr. Howard, who I'm sure by this time realized his tactical mistake, promised that would be the case.

Scheme Exposed

The next step was to get the witnesses off the plantation and then have the white reporters tell the DA and the prosecutors that we had them and that they were all willing to talk. We broke up the meeting on this note.

But the white reporters went to the authorities either that night or the first thing the next morning because when the trial recessed the next day the prosecutors had informed the judge and the Governor of the State about the new evidence and the trial came to an abrupt recess to allow the prosecutors to talk with the witnesses.

Now during cotton picking time in Mississippi you can't get a cotton picker to leave the plantation during the day unless a white man comes for him. If he does he is subjected to a good whipping.

Ruby Hurley knew this and knowing this she became immediately alarmed that we would not be able to get the witness[es] until that night and that since the prosecution already knew about it the defense would also find out about it and that meant that they were still on the spot.

Still with the idea of saving lives, we huddled together with Miss Hurley in Sumner's only tavern to decide what was the next move.

Ruby said there was only one thing to do. That was to go on the plantation and warn the witnesses to leave at once and come to Mound Bayou as soon as possible. But native Mississippians pointed out the problem of that.

Meant Trouble

They said it meant trouble if any strange colored people showed up on a plantation and then some of the plantation people disappeared. Since we had to go to the plantation of the defendants they considered it double trouble.

But Ruby was insistent and it was finally agreed that Ruby and a reporter, Moses Newsome of Memphis[,] would go out on the plantation to warn the people and set up a meeting place for that night and that we would all then meet in a certain place in Cleveland, Mississippi[,] where we would talk to the witnesses and then bring them to Mound Bayou eight miles away to meet the authorities and the white reporters.

Thus shortly after high noon Ruby and Newsome disguised themselves as sharecroppers (Moses who was 130 pounds went away wearing a size 46 pair of overalls and Ruby wearing a Mother Hubbard dress and a bandana and actually looked for the moment like a sharecropper.)

This may sound fantastic but this is all true and it is the only way the state produced what few witnesses it did produce with the exception of Mose Wright.

They left, borrowed an old battered auto and went out into the plantations.

With the trial recessed we then went back to Mound Bayou. The meeting place with the witnesses was in Cleveland, Mississippi[,] and we were to be there at dark.

When darkness fell I went to the meeting place. There I met a man who is an ardent worker in the NAACP. He told me to park my car and get into his car. Then he drove me to a house which turned out to be the real meeting place.

I later learned that this is the way they do it down there. They announce one place as a site. But when you arrive there it is really not the bonafide place. If you are the right person you are taken from there to the meeting place. If you are not, no one will admit knowing what you are talking about.

Fantastic! It seems that way. But you have to live in Mississippi under the threat of its violence to learn what people like Ruby Hurley and other NAACP leaders have learned.

The Mississippi Lynching Story: Luring Terrorized Witnesses from the Plantations Was Toughest Job
James L. Hicks, *Cleveland Call and Post*, 22 October 1955

When I arrived at the house I found Ruby Hurley and Newsome safe but they had a sad story to tell.

During the afternoon the authorities notified by the white reporters had gone to the plantations ahead of them and questioned the prospective witnesses. This had scared them to death and they felt that we had gone back on our promise to get them out of there before the white people were told.

The result was that they not only clammed up to the whites but they refused to come to the meeting with us.

We didn't know what to do then. A call came from Porteous saying that he was on his way down with the sheriffs in the various counties. A special investigator [was] sent by the Governor and other officials. And we had no witnesses to produce.

We went on, however, to the meeting place with the white authorities and Dr. Howard[,] who met with them[,] told them of how they had jumped the gun and what it meant.

He also pointed out the danger that the witnesses would be in when the story broke and he asked that they be taken off the farms and placed in protective custody. The various sheriffs and county supervisors, all of whom were here, said they did not feel the people involved were in any immediate danger but they said if Dr. Howard thought so they would go get them and bring them to Mound Bayou for safe keeping.

Meet Officials

Thus at about midnight we sat there in an insurance office with the following law officials of Mississippi, T. J. Townsend, prosecutor of Sunflower County, Gwin Cole, who had been flown to the trial that day on orders by Governor Hugh White as soon as the new evidence was presented, Sheriff George Smith of LeFlore County, District Attorney Stannie S[a]nders of Sunflower County and John Ed Cothran, chief deputy of Sunflower County. They said the Governor was interested in the case and they wanted to do anything Dr. Howard and the group suggested.

Dr. Howard insisted that the only thing to do was to go right then and get the people off the plantation. The law officials said they could not force them to leave but that they could take us out and let us talk to them and bring those out who wanted to come.

Things happened fast after that. The various sheriffs said they would get people in their own counties and before one could say Jackie Robinson cars were moving out in all directions.

Visit Plantations

Some key people of Mississippi who were in on the meeting but who still cannot be identified got into cars with the sheriffs. These people were the contact people with the people on the plantations. Various reporters took off after the sheriffs in cars of their own. As for me I started out behind the sheriff who was to bring in Willie Reed.

He went through Mound Bayou like a streak and turned right at the dirt road leading towards Drew. I hit the dirt road behind him as he roared into the cotton fields.

Now it's simply a part of this fantastic story to state that at times on that little dirt road leading out of Mound Bayou I was travelling in the dead of night at times at 70 miles an hour!

It's fantastic but true.

But at that speed I lost the sheriff[,] and a Jackson and Johnson publications photographer who was riding with me and I decided to go on to County Supervisor Townsend's office at Drew where all the witnesses picked up by the various sheriffs were to be brought before being taken to Mound Bayou.

Driving at 75 miles an hour when we hit the paved road leading into Drew we overtook Simeon Booker and Clark Porteous and Featherson [Featherstone]. They too had chased a sheriff and got lost on the Mississippi dirt road. The five of us then went to Townsend's office.

As we arrived there a white woman drove up in a car and a colored man got out. This proved to be Frank Young, one of the key witnesses in the case who never testified. The sheriff in that county had simply called the plantation owner on which Young worked and told her to bring Young in.

Kept Mum

Dr. Howard was to have followed us to Drew to be there when witnesses were questioned but for some reason he was delayed and though Young had talked freely before this, he refused to talk to anyone but Dr. Howard.

We waited a long time and then the white woman who had brought him in grew tired and she took Young back to the plantation, promising to have him in court the next day. Young never took the witness stand. They told me he came to the court and could not find the courthouse and went back. I never did get the straight of this.

One of the sheriffs had taken a colored minister with him to get Mandy Bradley. About two o'clock in the morning they returned without Mandy. Moses Newsome, a reporter who rode in the sheriff's car with the minister and the sheriff[,] said the sheriff had driven to the house, sent the minister in to talk with Mrs. Bradley and see if she would come to Mound Bayou.

She is said to have told him that she would not. That she did not know anything about the case. But later the same woman did testify in the case and has now left Mississippi and is in Chicago. I can only believe that the events of the day and night had frightened her nearly to death.

The various sheriffs talked to other witnesses but were able to get none to come forward that night. Finally in the early hours of the morning we went back to Mound Bayou over the lonely back road.

There is one point which I should mention here that I feel had a direct bearing on my future activities with the trial.

During the meeting at Mound Bayou with the various sheriffs, one of them asked Dr. Howard what were the names of the two men who had been seen on the truck with Emmett Till. At this point Dr. Howard and the sheriffs were in the room together and reporters waiting outside.

Put on Spot

But at this point Dr. Howard in a loud voice called out "Send Jimmy Hicks in here." I went into the room and before all these sheriffs and other officials of Mississippi, many of whom I did not trust, he pointed to me and said: "This is Jimmy Hicks of the Afro American papers. He has talked with the people who know 'Too Tight.' Hicks, what is 'Too Tight''s real name and what is the name of the man who was on that truck with him?"

I didn't want to answer. I didn't want to enter into that way whatever. But I couldn't let Dr. Howard down before all those people and I knew I was the only one who had the answer. So I said "'Too Tight''s real name is Leroy Collins and the other man is Henry Lee Loggins."

All their eyes were upon me as I left the room. And I got a funny feeling that the finger might also be on me too.

Watch Story

Back at the Mound Bayou hotel my colleagues were even more insistent that I lighten up on the type of story I was filing though Western Union.

From that point on it seemed that everyone in the courthouse knew what I had written the moment I filed it. I am not accusing Western Union. I do not believe that the operators were willfully letting anyone read my copy.

But the Western Union ticker was set up in the hallway of the courthouse and many of the local people had never seen one work. Those who could not get into the courtroom made it a habit to crowd around the open phones and the Western Union desk and listen to the reporters call in their stories on special wires set up for them.

It was very easy for them to also look over the shoulder of the Western Union operator and see what he was filing.

The owner of the only colored phone in Sumner told me himself that the white people listened in on everything said on his phones[,] so I ruled that one out with the exception of a few calls to my office during which time I never once said what part I was playing in the trial.

While I was debating on whether to sit down and tell it all an incident happened which caused me to finally agree to file what I was seeing and doing.

I drove to the trial at nine o'clock Wednesday morning and sat through the trial until it recessed at 1:30. Then I started to my car parked in front of the courthouse. As I reached the car with the key in my hand to get a notebook out of the car a white man stepped off the curb and said to me "Boy is this your car[?]" When I answered that it was, he snatched the key from my hand and said[,] "You come with me down to the Mayor's office."

I was never so shocked in my life when I saw his gun [and] I decided that I'd better go along.

Under Arrest

I began walking with the man to the "mayor's office." Neither of us said a word. But oh how I was thinking. I felt at the start that Sheriff Strider[,] whom I simply do not trust[,] had got wind of my activity in tracking down "Too Tight" and I figured that I might be stuck away in some jail and given a good going over until after the trial.

We walked a half block and turned into the office of the *Sumner Sentinel.* Inside the door stood Featherson[,] the Jackson, Mississippi reporter who had worked on the witnesses with us virtually all night the night before.

Featherson said to me[,] "Hi Hicks. How you doing?" I said to him[,] "Not so good. Looks like I'm in trouble."

He said[,] "What's the trouble" and I asked him to ask the deputy who had brought me in. All the deputy would tell him was that Sheriff Strider had ordered him to pick me up.

I'll never forget Featherson. He told the deputy[,] "Look, I'm from Jackson, Mississippi. I know this boy. He's all right. You must have the wrong man. This boy is down here covering the trial." The deputy ignored him.

About that time Simpson, editor of the *Sentinel*[,] came in. And I was glad that he had been the first man I had gone to when I hit town.

Simpson, like Featherson, greeted me warmly and asked me how things were going. I told him that I was under arrest but did not know the charges. Simpson then aggressively demanded of the deputy what he was holding me for. When he refused to tell him he said[,] "Well, by God. Let's get the sheriff over here and see. This man is here to cover the trial. Every reporter speaks highly of him because I checked up on him.["] He then ordered someone in his office to get the sheriff[,] who was in the courthouse across the street.

Newsmen Busy

But instead of the sheriff coming back about 40 newsmen hit the door of the *Sentinel*.

Their nose for news had already sniffed a news story and they were there to check on it and I was glad to see them there.

It was then and only then that the deputy suddenly realized that he knew the charges against me. He said[,] "He's charged with passing a school bus!"

Simpson exploded. "School bus[,]" he said. "For goodness sakes, turn that man loose. You're getting ready to give this town the highest black eye it has ever had."

He then turned to what I later found out was the justice of the peace who tried my case—the linotype operator in Simpson's printing plant!

Simpson suggested to the linotype operator that he dismiss the charges but the linotype operator[,] who was then talking to his boss, said, "This is my case and I'm going to try it."

I saw then that there was a little man who wanted to show his importance and I was so relieved that it was a traffic charge and nothing else that I told Alex Wilson of the *Memphis Tri State Defender* to buzz to the colored press that I was OK and could pay the fine and that I think I'd get off better if they left and made it appear that no one was putting any pressure on the little justice of the peace.

They left (and bless them all for having the courage to come), but some of the white reporters remained and continued to ask questions. One picked up a phone off Simpson's desk, called Memphis and began to dictating the story to his editor. The story later appeared on the center fold of the *Memphis Commercial Appeal.*

With Simpson talking to the JP, he said to me[,] "Come back here, boy." I went. He took me back to a linotype machine, wiped the ink off his hands, got out a law book and began reading a law to me.

When he finished he told me that under that law he could fine me $300 or give me six months in jail. But he said he was going to "give you a break" and dismiss the case. He asked me if I thought that would be a good break. I told him I certainly did. And then he dismissed the case and told me to "tell all those reporters out there that we gave you a break." I told him that I would—and I did.

By this time, however, I was getting the general idea that I was a marked man[,] for during his conversation with me the justice of the peace started telling me where I was staying, what time I got to the trial in the morning, where I parked my car and who I was going to have lunch with that day. (I was going to eat with a local woman who had promised some more information. She did not show up).

I haven't the slightest idea how he learned all this.

Jimmy Hicks Tells Inside Story of Infamous Mississippi Lynch Case
James L. Hicks, *Cleveland Call and Post,* 22 October 1955

The next day Willie Reed, Mandy Bradley and others took the stand and testified. I filed straight copy of their testimony but I was eating my heart out to file copy on the fact that "Too Tight" Leroy Collins was in the Charleston jail, that Sheriff Strider knew he was there and that he would not produce him.

After they testified word came that the prosecution was going to close down its arguments. I couldn't believe it. How could they close without trying to put "Too Tight" on the stand.

I went to the Prosecutor Gerald Chatham and asked if it were true. He said it was. I asked him how about "Too Tight." He said Sheriff Strider told him that "Too Tight" was not in the Charleston jail. He said he couldn't produce him if the sheriff would not produce him.

I asked him what did he think had happened to "Too Tight." He said[,] "I wouldn't like to say."

Witness Seen

That night I received information that there was a person in Charleston who had been to the jail the day before and talked with "Too Tight." The person was at a certain spot[;] an NAACP official was there too and they wanted to know what should be done.

He told the person to be ready to testify the next day. Then we got word to the prosecutors by phone of what we had learned. As tactfully as it could be done it was pointed out that perhaps Sheriff Strider had been mistaken.

But the next morning the prosecution stated again that despite the fact that someone was willing to go to the jail and identify "Too Tight" he could not go there because the sheriff of the jail had already said he was not there.

The case actually went to the jury on that note and to this day no one got a chance to go there and talk to "Too Tight" Collins.

I think he is still there. If he is not there I think Sheriff Strider should be made to tell where he is.

Could Clear Mystery

And I believe if either he or Loggins could be put on a witness stand they would clear up once and for all the mystery of what they were doing on that truck with Emmett Till and what happened to Emmett Till when he was taken into that barn on the night of August 28.

Perhaps the reader will still condemn me for not dashing off reports on the above story day by day and hour by hour as it happened.

I should like to add these additional facts, unrelated as they might seem:

On the night that I filed my first copy from Sumner I was in my hotel room at Mound Bayou rather sure that no one in Sumner knew where I was living.

I got a phone call from Sumner long after midnight. The voice said he was a reporter from Louisiana and that he had met me earlier in the day. When I said I didn't remember him he said it was not important. That what he really called was for me to go to Memphis with him. He said he was working on a new angle on the story and asked me if I wanted to come along.

He said he realized Mound Bayou was not on the road to Memphis but that he was sleepy and would gladly drive out of his way to come by for me if I would agree to go so that I would help him drive back.

I told him that I couldn't possibly break away to go. When I said that he began asking me how long would I be at my hotel in Mound Bayou. I told him that I was just preparing to go south to Greenville and work on a new lead I had found. He said he could reach Sumner in about a half hour and that he wanted to talk to me. I told him I was leaving right away.

Given a Weapon

When the conversation ended and I told some of our group what had transpired a local Mississippian went out to his car, returned to my room and gave me a loaded .38 Smith and Wesson pistol. "Here, boy," he said. "You sleep with this tonight." I did.

About an hour later a carload of people drove up the side of my hotel and knocked on my door.

I lay there with my hand clutching the loaded gun and said nothing. Then they went next door and knocked on the door of Simeon Booker. He did not answer either.

By this time I got up and came to the door. I tested the lock to make sure it was locked and then I began peeping with gun in hand through the three small windows up at the top of the door of my hotel.

Beneath the street light outside I could see a carload of colored people. I was close to them as 30 feet. The light was playing full on the face of a colored woman I had seen before as she sat on the front seat of the car with the door opened.

The man doing the knocking was standing talking with her with his back to me and I could not see his face. I heard him say[,] "He's not in there."

Then the man walked around the other side of the car still with his face from me and went around the motel to the home of Mrs. Anderson[,] who owns the motel. I crossed the room, still with the gun in my hand, and watched him ring the bell until she answered the door.

Then he left after talking with her a moment and came back to the car parked in front of my door. He got into the car from the driver's side and soon they drove south toward Cleveland.

I went back to bed with the gun under my pillow. Then next morning Mrs. Anderson told me that the people had asked her if she had any vacant rooms. What I couldn't understand and still don't was why they knocked on the door of my motel room instead of first going to the office of the motel.

Feared Trap

On another occasion Murray Kempton of the *New York Post* called me in Mound Bayou. I got his message and called him back. He was not in. But as soon as I hung up the phone rang for me. A voice on the other end of the wire in Clarksdale said his name was Ferguson and that he knew I had called Murray a few minutes ago. The voice said he and Murray were good friends and that I could tell him anything that I was going to tell Murray and that he would pass it on to Murray.

I told the voice that he was on the wrong track, that I had not been calling Murray to tell him anything but that I was simply returning a call Murray had put through to me from Clarksdale.

The voice insisted[,] "Come on Hicks. You know plenty. Let me in on it." He gave the impression that he was another newsman. I told him I simply did not have any leads to work on and he finally hung up.

Face Trickster

Then next day in Sumner I told Murray about the incident. We went to James Featherson and accused Featherson of trying to get me to give him some information under his name.

But the last day of the trial Featherson came up to me in Kempton's presence and swore that he had never talked with me by phone. I told Murray that the man on the other end had used the name Ferguson. And in reflection I'm not sure that it was not the voice of Featherson.

Who was it? I haven't the slightest idea.

One more incident. Sheriff Strider gave out press passes which were supposed to enable reporters to use the backstairs which the jury used in getting in and out of the courtroom to avoid going through the crowd.

Barred by Deputy

The day after I gave the sheriff the name of "Too Tight" Collins I started up the back steps to go to the courtroom. A deputy was standing on the narrow stairway and as I approached him with the card in hand he put one foot against the wall of the narrow stairway, leaned against the other and barred the way.

I said[,] "Press" and held the card up higher. He said to me[,] "No niggers are going up this stairway." I bit my tongue, turned around and started for the front stairs where one had to push his way through the hostile crowd.

On the way I met John Popham of the *Times* and I told him what had happened. I also told him what a loaded thing it was to push one's way through the hostile crowd. He suggested that we get together and try to go up.

With Popham leading the way we went back to the stairs. Several white reporters walked on past the deputy before we reached him.

Then Popham walked past him. I followed. But as I put my foot out to mount the first stair, up came the deputy's foot again and barred the way. Popham, who had already passed him turned and said[,] "He's a reporter. He's got a card. The sheriff said the press could go up this way."

The man snarled at me[,] "You're not going up this way. Go 'round." He had a gun. I had no choice. I went around.

No Action Taken

I know that this information was given to Strider. But we still never were able to use the back steps.

All of these things gradually beat me down at Sumner. A deputy threatened to knock Simeon Booker's "head off" because Booker held up the press card and asked the deputy to help him get through the crowd.

A man who walked up to the press table and called all of us "niggers" was sworn in five minutes later as the bailiff.

Reporter Fired Upon

An English correspondent who talked to a colored woman was later fired at twice the same night by the deputy who arrested me.

A cross was burned fifty yards from the courthouse during the trial. There was no investigation that I heard of.

They allotted us chairs at the Jim Crow press table but during the noon recess while we were trying to get our stories filed in a colored restaurant the crowd would come in and take the chairs from our table. I stood up more often than I sat down.

Congressman Diggs and Dr. Howard brought their own chairs to the Jim Crow press table. On the last day of the trial the crowd took them.

This was the trial at Sumner as I lived it. Other colored reporters will verify that portion of my story where our paths crossed, and they crossed often. There are other colored reporters who could possibly tell even more fantastic stories. But they are all true.

This was Sumner, USA.

Defender Tracks Down Mystery Till "Witnesses"
L. Alex Wilson, *Chicago Defender,* 8 October 1955

> L. Alex Wilson, editor of the Memphis *Tri-State Defender,* was the *Chicago
> Defender* correspondent for the Till trial. In the following article, Wilson re-
> veals how he did more than just report on the proceedings. After the trial,
> with the help of local contacts and activists, Wilson picked up where James
> L. Hicks left off. Whereas Hicks sought the whereabouts of "Too Tight"
> Collins, Henry Lee Loggins, and other missing witnesses during the trial,
> Wilson attempted to track them down after the jury passed its verdict. He
> succeeded in finding only one of the witnesses—"Too Tight" Collins—and
> spirited him away to Chicago for an in-depth interview. Despite Wilson's
> hope that the evidence he had uncovered would give Till's family a second
> chance at justice, Collins proved a tight-lipped witness and, in the end, the
> authorities refused to take further action.

I tracked down Leroy (actually Levy) "Too Tight" Collins after four harrowing,
danger-filled days, and brought him out of Mississippi to Memphis and from
there to Chicago.

The success of my mission—to bring out, without arousing suspicion, one
or both of the men believed to have been eye-witnesses in the brutal and cowardly slaying of Emmett L. Till—was made possible by the cooperation of the effective Negro underground system in Mississippi.

Henry Lee Loggins, a life-long friend of Collins, is the other person whom it
was believed witnessed the crime.

Both had been strangely missing during the trial from their usual haunts in
Glendora and Minter City, Miss., and from the farm where they worked, which
had been supervised by J. W. Milam, one of the defendants in the case.

Both had been sought by the prosecution and law enforcement officers to testify in the trial.

It was believed that their testimony, if they could be located, would clear up
all doubts about the slaying.

One person, who cannot be named, had reported seeing Collins in Sheriff H.
C. Strider's jail at Charleston, Miss., and the same person had been informed that
Loggins was being held in the same jail also.

Later, officials stated that the prison had been checked twice for the two, even
for anonymous listing of names, to no avail.

Last Monday, Sept. 26, a key figure in the Mississippi underground reported that Sheriff Strider had assured Loggins' father that his son would be home by Wednesday, Sept. 28.

That was the tip-off for the *Defender* publications to go into action; to have a newsman at the Charleston, Miss. Jail, if the men were being held there to witness the release; and to find the pair if they suddenly appeared in the community. Then, with their own agreement, take them out of the state of Mississippi for their own welfare.

After making contact with a leading figure in the Mississippi underground, informing him of the mission to be undertaken, I headed for the first rendevous about 100 miles away. I left Memphis about 8:30 P.M. on Sept. 26.

Aware of Danger

A brilliant, jagged streak of lightning flashed down the murky sky as I sped by auto to the destination. The deep resonant hum of the motor of my car moving at a high, but safe speed, was somehow reassuring.

But the smooth hum of the auto motor did not dispel the danger involved in the mission. I was not shaken by fear. I had decided before leaving home, and after communing with God, that if I could in any way help to contribute anything to justice in the shameful case by my effort, whatever the price, so be it.

I arrived at a place which can only be identified as "Rendevous" about 11:30 P.M. of the same evening. I learned from a leader of the underground that a contact, whom I shall identify as Contact A[,] had reported in about two hours earlier.

This person had seen Collins in a community located about 40 miles away that day. He had found out that both Loggins and Collins had made their first appearance in that community since before the trial on Sept. 26, in so far as he was able to ascertain.

That meant one big hurdle had been overcome. That is, there would be no necessity for gathering a stout-hearted group to be on hand at the Charleston jail.

The leader at headquarters suggested that we go to the home of another key figure and discuss the entire matter with him. We decided the first thing to do would be to select a person who could be trusted by us, and one who could make contact with Collins and Loggins to serve as a "go between."

Leader B, at whose home we were, recommended a man who was quite well acquainted with everyone in the community where the "witnesses" lived. We approved this recommendation. Leader B accepted the responsibility of briefing the man, whom I shall identify only as Contact B, the next morning. It was quite late by that time and we left that home.

The next morning, Tuesday, at headquarters the leader called on a friend to get the services of a man, Contact C, who had said during the Till trial that he knew both Collins and Loggins on sight.

This action was taken when I pointed out that there could not be any error in identification of the two men wanted. The friend of the leader came to head-quarters and left[,] promising that he would have Contact C come in, as soon as possible.

The efforts made by Contact B to find the two men were unrewarding. The day passed. Nothing had been achieved. The outlook was dim.

I wanted to go to Minter City where the men were seen. A stranger in a small town, driving a conspicuous car with an out-of-state license tag, would arouse sus-picion immediately. [Neither] The leader, nor his friend could expose himself.

So, we pinned our hopes on Contact C.

The next morning, Wednesday, Sept. 28, was a bad one. I failed to make any headway. Then, about 1 P.M. the breaks came fast. Contact C reported and after a briefing agreed to help. While I was talking with him, Contact A, who proved later to be vitally important, came to the headquarters. He is an intelligent, clear-thinking, practical person.

Contact A had known both men for years. He could associate with them with-out arousing suspicion. During the conference with him, I was given a vivid pic-ture of Collins and Loggins' personalities.

Of the two, Collins was the most trustworthy if approached properly. As much could not be stated of Loggins, he said.

It was during this conference that I learned Loggins had left Minter City for St. Louis. That eliminated him from the search in that area.

Expressing a desire to help get Collins out of town for his own well-being, be-fore J. W. Milam and Roy Bryant were released on bond, he outlined a course of action for that evening.

He had to go to Minter City to pick up several persons who were coming into the town where the underground headquarters was located, for a program. Collins liked to drive an automobile and he would invite him to come along and do so.

Once into town, he would drop all other persons off at the site of the program and permit Collins to drive him to the "rendevous" headquarters.

The plan had all the earmarks of a good one but it didn't work. When Con-tact A arrived in Minter City he found that Collins was working in the cottonfield and living in the rear of his employer's home.

Not actually living in the town, he couldn't afford to go on the property looking for Collins without some question arising. So contact A returned without the man.

A heavy down pour of rain lashed the cottonfields that evening. I asked contact A if he thought it would be dry enough to pick cotton the next day. He stated that he didn't think it would.

That being the case, I said, then Collins won't be working and will probably be lounging around in the joints at Minter City. He agreed to try the next morning to have Collins ride into the "rendevous" town. This effort failed.

It seemed that "Too Tight" Collins wanted to stay as far away from the town in which the rendevous headquarters is located as possible.

Soon after Contact A left, after promising to continue to do whatever he could, Contact C made the offer that later paid off.

He said Collins likes to gamble and if we can't get up to him any other way "I can gamble up to him and get him in a position where you can talk to him." That was Thursday afternoon, Sept. 29.

Friday morning, Contact A came to headquarters again. He had been unable to get Collins away from Minter City.

I outlined the plan of approach to Collins. Since he had a deep fondness for gambling we would lure him with that. Contact C would be given money with which to gamble, and Contact A would use his car as a means of transportation.

They were to go to Minter City and contact Collins. Point out to him that a big game would be on that night (Friday, Sept. 30) in the town where rendezvous headquarters is located and in a village some 30 miles distant. Go to either town selected by Collins. If he balked because of lack of money lend him some, pointing out that it is no more than one good gambler would do for another and that the three of them were out to clean up as a team.

This maneuver worked. About 7 P.M. Contact C called me from the village[,] stating briefly where to find him. I knew that at last Collins had been maneuvered into a position where direct contact could be made without arousing suspicion.

I, the leader of the rendevous headquarters and his friend, sped to the little town in my auto after a bit of nerve-wrecking delay.

When he arrived, Contact C breathed a sigh of relief. Five minutes longer and they would have had to go. There was no gambling in the town that night.

I made the direct contact with Collins, while he and a friend were seated in their car, by using the old ruse of asking for a match.

At first, he was upset and puzzled by a stranger offering to help him get out of town for his own safety. As I talked though[,] he found that I was sincere.

I was finally able to get him to crawl out of the car and come to mine where he listened to the three of us explain to him why he should leave Mississippi that night.

He refused to agree to leave that night but promised to have his family at the rendevous headquarters at 7 A.M. Saturday. On that we agreed and parted.

After I reached the home in which I was staying, and was preparing to turn in for the night, a telephone call came thru to me from the underground leader. He stated that Collins had changed his mind. He was at a bus station awaiting me, ready to leave for Chicago.

I quickly re-dressed, packed my clothing and went to the station. There I found him and a friend of his. His family had refused to leave the state, but agreed that he should for the time being.

Two hours later, we were in Memphis. We left Memphis at 3 A.M. Saturday morning for Chicago. During the 11-hour trip by auto, Collins eagerly assisted in driving.

That is how I, with the help of the underground, was able to get Levy "Too Tight" Collins out of Mississippi, in an effort to aid justice in the Till case.

Here Is What "Too Tight" Said
Chicago Defender, 8 October 1955

> In same issue as the Wilson article above, the *Chicago Defender* published the following interview with "Too Tight" Collins. As the editor's note mentions below, the interview was conducted by Colonel Euclid Louis Taylor, general counsel for the paper. Also in the room with Taylor were Wilson and John H. Sengstacke, publisher and editor of the *Defender.* Against the hopes of the paper, Collins proved to be an uncooperative witness who obviously had something to say, just not to the *Chicago Defender.*

Editor's Note: Colonel Euclid Louis Taylor, general counsel of the "Chicago Defender," questioned Levy 'Too Tight' Collins for two days. The questions and the answers have been reproduced below without changes in order that "Defender" readers might be able to evaluate the statements for themselves. The text of the interviews follows:

Taylor: Mr. Collins, my name is Euclid L. Taylor, general counsel for the *Chicago Defender*. You came to Chicago today from Memphis.
 Collins: Yes.

Q: You came here with a representative of the *Chicago Defender* from Memphis.

A: Yes—I drove up by automobile.

Q: You understand that the gentleman behind you is John H. Sengstacke, publisher and editor of the *Chicago Defender*. I would like to ask you some questions. If you want to answer them you can, if you don't want to answer them, that's okay. Nobody has abused you or threatened you since you arrived.

A: No.

Q: What is your name?

A: Levy Collins[.]

Q: Where do you live?

A: I live in Glendora. It's in Sunflower County, in Mississippi.

Q: Do you have a family?

A: I have a family. I have a wife and 4 children.

Q: What is your wife's name?

A: Triola. I don't know how to write it.

Q: Where are your wife and children?

A: They is in Glendora.

Q: Do you remember reading in the daily papers about the death of a boy by the name of Emmett Till who was supposed to have been killed in Mississippi?

A: I can't read but I heard them talking about it.

Q: Are you employed?

A: Employed? No.

Q: Are you working?

A: Yes.

Q: Were you working for J. W. Milam[?]

A: I was working for his brother-in-law—for Campbell.

Q: Who is Mr. Campbell?

A: Melvin Campbell.

Q: Where does he live?

A: He lives in Minter City.

Q: What kind of work did you do for him[?]

A: I ran the cotton picker.

Q: How long have you been employed?

A: 4 years.

Q: Did you ever work for J. W. Milam[?] (J. W. Milam was acquitted with Roy Bryant of the Till murder).

A: I drove his trucks.

Q: Was he in the trucking business?

A: He had 4 trucks.

Q: What was your salary?

A: I got $6 a day.

Q: How much did you get for running the truck[?]

A: Same thing—$6 a day.

Q: On Sunday nite, August 28, 1955, where were you[?]

A: Saturday nite I was working at the store. I came home and went to bed. Sunday I went to Greenwood.

Q: Then what did you do?

A: I came back to Glendora. Monday morning I went to work.

Q: At what time[?]

A: About 7 A.M. Mr. Milam came out for me.

Q: Who is Mr. Milam?

A: J. W. Milam. (The same Milam referred to above)

Q: Who was with him[?]

A: He was by himself in an automobile.

Q: What make of automobile?

A: It was a '53 Chevrolet.

Q: About what time of day was this?

A: 7 A.M.

Q: Were you in bed?

A: No—I was up.

Q: What did he say to you?

A: He said was I ready to come to work in his car[.]

Q: Was any body else in the car?

A: Nobody but me.

Q: How far is Glen[do]ra from the place where he picked you up?

A: I was living in town. He came out to my house in his car. We went to Minter City.

Q: How long did it take?

A: About 20 minutes.

Q: Didn't anybody get in the automobile in which you were riding?

A: Nobody.

Q: What did you do then?

A: I got on the cotton picker and went to work.

Q: Was there anybody else on the cotton picker?

A: Joe Willie Brown (another colored farm hand).

Q: Was there anybody else?

A: Nobody but me and Joe Willie.

Q: Did you see anybody else?

A: I didn't see anybody else.

Q: Anybody else on the farm?

A: Nobody else.

Q: You saw nobody else on the farm[?]

A: Not that day.

Q: Did you see Mr. Milam?

A: I saw Mr. Campbell not Mr. Milam.

Q: About what time was that?

A: I saw Mr. Campbell at 11:00 A.M.

Q: How did you know it was 11 A.M.?

A: He said it was 11 A.M.

Q: Do you have a watch?

A: No. We asked him what time it was.

Q: And you didn't see anybody else.

A: Nobody but us three.

Q: Then what did you do?

A: We went to work and he went back to the store. He brought us some gas.

Q: How much gas?

A: He brought 5 gals. apiece.

Q: And what did you do with the 5 gals?

A: We had a picker apiece. He left the gas for us.

Q: Did you see Mr. Milam any more that day[?]

A: No. I didn't see Mr. Milam at all that day.

Q: When was it you saw Mr. Milam?

A: I haven't saw Mr. Milam since that Monday morning. Tuesday they told me he was in jail. I saw Mr. Campbell that evening.

Q: Where was he?

A: He was at the store.

Q: Where did you get picked up by the truck?

A: Mrs. Campbell came by in a car.

Q: What kind of car did she have?

A: 53 Chevrolet. She drove it out into the field and got him. He left the pick up truck for us.

Q: Who drove it?

A: I drove in the cab with Joe.

Q: Did you see Mr. Loggins? (He is the other mystery "witness")

A: I saw him Tuesday, not Monday[.] Loggins didn't work Monday but I saw him Tuesday.

Q: How long have you known Mr. Loggins[?]

A: Oh—we were raised up together for about 12 years.

Q: You were close friends?

A: Yes, we were close friends[.]

Q: What did you and Jo Willie do?

Q: We were together Saturday night (Aug. 27, 1955.) He came over to Glendora. I paid some bills but where he went that Saturday nite I don't know. I didn't see him any more.

Q: Did you go get something to drink?

A: No, I don't drink and he don't drink.

Q: You don't drink at all[?]

A: I drink a little beer but not a whole lot to drink. I went home and went to bed.

Q: You didn't go out Saturday night?

A: No. I went out Sunday morning.

Q: By yourself?

A: No, Albert Buck came and got me. He was by himself.

Q: Is Albert Buck colored or white?

A: Albert Buck is colored. Me and him went to Greenwood together in a '55 Chevrolet.

Q: What did you do in Greenwood?

A: We went to Greenwood to see some girls.

Q: How long were you there?

A: Until about 10 or 11 P.M. that nite.

Q: Was it 10 P.M. or 11 P.M., or between 10 P.M. and 11 P.M.?

A: Between 10 P.M. and 11P.M.

Q: What were the names of the girls?

A: I don't know the names of the girls.

Q: You don't know the names of the girls you went to see[?]

A: No.

Q: Where do they live?

A: They live on Johnson Street.

Q: Johnson and what.

A: I don't know—just on Johnson Street.

Q: There must be some street that runs across Johnson Street—what is the name of that street?

A: I don't know. We went in the house but I didn't know anyone.

Q: Were the girls alone?

A: No—their mother was there with them.

Q: What is the mother's name[?]

A: I don't know the name of the mother.

Q: How did you get back home?

A: He brought me back in his car, let me out at the house and that was the last I saw of him. I went to bed and didn't get up until Monday morning.

Q: When did you see Loggins?

A: Not until Tuesday. (Aug. 30, 1955)

Q: Where did you see him?

A: I saw him in town. (Aug 29, 1955)

Q: About what time?

A: About 7:00 A.M. (The same time Collins previously stated that J. W. Milam picked him up to go to work.)

Q: Where was he?

A: In Glendora on the streets.

Q: Did you speak to him?

A: I didn't have time to talk with him. I didn't talk with him until Tuesday.

Q: Where was that?

A: Out in the field running the cotton picker.

Q: Was he running a cotton picker[?]

A: He was out running the cotton picker with me.

Q: Wasn't he supposed to have gone to St. Louis?

A: He was supposed to have went to St. Louis. That's last Monday is when he went.

Q: Where was he when you talked with him Tuesday?

A: He was working out in the field.

Q: You remember somebody by the name of Reed said he saw you and another man on a truck out at the farm. Has anyone asked you any questions at any time about whether or not you were on a truck[?]

A: No.

Q: I am the first to ask you about it[?]

A: Yes—you are the first to ask me.

Q: No Sheriff, no policeman or state's attorney has asked you about it[?]

A: No—nobody but you.

Q: I asked you for the first time on October 1, 1955 when I first saw you[?]

A: Yes.

Q: Where were you during the trial?

A: I was in Clarksdale, Miss.

Q: What were you doing?

A: Driving a gravel truck for Mr. Milam.

Q: Do you mean the same Mr. Milam?

A: I was driving this truck for Mr. Campbell[,] his brother-in-law.

Q: Did you see Mr. Campbell during the trial?

A: No.

Q: Who told you to go out to Clarksdale?

A: Mr. Campbell did.

Q: You worked up in Clarksdale driving this gravel truck. Did Mr. Campbell pay
   you for the time you worked in Clarksdale?

A: Sure did.

Q: He sent you to Clarksdale by yourself?

A: Henry Loggins was there at the time. Me and him both were sent up to work.

Q: Was anybody else sent up there?

A: Nobody but me and Loggins.

Q: When you came back from there was the trial over[?]

A: I guess it was but I didn't know about the trial.

Q: Did Mr. Campbell tell you it was over with?

A: He told me.

Q: What did you say to him[?]

A: I told him the job was finished and he told me to go back to the cotton picker
   that Saturday. That was two Saturdays ago. I worked up there all during the
   trial. When the trial was over I told him the work was finished.

Q: Were you and Mr. Loggins the only ones sent up from Glendora?

A: Yes.

Q: On Saturday nite just before you heard about the Till boy being killed and
   just before Mr. Milam was arrested, were you on a truck with Mr. Melvin
   Campbell or anybody with a colored boy along?

A: No not me.

Q: Did you see any strange colored boy that day on the truck [?]

A: No—I didn't see anybody.

Q: Just a few days ago you told us Mr. Loggins went to St. Louis. Now you and he were very good friends, is that right[?]

A: Yes.

Q: Did Loggins leave Sunday[?]

A: I don't know.

Q: Did you talk to him about it[?]

A: He told me he was going to St. Louis Monday. I told him to send back after me.

Q: What do you mean send after you?

A: I mean send me a ticket.

Q: You want to leave Mississippi?

A: Yes.

Q: Did anybody tell you to get out of Mississippi?

A: No.

Q: Did you ever talk to Loggins about the Till boy being killed?

A: No.

Q: Weren't you interested in the case?

A: No—nobody that I knew had been killed and in a case like that I didn't have anything to do with it. It was not my business. In a case like that where none of my color did it, I didn't say anything about it.

Q: How did you know a colored man didn't do it?

A: I don't know it. I just don't think a colored man would do a thing like that.

Q: Do you believe Mr. Milam would do a thing like that?

A: No, I believe he was too nice a man to do it. He treat too many colored people nice. He treat me and all the rest of the colored people nice. He was mean to white people, though.

Q: He was nice to the colored people but mean to the white people[?]

A: Yes.

Q: Did anybody tell you to say that?

A: Nobody told me to say anything.

Q: You have a father in Mississippi and a family. Do you intend to go back and get them[?]

A: Yes—I intend to go back and see if they would come away from Mississippi.

Q: Now, Mr. Collins, you want to tell the truth, don't you[?]

A: Yes, I want to tell you what I know.

Q: You stated you wanted to talk to H. Loggins, that is the H. Loggins that you were down in Mississippi with. Can you tell us why you want to talk with him[?]

A: I just want to talk with him.

Q: What do you want to talk to him about?

A: I can't tell you what I want to talk with him about. I just want to see him.

Q: Did you see any broken pieces of a cotton gin laying around the Milam or Campbell farm[?]

A: No.

Q: Did you see any broken pieces of a cotton gin at all?

A: No.

Q: Did you hear any of the fellows say there was any broken pieces of a cotton gin around[?]

A: No.

Q: How far in school did you go?

A: I stopped in the 3rd grade.

Q: You told me the 6th grade.

A: No—I told you 3rd grade. I was going to school in Glendora. I finished the 3rd grade and stopped going to school.

Q: Were you ever in jail in Mississippi?

A: Never been in jail in my life.

Q: Were you ever held in jail by anybody and told you couldn't leave?

A: No.

Q: Has anybody asked you whether or not you knew anything about the Till case?

A: No.

Q: None of the sheriffs, policemen or prosecutors?

A: No.

Q: You know that Mr. Reed said that either you or a man looking like you was on the truck at the farm of Mr. Campbell.

A: I heard them talking about it.

Q: You were never on the farm when Mr. Milam and Mr. Campbell had any strange boy with them[?]

A: That's right.

Q: Do you know where the Till place is?

A: No.

Q: Do you know where Money is?

A: Yes I know where it is.

Q: Do you know where the Till folks live?

A: I never go there very much.

Q: Did you ever go over there with Mr. Milam?

A: No.

Q: With Mr. Bryant? (Roy Bryant, the other acquitted defendant)

A: No.

Q: Did you ever go over there?

A: I don't know where they live at. I just know where Money is.

Q: Have you ever been to Money?

A: I drove over there but I went over there with some other boys.

Q: You want to talk to Mr. Loggins and then you want to talk to me again, is that right?

A: Yes, I just want to talk to him. I don't know anything else to tell you.

Q: You stayed in a hotel in Chicago last night.

A: That's right.

Q: Do you know the name of the man with whom you stayed?

A: I don't know his name. I forgot it.

Q: Do you see him in this room?

A: Yes, I see him in the room.

Q: Please point him out to me.

A: (Indicates Mr. L. Alex Wilson)

Q: That is Mr. L. Alex Wilson, our *Chicago Defender* editor in Memphis. Has anybody abused you, or mistreated you or promised you any reward of any kind?

A: No.

Q: Do you know Mr. Bryant—Milam's brother-in-law?

A: Roy Bryant—Yes I know him.

Q: How long have you known him?

A: I have known him about 3 or 4 months. I have not been around him very much to know him.

Q: Did you ever work for him?

A: I never worked for him in my life.

Q: From the time you worked around him did you ever form any opinion whether you think he would be the kind to do anything like this[?]

A: No.

Q: Was he mean to you?

A: No.

Q: Do you think he would do a thing of this kind?

A: I don't know what he would do.

Q: Do you know of anybody in Mississippi that would do a thing like this?

A: Not around here.

Q: Do you have any idea who you think did it?

A: I don't have any idea who did it.

Q: If we have this statement typed up, will you read it [and] sign it[?]

A: I can't read. If somebody writes my name I can copy it but I can't read.

Q: How do you spell your name?

A: Levy Collins.

Q: What is your father's name?

A: Walter.

Q: What do you call your wife?

A: Triola.

Q: Were you always paid in cash when you worked?

A: Always in cash.

Q: Never a check[?]

A: No.

Q: Do you ever go to the store and buy anything[?]

A: I never do go there and buy anything.

Q: Go where?

A: To the store.

Q: Do you count money?

A: Yes.

Q: You can add then.

A: I can't add.

Q: Then how can you count money?

A: They tell me how much it is.

Q: How do you know if you have the right amount?

A: I just know. I ask them how much it is and they tell me and give me my change.

Q: You can tell the difference between a $5.00 and a $10.00 bill.

A: Oh yeah, I know that.

Q: You know you have the right change after you ask them what it costs.

A: That's right.

Q: When Loggins dropped you off in front of your house Sunday night when you came back from Greenwood, where did he go?

A: Loggins didn't leave me off—Albert Buck did. I didn't see Loggins that night at all. I didn't see him until Monday morning (Aug. 29, 1955). He was on the streets and I was going to work. I haven't seen him any more until that Tuesday. We all worked up until that Saturday night.

Q: Did you talk to Loggins on Tuesday about Mr. Milam being put in jail?

A: I didn't say anything to him.

Q: He didn't say anything to you[?] Neither one of you discussed the fact that Mr. Milam had been put in jail[?]

A: No.

Q: You knew he was in jail.

A: I didn't say anything about it.

Q: And Loggins didn't say anything about it?

A: No.

Q: You were not interested[?]

A: I wasn't interested because I didn't believe he was in jail.

Q: They told you your boss man was in jail, didn't they?

A: Well, yeah, I had to believe it but I didn't see him any more. You see when white people get to talking about something, I don't stay to see what they are talking about. I get out.

Q: How long have you known Jo Willie Brown?

A: I know him about a year and a half.

Q: The three of you worked operating the cotton picker machine right along?

A: Yes.

Q: What happened to the other cotton picker when the two of you were in the field[?]

A: He was sitting down.

Q: That Tuesday morning how did you get to work?

A: We went in the truck. I drove it myself.

Q: How many trucks does Mr. Campbell have[?]

A: He has two.

Q: What makes?

A: A 54 and a 55 Chevrolet.

Q: What color is the 55 truck?

A: Blue—both of his trucks are blue.

Q: Was the 55 truck on the farm Monday morning?

A: It was out there when we went to work. One truck was at Minter City. That Monday morning (Aug. 29, 1955) Mr. Campbell took me to work and the 55 truck was out there. Mr. Campbell took me to Minter City in the truck and he went back to town.

Q: What time did you get to Minter City?

A: I don't know exactly what time.

Q: A very good friend of yours stated yesterday that you stated you knew more about the case than you were willing to tell. Is this true?

A: I don't know anything about it.

An Open Letter to U.S. Attorney General Herbert Brownell and FBI Chief J. Edgar Hoover
James L. Hicks, *Washington Afro-American,* 19 November 1955

James Hicks posted the following letter to Attorney General Herbert Brownell and FBI Director J. Edgar Hoover. In it, Hicks not only reasserts the claims he made in his exposé, but he also gives further names and details about the case. There is no evidence that either Brownell or Hoover responded to Hicks's letter or followed up on his leads. From the beginning, the federal government refused to investigate the case on the grounds of jurisdiction. Since no interstate crimes had been committed—so the argument went—the federal government had no grounds for intervention. Despite the fact that Hicks's letter makes it clear that the federal government did have an "in" in the case (when local law officers tamper with witnesses, the federal government can intervene), no action was taken by either the attorney general's office or the FBI.

Gentlemen:

As an American, I have been deeply disappointed that the arm of the Federal government, headed by your respective offices, has not seen fit to enter into the murder of 14-year-old Emmett Till of Chicago.

As a citizen interested in following the case, I have recently picked up rumors that at long last either one or both of your offices may finally intervene and investigate the case.

And as a newspaperman interested in simple justice, I submit herewith to your high offices certain information on the case which I know to be true.

I feel certain if aggressively pursued, it will prove to the world that four white men, aided by two colored men, killed Emmett Till and threw his body into the Tallahatchie River.

Here are the facts in detail:

The key to the murder is the little city called Glendora, Miss., about seven miles south of Sumner, Miss.

Send an FBI agent to Glendora. Tell him to find Reid's Café, located in the heart of the colored section of town. It's not hard to find.

Tell him to stand in front of the front door of Reid's Café, facing the door. On the right at three o'clock on a watch dial, there will be located a small one room shack about 40 yards from the café.

Tell your agent to knock on that door. Inside he will find a mother with three young children. Her name is Mrs. Henry Lee Loggins. She will tell you that she is not married to Henry Lee Loggins, but that she is his common-law wife and that he is the father of all three of her children.

Mrs. Loggins works for J. W. Milam, one of the defendants in the Till murder trial. She picks cotton on his plantation. Her husband[,] Henry Lee, drives a cotton picker for Milam.

If you question this woman she will tell you that at one time shortly before the death of Emmett Till a man named Levy (Too Tight) Collins lived with her and Loggins in the little house there in Glendora.

Too Tight also worked on the Milam farm.

She will further tell you that after Till was killed and shortly before the murder trial at Sumner, "the White folks" came and took both Too Tight and Loggins.

If you ask her where they took them, she will tell you that they told her that they were being taken to the Charleston jail at Charleston; that they were going to be kept there for about two weeks and that they were not going to be harmed.

Remember that name—the Charleston jail, for it is important. But just for the moment turn your attention again to Glendora.

Stand now directly in front of Mrs. Loggins' little shack. If you face the door on your right, directly at "three o'clock" will be a doorway leading into a brick building. This is the back door of a building on the main colored street.

Knock on that door. Inside you will find that this is an undertaker's parlor and the home offices of one of the many burial societies owned by colored people in Mississippi.

Talk to the people there. I'm not at liberty to call their names. But if you shop around you will be directed to other people who will tell you how to locate the father of Henry Lee Loggins.

Go to Loggins' father. Press him. He will be reluctant to talk and when you finally hear his story you will easily understand why he is reluctant to talk.

But when you finally get his story, he will tell you that his son Henry has confessed to him that he was on the murder truck the night Emmett Till was killed.

He can tell you that his son has named to him the four more white men—instead of two—who were involved in the kidnapping or murder.

He also will tell you that the other white men involved along with Roy Bryant and J. W. Milam were relatives of Milam, that one of them was a close relative who has already been named by Willie Reed and that the other is a relative who lives at Ita Bend [Itta Bena], Miss.

But don't stop with the testimony of Henry's father. Ask him about the minister. Ask him to give you the name of the colored minister to whom Henry has also confessed being on that murder truck.

NAACP officials have pleaded with this same minister to come forward and tell his story but he is afraid and will not do so. Get the name of this minister from Loggins' father.

If he will not give you his name, as a last resort, I will call an NAACP official in Clarksdale and beg him to release me from an "off the record" confidence and give it to you myself.

This NAACP official has literally begged the minister to tell the world what Loggins told him but he will not do so.

Go back now across the short space to the home of Mrs. Loggins. You can talk more intelligently now and when she discovers that you know something she will tell you more.

Ask her where her husband, Henry, is. She will tell you that he is on the Milam farm daily but that he does not come home every night. Ask her where you can put your finger on him.

Then ask her when was the last time she saw Too Tight Collins. See if she will not tell you that she has not seen him since Oct. 10, the date on which a Chicago newspaper released him and sent him back to Mississippi.

Make her tell you where Too Tight is and you will explode the lie that J. W. Milam is trying to spread throughout Mississippi that Too Tight is missing and has been missing since the newspaper took him north to Chicago.

Too Tight is still in Mississippi working for J. W. Milam.

Ask her where Too Tight's father is. She will point south and tell you that he is on a plantation just three miles away on the Eaglet farm. He can tell you a lot more about the strange actions and mysterious disappearances of his son since the death of Emmett Till.

Now, before you leave Glendora, drop in to Reid's Café. Talk to some of the cotton pickers hanging around there. Listen to them tell you of the big talk that has been made by Too Tight since he came back South from Chicago.

Listen to them tell how Too Tight boasts that the hole in the Till boy's head was not a bullet hole, but a hole drilled in his head with a brace and bit by one of the white men.

Go then on up to Sumner just seven miles north and drop into Jesse Griffin's place. Talk to the guys up there and hear the same thing from the cotton pickers who hang around.

Ask them to tell you, as they told me on my second visit to Sumner, how Too Tight sat around the tavern and related how at one time during that fateful morning he was on the back of the truck with Emmett Till and they found that despite the punishment, the boy was still not dead.

They will tell you that Too Tight told them that he decided that he had seen all he could stand and decided to get off of the truck. But [J.] W. Milam pulled his gun and said if he got off he would blow out his brains.

Now remember, I asked you to remember the name Charleston jail. Go on to the Charleston jail and find there a young colored woman named Sarah who is serving a life term for killing a rival woman about her husband.

Sarah is a "trusty" at the jail. She is rather young, not too bad looking and she cooks for the inmates of the jail. If you investigate Sarah closely, you will find that "cooking" is not the only thing that she does for the men in the jail.

She also performs other services for them including serving the sheriff.

For her services Sarah is given certain privileges which she does not wish to give up. Therefore Sarah will be reluctant to talk.

But make Sarah talk and she will tell you that during the Sumner murder trial when Sheriff H. C. Strider was saying that he could not locate Too Tight Collins, actually Collins was at that time locked up in the Charleston jail.

I have been informed that Federal Government is looking for an "in" through which to get into the Till murder case. I'm also informed that one of the ways the Federal Government can get into the case is by proving that at the time of the murder trial key witnesses were prevented by law officers from testifying.

I submit that Too Tight Co[ll]ins was a key witness. I submit that Sarah can prove that Collins was in jail during the trial. And I ask you: If Collins was in the Charleston jail, who put him in there? A law officer, of course. And who is the principle law officer? Sheriff H. C. Strider.

One final word. Mrs. Mandy Bradley is a courageous woman and took the stand to testify as to what she saw and heard during the killing of Young Till. But her husband, Alonzo Bradley, was not so courageous.

He was there with his wife and saw and heard all she heard and saw. But he was afraid to testify.

After Mrs. Bradley testified against J. W. Milam, we got her out of Mississippi. The night after she testified Alonzo Bradley went back to his home on the Milam farm—a foolish thing to do in Mississippi.

J. W. Milam came to his shack and ordered him to leave at once. Alonzo Bradley left. For days he scouted around in Mississippi, trying to raise enough money to get to Chicago and join his wife.

On my second trip to Mississippi I contacted Alonzo Bradley and helped him get out of Mississippi. He is now in Chicago with his wife.

Before he left he told me that Leslie Milam had ordered him off the Milam farm at gun point. He also told me some other things which would be of great help to you if you are investigating the Till murder. Talk with Alonzo Bradley.

There is one more man you should talk with. His name is Frank Young. On the night we rounded up witnesses in Mississippi, Mr. Young came forward to the office of County Supervisor Townsend at Drew, Miss.

He told us he had knowledge of the murder but before he talked, he wanted to first talk to Dr. T. R. M. Howard and get assured that he would not be harmed.

He made this statement in the offices of the county supervisor. He knew when he came there that he had been asked to come for only one purpose—to tell what he knew of the murder of Emmett Till.

Unfortunately, when Frank Young came in Dr. Howard was not there. He hung around until after 4:30 A.M., until finally the white woman who had brought him in off her plantation grew tired and took him back.

They promised that Frank Young would take the witness stand the following day. But he never did. Mr. Young has not been mentioned in connection with the trial since.

What did Frank Young have to say?

He is easy to locate. Just go to Drew, Miss[.], to the offices of County Supervisor Townsend. Mr. Townsend can pick up the telephone and call the plantation on which Mr. Young works and the white woman he works for will bring him in.

That's the way they did it that night.

And, finally, go to Henry Lee Loggins. Ask Loggins if it is not a fact that on the Saturday before the recent indictment proceedings he was scheduled to go to St. Louis on a trip, financed by a Chicago newspaper, and that on arrival there, was supposed to tell all he knew about the Till murder.

Ask him if it is not a fact that he was taken by reporters on a round of good-byes to all his girlfriends and that finally he was taken to his home to say good-bye to his mother.

And ask him if it is not a fact that his mother broke down and begged him not to go. And ask him if it's not a fact that he then decided to call the whole thing off, returned the spending money he had been given and stayed in Mississippi where he is now.

Ask him if is it is not a fact that he has admitted that he is afraid to tell all he knows about the Till murder because he himself was an accomplice in the crime.

If there is any additional service I can be to you two gentlemen, if and when you decide to go or send someone to investigate this murder in Mississippi, I stand ready at any time to help in whatever way possible.

Respectfully,

James L. Hicks

Emmett Till Is Alive

The American Anti-Communist Militia, November 1955

> According to the jurors in Sumner, Milam and Bryant were acquitted of all murder charges because Till's body had not been positively identified. No corpse, no murder. Even before the trial, unsubstantiated rumors about "a hoax" had surfaced: Emmett Till, many argued, was alive and well, and the body in the river nothing more than an elaborate plant by outside agitators trying to destroy the good name of Mississippi, "the most lied-about state in America." The following handbill, which appears to have been distributed after the trial and during Mrs. Bradley's West Coast speaking tour in November 1955, echoes these sentiments.

EMMETT TILL

IS ALIVE

Emmett Till is the impudent Chicago "Nigger" who grappled with a white Mississippi housewife and was duly punished by her legal protectors. The Communists immediately took advantage of this local fracas to create a national incident, so "Nigger" Till was whisked away into hiding by the NAACP. Till is alive in California where his mother is now visiting. (Above information on whereabouts of Till comes from numerous reliable sources).

The suspicion of patriotic Americans over the country is now justified in that it was generally assumed from the start, this entire incident was a hoax created by the Jewish inspired NAACP to implement racial hatred.

This bit of sensational news will never be broadcast to the general public. WHY, YOU ASK? —Because, Christian reader, the same Jews who sponsor the NAACP and plan to destroy America either own or control practically every means of communication, the press, radio and television and current magazines. (For documentation of the above statement see "American Jewish Committee Budget 1953–1954," pp. 41–52, pp. 76, 77)

AMERICAN ANTI-COMMUNIST MILITIA
National Headquarters
Kansas City 26, Missouri

The Shocking Story of Approved Killing in Mississippi
William Bradford Huie, *Look,* 24 January 1956

> William Bradford Huie, a seventh-generation Alabama novelist and journal-ist, was a rare breed: a southern conservative who was a crusader against racial injustice. Before investigating the Till case, he wrote, at the request of Zora Neale Hurston, a best-selling exposé about another race-murder and trial, *Ruby McCollum: Woman in the Suwannee Jail* (1954), for which he eventually served time for contempt of court. Later in his career, he investi-gated the murders of civil rights workers Michael Schwerner, James Chaney, and Andrew Goodman in Philadelphia (*Three Lives for Missis-sippi,* 1964) and Martin Luther King in Memphis (*He Slew the Dreamer,* 1969). He is often credited as being the "father of checkbook journalism," and his interview with Milam and Bryant—published to much fanfare in *Look* magazine in January 1956—is often cited as the first example of its kind. Huie paid the two men four thousand dollars for their story, an action he defended by claiming he was a "truth-seeker" who would, if he had to, even pay murderers to get at the truth. Huie's account, in which Till is de-

picted as brash and sexualized, remains both influential and controversial. Translated into several languages upon publication, the article—surprisingly—has never been reprinted in its entirety until now. In a 1959 book entitled *Wolf Whistle and Other Stories* (excerpted later in this anthology) Huie defended his conclusions.

Editor's Note: *In the long history of man's inhumanity to man, racial conflict has produced some of the most horrible examples of brutality. The recent slaying of Emmett Till in Mississippi is a case in point. The editors of "Look" are convinced that they are presenting here, for the first time, the real story of that killing—the story no jury heard and no newspaper reader saw.*

Disclosed here is the true account of the slaying in Mississippi of a Negro youth named Emmett Till.

Last September, in Sumner, Miss., a petit jury found the youth's admitted abductors not guilty of murder. In November, in Greenwood, a grand jury declined to indict them for kidnapping.

Of the murder trial, the *Memphis Commercial Appeal* said: "Evidence necessary for convicting on a murder charge was lacking." But with truth absent, hypocrisy and myth have flourished. Now, hypocrisy can be exposed: myth dispelled. Here are the facts.

Carolyn Holloway Bryant is 21, five feet tall, weighs 103 pounds. An Irish girl, with black hair and black eyes, she is a small-farmer's daughter who, at 17, quit high school at Indianola, Miss., to marry a soldier, Roy Bryant, then 20, now 24. The couple have two boys, three and two; and they operate a store at a dusty crossroads called Money: post office, filling station and three stores clustered around a school and a gin, and set in the vast, lonely cotton patch that is the Mississippi Delta.

Carolyn and Roy Bryant are poor: no car, no T. V. They live in the back of the store which Roy's brothers helped set up when he got out of the 82nd Airborne in 1953. They sell "snuff-and-fatback" to Negro field hands on credit; and they earn little because, for one reason, the government has begun giving the Negroes food they formerly bought.

Carolyn and Roy Bryant's social life is visits to their families, to the Baptist church and, whenever they can borrow a car, to a drive-in, with the kids sleeping in the back seat. They call *Shane* the best picture they ever saw.

For extra money, Carolyn tends store when Roy works outside—like truck driving for a brother. And he has many brothers. His mother had two husbands, 11 children. The first five—all boys—were "Milam children"; the next six—three boys, three girls—were "Bryant children."

This is a lusty and devoted clan. They work, fight, vote and play as a family. The "half" in their fraternity is forgotten. For years, they have operated a chain of cotton-field stores, as well as trucks and mechanical cotton pickers. In relation to the Negroes, they are somewhat like white traders in portions of Africa today; and they are determined to resist the revolt of colored men against white rule.

On Wednesday evening, August 24, 1955, Roy was in Texas, on a brother's truck. He had carted shrimp from New Orleans to San Antonio, proceeded to Brownsville. Carolyn was alone in the store. But back in the living quarters was her sister-in-law Juanita Milam, 27, with her own two small sons and Carolyn's two. The store was kept open until 9 on week nights, 11 on Saturday.

When her husband was away, Carolyn Bryant never slept in the store, never stayed there alone after dark. Moreover, in the Delta, no white woman or group of white women ever travels country roads after dark unattended by a man.

This meant that during Roy's absences—particularly since he had no car— there was family inconvenience. Each afternoon, a sister-in-law arrived to stay with Carolyn until closing time. Then, the two women, with their children, waited for a brother-in-law to convoy them to his home. Next morning, the sister-in-law drove Carolyn back.

Juanita Milam had driven from her home in Glendora. She had parked in front of the store and to the left; and under the front seat of this car was Roy Bryant's pistol, a .38 Colt automatic. Carolyn knew it was there. After 9, Juanita's husband, J. W. Milam, would arrive in his pickup to shepherd them to his home for the night.

About 7:30 P.M., eight young Negroes—seven boys and a girl—in a '46 Ford had stopped outside. They included sons, grandsons and a nephew of Moses (Preacher) Wright, 64, a cropper. They were between 13 and 19 years old. Four were natives of the Delta, and others, including the nephew, Emmett (Bobo) Till, were visiting from the Chicago area.

Bobo Till was 14 years old; born on July 25, 1941. He was stocky, muscular, weighing about 160, five feet four or five. Preacher later testified: "He looked like a man."

Bobo's party joined a dozen other young Negroes, including two other girls, in front of the store. Bryant had built checkerboards there. Some were playing checkers, others were wrestling and "kiddin' about girls."

Bobo bragged about his white girl. He showed the boys a picture of a white girl in his wallet; and, to their jeers and disbelief, he boasted of his success with her.

"You talkin' mighty big, Bo," one youth said. "There's a pretty little white woman in the store. Since you know how to handle white girls, let's see you go in and get a date with her?"

"You ain't chicken, are yuh, Bo?" another youth taunted him.

Bobo had to fire or fall back. He entered the store, alone, stopped at the candy case. Carolyn was behind the counter; Bobo in front. He asked for two cents worth of bubble gum. She handed it to him. He squeezed her hand and said: "How about a date, Baby?"

She jerked away and started for Juanita Milam. At the break between counters, Bobo jumped in front of her, perhaps caught her at the waist, and said: "You needn't be afraid o' me, Baby. I been with white girls before."

At this point, a cousin ran in, grabbed Bobo and began pulling him out of the store. Carolyn now ran, not for Juanita, but out the front, and got the pistol from the Milam car.

Outside, with Bobo being ushered off by his cousins, and with Carolyn getting the gun, Bobo executed the "wolf whistle" which gave the case its name.

That was the sum of the facts on which most newspaper readers based an opinion.

The Negroes drove away; and Carolyn, shaken, told Juanita. The two women determined to keep the incident from their "menfolks." They didn't tell J. W. Milam when he came to escort them home.

By Thursday afternoon, Carolyn Bryant could see the story was getting around. She spent Thursday night at the Milams, where at 4 A.M. (Friday) Roy got back from Texas. Since he had slept little for five nights, he went to bed at the Milams' while Carolyn returned to the store.

During Friday afternoon, Roy reached the store, and shortly thereafter a Negro told him what "the talk" was and told him that the "Chicago boy" was "vistin' Preacher." Carolyn then told Roy what had happened.

Once Roy Bryant knew, in his environment, in the opinion of most white people around him, for him to have done nothing would have marked him a coward and a fool.

On Friday night, he couldn't do anything. He and Carolyn were alone, and he had no car. Saturday was collection day, their busy day in the store. About 10:30 Saturday night, J. W. Milam drove by. Roy took him inside.

"I want you to come over early in the morning," he said, "I need a little transportation."

J. W. protested: "Sunday is the only morning I can sleep. Can't we make it around noon?"

Roy then told him.

"I'll be here," he said, "Early."

J. W. drove to another brother's store at Minter City, where he was working. He closed that store about 12:30 A.M., drove home to Glendora. Juanita was away, visiting her folks at Greenville. J. W. had been thinking. He decided not to go to bed. He pumped the pickup—a half-ton '55 Chevrolet—full of gas and headed for Money.

J. W. "Big Milam" is 36, six feet two, 235 pounds; an extrovert. Short boots accentuate his height; khaki trousers; red sports shirt; sun helmet. Dark-visaged; his lower lip curls when he chuckles; and though bald, his remaining hair is jet-black.

He is slavery's plantation overseer. Today, he rents Negro-driven mechanical cotton pickers to plantation owners. Those who know him say he can handle Negroes better than anybody in the county.

Big Milam soldiered in the Patton manner. With a ninth-grade education, he was commissioned in battle by the 75th Division. He was an expert platoon leader, expert street fighter, expert in night patrol, expert with the "grease gun," with every device for close-range killing. A German bullet tore clear through his chest; his body bears "multiple shrapnel wounds." Of his medals, he cherishes one: combat infantryman's badge.

Big Milam, like many soldiers, brought home his favorite gun: the .45 Colt automatic pistol.

"Best weapon the Army's got," he says. "Either for shootin' or sluggin.'"

Two hours after Big Milam got the word—the instant minute he could see the store—he was looking for the Chicago Negro.

Big Milam reached Money a few minutes shy of 2 A.M., Sunday, August 28. The Bryants were asleep; the store was dark but for the all-night light. He rapped at the back door, and when Roy came, he said: "Let's go. Let's make that trip now."

Roy dressed, brought a gun: this one was a .45 Colt. Both men were—and remained—cold sober. Big Milam had drunk a beer at Minter City around 9; Roy had had nothing.

There was no moon as they drove to Preacher's house: 2.8 miles east of Money.

Preacher's house stands 50 feet right of the gravel road, with cedar and persimmon trees in the yard. Big Milam drove the pickup in under the trees. He was bareheaded, carrying a five-cell flashlight in his left hand, the .45 in his right.

Roy Bryant pounded on the door.

Preacher: "Who's that?"

Bryant: "Mr. Bryant, from Money, Preacher."

Preacher: "All right, sir. Just a minute."

Preacher came out on the screened-in porch.

Bryant: "Preacher, you got a boy from Chicago here?"

Preacher: "Yessir."

Bryant: "I want to talk to him."

Preacher: "Yessir. I'll get him."

Preacher led them to a back bedroom where four youths were sleeping in two beds. In one was Bobo Till and Simeon Wright, Preacher's youngest son. Bryant had told Preacher to turn on the lights; Preacher had said they were out of order. So only the flashlight was used.

The visit was not a complete surprise. Preacher testified that he had heard of the "trouble," that he "sho' had" talked to his nephew about it. Bobo himself had been afraid; he had wanted to go home the day after the incident. The Negro girl in the party had urged that he leave. "They'll kill him," she had warned. But Preacher's wife, Elizabeth Wright, had decided that the danger was being magnified; she had urged Bobo to "finish yo' visit."

"I thought they might say something to him, but I didn't think they'd kill a boy," Preacher said.

Big Milam shined the light in Bobo's face, said: "You the nigger who did the talking?"

"Yeah," Bobo replied.

Milam: "Don't say 'Yeah' to me: I'll blow your head off. Get your clothes on."

Bobo had been sleeping in his shorts. He pulled on a shirt and trousers, then reached for his socks.

"Just the shoes," Milam hurried him.

"I don't wear shoes without socks," Bobo said; and he kept the gun-bearers waiting while he put on his socks, then a pair of canvas shoes with thick crepe soles.

Preacher and his wife tried two arguments in the boy's behalf.

"He ain't got good sense," Preacher begged. "He didn't know what he was doing. Don't take him."

"I'll pay you gentlemen for the damages," Elizabeth Wright said.

"You niggers go back to sleep," Milam replied.

They marched him into the yard, told him to get in the back of the pickup and lie down. He obeyed. They drove toward Money.

Elizabeth Wright rushed to the home of a white neighbor, who got up, looked around, but decided he could do nothing. Then, she and Preacher drove to the home of her brother, Crosby Smith, at Sumner; and Crosby Smith, on Sunday morning, went to the sheriff's office at Greenwood.

The other young Negroes stayed at Preacher's house until daylight, when Wheeler Parker telephoned his mother in Chicago, who in turn notified Bobo's mother, Mamie Bradley, 33, 6427 S. St. Lawrence.

Had there been any doubt as to the identity of the "Chicago boy who done the talkin'," Milam and Bryant would have stopped at the store for Carolyn to identify him. But there had been no denial. So they didn't stop at the store. At Money, they crossed the Tallahatchie River and drove west.

Their intention was to "just whip him . . . and scare some sense into him." And for this chore, Big Milam knew "the scariest place in the Delta." He had come upon it last year hunting wild geese. Over close to Rosedale, the Big River bends around under a bluff. "Brother, she's a 100-foot sheer drop, and she's a 100 feet deep after you hit."

Big Milam's idea was to stand him up there on that bluff, "whip" him with the .45, and then shine the light off down there toward that water and make him think you're gonna knock him in.

"Brother, if that won't scare the Chicago——, hell won't."

Searching for this bluff, they drove close to 75 miles. Through Shellmound, Schlater, Doddsville, Ruleville, Cleveland, to the intersection south of Rosedale. There they turned south on Mississippi No. 1, toward the entrance to Beulah Lake. They tried several dirt and gravel roads, drove along the levee. Finally, they gave up: in the darkness, Big Milam couldn't find his bluff.

They drove back to Milam's house at Glendora, and by now it was 5 A.M. They had been driving *nearly three hours,* with Milam and Bryant in the cab and Bobo lying in the back.

At some point when the truck slowed down, why hadn't Bobo jumped and run? He wasn't tied; nobody was holding him. A partial answer is that those Chevrolet pickups have a wraparound rear window the size of a windshield. Bryant could watch him. But the real answer is the remarkable part of the story.

Bobo wasn't afraid of them! He was tough as they were. He didn't think they had the guts to kill him.

Milam: "We never were able to scare him. They had just filled him so full of that poison he was hopeless."

Back of Milam's house is a tool house, with two rooms each about 12 feet square. They took him there and began "whipping" him, first Milam, then Bryant smashing him across the head with those .45's. Pistol-whipping: a court-martial offense in the Army . . . but MP's have been known to do it . . . and Milam got information out of German prisoners this way.

But under these blows, Bobo never hollered—and he kept making the perfect speeches to ensure martyrdom.

Bobo: "You bastards, I'm not afraid of you. I'm as good as you are. I've 'had' white women. My grandmother was a white woman."

Milam: "Well, what else could we do? He was hopeless. I'm no bully; I never hurt a nigger in my life. I like niggers—in their place—I know how to work 'em. But I just decided it was time a few people got put on notice. As long as I live and I can do anything about it, niggers are gonna stay in their place. Niggers ain't gonna vote where I live. If they did, they'd control the government. They ain't gonna go to school with my kids. And when a nigger even gets close to mentioning sex with a white woman, he's tired o' livin.' I'm likely to kill him. Me and my folks fought for this country, and we've got some rights. I stood there in that shed and listened to that nigger throw that poison at me, and I just made up my mind. 'Chicago boy,' I said, 'I'm tired of 'em sending your kind down here to stir up trouble. Goddam you, I'm going to make an example of you—just so everybody can know how me and my folks stand.'"

So big Milam decided to act. He needed a weight. He tried to think where he could get an anvil. Then he remembered a gin which had installed new equipment. He had seen two men lifting a discarded fan, a metal fan three feet high and circular, used in ginning cotton.

Bobo wasn't bleeding much. Pistol-whipping bruises more than it cuts. They ordered him back in the truck and headed west again. They passed through Doddsville, went to the Progressive Ginning Company. This gin is 3.4 miles east of Boyle: Boyle is two miles south of Cleveland. The road to this gin turns left off U. S. 61, after you cross the bayou bridge south of Boyle.

Milam: "When we got to that gin, it was daylight, and I was worried for the first time. Somebody might see us and accuse us of stealing the fan."

Bryant and Big Milam stood aside while Bobo loaded the fan. Weight: 74 pounds. The youth still thought they were bluffing.

They drove back to Glendora, then north toward Swan Lake and crossed the "new bridge" over the Tallahatchie. At the east end of this bridge, they turned right, along a dirt road which parallels the river. After about two miles, they crossed the property of L. W. Boyce, passing near his house.

About 1.5 miles southeast of the Boyce home is a lonely spot where Big Milam
has hunted squirrels. The river bank is steep. The truck stopped thirty yards
from the water.

Big Milam ordered Bobo to pick up the fan.

He staggered under its weight . . . carried it to the river bank. They stood
silently . . . just hating one another.

Milam: "Take off your clothes."

Slowly, Bobo sat down, pulled off his shoes, his socks. He stood up, unbut-
toned his shirt, dropped his pants, his shorts.

He stood there naked.

It was Sunday morning, a little before 7.

Milam: "You still as good as I am?"

Bobo: "Yeah."

Milam: "You've still 'had' white women?"

Bobo: "Yeah."

That big .45 jumped in Big Milam's hand. The youth turned to catch that big,
expanding bullet at his right ear. He dropped.

They barb-wired the gin fan to his neck, rolled him into 20 feet of water.

For three hours that morning, there was a fire in Big Milam's back yard: Bobo's
crepe-soled shoes were hard to burn.

Seventy-two hours later—eight miles downstream—boys were fishing. They
saw feet sticking out of the water. Bobo.

The majority—by no means *all,* but the *majority*—of the white people in Mississippi 1) either approve Big Milam's action or else 2) they don't disapprove
enough to risk giving their "enemies" the satisfaction of a conviction.

What's Happened to the Emmett Till Killers?
William Bradford Huie, *Look,* 22 January 1957

Huie returned to Mississippi a year after the trial and pursued an interesting
angle on the Till case: how the murder ended up ruining the lives of Milam
and Bryant. While this article does not enter any new evidence into consideration, it reinforces Huie's earlier theories about the case and thereby helps
to establish Huie's version of events as the most widely distributed of the
day. In contrast to the news articles by Hicks and Wilson, Huie's conclusions were disseminated to a large national audience over a period of several
years.

A year ago, *Look* published my report of how two white ex-soldiers in Mississippi, J. W. Milam, and his half brother, Roy Bryant, killed a Negro youth from Chicago, Emmett (Bobo) Till. Even though a jury had found the two not guilty of murder, it was a report that nobody could refute. Recently, I revisited Mississippi to learn how their crime has affected their lives.

Look readers will recall the salient points of the story:

Bobo Till, visiting his country cousins in the Delta in August, 1955, boasted of sexual relations with a Chicago white girl whose picture he carried. The local Negro youths, "just to show us how much you Chicago cats know about white girls," dared Bobo to enter a crossroads store at night and ask Bryant's young wife "for a date." While the Delta Negroes peered, in delicious awe, through the front windows, Bobo took the dare; Carolyn Bryant chased him with a pistol and, in a gesture of adolescent bravado, Bobo "wolf-whistled" at her.

Early in the morning of August 28, 1955, Milam and Bryant abducted Bobo from his uncle's farmhouse, intending to beat him and "chase him back to Chicago." But instead of cowering, Bobo taunted them about his relations with a white girl, whereupon they took him to the Tallahatchie River, where Milam killed him with one bullet from an Army .45. They fastened a gin fan to his neck and threw him in.

When the body was found, the most celebrated race-sex case since Scottsboro was born. Outsiders, both white and Negro, flooded the little town of Sumner, Miss.; and many Delta whites, including all five of Sumner's attorneys, "fought the invasion" by contributing money and voice to the defense. Milam and Bryant had admitted the abduction to arresting officers, denied the slaying; the prosecution had no witnesses to a murder; the defendants did not testify at the trial; and the jury found them not guilty.

To establish the truth, I traveled a year ago from my home in Alabama, first to Mississippi, then to Chicago. Facts which the prosecution had been unable to present at the trial, I found easily; the scene of the slaying; where the gin fan had been picked up; the time of the disposal of the body. Moreover—and to some people, this sounds incredible—Milam and Bryant were not reluctant to talk.

This didn't surprise me. Milam is a skilled mechanic, an expert, decorated soldier who won a battlefield commission in the Bulge: he is articulate. He and his younger brother don't feel they have anything to hide; they have never regarded themselves as being in legal jeopardy. Not even psychologically are they on the defensive. They took it for granted before the trial that every white neighbor, including every member of the jury and every defense attorney, had assumed that they had indeed killed the young Negro. And since the community had swarmed to their defense, Milam and Bryant assumed that the "community," including most responsible whites in Mississippi, had approved the killing.

Milam said: "I didn't intend to kill the nigger when we went and got him— just whip him and chase him back up yonder. But what the hell! He showed me the white gal's picture! Bragged o' what he's done to her! I counted pictures o' *three* white gals in his pocketbook before I burned it. What else could I do? No use lettin' him get no bigger!"

With that judgement, it was, and is, inconceivable to J. W. Milam that any "real American" would disagree—certainly no "red-blooded, Anglo-Saxon, Southern white man."

Why hadn't Milam and Bryant "talked" before I arrived? Nobody had asked them. Their "enemies" had assumed that they wouldn't talk; their "friends" had preferred that they say nothing.

In this category were the defense lawyers, who, concededly, are honorable men. Only one of the five, in preparing for the defense, dared ask Milam if he had, in fact, killed the young Negro. Milam cleared his throat to speak, but the lawyer, on second thought, stopped him.

The attorneys preferred, as was their legal right, to conduct the defense and erect smoke screens about the "forefathers" and the "Southern way of life" and to attack the "identification of the *corpus delecti*" without having asked their clients for the facts.

One lawyer told me: "No, I didn't question them. I guess I assumed they'd killed him; but my wife was worried, and every night after we turned out the light, she had been asking me if they were guilty and I'd been telling her no. So I figured the less I really knew the better."

That was the figuring of most of the literate Southerners who defended Milam and Bryant and "Mississippi." They preferred to "defend"—to "beat off their enemies"—without determining the truth. So, during the past year, they have had to adjust to a cruel irony: They won their battle with "outsiders"; they won an acquittal for Milam and Bryant; then, they had to face every detail of the truth.

Did I pay Milam and Bryant? I didn't pay them for the truth. I already had it. I did, later, purchase from them the right to portray them on the screen. I regard this story as the best of the race-sex cases with which to explain the nature of the racial conflict in America in 1957. I intend to film it. It isn't a story with "two sides"; but it does have an indivisible truth.

That truth is that the Southern white of the Milam type—and there are thousands of them—will not countenance even discussion of interracial commingling involving the sexes.

In the face of this situation, however, I have found that the Mississippi community in which Emmett Till was killed has developed a strong sense of repugnance to the whole episode.

On my recent trip to Mississippi, I talked with white men in Jackson, Greenwood, Sumner, Indianola, Glendora and Tutwiler. Then, early one morning, Milam met me in Ruleville. It was during the cotton-picking season, and he was servicing two mechanical pickers which were running in his own field nine miles from Ruleville. He was driving the same Chevrolet pickup in which he had hauled Bobo to his death; I got in the pickup and we drove back to his field. We sat talking and watching the two big pickers crawling up and down the rows. I asked him to help me reconstruct all that had happened to him and Bryant since the trial and publication of the story.

They have been disappointed. They have suffered disillusionment, ingratitude, resentment, misfortune.

Milam obviously isn't sorry he killed Bobo—to him, he had no choice—but it was an unlucky event for him.

For years before the slaying, the numerous Milam-Bryant clan had operated a chain of small stores in the Delta, stores dependent on Negro trade. At the time of the slaying, the mother had a store at Sharkey; Bryant had the store at Money in which the incident occurred, and Milam's brother-in-law, M. L. Campbell, had the store at Glendora in which Milam was working.

Now, all these stores have been closed or sold. The Negroes boycotted them and ruined them.

Many Negroes Won't Work for Milam

Milam, too, at that time, employed Negroes to operate his cotton pickers. He was reputed to be an expert in "working niggers." Now, many Negroes won't work for him, and he has to employ white men at higher pay.

When Bryant's store was closed, he had trouble getting a job. So now, with assistance under the GI Bill of Rights, he is going to welding school at the Bell Machine Shop, in Inverness. He and Carolyn and their two children live in Indianola, and he draws about $100 a month as a veteran. Had he been convicted of a felony, he would have been ineligible for this assistance.

"Roy'll have it tough, I'm afraid," Milam said. "It takes a long time to learn welding, and by the time you've learned it, you've ruined your eyes."

With the stores gone, Milam had to return to farming. He owns no land, and he was shocked when landowners who had contributed to his defense declined to rent to him.

Along with the land, he needed a "furnish" of $5,000 to put in a cotton crop. He had more equipment than the average renter, but despite this advantage, he had trouble getting a "furnish."

In all of Tallahatchie County—the county which had "swarmed" to his defense—he couldn't rent land. The Bank of Charleston, largest in the county, refused him a loan. (The county attorney, J. H. Caldwell, Jr., who had prosecuted Milam and Bryant, is influential at this bank.)

Finally, Milam, with his brother-in-law, M. L. Campbell, was able to rent 217.4 acres in Sunflower County, near the vast plantation owned by U. S. Sen. James O. Eastland. And at the last moment, he was able to get a $4,000 "furnish" at the Bank of Webb—in Tallahatchie County. It is unusual for a bank to "furnish" a crop outside its county; one explanation is that a member of the loan committee at the Bank of Webb is John W. Whitten, Jr., of the law firm of Breland and Whitten, the most powerful firm in Tallahatchie County, which defended Milam and Bryant.

"I had a lot of friends a year ago," Milam observed. "They contributed money to my defense fund—at least, they say they did. We never got half of what they say was contributed. I don't know what happened to it, but we never got it. Since then, some of those friends have been making excuses. I got letters from all over the country congratulating me on my 'fine Americanism'; but I don't get that kind of letters any more. Everything's gone against me—even the dry weather, which has hurt my cotton. I'm living in a share-crop with no water in it. My wife and kids are having it hard."

Perhaps the unkindest cut to Milam was struck by Sheriff E. D. Williams of Sunflower County. Milam carries at all times the big .45 automatic with which he killed Bobo. He can knock off a turtle's head at 50 feet. But after he moved to Sunflower County, the sheriff stopped him in Indianola and ordered him to quit carrying the gun.

Mississippi law is liberal on this point. If you can prove your life is being threatened, you can carry a weapon. Milam has no lack of such proof: The one type of letter he continues to receive from outside the state is the death threat to him or his children. Yet, despite these threats, he has had his ultimatum from the sheriff.

So Milam is confused. He understands why the Negroes have turned on him, but he feels that the whites still approve what he did. Why, then, should they be less co-operative than when they were patting him on the back, contributing money to him, and calling him a "fine, red-blooded American"?

The explanation was given to me by a responsible citizen of Tutwiler, in Tallahatchie County.

"Yeah, they came up here looking for land and a 'furnish,'" he said. "But we figured we might as well be rid of them. They're a tough bunch. And you know there's just one thing wrong with encouraging one o' these peckerwoods to kill a nigger. He don't know when to stop—and the rascal may wind up killing you."

Along the highways in Mississippi now, there are signs: MISSISSIPPI—THE MOST LIED ABOUT STATE IN THE UNION. And to try to counteract these alleged lies, the state recently entertained a group of New England editors. To these editors, Gov. James P. Coleman said: "We might have convicted the Till murderers if it hadn't been for Congressman Diggs and those other Negroes who came down here from the North."

That isn't quite true, as social conditions in Mississippi prove. Milam and Bryant can't be prosecuted for murder again—the Constitution protects them from that. They are still under bond on a charge of kidnaping Emmett Till, based on their own statements to arresting officers. But three grand juries have failed to indict them.

Why don't the grand juries indict, so the two men could then be tried? Jurors in Mississippi are male, white "qualified electors." And the state concedes the defense precious advantages in the selection of a trial jury.

The state of Mississippi can never convict Milam and Bryant of this crime before a jury. For, on any such jury, the defense can be certain of enough of what Milam calls "real, red-blooded, Anglo-Saxon, Southern white men" to at least insure a mistrial.

Milam and Bryant will not be tried again; but as landless white men in the Mississippi Delta, and bearing the mark of Cain, they will come to regard the dark morning of August 28, 1955, as the most unfortunate of their lives.

From *Time Bomb: Mississippi Exposed and the Full Story of Emmett Till*
Olive Arnold Adams, 1956

> When Olive Arnold Adams published *Time Bomb: Mississippi Exposed and the Full Story of Emmett Till,* she was editor of Global News Network, an

agency serving the black press, and her weekly column, "Straight Ahead,"
appeared in more than fifty African American newspapers. Her husband
was Julius J. Adams, who at the time of the Till murder was managing editor of the *New York Amsterdam News*. *Time Bomb* was written under the
sponsorship of the Mississippi Regional Council of Negro Leadership and
its founder, Dr. T. R. M. Howard of Mound Bayou. As a result, the pamphlet has a double focus: telling the inside story of the Till murder and re-
lating the good work being done in Mississippi by the MRCNL. The following selection represents only those parts of the pamphlet dealing with
the murder. Adams's conclusions support those of Hicks and Wilson and,
against Huie's interpretation, suggest once again that Milam and Bryant
used local black men to aid them in their heinous crime.

I

MISSISSIPPI, 1955
"Then said I unto them, Ye see the distress that we are in, how
Jerusalem lieth waste, and the gates thereof are burned with fire . . ."
Nehemiah 3:17

You are traveling north on Highway 49 out of Jackson, Mississippi. The tree-
shaded streets of Jackson's residential section are behind you and you are heading toward the rural areas. You have come to have a look at Mississippi and your
tour has only begun.

You have seen the glory of the South depicted in the relics assembled with loving care in the State Capitol in Jackson. Now you want to see the other relics of
the Confederacy—the feudal life that still exists despite the forward march of
America, the provincialism, the backwardness, the bitterness.

You have seen the fine monument to Jefferson Davis in the rotunda of the old
Capitol. Now you want to see the effects of the other monuments erected to the
Lost Cause—the racial barriers.

You have leafed through many volumes and viewed endless pictures, all keeping alive the beautiful memories of an era of gracious Southern living. But you
have come to see if there is any sign that Mississippi might stop looking back long
enough to find out where she is headed.

You have heard that there is a peculiar significance to the term "rural South,"
and now you know why. The Southern countryside is unique. It has an atmosphere unlike any other part of the country. The stranger gets the distinct feeling

that he is trespassing on private property and, in a sense, he is, for the clusters of shacks that dot the fields, here and there on either side of the highway, actually belong to plantations, and life on them is provincial, in many instances, backward. The stranger intrudes in still another sense: he is looked upon with considerable suspicion until the natives are fairly sure that his mission is harmless.

The names of some of the towns on the road signs seem amusing—"Tougaloo"—"Yazoo City"—"Eden"—"Tchula"—"Itta Bena"—"Money." A year or so ago, the sign reading "Money—10 Miles" might have elicited a smile. *Then* you might have thought, "What a funny name for a town!" But *now* "Money, Mississippi" rings a bell—or, more aptly, *tolls* a bell—for you have been sickened by the murder story that put Money on the front pages of newspapers all over the world, and on the lips of every newscaster.

It was a story with the impact of a Pearl Harbor. In fact, it was even more stunning, for it was difficult to fathom the kind of brutality displayed in this murder of a 14-year-old boy. Pearl Harbor and similar war atrocities have been committed by people in the fervor of patriotism. This foul deed could claim no such "distinction." This was not even a duel of honor, with weapons and seconds chosen in advance, and an hour appointed for a matched fight. This was a sneak attack on an innocent child—a bewildered child, dragged from his bed at gun point in the dead of night, and, vastly outnumbered, beaten to the point of death, then shot through the head like a mad dog. This was a cold-blooded, ruthless, base, utterly senseless sacrifice of human life, and you wanted to see what kind of atmosphere could breed such hatred. This was more than a killing for which two men went free. There was more involved here than could be corrected even by imposing the death sentence upon the murderers.

You agreed with the millions who said somebody ought to do something about Money, but you knew that in order to do something about it, you had to understand the who—the what—the why. What kind of men could do a thing like this? What manner of Negro could go along and give a hand? What kind of mother could condone the bestial murder of another mother's child? What kind of people could hesitate to condemn the perpetrators of the dastardly crime, but deplore the publicity involved?

To find some of the answers to these questions, you want to have a look at the South and to learn something about its "incestuous" existence, to look at life in its rural communities. So, you turn off at the sign that reads, "Money—10 Miles." It is well that you have kept an eye on your speedometer, because you might have missed the town. It is, as you have been informed by a native daughter, "just a wide place in the road." This group of frame buildings you see would hardly have qualified in your mind as a town. But there it is. The post office, the filling station, the little cluster of buildings. Money, Mississippi . . . all of it.

This little business section takes care of the needs of some 120 souls in the immediate vicinity, as well as a few hundred more scattered around on adjoining plantations. The center of activity is the grocery store—the local trading post not merely for staple supplies, but for local chit chat as well. The owners, Roy Bryant and his wife Carolyn, have made things fairly comfortable for the Negroes who patronize their store. On the porch there are several benches and a checker board or two—all of them put to pretty consistent use.

Bryant's store is Money's community center, and Bryant and his wife are dominant figures in the town's existence. Roy Bryant is known for miles around by both Negroes and whites, but much of his local fame stems from his relationship to his half-brother J. W. Milam, a contract cotton picker, who is known as a surly character and a brutal taskmaster. He, his two brothers, and his half-brother Bryant are described by some whites and Negroes—in the vernacular of the South—as "white trash." Still they have a certain amount of control over the little community—Bryant extends credit rather freely at his store, and Milam has the power to hire and fire. Both men, therefore, hold a whip hand.

This typical little Southern farm community is the very personification of the feudal life of the South. The large plantation owner leaves the management of his property to a man who supervises the entire operation and has complete control over the workers. The manager needs brawn and very little brain, and he helps to see to it that he has an abundance of workers who fit into this category. This is fairly simple. All he has to do is help keep Negroes from getting too much education by preventing them from voting for more or better schools. This is his contribution to the maintenance of the "status quo" in the South. In exchange, he has a certain amount of job security; he can operate his own little system of graft by underpaying his help, and he is free to do a little bootlegging and a few odd jobs on the side.

All the while, he knows he is looked down on as "white trash," but he compensates for this by grinding his heel on the neck of the Negro. That way, he can be better than somebody, or at least feel better. Actually, he questions his superiority. He knows he does not command respect, so he demands it through acts of violence and terror.

As for the Negroes who are used in this manner, they have little to fight with, even though they feel the injustice of the situation. Many of them eke out an existence on their little plots of ground, just barely making ends meet from one year to another. They have become more or less resigned to a life without citizenship rights, because the fight is just too big for the weapons they have. They attempt, therefore, to live as comfortably as they can within the narrow limits prescribed by their white overlords. Those who leave do so regretfully. It is their home and they love it. They would prefer to stay, but when life becomes unbearable they seek relief and opportunities elsewhere. They are, however, limited in the accomplishment of a better life because of little education in their early years.

Every cause, however, has its quislings, and the cause of the Negro is no exception. There exists a segment of the Negro population, very small to be sure, but whose influence is morally debilitating. This segment is referred to collectively as "white folks' niggers." Without mental and moral strength, they are easy prey for the white man who wants a few unpleasant errands run. Every boss has at his disposal at least two of these men. They have worked for him since they were boys. They have had little or no education, and depend upon the boss for their livelihood. They take his word for everything, including the amount of money he pays them. They cannot read, write, nor do simple arithmetic. All they know is that the boss provides the means of making their bread and butter. To fight for more than that is beyond their comprehension, because they have never had a taste of freedom. It is difficult for other Negroes to help them to see the light, because too often the position of these Negroes is not much better.

In a community such as this, law enforcement is still in a primitive state. The law, therefore, actually becomes the white man's whim of the moment, since White Supremacy is god. This was the primitive law of plantation life. Every white man used a shotgun to defend his property and to hunt for game. Even though the need no longer exists for this kind of protection, the ways of the Southerner are slow to change, and every man can go about armed if he chooses—and he usually does.

This is not to say that each county does not have its duly appointed or elected peace officer. Indeed it does. But in the majority of cases, such an officer is also a poor white who got his job by being somebody's errand boy. He is dedicated to the crude mores of the backward South, and besides, he is friendly with all the white people in the locality. His only function, then, seems to be to clear up any minor fracas between white people, or to punish a Negro if he breaks any minor law of the Southern jungle. Negroes can kill each other; white people can kill

Negroes, and the machinery of the law doesn't budge. There have been literally scores of Emmett Tills in Mississippi history, but nobody who could do anything about it cared, and those who cared couldn't do anything about it.

This is the kind of primal society into which Emmett Louis Till made an entrance last August. It appears on the surface much the same today. But because of him, it will never be the same again; for although you will be shocked by Mississippi before your tour is done, you will also be encouraged. Mississippi savagery has brought forth a new race, and beneath the seemingly quiet surface, there is a buzzing underground. This gives hope that 14-year-old Emmett Till's tragic end will serve a purpose.

II

EMMETT LOUIS TILL — HIS STORY
"For they eat the bread of wickedness, and drink the wine of violence."
Proverbs 4:17

The Southerner is a proud soul. He is sure Almighty God smiled with particular favor upon his beloved Southern homeland, and he boasts of its natural beauty, its fine people, its pioneers, its history. Even a Negro living in virtual serfdom displays passionate loyalty to his section of the country, and he is not likely to be outdone by anybody in praise of his native state.

It was only natural, therefore, that the Reverend Moses Wright of Mississippi when visiting Chicago last August—and while showing proper respect for the Merchandise Mart, the Loop, and the view from the Tribune Tower—felt constrained to boast a little too. Nowhere in the whole world, was he willing to wager, would one find such a fisherman's paradise as the spot near his home in Mississippi. Within the proverbial stone's throw from his cabin, he declared, there are four rivers —the Tallahatchie, the Sunflower, the Yalobusha, and the Yazoo. There are also about seven deep lakes, and the fisherman is always rewarded with a good catch.

Reverend Wright's word picture recalled to the mind of his nephew, Emmett Louis Till, still another virtue of the minister's Delta home. Emmett loved farm animals, and on two previous visits to his Uncle's farm, he had enjoyed feeding the cows and chickens. Mississippi seemed a perfect vacation spot, and Emmett and his cousin, Wheeler Parker, launched a campaign to get permission to spend the rest of the summer there. The boys' parents fell in with the idea, and it was agreed that when Reverend Wright returned to Mississippi the latter part of the month, the two boys would go with him.

Emmett was eagerly looking forward to the trip. His mother, Mrs. Mamie Bradley, was happy that Emmett could spend the last two weeks of his vacation in the fresh air and sunshine, fishing and loafing—a perfect ending to a mercilessly hot summer. She had been gratified to watch Emmett develop into a strapping youth. Stricken with polio when he was very young, he had been a frail youngster with a pronounced impediment in his speech. This had left Emmett shy and sensitive, but he was beginning to overcome his reticence, although he still stammered noticeably. It had been hard not to coddle Emmett, and his mother thought this vacation jaunt from her would be good for him. She was glad that Reverend Wright was willing to take the boys, because she had stated emphatically that she would not let Emmett travel alone.

Arrangements were made for the boys to leave with Uncle Moses on Saturday, August 20. The party was to board the train at La Salle Station in downtown Chicago, but Emmett was slightly delayed in his last minute preparations for the trip and his mother had sent word that he would join them at Englewood Station.

When the train pulled in at Englewood, Emmett was nowhere in sight. His Uncle Moses and Cousin Wheeler searched frantically for him. Reluctantly, they got back on the train when the conductor called "All Aboard," and had just about given up all hope, when they heard a bustling at the far end of the platform. It was Emmett. With the help of his mother, the porter and the conductor, he scrambled onto the last car just in time. The three were happily reunited, and many times during the long trip South, they talked of Emmett's good fortune in not having missed the train that was to take him on such a grand adventure.

No one has thought to ask if Emmett Till enjoyed fishing in the Tallahatchie River. The very question conjures up a grisly picture of his mutilated body which was found floating in the Tallahatchie, with feet in the air, his neck secured to a cotton gin fan with a length of barbed wire.

The events leading up to this horrible discovery are astounding. Millions of Americans were shocked, but many of them, well-meaning, assumed that Emmett Till must have done something to provoke punishment. Those who believe this are simply not acquainted with the savagery of the South. All Emmett Till had to do to arouse the ire of a backward Southerner was simply to be Emmett Till—a Northern Negro, well dressed, with a little vacation money to spend, and an air of security and confidence. This is enough to make "white trash" see red. It might give local Negroes "ideas."

The nauseating stories of the mock trial which resulted in clearing those accused of Till's murder, and the subsequent refusal of the grand jury to indict the two for the kidnaping they admitted, are now well known. Everyone suspected at the outset that Roy Bryant and J. W. Milam killed Emmett Till. They knew that the mores of the South prevented true justice. The recent boastful confession attributed to the two men in a national magazine article supports that conclusion. Their story probably set very well with others of their kind, and may even have convinced some people that at least Emmett Till was a fresh young upstart who had made improper advances toward a white woman, boasted about it, and stood his ground even at gun point, thus justifying his murder . . . at least in the minds of some Southerners. This, of course, was just more vicious propaganda, aimed at fitting Emmett Till into the "sexually depraved" category among the stereotypes into which Negroes are so often cast. It was an obvious attempt to dream up a crime to fit the punishment.

The fact is that the true, official Emmett Till story will never come to light until the day when the Mississippi Negro is free . . . when the laws that protect murderers also protect him . . . when he can appear on the witness stand, tell the truth, and be believed, without having to be spirited away from his home for fear of reprisals.

The principal witnesses for the prosecution in the Till case were Reverend Moses Wright, Mrs. Amanda Bradley, and 18-year-old Willie Reed. The appearance of Negroes in court, testifying against white men in an atmosphere charged with racial tension and hatred, was entirely new in the recent history of the South. Despite threats and intimidation, they stuck to their story, which was never categorically denied, since Bryant and Milam did not appear on the witness stand in their own defense. Willie Reed, now relatively safe in his self-imposed exile from Mississippi, has been able to throw some additional light on some of the events and incidents attested to in court by other witnesses. There are still others who remained in Mississippi and who have information, but who were never permitted to present it in court, and are now afraid to do so, for fear of their lives.

This is the story told in whispers about the case of Emmett Till. It does not come from Milam and Bryant, but from God-fearing, law-abiding citizens. The story has been gathered from talks with relatives of eye-witnesses to certain phases of the crime, and from eye-witnesses themselves. It is repeated here as a running narrative, sometimes from the vantage point of the defendants, sometimes from the vantage point of a witness. Regardless of court records or "confessions," this is the story that has already become the Till legend:

Emmett Till, his cousin Wheeler Parker, and Uncle Moses Wright arrived in

Mississippi on Sunday, August 21. On the following Wednesday, Emmett, Wheeler, Maurice and Simeon Wright, his Mississippi cousins, Ruthie May Crawford, and three other local boys decided to go to the country store to buy a treat. They drove the 2.8 miles from Reverend Wright's humble cabin to Bryant's store in Reverend Wright's aged Ford. When they arrived, there were four men on the porch, two of them in the midst of a checker game. The boys looked on for a while and then Emmett offered to treat his pals. They all wanted bubble gum and Emmett went in to buy some. Simeon Wright went with Emmett to the door and waited outside the door while Emmett made the purchase and put the money, in the exact amount, on the counter. As he was leaving the store, Emmett turned and before opening the screen door said, in his characteristic stammer:

"G-g-g-g-goodbye."

The local boys laughed at Emmett's stutter and as they walked down the steps and away from the store, one of them was heard to say:

"Bobo, don't you know you're not supposed to say goodbye to a white woman?"

Another said, "But she *was* good lookin', *wasn't* she?"

At that remark, Bobo puckered up and attempted to whistle. By that time, they were several yards from the store and no one else was in sight.

The boys went back to the store Friday and nothing was said in reference to their previous visit. It is believed, however, that the whistle incident was marked by one of the men who was within earshot. It is believed such a person may have sought a favor, or perhaps easy credit at the store, by distorting the story for the benefit of Roy Bryant who had been out of town during the week. The story apparently was well received by Bryant. It had all the ingredients to rile a Southern white man—a Northern Negro had come into their midst . . . a symbol of Northern superiority and Northern interference. This called for action.

At 2 A.M. Sunday, August 28, Roy Bryant, his half-brother, J. W. Milam, and two other persons, drove to Reverend Wright's cabin in a green Chevrolet pickup truck with the white top. Bryant and Milam went to the door. A person "with a little voice lighter than a man's" stayed in the truck, and the other, identified as a Negro, lurked outside.

Bryant and Milam knocked at the door and called, "Preacher."

When Reverend Wright asked who was there, Bryant answered, "This is Mr. Bryant from up at the store."

Reverend Wright opened the door and Milam pressed a gun against the minister's stomach and forced his way in, followed by Bryant.

"We came for the boy from Chicago," he said. Going in to the bed in which Emmett Till was sleeping, he demanded:

"Are you from Chicago?"

"Yes," said Emmett.

Milam was indignant and said, "Did you say 'yes' to me? If you say 'yes' to me again, I'll knock your —— brains out. Get up and put your clothes on."

Emmett got up and put on his shirt and trousers, and his new pair of leather-soled loafers. Reverend and Mrs. Wright pleaded with Bryant and Milam not to take the boy out. They said that if he had done anything he should be punished for, he would get a whipping, but they begged the men not to take the boy away.

(At the time of their arrest as suspects, Sheriff George Smith reportedly told newspapermen that Bryant and Milam had said they took Emmett from his uncle's home to question him about the "wolf-whistle" incident, but that they later turned him loose.)

Bryant and Milam took Emmett to the waiting truck, where he was identified as the boy who had been to the store the previous Wednesday. Milam, Bryant, and "the person with the light voice" who was thought to be a woman, got into the cab of the truck, and the Negro, whom we shall call "Wiggins" for the purpose of identification in this story, got into the back of the truck and was holding Emmett as if to keep him from getting away. The truck headed toward Money, where it was next seen. Later, it was seen in Glendora. The woman was no longer in it, but there were four white men in the cab, all of whom appeared to have been under the influence of intoxicating liquor. At one point, "Wiggins" had been left in the back of the truck with Till. Emmett had apparently become apprehensive and was difficult to handle. "Wiggins" is said to have asked for help in keeping the boy quiet, saying that he didn't think he could keep him from getting away. At a Negro night-spot in Glendora, they picked up another Negro named "Herbert" to help control the boy.

When the green Chevrolet pickup truck with the white top pulled out of Glendora early that Sunday morning, it had seven occupants—four white men were in the front, and Emmett Till, "Wiggins" and "Herbert" were in the back.

At 6:00 A.M., the green pickup truck made its way into Sunflower County, some 25 miles from Glendora, in the direction of the plantation managed by J. W. Milam's brother, Leslie.

This was too early for many people to be stirring, but 18-year-old Willie Reed had been awakened at the crack of dawn. His grandfather had forgotten to buy fresh meat for Sunday's dinner, and Willie was sent to the store to get some. The country store is approximately 2 miles from the Reed home by way of the asphalt road, but it is about 1¼ miles if one takes a shortcut across Leslie Milam's plantation.

When Willie Reed neared the dirt road that leads to the headquarters barn on Leslie Milam's plantation, he met the green Chevrolet pickup truck with the white top. He recognized two of the white men, but did not have a chance to see who the other two men were in the front seat. As the truck turned in at the plantation, it passed immediately in front of Willie Reed and he looked into the back of the truck directly into the face of Emmett Till. Emmett was seated with his back to the cab of the truck, flanked by "Wiggins" and "Herbert." Willie Reed was, therefore, the last person not connected with the crime to see Emmett Till alive.

As Willie Reed cut across the field, he heard a boy crying from inside the headquarters barn: "Lord, have mercy! Mama, save me!"

He also heard blows landing on a body. They sounded as if they were made with a heavy object such as the handle of a hoe or the butt of a pistol. Willie also heard men's voices cursing and yelling, "Get down, you black bastard."

Willie Reed became frightened and did not go to the barn, but went around it, to the home of Mrs. Amanda Bradley about 100 yards away. Mrs. Bradley was preparing Sunday breakfast. A family friend, "Fred Yonkers," was also there.

"Aunt Mandy, who are they beatin' down at the barn?" Willie asked.

The Milam brothers are famous for their "pistol whuppin'" and the sound of some Negro being roughed up by the Milam gang was not new to her. So she said:

"I don't guess they're beatin' anybody, Willie."

"But Aunt Mandy," Willie insisted, "it sounds like they're beatin' somebody to death down there!"

Mrs. Bradley immediately emptied the water bucket and asked Willie to go to the well, which was near the barn, and fetch her some water.

"But I'm afraid to go down there," Willie pleaded.

At this point, "Mr. Yonkers" took the bucket and together he and Willie Reed went to the well. On the way, they heard the cries again and again. They also heard the blows being struck. While they were at the well drawing the water, the cries grew fainter and fainter, and then there were no more.

As they started back to the house, they saw J. W. Milam, wearing khaki trousers and a yellow shirt with an open collar, come out of the storage room of the headquarters barn. He wore a pistol in a holster at his right side. He went to the same well and got a drink of water. When he went back to the storage room, the other three white men joined him. Shortly after this conference, a tractor near the side door of the storage room was moved and the green Chevrolet pickup truck with the white top was backed up to the side door.

By this time, Willie Reed and "Fred Yonkers" had retreated to the seclusion of Mrs. Bradley's kitchen, and with Mrs. Bradley they were watching the proceedings from the kitchen window. They saw what they believed to be a body placed in the back of the truck. They saw a tarpaulin thrown over it. Then they saw the truck as it pulled out.

While the truck was on its way, movement was detected under the tarpaulin. Numerous efforts were made by private individuals to determine what actually happened after the truck left the Milam plantation. John H. Sengstacke, publisher and editor of the *Chicago Defender,* interested himself in the case. Through one of his editors, Alex Wilson of Memphis, Tennessee, he succeeded in getting a young Negro, "Too Tight" Collins, out of Mississippi and to Chicago, where he was questioned at length about the case by the *Defender's* Counsel, Col. Euclid Louis Taylor. However, Collins failed to shed any material light on the murder. Both Taylor and Sengstacke said they believed Collins knew more than he was willing to tell. In the investigation the *Defender* group learned that another Negro, Henry Lee Loggins, would be able to tell an "interesting story" if he would talk, but neither Wilson nor anyone else could persuade Loggins either to leave Mississippi or to give them any information for publication.

This much is certain: between the time the truck left the plantation and the time his body was dragged from the Tallahatchie river, Emmett Till had been shot through the brain. One end of a piece of barbed wire about 40 inches long was tied around his neck and the other end was attached to a 90-pound gin fan.

A young unidentified Negro helper was asked to clean out the back of the pickup truck which was later seen in Glendora. The boy noticed bloodstains and asked what they were. The matter was tossed off lightly, and the boy was told:

"I just killed a deer. Don't say anything about it."

The boy noticed something else, however. He saw a pile of clothes on the ground near the barn. The boy was then sent off on an errand. When he returned, the clothes were reduced to ashes. Later, he secretly poked around in the ashes and discovered only one shoe. It is believed the other shoe may still be somewhere in the high weeds around the headquarters barn.

As for the gin fan that weighted down Emmett Till's body, there was in all the surrounding territory, only one such fan missing—from an abandoned gin located about 100 yards behind the store of one of the Milam brothers in Itta Bena.

Chapter 5 *Memoirs*

The story of Emmett Till did not fade away with the passing of his trial and the failure of the Sumner jury to convict his two murderers. In early November, a grand jury refused, without explanation, to bring indictments against Milam and Bryant on kidnapping charges. Considering that both men had confessed to kidnapping when they were first arrested by Sheriff Smith—thus in effect indicting themselves—the refusal of this grand jury to send the case to trial was yet another example of the South's increasingly defensive—and indefensible—position. While the grand jury's decision was applauded by all the usual suspects, some southern newspapers broke rank. For instance, in a November 11 editorial, the *Memphis Commercial Appeal* lamented the decision, citing it as a "breakdown in our system of due process of law." According to the *Appeal,* the grand jury's action "means that citizens of a state have agreed that under certain circumstances they will not require accused persons to face trial, even after those persons have admitted that they invaded another man's house, and that they took by force a person from that house." This action has been "weighed in the balance, and to our shame, it has been found wanting."

Despite the best efforts of many in the South, Till's story, much like his mutilated corpse, would not stay submerged in the deep waters of forgetfulness. Although many other examples of black victimization and white violence in the days before the civil rights movement have been unjustly forgotten, the memory of Till's lynching continues to cast a long and dark shadow. Many forces conspired to enable his story to sear itself into the collective memory of the nation. As a northern rather than a southern black man—and from a big city with a large black population and powerful political leaders—Emmett Till had an army of supporters with the freedom to challenge the institutionalized racism of the South. A southern black man would not have been in such a position. Moreover, Mamie Till Bradley's decision to bury her son back home, and—more importantly—to have him lie in state for three days in an open casket, was not only an act of defiance against the state of Mississippi, but also an open invitation to make his funeral—and thus the upcoming trial of his murderers—a national media event. Had she not invited "the whole world to see what they did to [her] boy"— and who can imagine what pain this must have caused her?—*Jet* magazine would never have been able to run the powerful photograph of Till's swollen, disfigured, and stitched-together face, a photograph published in black newspapers throughout the country and, by all accounts, an image which galvanized a generation of African Americans. Finally, Till's murder occurred only a few months before the Montgomery Bus Boycott, and thus unlike the other lynchings and murders that preceded it, Till's happened at a time when blacks were beginning to move out of the margins and onto the center stage of American history. At this time of unprecedented black agency, when African Americans were commencing the long march to freedom that would attempt to redeem the soul of America, Till's murder began in retrospect to look like the first step on that great journey and the sorest example of the sins for which the nation needed forgiveness and atonement.

The following selections trace out the trajectory of Till's legacy as it appears in autobiographies, letters, memoirs, interviews, and other nonfiction documents (fictional representations—poems, stories, song lyrics, and so on—will be taken up in the next chapter). Beginning with Mamie Till Bradley's own recollection of her son's life and death and ending with John Edgar Wideman's masterful and passionate confession that he still remains haunted by the face of Emmett Till more than forty years after his murder, this chapter pays tribute to the power of memory. Emmett Till may have lived only fourteen years, but through collective acts of remembrance he has managed to transcend his tragic and brutal death to be reborn again and again.

From "Mamie Bradley's Untold Story"
Mamie Till Bradley, as told to Ethel Payne, *Chicago Defender,* April–June, 1956

From April 21 to June 9, 1956, the *Chicago Defender* ran Mamie Till Bradley's "untold story" in eight weekly installments. Immediately after the murder trial, Mrs. Bradley, under the sponsorship of the NAACP, spoke to packed auditoriums and churches throughout the country, and thus long before her interview with Ethel Payne appeared in the *Defender* she had moved audiences with her account of the horrors she experienced in the fall of 1955. The following selection does not reprint all eight installments in their entirety because much of Mrs. Bradley's *Defender* story deals with her younger days and her marriage to Emmett's father, Louis Till. Rather, only those moments that deal directly with the events of August and September 1955 are included.

[Installment 1, 21 April 1956] Since that terrible day when my girl friend, Ollie Williams, broke the news to me about Bo, nothing has been the same. Ollie and I have known each other since school days in Argo, Ill. She works at Inland Steel Co. When word came that Bo was missing, the people out there were very concerned and they offered to do all they could.

The *Chicago Tribune* was the first to get the message by telephone that Bo's body had been found. They called Ollie on her job and asked her to break the news to me. People wonder why I am so calm, and some even think that I am cold.

What they don't realize is that when they brought back what was left of my boy, I prayed harder than I had ever done in my life for strength to go through with what I knew had to be done—I had to know for myself that this was really Bo. Nobody else could do it for me.

Advised Not to Look

Mr. Rainer (the undertaker) advised me not to look at the body. So did my friends and relatives. They thought it would be too horrible a shock, but after I prayed so hard, something told me, "Your heart will be encased in glass and no arrows can pierce it."

I looked at that horribly mangled monstrosity—the odor was terrible—what had been done to a human being created by God was a crime so foul, I don't have words to describe it. No sane, decent person could do that to another, only somebody possessed by the devil.

It looked like something from outer space, and it seemed like a weird nightmare, not a part of me.

There's My Heart

I looked at this and no tears came, only a deep, lonely feeling that time and space had crushed me and I was left in a vacuum. After Mr. Rayner had patched and fixed up the remains—and he did a wonderful job[—]it was I who insisted that the body be opened to the public.

I wanted people to see what hatred of a human being, just because of the color of his skin, can do. As I stood and looked down under the glass covering of the casket, I said to myself over and over. "There's my heart underneath that glass."

Sleep to Forget

Now, I find myself wanting to sleep, sleep, sleep. Sleep is an escape from reality—from the nagging persistence of the evil that must haunt all of us—that in a way, all of us are responsible for Bo's death, because we've let people like those killers have their way, and the decent people have just sat by.

I still get hundreds of letters and telephone calls from crackpots and cranks—they're all the same. — "Now maybe you niggers will stay in your place." Since that terrible article in *Look* magazine, full of Milam and Bryant's lies about my child[,] came out, the calls and letters have increased.

I'd like to get away, but there's no rest anywhere. Somehow, I've got to stay and fight. That's all there is left for me.

Sometimes, I lie awake at night and review my whole life and ask myself why just an ordinary person like myself, somebody who never thought of seeing her name and picture in the papers, should suddenly have been thrust so tragically and unwillingly into a limelight she never wanted.

The answer came to me that night of Aug. 20, but still I wonder. [. . .]

[Installment 6, 26 May 1956] Bo had been nagging at me to let him go to Mississippi. Some of his friends were going and he wanted to be with them.

At first, I flatly said no and told him not to bother me any more about the subject. Then Uncle Moses Wright came to Chicago to attend the funeral of a relative. He said he would be responsible for Bo and the rest of the boys.

Uncle Moses was sort of a patriarch in the family. In fact, everybody called him "Papa" Moses. So it was perfectly allright with me to let Bo go in his care because I felt he would be in good hands.

Once the matter was settled, I began lecturing and schooling Bo seriously on how to conduct himself in the South.

I emphasized over and over again to him that it was not the same as Argo or Chicago and he had to be extra careful to avoid getting in trouble with white people. The summer he was nine, I had taken him to Mississippi to visit some of my folks and he had got into a fight with a little boy.

I literally hammered it into him that he was 14 now and much bigger and he must not get into trouble. He understood me and agreed to behave himself according to the code I had laid down.

Bo left for Mississippi with Papa Moses and Wheeler Parker, Jr., the 20th of August. I was just starting my vacation.

I was then working with the Air Force as a voucher examiner. I had planned to go to Omaha to visit some relatives, but first I wanted to get things in order at home.

I went to the city dog pound and picked up Bo's dog "Mike." Mama came over to help me set the house straight.

By Tuesday, I was all ready to go, but I felt tired and decided to rest a day. I had a feeling of inertia which lasted through Friday. I couldn't do anything but sleep.

I would get up to get something to eat and then go right back to bed. By Saturday, I was so lonesome for Bo that I said I would wait for some word from him before I went anywhere.

His first letter came on Saturday afternoon and I decided then to go to Mississippi and come back with him. I called a cousin of mine to drive down there with me, but he didn't get the message. Ironically, he was in Argo hoping he could get somebody to go with him.

I thought Bo would come home maybe Saturday or Sunday. If not, then I planned to get the City of New Orleans Monday morning and go to Money. I showed this letter to Mama. She remarked: "It was so beautiful that I'm going to put this up carefully. This could be his obituary."

Late Saturday afternoon, I received a telephone call from my cousin, Allan Jackson, in Detroit and I told him that I was going to Mississippi Monday. Allan told my father of my plans.

My friend, Bertha Hollis, called me about 7 P.M. and we went out to a new place at 71st St and stayed until about 11 o'clock. I had been expecting some folks from Argo to come by the house.

When we got back, they had been trying to reach me. They came by and we stayed up so long talking and laughing that I fixed an early breakfast.

I was telling them about my letter from Bo and just bragging about my kid. I said, "If Bo Till could get his feet on Chicago soil, he would be one happy kid." There was a moment of complete silence.

Perplexed, I stopped to figure out why I had made that remark. Just as suddenly, everybody resumed talking and laughing and no further words were said about the matter.

After they left, I lay down intending to get up a little later and go to church. Around 9:30 that morning, the telephone rang. I picked up the receiver.

"Hello, Hello, Hello," a moment of silence.

Finally the voice came through. "This is Willie Mae (a cousin on the Westside) I don't know how to tell you. Bo—they came and got him last night."

She broke down crying and hung up. I guess I should explain that Willie Mae is Uncle Moses' oldest daughter by his first marriage.

I promptly called Mama and told her what Willie Mae had said. Mama ordered me to get over to her house as fast as I could. I hung up and mechanically started making my bed.

The thought came to me. "Why are you making the bed? That's not important[.] Bo's missing."

I called my friend Gene and told him what had happened and he said he would come right over and go with me to Mama's.

Frantic by now, I couldn't wait for him. So I dashed out of the house and around the back to get the car out of the garage. Gene drove up in his car and caught me just as I was backing out.

He left his car in front of my house and took the wheel of my car. In my state of anxiety, I thought he was going too slow.

At 63rd and Halsted, I asked him to pull over to the curb. I slid under the wheel and stepped on the accelerator as hard as I could. I guess I broke all speed records and went through every red light.

If a cop had stopped me I intended to ask for a police escort, but nobody did.

[Installment 7, 2 June 1956] When we got to Mama's we talked the situation over and decided what action to take. It was impossible to get a message through to Papa Moses, so Mama called her brother, Crosby Smith in Sumner, Miss.

Willa Mae came in and between tears she sobbed out more of the story. She said she had heard that Bo had whistled at a white woman. This didn't make any sense to us, because I for one couldn't imagine Bo doing anything like this.

All day Sunday, we called and stayed by the telephone hoping that somehow, Papa Moses could get through to us.

On Monday I visited the N. A. A. C. P. office and called the *Chicago Tribune*. The story of Bo's disappearance began to break in the papers. The NAACP referred me to Atty. William Huff[,] who is considered an authority on extradition cases and knows a lot about civil rights cases.

We were still trying to get Uncle Moses and I had determined by this time to get the fastest thing out of Chicago to Mississippi to find out at first hand what had happened to Bo.

In the back of my mind was the hope that Bo had slipped away from his abductors and was hiding, afraid, in the home of some colored people and I kept hugging this hope close to me. We got Uncle Crosby again and he asked us to give him time to try one more time to get Papa Moses before any of us started out for Mississippi.

There was no sleep for me. A young cousin of mine shared the bedroom in the attic of my mother's home. She was sleeping with her head at the foot of the bed. During the night, some dogs howled mournfully and nobody could stop them.

Around 5 o'clock in the morning, my little cousin woke up screaming like a mad woman and moaning. She had turned completely around in the bed. We got her quiet and then we asked her what was disturbing her. All she could say was "I don't know. It was a horrible dream with blood everywhere, but I don't remember."

Tuesday, we finally got through to Papa Moses[,] who told us the story of how these white men had come by the house in the dead of the night and ordered Bo to get up and get dressed and come with them.

Papa Moses said he had gone to the store run by Roy Bryant and he was told that they had let Bo go and they didn't know where he was.

We have learned since that there were actually four white men and two Negroes in the group. On Tuesday, Mama got three calls from the Chicago Police Department saying that Mississippi authorities had contacted them telling them that Bo was on the way home.

I had gone to the bank in Argo to draw out some money to send to Uncle Crosby. After I left there I stopped by Mr. Huff's office and he showed me copies of telegrams he had sent to Governor Stratton, the Attorney General, and Governor Hugh White of Mississippi.

I was so desperate for some kind of hope. I told Mr. Huff my theory that Bo was probably hiding in some home and he sympathized with me. Both of us were wishing that this would be so.

Back at Mama's

When I got back to Mama's she met me smiling at the door and said, "Sister, did you hear the news? Bo's on his way home." I didn't believe her. I kept asking questions about how she got the news and desperately asking, "Won't somebody tell me something?"

Finally, I called the police department to trace the messages. They directed me to the criminal division and the missing person's bureau. Neither one had any records of any calls.

Those calls had been a hoax on the part of someone, we don't know who. We got Uncle Crosby and he said give him a few more hours to find Bo and if not to get the City of New Orleans the next morning and come to Mississippi. I made preparations to go.

Breaks the News

Wednesday, the *Tribune* called me and asked if I had had any word and I said no. I, in turn, asked them if they had any news as they were keeping the wire services on the case. A little later, Ollie called me and broke the news. I was so stunned I was numb.

Papa Spearman worked at Inland Steel where she also worked, but it was Ollie whom the *Tribune* called to give her the news to me. They knew when I called them before, but the story was so horrible, they wanted someone close to me to tell me about it.

We learned from Uncle Crosby that they were trying to bury Bo in Mississippi and I told him to stop the burial at any cost and to bring my baby—what was left of him—out of Mississippi.

I did not want my child buried there. Uncle Crosby said he would get the body which had not been embalmed and bring it to Chicago if he had to get a truck and fill it full of ice and drive it himself.

After the first shock, I went to bed in the front part of Mom's house, and everybody else stayed in the back to let me rest.

[Installment 8, 9 June 1956] While I was lying there, wide awake, I pondered over the whole chain of events leading up to that fateful day. My mind went back and forth over my life like a roving camera searching, searching, for some reason why this had happened to me.

I was angry with God that He had let Bo be kidnapped and slain so brutally and aloud I demanded, "Why did You do this[?] Why are You so cruel that You would let this happen? Why do You allow this kind of persecution?"

Strange Experience

Then began one of the strangest experiences of my whole life. It was just as though someone had entered the room and we were carrying on a conversation. It was as real to me as though we were both flesh and blood.

The presence said to me, "Mamie, it was ordained from the beginning of time that Emmett Louis Till would die a violent death. You should be grateful to be the mother of a boy who died blameless like Christ. Bo Till will never be forgotten. There is a job for you to do now."

I sat up in bed and stretched out my hand. I was praying hard that nobody would come up front before the conversation was completed, because I wanted the answer and I wanted to finish talking this thing out.

I knew that if anyone came up there and heard me talking, they would instantly think I had gone out of my mind with grief.

Voice Gives Answer

"What shall I do?" I asked.

The voice replied, "Have courage and faith that in the end there will be redemption for the sufferings of your people and you are the instrument of this purpose. Work unceasingly to tell the story so that the truth will arouse men's consciences and right can at last prevail."

The Voice died away and the Presence left the room. I lay down and slept peacefully.

There is no need to go into all of the details of the killing and the funeral. I have read the magazine article purporting to be the real story of the Till Killing.

Roy Bryant and J. W. Milam went to great pains to manufacture those lies about Bo in order to try and justify the crime they committed.

No Rest, No Peace

What they said is the true reflection of the warped and twisted minds of people like them.

They are insane with hatred and that hate comes from fear and insecurity bred into them.

In their brazen admission of the killing, they had condemned themselves forever along with the state of Mississippi.

There will never be any rest or peace for them.

I could hate all white people for this, but I don't.

I think, however, that the large class of decent people in this country are guilty of the sins of omission when they fail to speak out for the right and take a stand against injustice. These are the people I am appealing to.

That's why I am telling the story of my life and Bo's.

He was a child, sweet and innocent. Nothing can change that, I sit and think. I have time for a lot of thinking.

Bo's Responsibility

I think back now about the elderly woman living on an old age pension by herself and how fond Bo was of her. He used to go by her house every day to see if she was all right and to run errands for her and he would never take any money from her. She was his special responsibility.

I think of Bo imitating the commercial announcers on TV and how funny he could be.

I think of our discussions and plans for his college education—and how that would lead into the inevitable thought that some day he would get married and have children of his own.

I used to get jealous at the thought of one day having a daughter-in-law and I would even fuss with Bo about her.

Bo's Future

He used to laugh so hard at me. He'd say, "You know what? I'm going to get a great big house to keep you both in and when you get to quarreling, I'll just pick you both up—one in each hand and I won't let you go until you both promise to be good."

Sometimes, I'd find myself actually pouting about Bo's future wife.

Then I had a dream. I saw a baby—the most beautiful child I had ever seen. It was Bo's baby and I fell in love with it.

When I woke up, I could still imagine myself holding this child—my grandchild and the thought made me feel all warm and good. After that, I found myself eagerly looking forward to Bo's marrying and having children. They would be my grandchildren.

What Is Left

I am alone now. I have my mother and father, my relatives and friends. Still I am alone with my thoughts and my heart buried in a pine box underneath glass.

I haven't started back to work yet, because I have not yet become adjusted to being without Bo.

There is work for me to do and I am thinking of the future. I may go back to school and prepare myself to teach.

At 33, I should have some useful years ahead and I think I would enjoy working with children.

The doctors tell me that I can marry again and have children. This, I don't know about. Right now, I'm alone with Bo and God.

From *Wolf Whistle and Other Stories*
William Bradford Huie (1959)

In 1956, *Look* magazine published William Bradford Huie's infamous interview with J. W. Milam and Roy Bryant—an interview in which they confessed to the murder—and a year later he followed up with another piece focusing on the declining fortunes of the two men (both reprinted in chapter 4 of this book). In 1959, Huie reworked these articles for a longer piece, adding some previously published civil rights journalism and telling in greater detail how he gathered facts about the murder and what he suffered as a result of publishing his exposé. The reworked piece was published in *Wolf Whistle and Other Stories,* a paperback original that also included two other examples of Huie's investigative journalism. The following selection from *Wolf Whistle* recounts how Huie investigated the case, verified or disproved the facts he was told, and then defended himself against accusations of bad faith from both sides of the civil rights movement.

A month after the trial I began work on the case. I knew only what I had read; therefore, in a sense, I knew very little. I knew much less than I have told here— to this point. For the trial revealed nothing about the human being named Bobo Till, or the human beings named Big Milam, Roy Bryant and Carolyn Bryant.

The scores of reporters had added little. No reporter established *why* Bobo entered the store, or what happened in the store to cause Carolyn to go after the gun and to cause Bobo's cousin to rush into the store and pull him out. Bobo's attitudes and motivations were neglected. The press stories began with "a Negro boy wolf-whistling at a white woman." The wolf whistle, in the press, caused the abduction.

No one explained why the abduction was delayed four days after the wolf whistle; or why Milam and Bryant "did their duty" at 2 A.M. on a Sunday. No one even hoped to dispel the mystery of why and how Bobo was murdered.

Here was a tragedy commanding world attention at a pivotal moment in racial conflict. It involved human beings who needed knowing. Yet the characters in the drama had not been delineated for the consideration of thoughtful men.

My motivation was curiosity. I was curious about Big Milam and Bobo and every other character in the drama. Moreover, I believe that progress in human relations is possible only after understanding. I drove alone at night across Mississippi. Reflecting, I realized my advantages. I was independent . . . and Southern . . . had my own money . . . and I knew about such cases from Roosevelt Wilson and Ruby McCollum and all the others. I knew enough to assume that Big Milam and Roy Bryant would tell me everything they knew and felt. No other reporter had assumed this. Even Southern editors and columnists—those who have lived too sheltered too long—were dumbfounded at my assumption.

I knew enough to assume that I could go to Chicago, with the co-operation of NAACP, and that the Negro youths who were Bobo's playmates would tell me all they knew and felt about Bobo—how he talked and felt and why he did whatever he did. No other reporter had gathered these young Negroes around him, put them at ease by using their four-letter words, communicated with them as one human being to another.

I make these comparisons, not boastfully, but to illustrate the melancholy deterioration of the press in America. The day of the initiating newspaper and the resourceful reporter is fast going if it isn't gone.

Why shouldn't Milam and Bryant tell me the truth? The trial was over; they can't be tried for murder again: the Constitution forbids it. No Mississippi grand jury will indict them for kidnaping. They were not and are not in jeopardy. They are not on the defensive, legally or psychologically. Since childhood they have heard racial separation preached in their churches. From 1894 to 1954 racial separation was the "law of the land," pronounced so by a Supreme Court whose members included Brandeis, Cardozo and Holmes. White Supremacy is the slogan of the Democratic Party. In their trial Milam and Bryant were defended, commended, slapped on the back, by community leaders who had never before spoken to them. Defense money came from Chicago, from New Jersey, from twenty different states.

At their trial Milam and Bryant assumed that every person in the courtroom— judge, jurors, lawyers, spectators—*knew* that they had killed Bobo Till. So Milam and Bryant assumed that the murder was *approved* by their relatives, their neighbors, their community leaders, their newspapers, their state—by every institution which they respect.

So why wouldn't they tell me everything? What was there to hide? Why hadn't somebody already asked them?

I was the first man to confront Milam and Bryant who wanted the truth, and knew enough about them and their society to assume I'd get it.

I didn't, however, go directly to them. I breakfasted early at Holiday Inn,

Greenwood, and at 8 A.M. I was sitting in the modern, red-brick offices of Breland & Whitten in Sumner. I had never been in Tallahatchie County, Mississippi, but I didn't have to ask anybody where to start.

Except that he is heir to the agrarian, biracial society of the Delta, John Whitten, thirty-six, is the decent, intelligent, young lawyer you can find most anywhere in America. He's cultured, educated, honest, a fine soldier, secretary of his county's Democratic Party organization, an Ole Miss alumnus.

He received me cordially: most of us old-time Southerners are kin. If we aren't fraternity brothers our brothers are. Or we met on some battlefield. Or our grandmothers were at Monteagle together escaping the fever. Or our granddaddies rode shoulder-to-shoulder at Gettysburg.

For a defeated people, a war never really ends.

After we had explored the lines of kinship, I said:

"John, I want the truth about the Till case. I want to publish it. Whatever our racial sins down here, I like to think we are less hypocritical than some of our enemies. I like to think that truth serves decent purposes better than mystery or propaganda.

"I assume this is about what happened," I continued. "Milam and Bryant got the Negro boy and took him somewhere to whip him. They didn't intend to kill him. But while they were whipping him, something went wrong. Maybe they were drunk. Perhaps, accidentally, they hit him too hard. Maybe they injured him and decided they had to kill him. In any case, they killed him and threw him in the river. Is that about right?"

"I'll tell you the first truth," John Whitten replied. "I don't know what happened. We never asked them. We defended them . . . you know why. But we didn't question them. I personally didn't ask them because . . . well, my wife was disturbed about it. She kept asking me every day if they had killed the Negro boy. To make it easier for her I kept telling her no. So I didn't want to hear the truth. They were entitled to defense; I defended them; but I didn't have to listen to them."

He paused, then added: "As to what happened, my assumption is about what yours is. You and I both know the taboo; and we know what the Court decision has done to our people."

I pulled photographs from my brief case.

"It's my guess also," I said, "that Milam was the killer and Bryant a coatholder. Milam is older; he won a battlefield commission; he looks like the family leader."

"I'd guess that, too," John Whitten said. "Milam was a good soldier: that's one of the claims he has on me. He's not a bad citizen . . . not rowdy or a disturber of the peace. He's the overseer type; he works Negroes, lives among them."

"I can proceed in either of two ways," I said. "By now they've talked. So I can hang around here, spend a little money, take a boat up that river, walk down a few roads at night, meet a few people in graveyards, and I can find out what happened. Or they can sit down and tell me. They won't be tried again; and even if they are, if they tell me, I won't testify against them. I want them to tell me the truth and help me verify it."

John Whitten thought for a moment, then said: "I don't see anything wrong with that."

It may be poor business for a writer to undersell his efforts, but that's how it was done. Or how it was begun. Over the period of a week I cross-examined Milam and Bryant through three long night sessions. During the days I wrote and worked on verification. In a boat I found the spot on the riverbank where they killed the youth and threw him in. I found witnesses who saw the pickup and who verified the time. I found where they got the barb-wire and the gin fan. In Mississippi—and later in Chicago—I verified the story in every verifiable detail. [. . .]

I flew to Chicago to see Mamie Bradley, Preacher and Elizabeth Wright, and the Negro youths who are Preacher's sons, grandsons and nephews. (Having had two wives, Preacher has teen-age grandsons and teen-age sons.) Preacher had abandoned his cotton crop and was living in Chicago, assisted by NAACP.

I told Roy Wilkins, head of NAACP, what I was doing, and his Chicago attorneys arranged for me to see Preacher. Since NAACP and Mamie were estranged, I reached her through my friends on *Ebony* and *Jet* magazines.

I went to Mamie's house about 11 P.M. She lives comfortably, upstairs in a two-family house. She is educated; and at thirty-four is an attractive, café-au-lait-colored woman. She has married three men—the first was Louis Till—and she is now a divorcee with a steady friend. Bobo was her only child.

Three Negro men were with her: her father, her friend, and a policeman assigned to guard her. She said "Mississippi people" wanted to kill her.

She talked about the boy—she called him "Bo." He had lived there with her and her husbands. He was in the ninth grade; he made average marks, seemed to be growing up rapidly. He had never been in trouble.

I clarified the dispute over his age and size. Milam and Bryant resented charges that they "murdered a child."

"That wasn't any *child* I killed," Milam protested. "His head came up to my shoulder and I'm six two. I didn't ask him his age, but he was muscled-up like a man. He could handle that hundred-pound gin fan. If he was just fourteen, he was the biggest fourteen-year-old I ever saw."

He *was* just fourteen. He was born in a Chicago hospital; his birth certificate is of record.

But he was one of those fourteen-year-olds who can be mistaken for eighteen. Mamie showed me his clothes. Her father is a medium-sized man. He told me he wore the boy's clothes. I'm five eight and weigh 155. I tried on his coat and it was a fair fit. Preacher testified in court: "He looked like a man."

I told Mamie only that I was "investigating the case." I didn't tell her Milam's story. So I was cautious when I asked her—and the men—about Bobo's sex life.

"Did he have a girl—girls?" I asked.

"He was at the age when boys are learning about girls," Mamie replied. "And when they talk and boast a lot."

"Do you think he had had a sexual relationship with any girls?

Mamie answered: "Mr. Huie, how would I know? That isn't the sort of thing a boy would discuss with his mother."

I turned to the men: "You gentlemen knew him. What would be your judgment?"

The friend, a good-natured man, chuckled. "I wouldn't say yes and I wouldn't say no," he said. "They start mighty early nowadays."

The six Negro youths and I sat in a vacant lot and talked. *Look*'s Chicago man, Jack Starr, was within earshot. I wanted him to check me, not only on what I heard but on my interpretations.

I asked the boys to tell me about Bobo and what they did in Mississippi during the week before the incident at the store.

They told me they rassled a lot: some said they could whip him, others admitted he could whip them. They told me he had not been afraid of white men: he said "Yeah" and "Naw" to white storekeepers and drew "hard looks" and they warned him. With no suggestion from me, they told me about "Bobo's white girl."

They showed me where the girl lived. I saw her in the front yard. I was tempted to talk with her, but prudence restrained me. Her father might resent a Kinsey inquiry.

"Tell me, fellows," I said, "you think Bobo ever really got any from her?"

They argued. The most responsive one said: "Naw, I don't think he'd ever really got any. He claimed he had, and he had her picture and he showed it to everybody and he talked big. He mighta been gettin' close, but I don't believe he'd ever been in her nest."

"Had he ever had any at all? Or was it just talk?"

"Oh, he'd got some. Yessir. He got some in Mississippi. He could do it, all right."

The boys remembered the scene at the store. With two girls they were in the '46 Ford going to a "jook." But the "jook" wasn't open yet, so they stopped in front of Bryant's.

"Mr. Bryant was O.K.," one of them said. "I played checkers with him. He let me have cokes on credit."

They told me how—with everybody horsing around in front of the store—Bobo displayed his white girl's picture and was dared to "try to get a date" with Carolyn Bryant.

"I told him not to go in there," an older boy said. "We watched him, and when he jumped in front o' Mrs. Bryant I run in and got him. He didn't mean no harm, but he didn't know where he was."

I asked them why, after the incident, they hadn't warned Bobo to leave Mississippi.

"I did," one of them insisted. "I told him to make tracks."

"I didn't think they'd come after him," another added. "I told him Mr. Bryant would beat his ass if he caught him around the store again. But I didn't think they'd come looking him up."

Elizabeth Wright is a good woman, a sharecropper's second wife with little education but much human understanding. She talked easily as we sat in a crowded kitchen in Argo, near Chicago.

"I feel partly responsible for the boy's death," she said. "He could'a been in Chicago when they come after him. I just didn't get the straight of what happened at the store. I've lived my life in the South, just like you, Mr. Huie. We both know how things are. From what I could worm out of the boys, it seemed like a kind'a prank. Bobo shouldn'a done it. I told him so; and Preacher told him so. The boys shouldn'a let him do it. But he didn't know what he was doing—and I guess I thought the white folks'd realize that. And when they didn't come lookin' for him right off, I figgered maybe they'd forget it."

Preacher said: "When they come and got him, I figgered they'd whup him. But I *nevah in this world* figgered they'd kill him. An' I can't figger yet what happened to make 'em *kill* that boy."

And in Mississippi Mr. Breland said to me: "They shouldn't have killed him. They should have striped him, told him to get the hell back Up Yonder. But they shouldn't have killed him. And they wouldn't have killed him except for Black Monday. The Supreme Court of the United States is responsible for the murder of Emmett Till."

"Maybe you and I are a little responsible, too," I said.

"No," he replied. "I don't think so. We know how things are. We have a workable way of life. It's those boys on the Supreme Court who want to go the unnatural and unconstitutional way. As a lawyer I respect the law. But I got no respect for the present members of the Court. They are responsible for the Till murder and for all the other murders we're bound to have."

There, for the objective mind, is the true story of the murder.

Emmett Till was not a *bad* youth. He can be called a *good* youth. You can call him a child—if you call 160-pound boys who have had sexual experience *children*. He was at the age when many youths are preoccupied with sex. He lived in an environment where he was "gettin' close" to sex with a white girl.

His conduct at the store was . . . reckless. Few would approve of it. Nothing in his experience had taught him to understand the risk of his "messin' around" with Carolyn Bryant.

I found no reason to criticize Caroyln's conduct. I met her in Mississippi. She impressed both me and my New York attorney as a responsible—and extraordinarily pretty—young woman. She tried to "prevent trouble." You don't have to take her word for it; the proof is in the facts. She saw Milam an hour after the incident. Had she told him, the reckoning would have come next day—not four days later.

Moreover, Negroes established that Bryant was "told" by a "Judas nigger." A Negro "crusader" is Dr. T. R. M. Howard, formerly of Mound Bayou, Mississippi, now of Chicago. Dr. Howard addresses fund-raising meetings in the North. His target in the Till case is the "Judas nigger."

"He was a two-bit nigger who wanted four bits' worth of credit," Dr. Howard exclaims.

So what can Carolyn Bryant be blamed for? At the trial she offered to testify that Bobo used "obscene words" to her. This may or may not have been true; but it was immaterial. She did not so testify before the jury.

Roy Bryant is pathetic. He's a scrapper, but no killer. He "had" to "whip the niggah's ass." But I don't believe Bryant would have killed him, even after the boasts about the white girl.

There is no reason to believe that Milam and Bryant intended to kill. Had Bobo acted as they expected him to act, he would have escaped with a "whipping." It would have been brutal, since Milam learned to "pistol-whip" in the Army. But Bobo would have escaped severe injury.

Some persons point to the time of the abduction—2 A.M.—as evidence that Milam intended to murder him. The time has no significance. These men are accustomed to working all night. Mechanical cotton pickers are operated until the dew falls. Then they are serviced at night to have them ready to operate at sunup. Trucks run all night.

Bryant had gone to bed. Milam selected the time because (1) he had just learned of the incident, (2) it was a convenient time for him, and (3) it was the "best time to catch the niggah." Had Milam and Bryant arrived at Preacher's much earlier they would have "missed him." For it was Saturday night and the boys didn't get home from Greenwood until 1 A.M.

Had Milam intended to kill he wouldn't have waited until daylight to obtain the gin fan. He was observed getting the fan. Also: the drive to and from the Big River, looking for a "scary bluff," was not the action of men determined to murder. Returning from that drive, Milam passed near the spot where he later obtained the fan. After he decided to kill, to obtain the fan he doubled back on a route he had already traveled.

Moreover, had Milam from the start intended to kill, he would not have taken the youth to his own tool shed. He would have driven directly to the river and been done with his crime before daylight.

So the decision to kill was Milam's, and it was made in the tool shed. That Bobo showed Milam his white girl and made his claims is in character. This is what Bobo had been doing for a week.

The murder resulted from coincidence. Just as nothing in his experience had equipped him to understand the recklessness of his prank in the store, so had nothing equipped Bobo to understand a character like Big Milam. Until he reached the riverbank, Bobo believed Milam was bluffing. Milam said: "I guess he'd just never run into anybody like me." He hadn't.

Bobo showed the girl's picture once too often. He showed it in the wrong place to the wrong man, too soon after the Supreme Court had decreed a change in the Delta "way of life."

Not once did I hear the term "wolf whistle." In the excitement at the store Carolyn Bryant didn't notice a whistle. Milam and Bryant knew nothing of a whistle. They abducted Bobo for what he "said" in the store; and Milam killed him, not for any act or word or whistle at the store, but for what Bobo said he did to a white girl in Chicago.

Nor did the Negro boys mention the wolf whistle. I finally asked them about it, after which they agreed that Bobo may have whistled, at the store. But it had not struck them as important.

Yet the case is known as The Wolf-Whistle Murder Case. Such is the yearning for simplicity.

When *Look* published some of these revelations, the reactions were startling.

The Associated Press refused to transmit comment. The assumption was that I had tape recordings; that *Look* published the material as a "calculated risk" . . . that we expected to be sued . . . that any paper which "touched" the story would risk being party to a suit.

AP reporters reached Milam, and when he said he never heard of Huie, AP carried his quotes without reservation. It occurred to no one that Milam was making comments I wrote for him.

Then came the Southern onslaught. An example is a columnist for a dozen newspapers, a confused, embittered man named John Temple Graves. His attacks on me and *Look* were savage.

". . . A Southern renegade . . . a masterly and dastardly imaginist . . . telling this story as he imagines it . . . the defendants are made guilty in unknowable detail, with no chance overlooked to incite feeling against Mississippi and the South. . . . Nothing in the Huie recital lets the reader know a jury acquitted these defendants . . . this shames the magazine world . . . write your protests to *Look* magazine, then fumigate your pen."

That Milam and Bryant and Carolyn Bryant sat across a table from me and *Look*'s attorney; that after I obtained the story, I purchased rights to portray them in a film; that I was assisted by able citizens of Mississippi—this was incomprehensible for Mr. Graves and those like him. Black Monday has unbalanced them.

When my lawyers finished with Mr. Graves and dictated his retraction, he was the Southern colonel who has smashed into a freight train. He still makes war on the windmills—but not on me.

The opposite extremists reacted like Mr. Graves. One Negro newspaper tried to promote a suit against me for "libeling a child and a race," for "confusing the racial conflict," for "giving comfort to the racists." A few white men felt I was "part of a plot to whitewash the killers and drag in sex."

To them I replied:

If I am *comforting* any racists, I wish you'd convince them of it so they'll quit trying to put me in jail. . . . I drew Emmett Till's portrait with the help of his mother
and his playmates. Witnesses heard the conversations. NAACP assisted me . . . . Roy
Wilkins told me that he and his wife read my story, found it "fair and reasonable."

Five thousand letters reached me. About half are appreciative.

The writers of a few of these appreciative letters, however, feel that the truth
justifies the murder, and these writers have sent money to Big Milam.

A fourth of the letters curse me as a "nigger-lover" and "traitor to the white
race." A significant number of these are from Illinois and New Jersey. The other
fourth curse me for the opposite reason: "for trying to make a Negro child into
something detestable."

I realized how diverse we are in the United States when television reporters
telephoned me from Northern cities where I have spoken. They wondered how
I can continue to live in the South. They assumed I am a pariah, that my home is
guarded, that Milam and the Ku Klux must be "looking" for me.

"You make me feel as if we are separated by an ocean," I told them. "My people
and I have lived in this county more than a century. This morning I walked to
the post office. This afternoon I played golf at the Decatur Country Club with the
club pro and two bankers. The lock on my house hasn't been used since the last
Yankee soldier went home in 1876. My neighbors don't care what I write. What
matters in my county is whether the fish are biting or the ducks are flying."

The disturbing reaction comes from a Negro woman writer in the North,
whom I respect. She wrote:

Your story is a disaster. The Till case has been of immense propaganda and fund-
raising value to Negroes and their white supporters in the race struggle. Most persons, other than the racists, could feel sorry for "the little colored boy who whistled at the white woman and then was lynched for it." Now you have spoiled the
image. Not only have you made Emmett Till into a less sympathetic character, but
after I read your account I felt sorry for *everybody:* for the murderers as well as the
brash young Negro. You knocked some of the crusading zeal out of me: I just
wanted to sit down and weep for the whole human race. But that's a luxury I can't
afford because I'm a Negro and I must fight. You *can* afford it: you can afford to
understand the tragedy of both the executioner and the victim. But I can't. So I
wish you had been just too busy to have bothered with the Till case. For while
you did not intend it, the effect of your effort has been to discourage me and to
neutralize a valuable propaganda weapon in the fight for racial justice.

To whom I replied:

Humanity needs crusaders; Causes need partisans. Crusaders and partisans prefer propaganda as their weapon, not truth. But humanity also needs understanding. And truth, not propaganda, promotes understanding.

To me a brash young Negro preoccupied with sex is not an unsympathetic character. And when I explain a murderer, I am not seeking forgiveness for him; I am seeking a cure, for him and for those who come after him. Will cancer be cured by making propaganda against it?

You have described the effect of my story on you; but you may be wrong in your evaluation of its effect on the "public." We truth-seekers have more respect for the "public" than you propagandists have. Your propaganda presented this case as the wanton murder of a "child" by apes. My truth presents it as the deliberate murder of a youth by a man who is not an ape, but who was sober, who holds a commission in the United States Army Reserve, and who, when he fired an expanding bullet through Emmett Till's head, thought he was doing *right*. And many Americans, not all of them Southern, have commended him.

Now I ask you: which of our pictures of this murder is the more disturbing? I have two thousand letters from thoughtful Americans who say that the crime, in the light of what I have written, is "even more terrible . . . shattering . . . awful in that one man, on such provocation from a youth, should arrogate to himself the power of life and death over a human being."

Wanting to weep for the whole human race need not be a disastrous impulse, even for a crusader. You'll regain any zeal you say I have knocked out of you. You may even come to regard truth as an effective weapon in crusades. [. . .]

A year after the Till murder I went back to Mississippi. I met Milam in Ruleville. It was during cotton-picking, and he was servicing two mechanical pickers which were running in his field 9 miles from Ruleville. He was driving the same Chevrolet pickup in which he hauled Bobo to his death. I got in the pickup and we drove to his field. We sat talking and watching the pickers crawl up and down the rows.

"I see white men are driving your pickers," I said.

"Yeah," he replied, "I don't work niggahs no more. They're leaving here by the thousands, going to Chicago."

After the murder Negroes boycotted the Milam-Bryant stores, forced their sale or closing. When Roy Bryant closed his store, he couldn't get a job. Now he was going to welding school under the GI Bill of Rights, drawing about $100 a month from the government. Had he been convicted of a felony, he'd have been ineligible for this assistance.

"Roy'll have it tough," Milam said. "It takes a long time to learn welding, and by the time you've learned it, you've ruined your eyes."

With the stores gone, Milam turned to farming. He was shocked when landowners who had contributed to his defense declined to rent to him. In all of Tallahatchie County—the county which had "swarmed" to his defense—he couldn't rent land.

Along with land, he needed a bank loan or "furnish" to put in a cotton crop. Even though he owned more equipment than the average renter, banks refused to "furnish" him.

When Milam had nowhere else to turn, John Whitten helped him rent 217 acres in Sunflower County; and the Bank of Webb, in which Whitten is on the loan committee, "furnished" him 4,000 dollars.

(John Whitten told me: "Yes, I helped him. He was a good soldier. In a mine field at night when other men were running and leaving you to do the killing, J. W. Milam stood with you. When a man like that comes to you and his kids are hungry, you don't turn him down."[)]

"I had a lot of friends a year ago," Milam continued. "They contributed to my defense fund—or they said they did. Bankers and plantation owners slapped me on the back. I got letters from all over the country congratulating me on my 'fine Americanism.' Now . . . I don't get those letters any more and bankers are too busy to talk to me. Everything has gone against me—even the dry weather which has hurt my cotton. I'm living in a share-crop house with no water in it. My wife and kids are having it tough."

I watched him. He looked older, confused, uncertain. The poor, landless "redneck" with the mark of Cain on him.

"Tell me this, J. W.," I said. "When you think back on that dark night of August 28, 1955 . . . the night you loaded the Chicago boy into this pickup and took him down to the river and killed him and threw him in . . . you ever have any regrets?"

He shook his head.

"No," he answered slowly, "I ain't sorry. What else could I'a done under the circumstances? Everybody thinks I done right. So I ain't sorry. But I guess it was about the unluckiest night of my life. You know why? Well, it's som'pin I learned. You can do som'pin that everybody says you ought'a done. Like killin' a German . . . or killin' a niggah who gets out'a place. Everybody slaps you on the back for it. Hell, they give you a medal! Then . . . after a while . . . those same folks won't come around you . . . they won't *even like* you . . . because you done it."

He inhaled a long breath on his cigarette, then blew smoke out the window.

"It's a goddamn funny thing, ain't it?" he said. "They want you to do it. They are glad you done it. Then they don't like you for doing it. . . . Crazy goddamn situation, ain't it?"

From *For Us, the Living*
Mrs. Medgar Evers [Myrlie Evers-Williams] (1967)

From 1995 to 1999, Myrlie Evers-Williams, a long-time civil rights activist, served as the chairperson of the National Association for the Advancement of Colored People. In 1963, she was married to Medgar Evers, an NAACP activist who in November of that year was shot by a white assassin named Byron De La Beckwith. Despite the national and international spotlight put on the case, Beckwith twice escaped conviction after mistrials. Finally, in 1994 (and due in great part to the diligence of Evers-Williams), he was convicted of first-degree murder. In the following excerpt from her autobiography, Evers-Williams not only recounts her slain husband's efforts to track down evidence to convict the murderers of Emmett Till, but she also offers up her own meditations on the meaning and import of the crime.

Even before that predictable end [when a grand jury refused to indict the men who killed black farmer Lamar Smith for attempting to vote], almost as though the state of Mississippi had officially declared an open season on Negroes, murderers struck again. This time the victim was a fourteen-year-old Negro boy from Chicago, Emmett Till, visiting his uncle in the Mississippi Delta. The purported reason for the killing, widely disseminated by the press, was that Till had asked for a date with a married white woman seven years his senior.

There were, of course, embellishments on this theme, though no one ever charged the youth with more than a lewd suggestion or a "wolf whistle." But because of the overtones of sex, by which Mississippi often justifies its use of violence against male Negroes, it could have been just another Mississippi lynching. It wasn't. This one somehow struck a spark of indignation that ignited protests around the world. Kidnaped forcibly in the middle of the night, pistol-whipped, stripped naked, shot through the head with a .45-caliber Colt automatic, barb-wired to a seventy-four-pound cotton gin fan, and dumped into twenty feet of water in the Tallahatchie River, young Emmett Till became in death what he could never have been in life: a rallying cry and a cause.

Two white men were arrested for the sadistic murder: J. W. Milam, thirty-six, and his half-brother, Roy Bryant, twenty-four. Both were identified as the men who took young Till at gun-point from his uncle's home. Both admitted having taken him but only for the purpose of frightening him. Indicted and tried for murder in Sumner, Mississippi, they were acquitted by an all-white jury that deliberated one hour and seven minutes. Two months later a grand jury in Greenwood refused even to indict them for the abduction both had publicly admitted. Two months after that, in case anyone was still in doubt, reporter William Bradford Huie, in an article in *Look,* quoted both men on the exact details of the murder they now calmly described. Acquitted once, they could not, of course, be tried again.

These were sensational climaxes to a sensational murder, but, even before they were reached, the Till case attracted the kind of world and national attention Medgar had brooded about those many months before when he had speculated privately about a Mississippi Mau Mau. For weeks before the murder trial, newsmen from all over the country probed the psyche of the Delta, interviewing whites and Negroes, turning up some of the conditions of the benighted area. Angry and frustrated over this particularly vicious killing, Medgar made it his mission to see that word of it was spread as widely and accurately as possible. Publicizing the crime and the subsequent defeat of justice became a major NAACP effort.

Those were weeks of frenzied activities, weeks of special danger, for Medgar made many trips to the Delta, investigating, questioning, searching out witnesses before they could be frightened into silence. There were wild night drives to Memphis, where witnesses were put on planes for safer places until their presence would be needed at the trial. And, more than once, there were chases along the long, straight, unlighted highways that led from the Delta back to Jackson.

Medgar was by this time well known throughout the state, and his car was often sighted by police and sheriff's men minutes after he entered a Delta county. Frequently he was followed throughout his trips around the Delta. He had already begun to make it a practice to return to Jackson each night if possible, as much for the safety of the people he would otherwise have stayed with as for himself. Several times, when he started back after dark, he had to jam the accelerator to the floorboard to "shake the car's tail," as he put it, in the faces of anonymous pursuers.

Medgar never pretended he wasn't frightened at such experiences, though he often concealed the details from me. Usually I found out later, when the subject came up at the office with someone else or when a friend who had been with him let the secret drop. There was no hiding the extra precautions he sometimes took. When Emmett Till's body was found, Medgar and Amzie Moore, an NAACP leader from Cleveland, Mississippi, set off from our house one morning with Ruby Hurley, down from Birmingham, to investigate. All of them were dressed in overalls and beat-up shoes, with Mrs. Hurley wearing a red bandanna over her head. To complete the disguise, Amzie had borrowed a car with license plates from a Delta county. Watching them leave, knowing the tension and hate that gripped the Delta, I lived through the day in a daze of fear until their safe return that night.

While Medgar worked in the Delta, I was swamped at the office with telephone calls from the press, from friends, from unknown Negroes who wanted to know what was happening. I had to buy and read six or seven newspapers a day, clipping every word about the Till case for our own files and for the national office in New York. If Medgar's name had been mentioned in one of the papers, I could anticipate a spate of obscene and abusive phone calls.

Looking back, I know that from that time on I never lost the fear that Medgar himself would be killed. It was like a physical presence inside me, now subdued, now alive and aching, a parasite of terror that woke to remind me of its existence whenever things were particularly bad. Medgar would leave the house for one of his trips to the Delta, and I could feel my stomach contract in cold fear that I would never see him again. When he was home, when he spent a whole day in the office, it was like a reprieve, for I somehow had the absurd idea that nothing could happen to him if we were together. It was about this time that I began trying to live each day for itself, to count as special blessings those days when I knew he was in no special danger. It is a philosophy more easily preached than practiced, but I made a thousand conscious attempts to live it in the years that followed, knowing that the only alternative was some kind of breakdown.

I never completely understood what it was that made the murder of Emmett Till so different from the ones that had preceded it. In part, I suppose it was his youth. Medgar was convinced that the existence of our office in Jackson and the enormous efforts of the NAACP to get out the news made a tremendous difference. Whatever the answer, it was the murder of this fourteen-year-old out-of-state visitor that touched off the world-wide clamor and cast the glare of a world spotlight on Mississippi's racism. Ironically, the deaths of George Lee and Lamar Smith, both directly connected with the struggle for civil rights, had caused nothing like the public attention attracted by the Till case.

And perhaps that was the explanation. George Lee and Lamar Smith had been murdered for doing what everyone knew Negroes were murdered for doing. Neither murder had the shock effect of the brutal slaying of a fourteen-year-old boy who had certainly done nothing more than act fresh. The Till case, in a way, was the story in microcosm of every Negro in Mississippi. For it was the proof that even youth was no defense against the ultimate terror, that lynching was still the final means by which white supremacy would be upheld, that whites could still murder Negroes with impunity, and that the upper- and middle-class white people of the state would uphold such killings through their police and newspapers and courts of law. It was the proof that Mississippi had no intention of changing its ways, that no Negro's life was really safe, and that the federal government was either powerless, as it claimed, or simply unwilling to step in to erase this blot on the nation's reputation for decency and justice. It was the proof, if proof were needed, that there would be no real change in Mississippi until the rest of the country decided that change there must be and then forced it.

From *Coming of Age in Mississippi*
Anne Moody (1968)

> Anne Moody's *Coming of Age in Mississippi* is considered one of the classic texts of the civil rights movement. A daughter of sharecroppers, Moody was fifteen years old when Emmett Till was murdered, and in her memoir she writes movingly of the effect his lynching had on her understanding of the racial animosity in her home state. A few years later, she became active in the civil rights movement while attending Tougaloo College in Jackson, where she was one of the leading organizers of the Congress of Racial Equality (CORE) and an active participant in movements led by the NAACP and the Student Non-Violent Coordinating Committee (SNCC). She was also involved in the famous Woolworth's lunch counter sit-in demonstration in Jackson in 1963 and later that year joined the March on Washington. Winner of the Brotherhood Award from the National Council of Christians and Jews and the Best Book of the Year Award from the National Library Association, *Coming of Age in Mississippi* continues to be one of the most widely read memoirs of the movement.

Not only did I enter high school with a new name, but also with a completely new insight into the life of Negroes in Mississippi. I was now working for one of the meanest white women in town, and a week before school started Emmett Till was killed.

Up until his death, I had heard of Negroes found floating in a river or dead somewhere with their bodies riddled with bullets. But I didn't know the mystery behind these killings then. I remember once when I was only seven I heard Mama and one of my aunts talking about some Negro who had been beaten to death. "Just like them low-down skunks killed him they will do the same to us," Mama had said. When I asked her who killed the man and why, she said, "An Evil Spirit killed him. You gotta be a good girl or it will kill you too." So since I was seven, I had lived in fear of the "Evil Spirit." It took me eight years to learn what that spirit was.

I was coming from school the evening I heard about Emmett Till's death. There was a whole group of us, girls and boys, walking down the road headed home. A group of about six high school boys were walking a few paces ahead of me and several other girls. We were laughing and talking about something that had happened in school that day. However, the six boys in front of us weren't talking very loud. Usually they kept up so much noise. But today they were just walking and talking among themselves. All of a sudden they began to shout at each other.

"Man, what in the hell do you mean?"

"What I mean is these goddamned white folks is gonna start some shit here you just watch!"

"That boy wasn't but fourteen years old and they killed him. Now what kin a fourteen-year-old boy do with a white woman? What if he did whistle at her, he might have thought the whore was pretty."

"Look at all these white men here that's fucking over our women. Everybody knows it too and what's done about that? Look how many white babies we got walking around in our neighborhoods. Their mama's ain't white either. That boy was from Chicago, shit, everybody fuck everybody up there. He probably didn't even think of the bitch as white."

What they were saying shocked me. I knew all of those boys and I had never heard them talk like that. We walked on behind them for a while listening. Questions about who was killed, where, and why started running through my mind. I walked up to one of the boys.

"Eddie, what boy was killed?"

"Moody, where've you been?" he asked me. "Everybody talking about that fourteen-year-old boy who was killed in Greenwood by some white men. You don't know nothing that's going on besides what's in them books of yours, huh?"

Standing there before the rest of the girls, I felt so stupid. It was then that I realized I really didn't know what was going on all around me. It wasn't that I was dumb. It was just that ever since I was nine, I'd had to work after school and do my lessons on lunch hour. I never had time to learn anything, to hang around with people my own age. And you never were told anything by adults.

That evening when I stopped off at the house on my way to Mrs. Burke's, Mama was singing. Any other day she would have been yelling at Adline and Junior them to take off their school clothes. I wondered if she knew about Emmett Till. The way she was singing she had something on her mind and it wasn't pleasant either.

> *I got a shoe, you got a shoe,*
> *All of God's chillun got shoes;*
> *When I get to hebben, I'm gonna put on my shoes,*
> *And gonna tromp all over God's hebben.*
> *When I get to hebben I'm gonna put on my shoes,*
> *And gonna walk all over God's hebben.*

Mama was dishing up beans like she didn't know anyone was home. Adline, Junior, and James had just thrown their books down and sat themselves at the table. I didn't usually eat before I went to work. But I wanted to ask Mama about Emmett Till. So I ate and thought of some way of asking her.

"These beans are some good, Mama," I said, trying to sense her mood.

"Why is you eating anyway? You gonna be late for work. You know how Miss Burke is," she said to me.

"I don't have much to do this evening. I kin get it done before I leave work," I said.

The conversation stopped after that. Then Mama started humming that song again.

> *When I get to hebben, I'm gonna put on my shoes,*
> *And gonna tromp all over God's hebben.*

She put a plate on the floor for Jennie Ann and Jerry.

"Jennie Ann! you and Jerry sit down here and eat and don't put beans all over this floor."

Ralph, the baby, started crying, and she went in the bedroom to give him his bottle. I got up and followed her.

"Mama, did you hear about that fourteen-year-old Negro boy who was killed a little over a week ago by some white men?" I asked her.

"Where did you hear that?" she said angrily.

"Boy, everybody really thinks I am dumb or deaf or something. I heard Eddie them talking about it this evening coming from school."

"Eddie them better watch how they go around here talking. These white folks git a hold of it they gonna be in trouble," she said.

"What are they gonna be in trouble about, Mama? People got a right to talk, ain't they?"

"You go on to work before you is late. And don't you let on like you know nothing about that boy being killed before Miss Burke them. Just do your work like you don't know nothing," she said. "That boy's a lot better off in heaven than he is here," she continued and then started singing again.

On my way to Mrs. Burke's that evening, Mama's words kept running through my mind. "Just do your work like you don't know nothing." "Why is Mama acting so scared?" I thought. "And what if Mrs. Burke knew we knew? Why must I pretend I don't know? Why are these people killing Negroes? What did Emmett Till do besides whistle at that woman?"

By the time I got to work, I had worked my nerves up some. I was shaking as I walked up on the porch. "Do your work like you don't know nothing." But once I got inside, I couldn't have acted normal if Mrs. Burke were paying me to be myself.

I was so nervous, I spent most of the evening avoiding them going about the house dusting and sweeping. Everything went along fairly well until dinner was served.

"Don, Wayne, and Mama, y'all come on to dinner. Essie, you can wash up the pots and dishes in the sink now. Then after dinner you won't have as many," Mrs. Burke called to me.

If I had the power to mysteriously disappear at that moment, I would have. They used the breakfast table in the kitchen for most of their meals. The dining room was only used for Sunday dinner or when they had company. I wished they had company tonight so they could eat in the dining room while I was at the kitchen sink.

"I forgot the bread," Mrs. Burke said when they were all seated. "Essie, will you cut it and put it on the table for me?"

I took the cornbread, cut it in squares, and put it on a small round dish. Just as I was about to set it on the table, Wayne yelled at the cat. I dropped the plate and the bread went all over the floor.

"Never mind, Essie," Mrs. Burke said angrily as she got up and got some white bread from the breadbox.

I didn't say anything. I picked up the cornbread from around the table and went back to the dishes. As soon as I got to the sink, I dropped a saucer on the floor and broke it. Didn't anyone say a word until I had picked up the pieces.

"Essie, I bought some new cleanser today. It's setting on the bathroom shelf. See if it will remove the stains in the tub," Mrs. Burke said.

I went to the bathroom to clean the tub. By the time I got through with it, it was snow white. I spent a whole hour scrubbing it. I had removed the stains in no time but I kept scrubbing until they finished dinner.

When they had finished and gone into the living room as usual to watch TV, Mrs. Burke called me to eat. I took a clean plate out of the cabinet and sat down. Just as I was putting the first forkful of food in my mouth, Mrs. Burke entered the kitchen.

"Essie, did you hear about that fourteen-year-old boy who was killed in Greenwood?" she asked me, sitting down in one of the chairs opposite me.

"No, I didn't hear that," I answered, almost choking on the food.

"Do you know why he was killed?" she asked and I didn't answer.

"He was killed because he got out of his place with a white woman. A boy from Mississippi would have known better than that. This boy was from Chicago. Negroes up North have no respect for people. They think they can get away with anything. He just came to Mississippi and put a whole lot of notions in the boys' heads here and stirred up a lot of trouble," she said passionately.

"How old are you, Essie?" she asked me after a pause.

"Fourteen. I will soon be fifteen though," I said.

"See, that boy was just fourteen too. It's a shame he had to die so soon." She was so red in the face, she looked as if she was on fire.

When she left the kitchen I sat there with my mouth open and my food untouched. I couldn't have eaten now if I were starving. "Just do your work like you don't know nothing" ran through my mind again and I began washing the dishes.

I went home shaking like a leaf on a tree. For the first time out of all her trying, Mrs. Burke had made me feel like rotten garbage. Many times she had tried to instill fear within me and subdue me and had given up. But when she talked about Emmett Till there was something in her voice that sent chills and fear all over me.

Before Emmett Till's murder, I had known the fear of hunger, hell, and the Devil. But now there was a new fear known to me—the fear of being killed just because I was black. This was the worst of my fears. I knew once I got food, the fear of starving to death would leave. I also was told that if I were a good girl, I wouldn't have to fear the Devil or hell. But I didn't know what one had to do or not do as a Negro not to be killed. Probably just being a Negro period was enough, I thought.

A few days later, I went to work and Mrs. Burke had about eight women over for tea. They were all sitting around in the living room when I got there. She told me she was having a "guild meeting," and asked me to help her serve the cookies and tea.

After helping her, I started cleaning the house. I always swept the hallway and porch first. As I was sweeping the hall, I could hear them talking. When I heard the word "nigger," I stopped sweeping and listened. Mrs. Burke must have sensed this, because she suddenly came to the door.

"Essie, finish the hall and clean the bathroom," she said hesitantly. "Then you can go for the day. I am not making dinner tonight." Then she went back in the living room with the rest of the ladies.

Before she interrupted my listening, I had picked up the words "NAACP" and "that organization." Because they were talking about niggers, I knew NAACP had something to do with Negroes. All that night I kept wondering what could that NAACP mean?

Later when I was sitting in the kitchen at home doing my lessons, I decided to ask Mama. It was about twelve-thirty. Everyone was in bed but me. When Mama came in to put some milk in Ralph's bottle, I said, "Mama, what do NAACP mean?"

"Where did you git that from?" she asked me, spilling milk all over the floor.

"Mrs. Burke had a meeting tonigh—"

"What kind of meeting?" she asked, cutting me off.

"I don't know. She had some women over—she said it was a guild meeting," I said.

"A guild meeting," she repeated.

"Yes, they were talking about Negroes and I heard some woman say 'that NAACP' and another 'that organization,' meaning the same thing."

"What else did they say?" she asked me.

"That's all I heard. Mrs. Burke must have thought I was listening, so she told me to clean the bathroom and leave."

"Don't you ever mention that word around Mrs. Burke or no other white person, you heah! Finish your lesson and cut that light out and go to bed," Mama said angrily and left the kitchen.

"With a Mama like that you'll never learn anything," I thought as I got into bed. All night long I thought about Emmet[t] Till and the NAACP. I even got up to look up NAACP in my little concise dictionary. But I didn't find it.

The next day at school, I decided to ask my homeroom teacher Mrs. Rice the meaning of NAACP. When the bell sounded for lunch, I remained in my seat as the other students left the room.

"Are you going to spend your lunch hour studying again today, Moody?" Mrs. Rice asked me.

"Can I ask you a question, Mrs. Rice?" I asked her.

"You *may* ask me a question, yes, but I don't know if you *can* or not," she said.

"What does the word NAACP mean?" I asked.

"Why do you want to know?"

"The lady I worked for had a meeting and I overheard the word mentioned."

"What else did you hear?"

"Nothing. I didn't know what NAACP meant, that's all." I felt like I was on the witness stand or something.

"Well, next time your boss has another meeting you listen more carefully. NAACP is a Negro organization that was established a long time ago to help Negroes gain a few basic rights," she said.

"What's it gotta do with the Emmett Till murder?" I asked.

"They are trying to get a conviction in Emmett Till's case. You see the NAACP is trying to do a lot for the Negroes and get the right to vote for Negroes in the South. I shouldn't be telling you all this. And don't you dare breathe a word of what I said. It could cost me my job if word got out I was teaching my students such. I gotta go to lunch and you should go outside too because it's nice and sunny out today," she said leaving the room. "We'll talk more when I have time."

About a week later, Mrs. Rice had me over for Sunday dinner, and I spent about five hours with her. Within that time, I digested a good meal and accumulated a whole new pool of knowledge about Negroes being butchered and slaughtered by whites in the South. After Mrs. Rice had told me all this, I felt like the lowest animal on earth. At least when other animals (hogs, cows, etc.) were killed by man, they were used as food. But when man was butchered or killed by man, in the case of Negroes by whites, they were left lying on a road or found floating in a river or something.

Mrs. Rice got to be something like a mother to me. She told me anything I wanted to know. And made me promise that I would keep all this information she was passing on to me to myself. She said she couldn't, rather didn't, want to talk about these things to the other teachers, that they would tell Mr. Willis and she would be fired. At the end of that year she was fired. I never found out why. I haven't seen her since then.

From *Soul on Ice*
Eldridge Cleaver (1968)

Raised in the Watts district of Los Angeles, Eldridge Cleaver spent a troubled youth in and out of juvenile reformatories. In 1954, he was convicted of marijuana possession and sent to Soledad State Prison, and in 1957, soon after serving out his two-year sentence, he was convicted of rape with intent to commit murder and sentenced to fourteen years at Folsom State Prison. While there, Cleaver joined the Black Muslims, and in 1965 began writing the autobiographical sketches, political commentaries, and cultural analyses that would eventually become *Soul on Ice.* Because his work began to appear in the leftist magazine *Ramparts* while he was still in prison, Cleaver garnered the support of influential literary figures who eventually helped secure his parole in 1966. *Soul on Ice* was an immediate best-seller, but Cleaver was not able to enjoy fully the success and prominence the book could have brought him. After an abortive attempt to run for president on the Peace and Freedom party ticket in 1968, Cleaver was convicted of breaking parole, fled the country, and remained abroad until 1975. In the following excerpt, Cleaver recounts how he learned of Till's murder while serving his two-year sentence in Soledad and how the details of that murder not only triggered a nervous breakdown but also paved the way for his future crimes.

From our discussion, which began that evening and has never yet ended, we went on to notice how thoroughly, as a matter of course, a black growing up in America is indoctrinated with the white race's standard of beauty. Not that the whites made a conscious, calculated effort to do this, we thought, but since they constituted the majority the whites brainwashed the blacks by the very processes the whites employed to indoctrinate themselves with their own group standards. It intensified my frustrations to know that I was indoctrinated to see the white woman as more beautiful and desirable than my own black woman. It drove me into books seeking light on the subject. In Richard Wright's *Native Son,* I found Bigger Thomas and a keen insight into the problem.

My interest in this area persisted undiminished and then, in 1955, an event took place in Mississippi which turned me inside out: Emmett Till, a young Negro down from Chicago on a visit, was murdered, allegedly for flirting with a white woman. He had been shot, his head crushed from repeated blows with a blunt instrument, and his badly decomposed body was recovered from the river with a heavy weight on it. I was, of course, angry over the whole bit, but one day I saw in a magazine a picture of the white woman with whom Emmett Till was said to have flirted. While looking at the picture, I felt that little tension in the center of my chest I experience when a woman appeals to me. Here was a woman who had caused the death of a black, possibly because, when he looked at her, he also felt the same tensions of lust and desire in his chest—and probably for the same general reasons that I felt then. It was all unacceptable to me. I looked at the picture again and again, and in spite of everything and against my will and the hate I felt for the woman and all that she represented, she appealed to me. I flew into a rage at myself, at America, at white women, at the history that had placed those tensions of lust and desire in my chest.

Two days later, I had a "nervous breakdown." For several days I ranted and raved against the white race, against white women in particular, against white America in general. When I came to myself, I was locked in a padded cell with not even the vaguest memory of how I got there. All I could recall was an eternity of pacing back and forth in the cell, preaching to the unhearing walls.

I had several sessions with a psychiatrist. His conclusion was that I hated my mother. How he arrived at this conclusion I'll never know, because he knew nothing about my mother; and when he'd ask me questions I would answer him with absurd lies. What revolted me about him was that he had heard me denouncing the whites, yet each time he interviewed me he deliberately guided the conversation back to my family life, to my childhood. That in itself was all right, but he deliberately blocked all my attempts to bring out the racial question, and he made it clear that he was not interested in my attitude toward whites. This was a Pandora's box he did not care to open. After I ceased my diatribes against the whites, I was let out of the hospital, back into the general inmate population just as if nothing had happened. I continued to brood over these events and over the dynamics of race relations in America.

During this period I was concentrating my reading in the field of economics. Having previously dabbled in the theories and writings of Rousseau, Thomas Paine, and Voltaire, I had added a little polish to my iconoclastic stance, without, however, bothering too much to understand their affirmative positions. In economics, because everybody seemed to find it necessary to attack and condemn

Karl Marx in their writings, I sought out his books, and although he kept me with a headache, I took him for my authority. I was not prepared to understand him, but I was able to see in him a thoroughgoing critique and condemnation of capitalism. It was like taking medicine for me to find that, indeed, American capitalism deserved all the hatred and contempt that I felt for it in my heart. This had a positive, stabilizing effect upon me—to an extent because I was not about to become stable—and it diverted me from my previous preoccupation: morbid broodings on the black man and the white woman. Pursuing my readings into the history of socialism, I read, with very little understanding, some of the passionate, exhortatory writings of Lenin; and I fell in love with Bakunin and Nechayev's *Catechism of the Revolutionist*—the principles of which, along with some of Machiavelli's advice, I sought to incorporate into my own behavior. I took the *Catechism* for my bible and, standing on a one-man platform that had nothing to do with the reconstruction of society, I began consciously incorporating these principles into my daily life, to employ tactics of ruthlessness in my dealings with everyone with whom I came into contact. And I began to look at white America through these new eyes.

Somehow I arrived at the conclusion that, as a matter of principle, it was of paramount importance for me to have an antagonistic, ruthless attitude toward white women. The term *outlaw* appealed to me and at the time my parole date was drawing near, I considered myself to be mentally free—I was an "outlaw." I had stepped outside of the white man's law, which I repudiated with scorn and self-satisfaction. I became a law unto myself—my own legislature, my own supreme court, my own executive. At the moment I walked out of the prison gate, my feelings toward white women in general could be summed up in the following lines:

To a White Girl

I love you
Because you're white,
Not because you're charming
Or bright.
Your whiteness
Is a silky thread
Snaking through my thoughts
In redhot patterns
Of lust and desire.

I hate you
Because you're white,

Your white meat
Is nightmare food.
White is
The skin of Evil.
You're my Moby Dick,
White Witch,
Symbol of the rope and hanging tree,
Of the burning cross.
Loving you thus
And hating you so,
My heart is torn in two.
Crucified.

I became a rapist. To refine my technique and *modus operandi,* I started out by practicing on black girls in the ghetto—in the black ghetto where dark and vicious deeds appear not as aberrations or deviations from the norm, but as part of the sufficiency of the Evil of a day—and when I considered myself smooth enough, I crossed the tracks and sought out white prey. I did this consciously, deliberately, willfully, methodically—though looking back I see that I was in a frantic, wild, and completely abandoned frame of mind.

Rape was an insurrectionary act. It delighted me that I was defying and trampling upon the white man's law, upon his system of values, and that I was defiling his women—and this point, I believe, was the most satisfying to me because I was very resentful over the historical fact of how the white man has used the black woman. I felt I was getting revenge. From the site of the act of rape, consternation spreads outwardly in concentric circles. I wanted to send waves of consternation throughout the white race. Recently, I came upon a quotation from one of LeRoi Jones' poems, taken from his book *The Dead Lecturer:*

> A cult of death need of the simple striking arm under the street lamp. The cutters from under their rented earth. Come up, black dada nihilismus. Rape the white girls. Rape their fathers. Cut the mothers' throats.

I have lived those lines and I know that if I had not been apprehended I would have slit some white throats. There are, of course, many young blacks out there right now who are slitting white throats and raping the white girl. They are not doing this because they read LeRoi Jones' poetry, as some of his critics seem to believe. Rather, LeRoi is expressing the funky facts of life.

After I returned to prison, I took a long look at myself and, for the first time in my life, admitted that I was wrong, that I had gone astray—astray not so much from the white man's law as from being human, civilized—for I could not approve the act of rape. Even though I had some insight into my own motivations, I did not feel justified. I lost my self-respect. My pride as a man dissolved and my whole fragile moral structure seemed to collapse, completely shattered.

That is why I started to write. To save myself.

I realized that no one could save me but myself. The prison authorities were both uninterested and unable to help me. I had to seek out the truth and unravel the snarled web of my motivations. I had to find out who I am and what I want to be, what type of man I should be, and what I could do to become the best of which I was capable. I understood that what had happened to me had also happened to countless other blacks and it would happen to many, many more.

I learned that I had been taking the easy way out, running away from problems. I also learned that it is easier to do evil than it is to do good. And I have been terribly impressed by the youth of America, black and white. I am proud of them because they have reaffirmed my faith in humanity. I have come to feel what must be love for the young people of America and I want to be part of the good and greatness that they want for all people. From my prison cell, I have watched America slowly coming awake. It is not fully awake yet, but there is soul in the air and everywhere I see beauty. I have watched the sit-ins, the freedom rides, the Mississippi Blood Summers, demonstrations all over the country, the FSM movement, the teach-ins, and the mounting protest over Lyndon Strangelove's foreign policy—all of this, the thousands of little details, show me it is time to straighten up and fly right. That is why I decided to concentrate on my writings and efforts in this area. We are a very sick country—I, perhaps, am sicker than most. But I accept that. I told you in the beginning that I am extremist by nature—so it is only right that I should be extremely sick.

I was very familiar with the Eldridge who came to prison, but that Eldridge no longer exists. And the one I am now is in some ways a stranger to me. You may find this difficult to understand but it is very easy for one in prison to lose his sense of self. And if he has been undergoing all kinds of extreme, involved, and unregulated changes, then he ends up not knowing who he is. Take the point of being attractive to women. You can easily see how a man can lose his arrogance or certainty on that point while in prison! When he's in the free world, he gets constant feedback on how he looks from the number of female heads he turns when he walks down the street. In prison he gets only hate-stares and sour frowns. Years and years of bitter looks. Individuality is not nourished in prison, neither by the officials nor by the convicts. It is a deep hole out of which to climb.

What must be done, I believe, is that all these problems—particularly the sickness between the white woman and the black man—must be brought out into the open, dealt with and resolved. I know that the black man's sick attitude toward the white woman is a revolutionary sickness: it keeps him perpetually out of harmony with the system that is oppressing him. Many whites flatter themselves with the idea that the Negro male's lust and desire for the white dream girl is purely an esthetic attraction, but nothing could be farther from the truth. His motivation is often of such a bloody, hateful, bitter, and malignant nature that whites would really be hard pressed to find it flattering. I have discussed these points with prisoners who were convicted of rape, and their motivations are very plain. But they are very reluctant to discuss these things with white men who, by and large, make up the prison staffs. I believe that in the experience of these men lies the knowledge and wisdom that must be utilized to help other youngsters who are heading in the same direction. I think all of us, the entire nation, will be better off if we bring it all out front. A lot of people's feelings will be hurt, but that is the price that must be paid.

It may be that I can harm myself by speaking frankly and directly, but I do not care about that at all. Of course I want to get out of prison, badly, but I shall get out some day. I am more concerned with what I am going to be after I get out. I know that by following the course which I have charted I will find my salvation. If I had followed the path laid down for me by the officials, I'd undoubtedly have long since been out of prison—but I'd be less of a man. I'd be weaker and less certain of where I want to go, what I want to do, and how to go about it.

The price of hating other human beings is loving oneself less.

From *The River of No Return: The Autobiography of a Black Militant and the Life and Death of SNCC*
Cleveland Sellers (with Robert Terrell; 1973)

A native of South Carolina, Cleveland Sellers was only twelve years old when Emmett Till was murdered. In this brief excerpt from his autobiography, Sellers tells how Till's death profoundly impacted him. His memory of the newspaper photos of Till's bloated corpse coincides with many other memories from the period, especially from young adults. As the subtitle to his autobiography suggests, Sellers was an active member of SNCC and a self-styled black militant.

The atrocity that affected me the most was Emmett Till's lynching. Emmett Till, a fourteen-year-old black youth, was lynched in Money, Mississippi, on August 28, 1955. The grapevine carried all the details of his tragic death. Emmett was spending the summer with relatives in Mississippi. Being from the North, he was not familiar with the "folkways and mores" of the area he was visiting.

One afternoon he went to a local store with a group of friends. There was an attractive young white woman in the store: Mrs. Roy Bryant, the twenty-one-year-old wife of a local redneck. Emmett whistled at her. When Mrs. Bryant's husband heard about Emmett's whistling, he became enraged. That night someone kidnapped Emmett.

Three days after the incident, a local fisherman found Emmett Till's corpse floating in the Tallahatchie River with a huge electrical fan tied to the neck. The fan had not been heavy enough to hold the bloated corpse on the bottom of the river. Emmett Till had been beaten unmercifully before he was thrown into the river. The local sheriff announced after examining the mutilated corpse that it looked like someone had used an ax on it, "the cuts were so deep." Many black newspapers and magazines carried pictures of the corpse. I can still remember them. They showed terrible gashes and tears in the flesh. It gave the appearance of a ragged, rotting sponge.

Mrs. Bryant's husband and his half brother, J. W. Milam, were arrested and charged with the killing. There was a trial. All the jurors in the court were white. Over six thousand dollars was collected from whites across the South to support the two defendants. The trial did not last very long. The two men denied that they had killed Emmett Till. The jury accepted their story and the two men were released. Blacks across the country were outraged, but powerless to do anything.

Emmett Till was only three years older than me and I identified with him. I tried to put myself in his place and imagine what he was thinking when those white men took him from his home that night. I wondered how I would have handled the situation. I read and reread the newspaper and magazine accounts. I couldn't get over the fact that the men who were accused of killing him had not been punished at all.

There was something about the cold-blooded callousness of Emmett Till's lynching that touched everyone in the community. We had all heard atrocity accounts before, but there was something special about this one. For weeks after it happened, people continued to discuss it. It was impossible to go into a barber shop or corner grocery without hearing someone deploring Emmett Till's lynching.

From *My Soul Is Rested: Movement Days in the Deep South Remembered*
Ruby Hurley (interviewed by Howell Raines, 1973)

> In 1951, Ruby Hurley moved from New York to Birmingham to establish the first permanent NAACP office in that city. When Alabama outlawed the NAACP in 1956, Hurley was forced to leave the state. The year before, however, she was intimately involved in the Emmett Till case, having been sent to Mississippi by the NAACP to investigate the murder (see L. Alex Wilson's account of Hurley's work in chapter 4). The following account is excerpted from *My Soul is Rested,* a collection of interviews by award-winning newspaperman Howell Raines. The italicized passage in the selection is a notation added by Raines; ellipses and bracketed insertions in the text are his as well.

In the Emmett Till [murder] case, . . . I went to the trial to see how it was going. It was just like a circus. The defendants were sitting up there eating ice-cream cones and playing with their children in court just like they were out on a picnic. Everybody was searched going into the courtroom to make sure that none of the Negroes carried any weapons. White folks were not searched. It was again something that I won't forget and that was back twenty years ago. All because Negroes wanted freedom in Mississippi.

She investigated the Till case, the most celebrated lynching of the fifties, for the NAACP magazine "Crisis."

The boy was a fourteen-year-old who had infantile paralysis as a child and could not speak clearly. He whistled when he tried to enunciate words, rather than speak clearly. And this was the charge that was made against him, that he had whistled at [a white man's] wife in the store when he went in to get something for his little cousins. Now I talked with his cousins, and they told me what they thought had happened, and the boys were too young to make up or to fabricate. There's no question in my mind that [the two white men] . . . decided that they were going to "get a nigger." That's all, and that's they way they behaved, the way they reacted in those days. They took that child out and beat him, and then they tied him up with the chain from a cotton gin and dumped his body in the Tallahatchie River. And I always say, the Lord moves in mysterious ways wonders to perform, because his body was not supposed to come up the way it was weighted down. But it did come up, and a little teenager, white teenager, found the body on a Sunday morning as he was fishing in the Tallahatchie River.

But [they] were acquitted, and there were witnesses to the fact that they had the boy in the pickup truck with them and [that] they went on to the plantation of a brother of [one of the men], and when they left, the boy was not seen, but the tarpaulin was pulled down over the back of the pickup truck. The witnesses who saw this and heard the screaming from the barn where the beatings were taking place, a youngster of sixteen or seventeen and a woman from across the road, sent word that they wanted to talk to me and tell me some information.

I got the information on who saw that. . . . Those persons heard by way of the grapevine that I was investigating the case, and they passed the word back to me that they wouldn't talk to anybody but me. So I had to put on some cotton-pickin' clothes, literal cotton-pickin' clothes for those days, and make my way on to the plantation. . . . I really got a feeling of what the Underground Railroad during the days of slavery was all about—how word would be passed by just the look in an eye, never the exact phraseology being used, never the clear language, always in some form that you have to sorta try to figure out what the people meant. And it was only after going through, as I remember, four different families, going to four different places, did I finally get to the people who had sent word that they wanted to talk to me. You never went directly to a place. You had to go through . . . you were cleared all the way. Protection was there for me all the way and I didn't know it until many years later. There were men around with shotguns standing in various spots to be sure that I got where I was going and got back.

From "On Being Black and Middle Class"
Shelby Steele (1988)

Shelby Steele is the award-winning author of *The Content of Our Character: A New Vision of Race in America* (1990) and *A Dream Deferred: The Second Betrayal of Black Freedom in America* (1999). A self-described black conservative, he is a senior fellow at the Hoover Institute at Stanford University. In the following excerpt from "On Being Black and Middle

Class" (first published in *Commentary* and later included in *The Content of Our Character*), Steele recalls his memories of Emmett Till in order to probe one of his favorite subjects: the empowerment politics of victimization.

To overcome his marginal status, the middle-class black had to identify with a degree of victimization that was beyond his actual experience. In college (and well beyond) we used to play a game called "nap matching." It was a game of one-upmanship, in which we sat around outdoing each other with stories of racial victimization, symbolically measured by the naps in our hair. Most of us were middle-class and so had few personal stories to relate, but if we could not match naps with our own biographies we would move on to those legendary tales of victimization that came to us from the public domain.

The single story that sat atop the pinnacle of racial victimization for us was that of Emmett Till, the Northern black teen-ager who, on a visit to the South in 1955, was killed and grotesquely mutilated for supposedly looking at or whistling at (we were never sure which, though we argued the point endlessly) a white woman. Oh, how we probed his story, finding in his youth and Northern upbringing the quintessential embodiment of black innocence, brought down by a white evil so portentous and apocalyptic, so gnarled and hideous, that it left us with a feeling not far from awe. By telling his story and others like it, we came to *feel* the immutability of our victimization, its utter indigenousness, as a thing on this earth like dirt or sand or water.

Of course, these sessions were a ritual of group identification, a means by which we, as middle-class blacks, could be at one with our race. But why were we, who had only a moderate experience of victimization (and that offset by opportunities our parents never had), so intent on assimilating or appropriating an identity that in so many ways contradicted our own? Because, I think, the sense of innocence that is always entailed in feeling victimized filled us with a corresponding feeling of entitlement, or even license, that helped us endure our vulnerability on a largely white campus.

Remembering Emmett Till
Michael Eric Dyson (1991)

> On July 25, 1991, the city of Chicago renamed parts of Seventy-first Avenue in honor of Emmett Till. Michael Eric Dyson, a leading cultural critic and author of such works as *Race Rules: Navigating the Color Line* and *Between God and Gangsta Rap,* delivered the following remarks during the dedica-

tion ceremony. In his remarks, Dyson not only recalls some of the earliest assessments of Till's murder—ones that emphasized the young boy's Christlike martyrdom—but he also situates the meaning of murder within a contemporary climate of black-on-black violence and urban neglect, thus prefiguring the essay by John Edgar Wideman ("The Killing of Black Boys") published later in this anthology. Dyson's most recent work is *"I May Not Get There with You": The True Martin Luther King, Jr.* (2000), and he is currently the Ida B. Wells professor of African-American studies at DePaul University.

The meaning of Emmett Till's brief life and tragic death is so monumental we can scarcely grasp hold of it. Our attempts to honor his memory today—although necessary and appropriate—are poor recompense for his noble sacrifice of life under obscene and absurd circumstances. And our efforts are pitifully inadequate to give gratitude to Mrs. Mamie Till Mobley, who without her knowledge or consent was called upon to sacrifice her only-begotten son. When Emmett lost his life in tender youth, the world shuddered in angry disbelief at the barbarous passions that could accomplish such a deed. But no American who had not spent energy to retard racism's unruly spread, who had not sought somehow to untangle the lethal knot of fear and ignorance that produce prejudice, could claim innocence. The blood of Emmett Till was on the hands of every person who watched in malignant silence as black men were lynched, black women were raped, and black children were intimidated and even murdered.

By choosing to honor the memory of Emmett Till, we make a covenant with our past to own its pain as our responsibility and to forgive its failures only if the wisdom we derive from their doing is made a conscious part of our present pacts of racial peace. After all, the repression of uncomfortable memories of racial calamity and the avoidance of past racial injustice have become all too common and convenient. But the only way old and deep wounds are healed is to confront their existence and to acknowledge their power to inflict even more suffering and harm if they go unchecked. By remembering Emmett Till's death, we confess that we are not yet done with the work of racial reconciliation, and that although important progress has been made, vast spaces of racial ignorance and animosity remain to be conquered before real justice is achieved.

We do no service to ourselves, and only great harm to Emmett's memory, if we overlook the specific events that caused his sainted sacrifice to acquire a luminous and universal symbolism. Emmett, who was nicknamed "Bo," enjoyed a normal childhood except for one distinguishing illness, which would later have an ominous effect on his short life: he contracted polio at the age of five, leaving him with a severe stutter. After visiting numerous physicians and trying several approaches to remedy his impediment of speech, Emmett's mother finally came upon a solution that worked. She instructed Emmett to whistle when he felt a stutter coming on, after which he was able to speak clearly.

On the surface, being a black teen with a stutter bore no power to shape one's destiny or to revolutionize the racial future of a nation. But with Emmett it was different. In the prime of his evolving adolescence Emmett faced the lethal limits imposed upon all black life, condensed to a single act of senseless murder. While completing a purchase in the grocery story in Money, Mississippi, where he had gone to visit his relatives, he made what appeared to be a whistling noise, which was interpreted as a "wolf whistle" to the white proprietor's wife.

If this indeed happened, what followed is still undeniably absurd. But in light of the fateful trajectory of Southern race relations, Emmett's stutter acquired a fatal meaning. His accidental biological trait, much like his race, collided with an ancient inter-racial sexual taboo that he barely understood, and in his northern freedom, had not learned to fear. Ironically, his very freedom from artificial racial distinctions was his doom.

For his unpardonable sin, Emmett was violently abducted from his uncle's house, brutally beaten, shot in the head, and tossed in the Tallahatchie River with a two-hundred pound cotton gin motor tied around his neck. When his body was pulled from the water, his mother Mamie successfully prevented him from being buried in Mississippi, as the local sheriff had deviously planned. Instead, she brought Emmett's body back to Chicago, and for five days she held an open casket vigil that was eventually viewed by more than six hundred thousand people.

The unspeakable horror of Emmett's death caused shock to ripple through the entire nation. More importantly, his death galvanized a people perched on the fragile border between heroism and fear to courageously pursue meaningful and complete equality. In the curious mix of fortuity and destiny that infuse all events of epic meaning, Emmett's death gained a transcendent metaphoric value. Rosa Parks drew strength from his unintended martyrdom when she sat down with dignity so that all black people could stand up with pride. Medgar Evers cried bitter tears of frustration and pain, and he was charged to gird his loins and renew his commitment to shout justice in Mississippi's Dark Delta, leading to his own death and a rightful place at Emmett's side in the sacred pantheon of mur-

dered martyrs. And Emmett's death gave Martin Luther King, Jr., the great social prophet and American visionary who himself answered the highest call to
service and paid the greatest price of sacrifice, an irresistible symbol for the civil
rights movement. And it continues to give contemporary fighters for freedom the
inspiration and courage to love mercy and to help do justice.

And so what we do here today is in memory of all who have given their lives
so that justice, freedom, and equality would not remain abstract principles on
parchment, but become living ideas in action. For the purpose of monuments,
whether statues of stone or street signs of steel, whether large or small, is to evoke
the sacrament of remembrance. Monuments embody a communal choice to remember and to make intangible dreams permanent and concrete. But their real
beauty consists in their power to complete the cycle of memory, and to transcend
stone and steel and renew our hearts and illumine our minds with the passion
and ideals for which they stand.

But above all, what we do here today is for all innocent children who, like Emmett Till, are the unwitting victims of sacrifice. It is for babies born to mothers
addicted to crack; it is for children who are mentally and physically disabled; it
is for children who endure emotional and bodily abuse in silent suffering; it is for
orphaned and foster children who are robbed of parental wisdom; it is for home-
less children who have no shelter from nature's changes or who are daily reminded by social theory or public policy that their lives are expendable and their
basic needs unaffordable.

And in the harshest irony of all, it is for the young black Emmett Tills who are
killed by other young black Emmett Tills in a culture of crime and violence that
is the cruelest challenge to Emmett Till's great legacy. The disintegration of the
moral fabric of urban communities, the thriving of the "political economy of
crack," and the obscene incidence of black-on-black homicide threaten to make
Emmett's untimely sacrificial death empty. Both black communities and American institutions must be held responsible. Black communities must develop cultural resources to restore ethical responsibility, place human regard for life at their
center once again, and generate transformative visions of black manhood that do
not lead to self-destruction. American institutions, including government, school,
and business, must restructure political economic practices that devalue black
male labor, reshape academic settings that needlessly exacerbate and reinforce
low self-esteem, and reconstruct practices such as police brutality that target
black men with vicious particularity.

In reality, all black children who become men and women, who have benefited from the freedom to explore the entire range of their talents, owe a debt to Emmett Till, who was denied the opportunity to fully blossom. In the city of Emmett's birth, there would be no possibility for the nearly superhuman athletic feats of Michael Jordan or for the stunning two sports exploits of Bo Jackson without Emmett "Bo" Till's short life and tragic death. His sacrifice helped opened doors for them. And if we continue to recall his life and death, the memory of Emmett Till will continue to open doors of painful truth and tragic but redemptive history for us all.

Growing Up White in the South: An Essay
Lewis Nordan (1993)

> A native of the Mississippi Delta, Lewis Nordan is the author of seven
> works of fiction and one memoir. Like several other writers in this chapter,
> Nordan was a young boy at the time of Till's murder. In 1993, he won the
> Southern Book Critics Circle Award for *Wolf Whistle,* a dark, comic novel
> based on the lynching. In the following essay—published by Algonquin
> Press as part of the promotional material for *Wolf Whistle*—Nordan recalls
> the strange genesis of his novel and the haunting need he had to write about
> Emmett Till. Nordan currently teaches at the University of Pittsburgh.

As I began the first leg of a book tour to promote *Music of the Swamp,* I made a joke to a friend that I was traveling around the country explaining how tough it was to grow up white in the South. In fact, despite the irony, that is what that book is about.

It tells about a white boy, Sugar Mecklin, who senses the tragic limitations of a society defined by racial hatred and alcoholism and geographical isolation.

An unexpected answer

So, anyway, early one morning on this book tour, I took a cab from my hotel in Atlanta to a local television station where I was scheduled to be interviewed. I found myself more anxious than usual when I learned that the show was being taped before an audience.

The guest preceding me was a popular entertainer, a handsome black recording star promoting a new album. I could hear him out there, belting out song after song, and the audience was eating out of his hand, cheering for more.

It was intimidating. A nervous, bookish, gray-bearded old cuss in spectacles—

me I mean—didn't have a chance following this guy, this singer. In fact, I was wondering whether he would hang around long enough for me to ask for his autograph.

Then, when the applause had died down, somebody—the director, the stage manager, I'm not sure who—told me to get ready, it was my turn, they were getting ready to announce me.

I heard my name called, and so, in fear, walked out onto the stage, in front of those cameras, beneath all those shocking lights, suspicious that my message about growing up white in the South was about to fall flat.

Once I was out there, I discovered one further intimidating detail. The interviewer and every member of this large television audience were black.

My whiteness dimmed the lights. My silly message about Sugar Mecklin's white-bread tragedy seemed altogether fatuous.

In any case, as part of the talk-show format, the audience was invited to ask questions from microphones placed throughout the studio. In my giddy state, I found myself giving a completely unexpected answer to one of the questions. Unexpected to me, I mean.

A woman stood at the microphone in the audience and said, "What will your next book be about?"

I said, confidently, "It will deal with the death of Emmett Till."

What? It would deal with what? Who said that?

I added, "Emmett Till was a black child who was murdered near my hometown when I was a boy. The trial of his murderers became a landmark in the civil rights movement." Words to that effect, anyway.

The remainder of the half hour was taken up with questions and answers related to the unexpected announcement of this work-in-progress.

An anonymous white boy

And now a year later, *Wolf Whistle,* the book I described on that television show, goes to press. It is the book I seem to have been preparing to write for a long time, and yet until the words came out of my mouth I had had no conscious intention of writing such a book.

There is, however, a detail in *Music of the Swamp* that might have predicted it. Two children in a boat see the feet and legs of a dead body sticking up from the water in a drift of brush beyond the Roebuck Lake spillway.

The narrator reports the body to be that of an old man who had "spells." I knew it was not. Though I had not given a thought to any future book I might write, I knew when I wrote the chapter that this dead person was none other than Emmett Till, floating upside down at the end of a barbed wire tether that was tied at one end to a hundred-pound gin fan and at the other, around the child's neck.

The description of the feet and legs of the body, poking up out of the water and the barbed wire and the gin fan, and even the phrase "a drift of brush," survive in my memory from a newspaper article of thirty-six years ago. Those helpless feet and legs, upside down, almost comic, have haunted me all my life.

Something else has haunted me as well, an invisibility, the anonymous white boy in the boat, checking his hooks for catfish, when he found the body of Emmett Till. Still, I wonder who he was, what became of him, how his life was changed.

The unreality of fiction

The novel that I have written is pure invention, because when I began my memory of the events surrounding the murder and the trial was very limited. Mainly I remembered the news article about the body in the drift of brush, and that the child was killed as a result of wolf whistling at a white woman.

The big blank spots in my memory were something of a blessing during the writing of the book. With no memory of the identity of the persons actually involved, I was free to set the novel in my already-invented fictional geography and population of Arrow Catcher, Mississippi. I used some characters that I'd invented and I made up new characters as they were needed.

I already knew most of the white people in my story, residents of my earlier books, and their relatives. The more I wrote, the more I invented, including a population of vaguely magical animals. A flock of buzzards, each vulture named after a former governor of the state of Mississippi; a tamed hellhound (whatever that is!) that lives behind a bootleg whiskey store; a one-handed monkey named after the president of the Confederacy; a parrot who cannot speak but can only make a noise like a cash register; all these things, and more, drove the story into that fictional realm where my work lives most comfortably.

The point of view of the novel is comprehensive, including not only major and minor characters, black and white, male and female, dead and alive, but even the buzzards on their telephone poles and pigeons in the rafters. It is a serious story, about death and grief and broken hearts, and in which credibility is a key, but it exists on a plane, sometimes comic, even burlesque, just askew of the "real," historical universe. That is my intention and my point: to render the natural world as itself and, at the same time, as unearthly.

The reality of Emmett Till

In one area, however, I discovered myself unwilling to allow the universe of my story to wobble on its axis, let alone to spin away from it. I found myself sticking tight to the few memories I held of Emmett Till. Other inventions came easily, but my mind would not let go of the historical Emmett.

As I worked with the material, other memories came to me. In addition to his upside down body in the brush pile, I remembered his age, fourteen, a year younger than I was when he died. I remembered that he had gone into the store, where he supposedly whistled at the white woman, to buy bubble gum. I remembered that he was from Chicago, that his father was dead, that he had been visiting a great-uncle and aunt, that the uncle's name was Mose.

In the early drafts of the novel, I kept all the remembered details—including Emmett's real name, Mose's real name, and much more. Even those private things that I made up about the family are grounded solidly in "real world" possibilities—I'm thinking especially of the lovemaking scene between the boy's uncle and aunt—where there is no room for caricature or anything unearthly.

Eventually, my editor asked me about this impulse to preserve Emmett Till intact, as real. Why was invention so bountiful, so extravagant in fact, in all the rest of the novel, and so skimpy when it came to the character that represented Emmett Till?

To tell the truth, the question scared me a little. Generally my thinking does not run to the abstract—I mean, I work by instinct and intuition, from which I create geographies and characters, and in the process seldom ask myself questions of "aesthetics."

Having been asked, though, I wondered. Was it merely reverence for the dead? Was it a streak of sentimentality? Was it some Faulknerian something-or-another, blood-guilt, that made everyone in my story, except Emmett, fair game for irony and satire and caricature?

At first I thought so, frankly. It is true that I revere the memory of Emmett Till. His death marked not only a turning point in civil rights but, in a very personal way, in my own life as well. And though I usually run away and hide from comparisons with Faulkner and his old-fashioned ideas about blood-guilt, my racial identification with the murderers of Emmett Till still troubles me.

But even as I acknowledge some culpability, I know that there is an aesthetic issue that supercedes these considerations.

This book, like every honest book, demands a moral center—and also an emotional, psychological, detail-based center—firm ground on which a reader may stand in complete confidence that it will not move. Especially this is true in a book like *Wolf Whistle,* where the ground of reality is so unstable, so likely to shift away from conventional expectations of reality.

Emmett (Bobo, in the fiction) and his family are the moral, emotional, psychological, life-affirming core of this novel which a reader may trust to be permanent, and around which all the rest of the world may go mad. The aesthetic need to maintain the solid ground was manifested in my early reluctance to change even the smallest details of my memory of the real event, including Emmett's name. Not until the last draft of the book did Emmett become Bobo—and he became Bobo in the novel only because that was the nickname by which, in real life, Emmett Till was known.

Just before I appeared on that television show in Atlanta last year, I chose a necktie from my suitcase and knotted it so tight around my neck that my face turned blue. My hair I plastered into place with great globs of a product called Mega Gel. (The tube advises, Extreme Hold for Design and Control.) My shoes were shined. My beard was trimmed. I shaved the tops of my ears. I plucked my nose hairs. My belt was pulled to the last hole. My breath said Scope! at long distances. Mega Gel had the idea: extreme hold for control.

Never mind the details, and don't imagine that I am asking for sympathy, but only believe that one week before this television interview, my own personal life had fallen into chaos. Everything was haywire, helter-skelter, inside out. Unlike Mega Gel, I had lost all control, and could discern no design in the scheme of things.

Looking back now I understand a few things better. All my cosmetics and my strict adherence to a self-imposed dress code were attempts to gain control of a world flying off its axis. When that anonymous woman at the microphone asked me about my next book, I reached down to the core of myself for something substantial to answer her with.

What I found there was Emmett Till. As soon as I spoke his name, I knew that I had found a buried chunk of my self's permanent foundation, the granite cornerstone of something formative and durable and true.

A few times over the years Emmett had surfaced, as he did briefly and anonymously in *Music of the Swamp.* And, in a way, he took me back to an even earlier, formative time, when I myself was a fatherless child, as Emmett had been, unaware of my loss and my grief. On that television program, Emmett emerged suddenly as the unshakable ground of *me,* where I could stand to watch in safety the rags and tags of my personal life flying away in the whirlwind, in confidence that they would all return or that what did not return could be lived without.

In *Wolf Whistle,* Emmett, Bobo, holds the same position as he held in my heart. He is the fixed center, in the midst of other lives that have been turned inside out. In the directionless fictional histories of the characters of *Wolf Whistle,* there are hints of what happened in my own history, and perhaps in the history of all human beings—death, heartbreak, betrayal, lost love, and lost hope.

Emmett, though, is *terra firma.* He is the reality, he is the rock. Everyone else in the book flies with the whirlwind, except, in the end, maybe the school teacher, Alice, whose life Emmett touched, as he touched mine, without either Alice or I ever meeting him. [Pittsburgh, January 1993]

From *Life on the Color Line: The True Story of a White Boy Who Discovered He Was Black*
Gregory Howard Williams (1995)

As a young boy growing up in Virginia in the 1950s, Gregory Howard Williams thought he was white. But when his parents' marriage broke up, and he moved to his father's hometown of Muncie, Indiana, Williams discovered that he was black. His dark-skinned father, he quickly learned, had been "passing" as an Italian-American. But now back in Muncie, Williams's father became black again, and Williams himself had to learn—and learn quickly—the truth about his heritage. In the following excerpt, Williams is talking with one of his grandmothers about the murder of Emmett Till, and in this brief conversation he learns a hard lesson about the depths of white racism and the challenges now facing him as a black man in a white man's world.

A few afternoons later I walked through Grandma Sallie's door and noticed a newspaper tucked in a bag of groceries on the table. Though Grandma was unable to read or write, she sometimes made an elaborate gesture of buying a paper to impress her neighbors. She often asked me to read it to her. She preferred articles about our neighborhood, but it was rare to find anything about Negroes in the Muncie paper. At one time it carried a social column called "The Colored Circle," but that had been discontinued. I sat at the kitchen table while Grandma rested on her bed. As she removed her shoes and began to rub her feet, I scanned the paper. In disbelief I read aloud of a fourteen-year-old black Chicago youth murdered while visiting relatives in Money, Mississippi. Apparently, he had whistled at a white woman. Kidnappers broke into his relatives' house in the middle of the night and abducted Emmett Till at gunpoint. Searchers later discovered his body in the Tallahatchie River. The youth had been shot in the head, lynched, and had a seventy-pound cotton gin fan tied around his body.

Laying the paper on the table, I turned to face Grandma, hoping she would tell me that nothing like Emmett Till's death could really happen in America.

"Billy, you don't know nothing about peckawoods. That's the reason I was always scared about Buster being in Virginia. They might have found him out and lynched him."

"Nobody would've bothered Dad," I insisted. "He owned a restaurant and tavern and made a lot of money."

"It don't make no difference what he owned. He was still a nigger, and if they found him out, he would'a been a dead nigger. You better watch out too, boy, and not mess around wit' no white girls. It was the ruination of your daddy. I bet them killers don't get a day. Anybody that growed up in the South know they ain't going to jail. And probably wouldn't, even if they done it here."

White men were charged with Emmett Till's murder and tried in front of an all-white jury. In September 1955, I read the news of the acquittal to Grandma as she sat in her kitchen.

"Maybe now you'll believe I know about politics, Billy," she said as she soaked her feet in a metal washtub after a long day cooking in the basement of the drive-in.

From *Black Profiles in Courage*
Kareem Abdul-Jabbar (1996)

> Kareem Abdul-Jabbar's *Black Profiles in Courage* is a readable and passionate account of African American men and women who, through their sufferings and their triumphs, have both challenged and strengthened the promise of American democracy. In the following passage, Abdul-Jabbar, best known as one of college and professional basketball's greatest players, recounts how Till's murder caused him to lose his "childish innocence" about race in America.

In the late sixties, when I was at UCLA, I read an amazing book that affected me profoundly. It was Anne Moody's autobiography *Coming of Age in Mississippi*. Moody was fourteen when Emmett Till was lynched. His murder was so savage, it petrified her. This passage about it in her autobiography has never left me:

Before Emmett Till's murder, I had known the fear of hunger, hell, and the Devil. But now there was a new fear known to me—the fear of being killed just because I was black. This was the worst of my fears. I knew once I got food, the fear of starving to death would leave. I also was told that if I were a good girl, I wouldn't have to fear the Devil or hell. But I didn't know what one had to do or not do as a Negro not to be killed. Probably just being a Negro period was enough, I thought.

I remember when I first read this, it gave me chills. I felt like I was living inside Anne Moody's skin. It made me recall, vividly, how Emmett Till's lynching affected *me* when it happened. And I starting feeling uneasy all over again. I was eight years old when I saw a photo of Emmett's body in *Jet* magazine. It made me sick. His face was distorted, gruesomely bloated. I had no idea what happened to him, but my parents discussed it at length; and the *Jet* photo left an indelible image I could never forget.

But that was the point; Emmett's mother had insisted on an open casket and a public viewing because she wanted people to see what senseless racism had done to her child. The day of his funeral, she was addressing the *world* as she asked reporters: "Have you ever sent a loved son on vacation and had him returned in a pine box so horribly battered and waterlogged that someone needs to tell you this sickening sight is your son—lynched?"

That was *her* way of putting people on notice.

And it worked. Thousands of Chicagoans viewed Emmett's body that day and millions saw the grisly photo from *Jet*. (In 1955 black newspapers, like the *Chicago Defender, Amsterdam News, Pittsburgh Courier,* and *Baltimore Afro-American,* and magazines like *Jet* and *Ebony,* were among more than two hundred black publications reaching African Americans.)

The murder shocked me; I began thinking of myself as a black person for the first time, not just a person. And I grew more distrustful and wary. I remember thinking: *They killed him because of his color.* In a way, I lost my childish innocence. I felt like I was living in Transylvania; all of a sudden, the color of my skin represented danger. From then on, I was always aware, like Anne Moody, that I could be hurt or even killed just for being black.

Pretty soon, my relationships started changing in school. For example, I remember that the day we had to rearrange our desks in sixth grade, I was out of the classroom. When I came back, my desk was the only one set apart. One of the kids said, "Yeah, he's *segregated!*" And everyone thought it was funny, except me and the only other black kid in the class. I think the reason I remember the innocuous incident is because it was part of an aftershock from Emmett Till.

The Killing of Black Boys
John Edgar Wideman (1997)

> In this, one of the most complex meditations on Emmett Till, novelist and critic John Edgar Wideman confesses that Till's face—"crushed, chewed, mutilated, gray and swollen"—has long haunted his sleep. The same age as Till in the summer of 1955, Wideman draws parallels between his life and Till's, and then Till's life and the lives of thousands of black boys who are still dying of violence in America. In prose as inventive as the best of his fiction, Wideman weaves a memoir of dazzling passion and intensity. The first author to twice receive the PEN/Faulkner Award for Fiction (for the novels *Sent for You Yesterday* [1983] and *Philadelphia Fire* [1990]), Wideman currently teaches at the University of Massachusetts at Amherst.

I am a man. A first-time grandfather recently. Yet a nightmare from my childhood still haunts my sleep. A monster chases me. Some creature whose shape and face are too terrible for the nightmare to reveal. I can't escape. Run headlong down an unfamiliar street, duck into an alley, dart along shortcuts, dash in and out of all the hiding places in my old neighborhood. The monster still lumbers behind me and also sits, patient and hideous, waiting to seize me when I turn the next corner.

Trapped by the dream, I try to scream my way out. There is no way out, but I scream anyway. One scream or many. Screaming for mercy. Screaming for the worst to happen, anything, just so the nightmare ends. Muscles of my throat constrict. I can't breathe. One last choked yell as the face of death looms closer.

I die. Awaken again to whimpers and panting, the rapid, lonely thump of my heart, noises that survive one world's extinction, another world's birth, and I lie in my warm bed shivering, listening to myself, wondering how my wife slept through the tumult.

Sometimes she doesn't. A scream can startle her awake. Her fear, the first thing I see when I open my eyes.

Though the nightmare is as old as anything I can remember about myself, I've come to believe the face in the dream I can't bear to look upon is Emmett Till's. Emmett Till's face crushed, chewed, mutilated, gray and swollen, water dripping from holes punched in his skull. Warm gray water on that August day in 1955 when they dragged his corpse from the Tallahatchie River.

Both of us 14 the summer they murdered Emmett Till. My nightmare, an old acquaintance by then. The fact that the nightmare predates by many years the afternoon in Pittsburgh I came across Emmett Till's photograph in *Jet* magazine confounds me and seems to matter not at all, part of the mystery I must abide to heal myself.

I certainly hadn't been searching for Emmett Till's face when it found me. I peeked quickly, focused my eyes just enough to ascertain something awful on the page, a mottled, grayish something resembling an aerial shot of a landscape cratered by bombs or ravaged by natural disaster—something I registered with a sort of simultaneous glance at and glance away.

Refusing to look, lacking the power to look, to this day, shames me. That afternoon in Pittsburgh I think I sensed vaguely why a wrecked boy's face was displayed in the pages of a magazine. Guessed it would be dangerous not to look. Emmett Till had died instead of me and I needed to know how, why. Not returning his eyeless stare blinded me. In a faint, skittish fashion, I intuited all of this. Understood obscurely how the murdered boy's picture raised issues of responsibility, accountability. But Emmett Till was also just too dead, too horribly, unalterably dead to look at. I sensed that too.

Like Emmett Till, in 1955 I had just graduated from junior high. I'm trying to remember if, like Emmett Till, I carried pictures of White girls in my wallet. Can't recall whether I owned a wallet in 1955. Certainly it wouldn't have been a necessity because the little bit of cash I managed to get hold of passed rapidly through my hands. *Money burns a hole in your pocket, boy,* my mom said. Wanting to feel grown-up, wanting to radiate at least a show of what seemed to represent manliness, I probably stuffed some sort of hand-me-down billfold in my hip pocket. The same urge may have prompted me to carry around a White girl's picture. No doubt about it, possessing a White girl's photo was a merit badge for a Black boy. A sign of power. Your footprint in "their" world. Proof you could handle its opportunities and dangers. Any actual romance with a White girl would have to be underground, clandestine, so a photo served as prime evidence of things unseen. A ticket to status in my clan of brown boys in White Shadyside, a trophy copped in another country I could flaunt in Black Homewood. So I may have owned a wallet with pictures of White girlfriends or classmates in it, and if I'd traveled to Promised Land, South Carolina, with my grandfather Harry

Wideman one of those summers he offered to take me down home to his briar patch, who knows? I was a bit of a smart aleck like Emmett Till. I liked to brag. Take on dares like him.

Okay, Emmett Till. You so bad. You talkin 'bout all those White gals you got up in Chicago. Bet you won't say boo to that White lady in the store.

Those of us who survived it understood in our bones that Emmett Till's murder was an attempt to slay an entire generation. Push us backward to the bad old days when the lives of Black people seemed to belong to Whites. When White power and racist ideology seemed unchallengeable forces of nature.

Emmett Till's dead body reminded us that the bad old days are never farther away than the thickness of skin, dark skin that some pale-skinned people claim the prerogative to strip away, burn or cut or shoot full of holes. It is not an accident that the hacked, dead face of Emmett Till looks inhuman. The point of killing and mutilating him, inflicting the agony of his last moments, was to prove he was not human.

And it almost worked. Comes close to working every time. Disfigured by drugs, crime, disease, homelessness, pathological poverty, drenched in hot-blooded or cold-blooded statistics, the brutalized Black body displayed in the media loses all vestiges of humanity. We are set back on our collective heels by the evidence, the warning, the prophecy that beneath Black skin something *other*, something less than human lurks. A so-called lost generation of young Black men dying in the streets today points backward, the way Emmett Till's battered corpse points backward, history and prophecy at once: This is the way things have always been, will always be, the way they're supposed to be.

The circle of racism, its perverse logic, is unbroken. Emmett Till violates the rules. Young Black men are born breaking the rules and thus forfeit all rights White people are bound to respect. Ugly consequences are inevitable. Why not jail Blacks, lynch them? Why not construct walls to separate them from decent citizens?

An apartheid mentality reigns in this country, not because most Americans consciously embrace racist attitudes or wish ill on their neighbors of African descent. Emmett Till dies again and again because his murder and the conditions that ensure and perpetuate it are more acceptable to the majority than placing themselves, their dominant position, at risk. Any serious attempt to achieve true economic, social and political equality must begin not with opening doors to selected minorities, but with the majority's willingness to relinquish a significant measure of power and privilege. There have always been open doors, of sorts—

emancipation, emigration, education, economic success in sport or business. What's been missing is an unambiguous private and public decision by a majority of the majority to dismantle the wall, to give up the doors and keys, the identity and protection that comes with the wall.

Like the body of Emmett Till, the Black victims of drug and territory wars raging today are not taken as signs of a fatally flawed society failing its children. Once more the bodies of dead Black men, imprisoned Black men, jobless Black men, addicted Black men are being used to justify increasingly brutal policing of the racial divide.

In 1955, one year after the Supreme Court's *Brown v Board of Education* school-desegregation decision, as the last great campaign to secure civil rights for Black people commenced in the southern United States, the murder of Emmett Till clarified exactly what was at stake: life or death. And as long as race continues to legitimize one group's life-and-death power over another, the stolen face of Emmett Till will haunt the unresolved middle ground between so-called Whites and so-called Blacks, his face unburied, unmourned, unloved in the netherworld where incompatible versions of reality clash.

It was hard to bury Emmett Till, hard to bury Carole Robertson, Addie Mae Collins, Denice McNair and Cynthia Wesley, the four girls killed by a bomb in a Birmingham, Alabama, church. So hard an entire nation began to register the convulsions of Black mourning. The deaths of our children in the civil-rights campaigns changed us. Grief was collective; began to unify us, clarify our thinking, roll back the rock of our fear. Emmett Till's mangled face could belong to anybody's Black son who transgressed racial laws; anyone's little girl could be crushed in the rubble of a bombed church. We read the terrorist message inscribed upon Emmett Till's flesh and were shaken, but refused to comply with the terms it set forth.

Because we knew the killing of children was an effort to murder our future, we mourned our young martyrs but also fought with ferocity and dignity in the courts, churches and streets to protect them. Young people, after all, were the shock troops of the movement for social justice, on the front lines, the hottest, most dangerous spots in Alabama and Mississippi. And though they had the most to gain and the most to lose, they also carried on their shoulders the hopes of older generations and generations unborn.

Now in our rituals of mourning for our lost children, there seems to be no sense of a communal, general loss, no comprehension of larger forces or of the relationship of our immediate trials—drugs, gang violence, empty schools, empty minds, empty homes, empty values—to the ongoing struggle to liberate ourselves from the oppressive legacies of slavery and apartheid. Funerals for our young are daily, lonely occurrences. In some urban ghetto or another somewhere in America, at least once a day a small Black congregation will gather together to try and repair the hole in a brother or mother's soul with the balm of gospel singing, prayer, the laying on of dark hands on darkened spirits.

How many a week, how many repetitions of the same sad ceremony must there be? The hush afterward when the true dimensions of loss and futility begin to set in. A sense of isolation and powerlessness dogs the survivors who are burdened not only by the sudden death of a loved one but also with the knowledge it's going to happen again, today or tomorrow, and it's supposed to happen in a world where Black lives are expendable, can disappear, *click,* just like that, without a trace, so it seems almost as if the son or sister were hardly here at all and maybe Black people really ain't worth shit just like you've been hearing your whole sorry life.

Curtis Jones, a cousin who accompanied Emmett Till on the trip from Chicago to Leflore County, Mississippi, in August 1955, relates how close Emmett Till came to missing their train, reminding us how close Emmett Till's story came to not happening, or being another story altogether, and that in turn should remind us how any story, sad or happy, is always precariously close to being other than it is. Doesn't take much to turn a familiar scene into chaos. Difficult as it is to remember what does occur, we must also try to keep alive what doesn't—the missed trains, squandered opportunities, warnings not heeded. We carry forward these fictions because *what might have been* is part of what gives shape to our stories. We depend on memory's capacity to hold many lives, not just the one we appear to be leading at the moment. Memory is space for storing lives we didn't lead; it's room where they remain alive, room for mourning them, forgiving them. Memory is like all stories we tell, a tissue of remembering and forgetting, of *what if* and *once upon a time,* burying our dead so the dead may rise.

Curtis Jones goes on to tell us about everybody piling into Mose Wright's automobile and trundling down the dusty road to church. How he and his cousin Emmett Till took the car into Money that afternoon while Mose Wright preached.

A bunch of boys loafing outside Bryant's general store on Money's main drag. Sho' nuff country town. Wooden storefronts with wooden porches. Wooden sidewalks. Overhanging wooden signs. With its smatter of Black boys out front, its frieze of tire-size Coca Cola signs running around the eaves of its porch, Bryant's was probably the only game in town, Emmett Till guessed.

Climbing out of Mose Wright's old Ford, he sports the broad smile I recall from another photo, the one of him leaning, elbow atop a TV set, clean as a string bean in his white dress shirt and stylized checkerboard-stripe tie, his chest thrust out mannishly, baby fat in his cheeks, a softish, still-forming boy whose energy, intelligence and expectations of life are evident in the pose he's striking for the camera, just enough in-your-face swagger so you can't help smiling back at the wary eagerness-to-please of his smile.

To Emmett Till, the Black boys are a cluster of down-home country cousins. He sees a stage beckoning on which he can perform. Steps up on the sidewalk with his cousin Curtis, to whom he is *Bo* or *Bobo,* greets his audience. Like a magician, Emmett Till pulls a White girl from his wallet. Silences everybody. Mesmerizes them with tales of what they're missing living down here in the woods. If he'd been selling magic beans, all the boys would have dug into their overalls and extracted their last hot penny to buy some. They watch his fingers slip into his shirt pocket. Hold their breath waiting for the next trick.

Emmett Till's on a roll, can't help rubbing it in a little. What he's saying about himself sounds real good, so good he wants to hear more. All he wants really is for these brown faces to love him. As much as he's loved by the Black faces and White faces in the junior-high graduation pictures from Chicago he's showing around.

He winks at the half-dozen or so boys gathered round him. Nods. Smiles. Points to the prettiest girl, the Whitest, fairest, longest-haired one of all you can easily see, even though the faces in the class picture are tiny and gray. Emmett Till says she is the prettiest, anyway, so why not? Why not believe he's courted and won her and ain't youall lucky he came down here bringing youall the good news?

Though Emmett Till remains the center of attention, the other kids giggle, scratch their naps, stroke their chins, turn their heads this way and that around the circle, commence little conversations of eye-cutting and teeth-sucking and slack-jawed awe. Somebody pops a finger against somebody's shaved skull, somebody's hip bumps somebody else, a tall boy whistles a blues line and someone's been humming softly the whole time. Emmett Till's the preacher and it's Sunday morning and the sermon is righteous. Everybody's ready for a hymn or a responsive reading, even a collection plate circulating so they can participate, stretch a little, hear their own voices.

You sure is something, boy. You say you bad, Emmett Till. Got all them White gals up North, you say. Bet you won't say boo to the White lady in the store.

Curtis Jones is playing checkers with old Uncle Edmund on a barrel set in the shade around the corner from the main drag. One of the boys who sauntered into the store with Emmett Till to buy candy comes running. *He did it. Emmett Till did it. That cousin of yours crazy, boy. Said,* Bye-bye, Baby, *to Miss Bryant!* The old man gets up so fast he knocks over the crate he's been sitting on. *Lord have mercy. I know the boy didn't do nothing like that. Huh uh. No. No he didn't. Youall better get out here. That lady come out that store blow youalls' brains off.*

Several months later, after an all-White jury in the town of Sumner, Mississippi, had deliberated an hour—*would have been less, if we hadn't took time for lunch*—and found Roy Bryant and J. W. Milam not guilty of murdering Emmett Till, the two men were paid $4,000 by a journalist, William Bradford Huie, to tell the story of abducting, beating and shooting Emmett Till.

To get rid of his body they used barbed wire to lash a 100-pound cotton-gin fan to Emmett Till's neck and threw him in the Tallahatchie River. The journalist in a videotaped interview said: "It seems to a rational mind today, it seems impossible that they could have killed him."

The reporter muses for a moment, then remembers: "But J. W. Milam looked up at me and he says, 'Well, when he told me about this White girl he had, my friend, well, that's what this war's about down here now, that's what we got to fight to protect, and I just looked at him and say, '*Boy, you ain't never gone to see the sun come up again.*'"

To the very end, Emmett Till didn't believe the crackers would kill him. He was 14, from Chicago, he'd hurt no one; these strange, funny-talking White men were a nightmare he'd awaken from sooner or later. Milam found the boy's lack of fear shocking. Called it "belligerence." Here was this nigger should be shitting his drawers. Instead, he was making J. W. Milam uncomfortable. Brave or foolhardy or ignorant or blessed to be already in another place, a place these sick, sick men could never touch, whatever enabled Emmett Till to stand his ground, to be himself until the first deadly blow landed, be himself even after it landed, I hope Emmett Till understood that Milam or Bryant, whoever struck first with the intent to kill, was the one who flinched, not he.

When such thoughts come to me, I pile them like sandbags along the levees that protect my sleep. I should know better than to waste my time.

I ask my wife, Judy, who is flesh-and-blood embodiment of the nightmare

J. W. Milam discovered in Emmett Till's wallet, what she thinks of when she hears *Emmett Till*.

"A Black kid whistling at a White woman somewhere down South and being killed for it is what I think," she says.

"He didn't whistle," I reply. I've heard the whistling story all my life and another that has him not moving aside for a White woman walking down the sidewalk. Both are part of the myth, but neither's probably true. The story Till's cousin Curtis Jones tells is different. And for what it's worth, his cousin was there. Something Emmett Till said to a White woman inside a store is what caused the shit to hit the fan.

She wants to know where I heard the cousin's version, and I launch into a riff on my sources—*Voices of Freedom,* an oral history of the Civil Rights Movement, Henry Hampton's video documentary *Eyes on the Prize,* a book *Representations of Black Masculinity in Contemporary American Art* organized around a museum exhibit of Black-male images. Then I realize I'm doing all the talking, when what I'd intended to elicit was Judy's spontaneous witness. What her memory carried forward, what it lost.

She's busy with something of her own—a law-school exam—and we just happened to cross paths a moment in the kitchen and she's gone before I get what I wanted. Gone before I know what I wanted. Except standing there next to the refrigerator, in the silence released by its hum, I feel utterly defeated. All the stuff spread out on my desk upstairs isn't getting me any closer to Emmett Till or a cure. Neither will man-in-the-street, woman-in-the-kitchen interviews. Only one other voice is required for the story I'm constructing to overcome a bad dream, and they shut him up a long time ago, didn't they?

Here's what happened. Four nights after the candy-buying and Bye-bye, Baby scene in Money, at 2:00 A.M. on August 28, 1955, Roy Bryant with a pistol in one hand and a flashlight in the other appears at Mose Wright's door. "This is Mr. Bryant," he calls into the darkness. Then demands to know if Mose Wright has two niggers from Chicago inside. He says he wants the nigger done all that talk.

When Emmett Till is delivered, Bryant marches him to a pickup truck and asks someone inside, "This is the right nigger?" And somebody says, "Yes he is."

Next time Mose Wright sees Emmett Till is three days later when the sheriff summons him to identify a corpse. The body's naked and too badly damaged to tell who it is until Mose Wright notices the initialed ring on his nephew's finger.

Where were you when JFK was shot? Where were you when a man landed on the moon? When Martin Luther King, Jr., was shot? When the Rodney King verdict was announced? Where were you when Emmett Till floated up to the surface of the Tallahatchie River for Bye-bye, Babying a White woman?

How many places can I be in at once? A Black boy asleep in my bed. A White man in the darkness outside a tar-paper cabin announcing the terror of my name, gripping a flashlight that yesterday was a flaming torch brandished in the fists of a white-sheeted ghost, a heavy-duty flashlight stuffed with thick D batteries that will soon become a club for bashing Emmett Till's skull. An old Black man in the shanty crammed with bodies, instantly alert when I hear *You got those niggers from Chicago in there with you?* An old man figuring the deadly odds, how many lives bought if one handed over. Calculating the rage of his ancient enemy, weighing the risk of saying words the other in his charge must hear, Emmett Till must hear, no matter what terrible things happen next.

Got my two grandsons and a nephew in here.

Black boy inside the cabin, a boy my age whose name I don't know yet, who will never know mine, rubbing his eyes, not sure he's awake or dreaming a scary dream, one of the tales buried deep, deep. He's been hearing since before he was born, about the old days in the Deep South when they cut off niggers' nuts and lynched niggers and roasted niggers over fires like marshmallows.

Black man in my bed, lying beside a pale, beautiful, long-haired woman rubbing my shoulder, a woman whose presence sometimes is as strange and unaccountable to me as mine must be to her, as snow would be falling softly through the bedroom ceiling, accumulating in drifts on the down comforter. Miracles and cheap trick of being many places, many people at once. Conjuring with words what I need, what I'm missing, what's lost. The nightmare dissolving as I decide she's real, as I pretend this loving moment together might last and last.

The name *Emmett* is spoiled for me. In any of its spellings. How could Black parents name a son Emmett? As big a kick as I get watching Emmitt Smith rush the football for the Dallas Cowboys, there is also the moment after a bone-shattering collision, and he's sprawled lifeless on the turf or the moment after he's stumbled or fumbled and slumps to the bench and lifts his helmet and I see a Black mother's son, a small, dark, round face, a boy's big, wide, scared eyes. All those yards gained, all that wealth, but like O.J., he'll never run far enough or fast enough. Inches behind them, the worst thing the people who hate him can imagine hounds him like a shadow.

Sometimes I think the only way to end this would be with Andy Warhol–like strips of images, the same face, Emmett Till's face, replicated 12, 24, 48, 96 times on a wall-size canvas. Like giant postage stamps end to end, top to bottom, each version of the face exactly like the other but different names printed below each one. Martin Till. Malcolm Till. Medgar Till. Nat Till. Gabriel Till. Huey Till. Bigger Till. Nelson Till. Mumia Till. Colin Till. Jesse Till. Your daddy, your mama, your sister, brother aunt cousin uncle niece nephew Till . . .

Instead of the nightmare one night, this is what I dream: I'm marching with many, many men, a multitude of Black men of all colors, marching past the bier on which the body of Emmett Till rests. The casket, as his mother demanded, is open. *I want the world to see what they did to my baby.* One by one, from an endless line, the men detach themselves, pause, peer down into the satin-lined box. Pinned inside its upright lid, a snapshot of Emmett Till, young, smiling, whole, a jaunty Stetson cocked high across his brow. In the casket he is dressed in a dark suit, jacket wings spread to expose a snowy shroud pulled up to his chin. Then the awful face, patched together with string and wire, awaits each mourner.

My turn is coming soon. I'm grateful. Will not shy away this time. Will look hard. The line of my brothers and fathers and sons stretches ahead of me, behind me. I am drawn by them, pushed by them, steadied as we move each other along. We are a horizon girding the earth, holding the sky down. So many of us at one time in one place, it scares me. More than a million of us marching through this city of monumental buildings and dark alleys. Not very long ago we were singing, but now we march silently, more shuffle than brisk step as we approach the bier, wait our turn. Singing's over but it holds silently in the air, tangible as weather, as the bright sun disintegrating marble buildings, emptying alleys of shadows, warming us on a perfect October day we had no right to expect but would have been profoundly disappointed had it fallen out otherwise.

What I say when I lean over and speak one last time to Emmett Till is: *I love you. I'm sorry. I won't allow it to happen ever again.* And my voice is small and quiet when I say the words, not nearly as humble as it should be, fearful almost to pledge any good after so much bad. My small voice and short turn and then the next man and the next, close together, leading, following one another so the murmur of our voices beside the bier never stops. And immensity, a continuous muted shout and chant and benediction, a river gliding past the stillness of Emmett Till. Past this city, this hour, this place. River sound of blood I'm almost close enough to hear coursing in the veins of the next man.

In the dream we do not say, *Forgive us.* We are taking, not asking for something today. There is no time left to ask for things, even things as precious as forgiveness, only time to take one step, then the next and the next, alone in this great body of men, each one standing on his own feet, moving, our shadows linked, a coolness, a shield stretching nearly unbroken across the last bed where Emmett Till sleeps.

Where we bow and hope and pray he frees us. Ourselves seen sinking, then rising as in a mirror, then stepping away.

And then. And then this vision fades, too. I am there and not there. Not in Washington, D.C., marching with a million other Black men. My son Dan, my new granddaughter Qasima's father, marched. He was a witness, and the arc of his witness included me, as mine includes his, so yes, I was there in a sense, but not there to view the face of Emmett Till because Emmett Till was not there either, not in an open casket displayed to the glory of the heavens, the glories of this Republic, not there except as a shadow, a stain, a wound in the million faces of the marchers, the faces of their fathers, sons and brothers.

We have yet to look upon Emmett Till's face. No apocalyptic encounter, no ritual unveiling, no epiphany has freed us. The nightmare is not cured.

I cannot wish away Emmett Till's face. The horrific death mask of his erased features marks a place I ignore at my peril. The sight of a grievous wound. A wound unhealed because untended. Beneath our nation's pieties, our lies and self-delusions, our denials and distortions of history, our professed certainties about race, lies chaos. The whirlwind that swept Emmett Till away and brings him back.

Chapter 6 *Literary Explorations*

The literary response to Emmett Till's murder was immediate. The first piece, a short narrative poem that appeared in the Communist *Daily Worker,* was published on September 12, a mere two weeks after the crime. By the end of the year, more than twenty other poems had been published, most by average Americans who submitted their work to local newspapers, some by more famous writers, such as Langston Hughes. While the production of literary texts about the murder has inevitably slowed down, it has remained a steady source of artistic inspiration for the past forty-seven years. In the 1990s alone, more than a dozen works focused on or made reference to the case, and the year 2000 was marked by the production of two new plays about Till's life (*The Guardian,* by Eugene McDaniel and Jonathan Muhammed, and *The State of Mississippi vs. Emmett Till* [first produced, 1999; revised 2000], by David Barr).

The first novel based on the case was the opportunistic *Dark Don't Catch Me* (1956) by Vin Packer (a.k.a. M. E. Kerr), a salacious paperback sex-thriller about a brash New York City black youth who is burned alive for "clucking" at a white woman in Paradise, Georgia. Since the appearance of Packer's novel, four other longer and more important works have been loosely based on the murder: Rod Serling's 1956 teledrama "Noon on Doomsday" (altered by nervous network executives so as to make its relation to the Till case almost undetectable), James Baldwin's 1964 play *Blues for Mister Charlie,* and two novels from the 1990s, Bebe Moore Campbell's *Your Blues Ain't Like Mine* (1992) and Lewis Nordan's *Wolf Whistle* (1993). Still another work, Ishmael Reed's 1986 novel *Reckless Eyeballing,* alludes heavily to the case, and indirect echoes of the lynching have been detected in Richard Wright's *The Long Dream* (novel, 1958), Eudora Welty's *Losing Battles* (novel, 1970), and Madison Jones's *Cry of Absence* (novel, 1972).

In contrast to those writers who based their works loosely on the events of 1955 are another group of artists who have chosen to address those events more directly. Among the poets who have written about the murder are Langston

Hughes ("Mississippi—1955," 1955), Gwendolyn Brooks ("A Bronzeville Mother Loiters in Mississippi. Meanwhile, A Mississippi Mother Burns Bacon," 1960), James A. Emanuel ("Emmett Till," 1963), Nicolas Guillén ("Elegías a Emmett Till," 1977), Audre Lorde ("Afterimages," 1981), Wanda Coleman ("Emmett Till," 1986), Anthony Walton ("The Lovesong of Emmett Till," 1996), and Pamela Sneed ("Eyes on the Prize," 1998). A handful of songs have reflected on Till's legacy, such as Langston Hughes and Jobe Huntley's "Money, Mississippi, Blues" (1955), Bob Dylan's "The Death of Emmett Till" (1962), Russell Malone's "Flowers for Emmett Till" (1992) and DJ Nasty Knock's "Emmett Till" (1996). Stage treatments include Richard Davidson's *Mississippi* (1955), Ossie Davis and Ruby Dee's *What Can You Say to Mississippi?* (1956), and Toni Morrison's *Dreaming Emmett* (1986). There is even an unproduced screenplay: William Bradford Huie's *Wolf Whistle* (1960).

It would be impossible, of course, to include complete versions of—or even selections from—all the literary representations of the case. First off, several of them are unpublished and appear not even to exist in manuscript form; they are known only through references in letters, autobiographies, or playbills. Such works include Davidson's *Mississippi,* Wade Dente's play *A Good Place to Raise a Boy* (1956?), Davis and Dee's *What Can You Say to Mississippi?,* and an untitled play performed by the Jewish Cultural Club in Cleveland, Ohio, on October 8, 1955. Toni Morrison's *Dreaming Emmett,* performed at the Albany, New York, Repertory Theatre in 1986, is the only play by the Nobel Prize–winning novelist; however, according to the APT, Morrison had all copies of the play destroyed, thus making it impossible to sample the work in this anthology. In other cases, permission restrictions prevent republication of works. For instance, Henry Dumas's 1965 *Negro Digest* story "The Crossing" is one of the most interesting fictions about the case, but Johnson Publishing has declined to permit reprinting of any work about Emmett Till to which it holds the rights (the reason why there are no selections from *Jet* or *Ebony* in this anthology). Finally, some of the longer works—Serling's *Noon on Doomsday,* Baldwin's *Blues for Mister Charlie,* Nordan's *Wolf Whistle,* and Campbell's *Your Blues Ain't Like Mine,* for instance—do not lend themselves to accessible excerpting.

Nonetheless, this chapter contains a judicious sampling of literary texts about Emmett Till, a selection that gives voice to the well-known, the never-known, and the forgotten. A good many of the works in this chapter appeared in sources that are hard to access, such as old newspapers and journals, and thus are being given a larger audience for the first time. Most of them have never been reprinted before, and one of them (Langston Hughes's "Money, Mississippi, Blues") is making its first appearance in print.

Requiem for a Fourteen-Year-Old
Richard Davidson, *Daily Worker*, 12 September 1955

Richard Davidson, a Jewish poet and playwright from New York City, contributed regularly to such periodicals as the *Daily Worker* and *Masses and Mainstream.* An active member of the Communist Party, Davidson wrote several works about the Till case; the following poem appears to have been the first creative work published about the murder. A second poem, entitled "A Cause for Justice" (reprinted later in this chapter), was also published in the *Daily Worker.* A play by Davidson entitled "Mississippi" ran for three nights at the Pantomime Theatre in New York City in January 1956, but no extant copies of it can be found. Davidson died in 1999.

Ten thousand heard the service which gave him
To the cooling earth.
    (The Church seats much less. The others
      Stood outside on sidewalks listening to the words piped over speakers.)
Ten thousand on two or three crowded streets
Watching slim years cut down, wrapped neatly
in the undertaking rooms.
Somebody sang out, "Yes God, praise his name."

    The street remembers him
    Knocking around with his bike
    Or running errands or grabbing
    For ice cream.
    He liked school
    And maybe was planning to be an engineer
    Or a cop on the beat
    Or play those notes that Louie Armstrong
    Sends twirling into space
(He was saving for a trumpet or was thinking about it.)
Man, he could feel the ground real easy under his shoes.
There was a lot of fun in growing up.
Except maybe when some damn fool made a crack
About being colored

Or the time the waiter left him and his mother
    waiting with those smart eyes of the manager
    pointing at the door.
(A lot of those ten thousand know about that.)

There were no earth shaking last words
Except a simple note.
    "Hi mom, having fun, send my bike, need
    dough, lots of love.["]
He missed his two wheeler on those
Long, hot southern streets.
[(]He had gone down to visit his uncle.)
    He promised his mother
    To pay her back.
(A guy can't get in a movie on confederate money.)
He wiped his eyes from the hot sun
And was anxious to get going.
He planned a quick graduation
And thought about college.

There is talking among the ten thousand.
Some are crying, some with eyes closed
Just thinking.
A little kid wonders why and doesn't quite understand.
A Bishop thunders words across the wires.
People look up and listen.
    (Nobody will forget how it happened.
    Finding his body banged up.
Finding murder on the long, hot streets.
    Somebody said he had the absolute nerve
    Whistling at a white woman that way.
Somebody said he was a damn young punk.)

Others remember him.
A nice kid with his cap slung back on his head
Used to go to dances at school
Make some jokes, buy a hot dog after, was sweet
on a girl lived down the block.
Once he wrote a poem to her

He kept it out of sight
Hid it underneath his school books.
Man, if his friends found out
They'd kid the pants off him for a month.
Somebody in the ten thousand called his name out and sang louder.

The crowd is orderly and the sermons ring
In the city air.
His buddies standing on the curb or sitting inside
May remember he liked to hear a good Lena Horne record
Or go out to Sox Park on those Sundays in June.
  (He used to like to get in the upper bleachers and yell his head off.)
He told them about a new idea for the football team
As soon as he got back they'd work on it.

The sermon is about over.
  (Authorities have promised quick action in the case.)
His mother asked for a song
"I Don't Know Why I Have To Cry Sometimes."
Some of the crowd is turning homeward now.
A few of his buddies walked down the block
Whistling a low moaning blues.
In Washington that night somebody remarked
about the need for a strong colonial policy.

Mississippi—1955
Langston Hughes (23 September 1955)

Langston Hughes, the best-known and most honored African American poet of his generation, published more than twenty volumes of poetry, fiction, drama, song lyrics, and memoirs. A political activist as well as an accomplished artist, Hughes also wrote a weekly column for the *Chicago Defender* from 1942 to 1965 in which he addressed issues of timely social, cultural, and political importance. The following poem was completed on September 23, but first appeared in Hughes's column on October 1 (see "Langston Hughes Wonders Why No Lynchings Probes," reprinted in chapter 3 of this anthology). Unfortunately, the poem was incorrectly transcribed by the editors at the *Chicago Defender* and thus contains many errors. Similar, though less formidable, errors mark the appearance of this work in other African American newspapers. Fortunately, a copy of the poem exists in the Papers of the NAACP at the Library of Congress, from which this version of the poem is drawn. Hughes died in 1968.

(To the Memory of Emmett Till)

Oh, what sorrow!
Oh, what pity!
Oh, what pain
That tears and blood
Should mix like rain
And terror come again
To Mississippi.

Come again?
Where has terror been?
On vacation? Up North?
In some other section
Of the nation,
Lying low, unpublicized?
Masked — with only
Jaundiced eyes
Showing through the mask?

Oh, what sorrow,
Pity, pain,
That tears and blood
Should mix like rain
In Mississippi!
And terror, fetid hot,
Yet clammy cold
Remain.

The Money, Mississippi, Blues
Langston Hughes and Jobe Huntley (October 1955)

A literary polymath, Langston Hughes worked comfortably within many genres, and his interest in blues music spanned the length of his distinguished career. His first collection of poetry, *The Weary Blues* (1926), bears testament to this interest, and later in his career he continued to explore the blues as an art form and a source of inspiration. The following work—never before published—is another example of Hughes's work as a blues song-smith. The song (with lyrics by Hughes and music by Jobe Huntley) was found among the Papers of the NAACP in the Library of Congress and is reprinted with the permission of the Hughes estate. As a preface to the poem, Hughes's letter to Henry Lee Moon, Public Relations Director of the NAACP, has also been included. In this letter, Hughes tells of the song's genesis and expresses his wish that it be used to help generate funds for the NAACP. There is no record of the song ever being produced, and unfortunately musical notations were not included with Hughes's letter.

October 4, 1955

Mr. Henry Lee Moon,
N. A. A. C. P.
20 West 40th Street,
New York 18, N.Y.

Dear Henry:

Several people at the rally Sunday at Lawson's Auditorium in 125th Street spoke to me about liking the poem which they had seen in the colored papers ["Mississippi—1955"]. Thank you for such good coverage. I heard Billy Holiday sing "Strange Fruit" there. And it occur[r]ed to me how many more people are r[e]ached when poetry is combined with music (the record of "Strange Fruit" is still selling after 20 years). So from the theme of my poem, I've made a song—but in popular style—the MONEY, MISSISSIPPI, BLUES, and the young Negro composer, Jobe Huntley, has set it to a simple singable melody.

The few people who have heard it today think it is very effective. I am enclosing the lyrics for you, and can arrange for you to hear the music anytime it is convenient for you, since perhaps the song might be useful to the N.A.A.C.P. in its fund raising campaigns. Either Josh White or Billy Holiday might be persuaded to make a record of the song without charge for the N.A.A.C.P. to be sold by the N. A. A. C. P. and distributed generally, all profits from this record to go to the

N.A.A.C.P., as the composer and I would donate our composition—reserving, of course, the rights to any other recordings (should any ever be made) and to the sheet music sales, if any.

Both Jobe Huntley and I know Josh White pretty well and could appro[a]ch him on this, should the idea appeal to you. I don't know Billy Holiday, and would consider her a second choice anyhow. But I do think such a recording right now by a name artist would have a sale to both Negroes and whites—and so might bring you in some funds.

If you and Roy like this idea, let me know, and I'll get busy contacting Josh who's in Boston this week performing, but will be back in New York next week.

If you see Mrs. Hurley, please tell her for me that I thought her talk at the rally most effective, and her appearance on the Barry Gray show equally good.

Best to Molly, and I hope I see you-all once in a blue moon again. At the moment I'[m] house-bound on TWO big deadlines due in at the publishers this fall. One is that autobiography—already over 500 pages and not done yet. Your famous Odessa line is in there, but none of the 22 (but me) are named, and the whole movie episode is played for comedy mostly. If you're in the neighborhood, drop by and glance over the script.

Best ever,

    Sincerely,
    Langston

THE MONEY, MISSISSIPPI, BLUES
Lyrics by Langston Hughes, Music by Jobe Huntley

> I don't want to go to Money, honey,
> not Money, Mississippi!
> no, I wouldn't go to Money, honey,
> down in Mississippi.
> There's pity, sorrow, and pain

in Money, Mississippi.
Tears and blood like rain
in Money, Mississippi,
in Money, Mississippi!

His father died for democracy
fighting in the army over the sea.
His father died for the U. S. A.
Why did they treat his son this a-way?
in Money, Money, Mississippi,
Money, Mississippi.

His mother worked to raise her child,
dressed him neat, kept him from running wild.
She sent him to the country when vacation came,
but he never got back to Chicago the same.
They sent him back in a wooden box——
from Money, Money, Mississippi,
Money, Mississippi.

Little old boy, just fourteen years old,
shot, kicked, and beaten 'cause he was so bold
to whistle at a woman who was white.
He was throwed in the river in the dead of night
in Money, Money, Mississippi,
Money, Mississippi.

I don't want to go to Money, honey,
not Money, Mississippi.
No, I wouldn't want to go to Money, honey,
down in Mississippi.
There's pity, sorrow, and pain
in Money, Mississippi!
Tears and blood like rain
in Money, Mississippi,
in Money, Mississippi!

No, I wouldn't want to go——
for no kind o' Money——

to Money, Mississippi,
not Money, Mississippi!

Money, Mississippi!

(Blues guitar accompaniment)

A Cause for Justice
Richard Davidson, *Daily Worker,* 11 October 1955

Davidson's second poem about Emmett Till to appear in the *Daily Worker*
was written after the verdict. It is the first literary document to suggest that
Till's murder will become a rallying cry for the nascent civil rights movement.

Mr. and Mrs. XX sat snugly in the hot courtroom
Waving a small fan in front of them smothering
The heat that crept through the turning fans.
They listen to the words and nudge each other
And glance at neighbors with familiar looks.
The jury would not be long and then the short walk home.
The triumph and the comforting smile over cocktails and small crackers.
Mr. XX slaps against a fly perching on his hand
He glances at his watch and measures off the minutes
And makes a small bet to himself how soon the verdict on the two men accused
    will make its entrance in the room where decision waits.
And then it comes, "not guilty" after an hour it comes
And Mr. and Mrs. XX rise slowly up, stretch their legs
Brush away unsuspecting insects
And walk casually to the main door and the wondering street.

(Far from that courtroom down in Mississippi
There is a soft grave and silent trees
And the echo of a boy's voice that is not lost in the headlines of yesterday
But is alive and clear and commands
Our attention.
The clocks of his life stop at fourteen years
And stopped are his dreams
That his flesh might have borne.
Stopped are his rightful hopes and even

Mistakes that youth's blood always shall allow.
Stopped are the gropings and fresh yells
That make a man.
They are stopped and his voice rises
Out of his murdered body, out of a killing
That was settled in a quick hour.)

Mr. and Mrs. XX settle down in their easy chairs
And guests pop in for a few good drinks and talk
About the trial and notice how the weather is and the
Fact that the defense attorney was quite interesting
And didn't Mrs. XX look fine in that autumn hat and was there
Really a reporter from *Time* there?
And what was all the shouting about and if there was a crime
Certainly it would have come out in the proceedings.
Mr. and Mrs. XX nod happily and yawn and it[']s been a long, long day
And they wonder secretly if pictures were taken and were
They seated in the right place?
They would purchase the morning papers and see.
Mr. XX goes to the front door, says goodnight, locks it, smokes a final cigarette,
    and walks casually to bed.
To his wife's arms and to sleep and to forget.

(Birds rest on a soft grave near silent trees
In air that is not silent;
The sky is a movement of footballs
And spilling bodies.
Shouts of a fourteen-year old running with
The glory of life just begun.
Smelling the first flower or cracking the ice of winter.
These fill the unsilent air.
All that he was is part of the high grass now
And the earth underneath.
And the voice now rising out of his death
Pointing to the stone and trying to accept it.
To accept an end that was not ready for years not lived.
Birds rest on a soft grave near silent trees
In air that is not silent.)

Mr. and Mrs. XX greet the morning with pouring
Coffee and the waiting cornflakes.
They scan the local paper and there are pictures
But they just missed them, the camera touching the row ahead.
Mr. XX grabs his hat, kisses his wife goodbye, and starts the car for the office and
    the bright, new day.
Mrs. XX makes an early appointment at the hairdresser.
Switches on the radio and wonders why all that excitement still goes on.
A trial is a trial and somehow the news of yesterday
Gets lost with hairstyles for tomorrow.

(His voice grows louder now and we remember
The last sermons and the song they played
Him into the dark grass.
"When the Saints Go Marching In."
We remember the prayers said and the slow, burning ache in a mother's heart.
We remember the young eyes and the dreams just turning from birth.)

We will not forget Emmett Louis Till
In tomorrow's problems or last week's good news.
We will not forget him in breakfast food
Or in the rush of winter bells.
We promise the voice that commands our attention
The earth that was his earth
Will not wilt and die in a quick hour's decision.

Our anger does not rest in a soft grave near silent trees
But grows as his young voice grows
His death becomes a part of our living flesh.
His killing a waking cry of our conscience.
His murder a country's shame and our fight
To erase that shame and to promise a rising voice
That justice will be done
    BE DONE!
    BE DONE!

For Emmett Till

Mary Parks, *Daily Worker*, 13 October 1955

Little else is known about Mary Parks besides her authorship of this poem. However, it was given a prominent place in the issue and was neither included in the letters to the editor section nor published under a "Poems from Readers" heading. This suggests that she was a regular, or at least a notable, contributor to the paper, and not simply a reader of the *Daily Worker*. In this poem, Parks situates Till's murder in the larger fabric of African American history and calls for it to become part of the nation's collective memory.

Boyhood years are a time to sing
Of birch tree leaf and a blue bird wing—
For summer days and a lad exploring,
For a high blue sky with a baseball soaring.
Boyhood years are a time for learning,
School each year when the leaves are turning,
Dreaming the long bright years ahead—
But not a time for a boy to be dead.

The teacher spoke about Plymouth Rock,
The Pilgrims, the Mayflower; was it to mock
Those others who came on the slavers' ships,
Braver than lions, tougher than whips?
Our country threw out the English king,
But we never threw out that other thing.
We hold these truths, the teacher said
To be self-evident—and dead.

She said all men were created equal.
But what of the slaves? What was the sequel?
Plantation ladies wore blue sashes,
Back-talking slaves got twenty lashes;
Proudly the white men's country rose
While black men toiled in the cotton rows;
But terrible rivers of blood were shed
To prevent such things as this boy being dead.

Did the teacher tell how, in Boston town,
William Lloyd Garrison was put down—
Defying the rope around his neck
To prevent the Underground Railway's wreck?
How many boys in Chicago knew
That Turner and Vesey were heroes, too?
That Negroes perished with John Brown's son?
How Harriet Tubman carried a gun?

Land where our fathers lived and died,
Boyhood years are a time for pride.
Now a boy can hope, in his manhood years
To be accepted among his peers;
In dreams a lad can follow his bent
And rise from porter to president;
Because of the falling color bars
A boy can walk with his head in the stars.

But not this boy with a shattered head,
Who died in a muddy river bed.
Remember him, every living thing,
Each birch tree leaf and blue bird wing—
Remember him stars, remember him sun,
Remember him, People—he was our son.
Avenge him together, O black and white—
That the sun may rise on this monstrous night.

Blood on Mississippi
Ernest Wakefield Stevens, *Cleveland Call and Post,* 15 October 1955

In this contribution to his hometown newspaper, Ernest Wakefield Stevens accuses Mississippi of savagery, giving poetic expression to a common indictment of the state in the national press. Moreover, he also draws attention to the international ramifications of the lynching.

Search the most benighted jungle,
Find the creature most insane,
And the Mississippi savage
Will, then, put the wretch to shame.

Murder always will be murder
But of all the ways to kill—
It was down right most revolting—
How they slaughtered Emmett Till—

All the world must look and shudder!
Decent people have been riled
Everywhere—of every color—
At the lynching of a child.

Lord of mankind everywhere,
How can any nation flood
Other lands with purer air
When its own is drenched in blood?

Bow your head low, Mississippi,
For the damage you have done
To the efforts of our country
In its fight for everyone.

What a mockery of Justice!
What a stinking, rotten smell!
Only down in Mississippi
Can one really prevue Hell.

Mississippi
Martha Millet, *Masses and Mainstream,* October 1955

Martha Millet's "Mississippi" appeared in the October 1955 issue of *Masses and Mainstream,* a journal affiliated with the Communist Party. Millet, who would later be better known as Martha Millet Garlin—wife of leftist intellectual Service Garlin—expressed such rage against the state of Mississippi that another *Masses and Mainstream* contributor, the famed African American historian Herbert Aptheker, responded in the next issue of the journal by calling for a more temperate condemnation of Mississippi.

The blood cries out

speaking truth to your lies,
Mississippi.

Indians named you "great waters";
the Spaniard de Soto after them
looking upon your river,
dark, impassive, suspect,
prophetic with blood of first Americans
slaughtered for empire, for gold,
for the gold of men's sweat;
prophetic with blood of the black man
dropping relentless into the flood
under the lash of Bourbon and cotton forever . . .

The blood cries out.

"What have they done to me?"
cries the voice of the child—
"What have they done?"

"Did I come from the North,
from my mother's embrace
to fall beneath the two-pronged fang
of the serpent that goes like a man . . .
striking and striking
into my just-formed flesh,
destroying of nature and man,
crushing my brain and my small
marvelous organs and bones
into the seal of their sadist
hate . . . ?"

Mississippi, stronghold of the Old South,
like a cancer spread over
a shuddering world,
over the straightforward sweetness
of early freedom roots—

Mississippi
madman who holds the time bomb, swaggering dwarf,
with your knout of fire . . .

> In the invisible congress of these States
> united—
> which exists—
> it is us—
breaks out a voice of held-in power
> over the coil of flame that snarls
> from Mississippi's borders—
> voice of John Brown, Thoreau, Mamie Bradley,
> demanding:

> "This day shall forever be proclaimed
> a day of national mourning
> and retribution!"

"What have they done?" cries the child.
"Why have they beaten me, tortured me,
wound me in wire from the cotton gin
that tore our years across,
that made them rich . . .
sunk me deep in the river of no forgetting . . .?"

O Mississippi——

Out of the folds of the Father of Rivers,
heavy with juices of black men
rearing a feudal domain on breaking backs,
the body propels upward.
Light abandons the world.
It is all gathered here, on this spot,
focused in horror and
supreme reckoning.

crying out
crying out

"Do unto others . . ."

yes

this nation under

God!

In the courtroom, she, the mother,
    stared, a hairbreadth away
    from the killers, the willing fingers
    of ghoulmakers in
    a southern Third Reich.

    O Mamie Bradley, how you stood
    in the courtroom confronting them,
    where every white calls the juryman
    cousin, and slips wink.

    You, stand up. You are proud. The blood of your child
    rose up in you for their damnation.

    Yours is the immemorial
    hammer of God,
    God of men.

    Does the river know colors of men,
    arms heaping sandbags,
    throwing up
    resistance of man,
    thrusting the rage of waters back?

    Survivors cling to the trembling roofs.
    Rescuers come,
    strongly moving the boats
    with weary arms
    through liquid avenues.
    Do they ask the color—savers, the saved?

When the river floods
What can stand it off?
Only man.

Mississippi,
huddling in arrogance
with your tobacco-spitting words
that rot the air—

Shut your eyes of death.
The child comes
vaster than any sun
that burned down on your cotton fields,
while you drove hard bargains at county seats,
piling land, cotton gold;
told your exploits under shade trees,
under magnolia essence—your flower,
like a palliative applied to a corpse
in the embalming room . . .

fathering forcibly young
on the black woman in nights
your romances do not record,
never record;
selling the fruit of your lust
under the hammer . . . goods
like your cotton, corn . . .

Mississippi
the judgement hangs over you,
the storm long warned of.
Will all your stone cellars suffice?
Will your strongest locks hold up?

Where are you, O federal government
with your laws, your justice forces;
laws that were made *for* men, *by* men,
not in man's despite . . . ?
Where have you hurried away

that scrap of paper, our
Constitution, written in blood
on drumheads on this soil
that was lava with men's
high hopes, brightness, love . . . ?
What have you done with equal rights
of all Americans
to life, to liberty, to
the pursuit of happiness . . . ?

Mississippi—

Distant and near the grief-rage
spills into your waters, onto
your soil of sweat

selling democracy everywhere,
at home
lynching it . . .

Emmett Till
Emmett Till . . .

You too Mamie Bradley
in the one-gallus courtroom
where jokes are cracked
where the killers pose
for family photos; where
a body bleeds mutilations.

Where is the boy?
What is this thing
You send back to me?

"And do you positively
identify the body
as that of your son,
Emmett Till . . .

Swear on the Bible——
Swear."

They swear on the Good Book still
with the old southern flourish
that whips a slave to death
between juleps.

Mississippi

when the avenger comes among you,
what will you do,
where will you hide,
what crevice of earth will receive you?

The blood cries out.

What have they done to you,
Emmett Till——?

What curse is it that causes
the southerner, Faulkner, to cry:
*We do not deserve to survive
and probably we won't.*

Mississippi,
in what grave
will you hide your curse;
in what eternity . . . ?

The blood cries out.

A Tribute to Emmett Till
Mary Carson Cooper, *Cleveland Call and Post*, 22 October 1955

In hopes of expressing her "deep concern over the Emmett Till slaying," Mary Carson Cooper of Akron, Ohio, contributed the following poem to the *Cleveland Call and Post*. While its call for militant action in response to the murder makes it unique among early poems about the case, it nonetheless expresses a sentiment voiced by many readers of African American newspapers.

Some southern demons lynched a child.
A mother's only son.
God sits on high and frowns at such
They'll pay for what they've done!
Young Emmett Till will never know
To God all men are equal
And no race is supreme.
It's time all Negroes did fight back
With their own lynching team!

For Moses Wright (Uncle of Emmett Louis Till)
"I.S.," *Daily Worker*, 14 November 1955

"I.S." is identified only as a reader from Brooklyn. In singling out the heroism of Moses Wright, "I.S." prefigures the way in which the Till story will be told more than thirty years later in the award-winning documentary *Eyes on the Prize*. In that documentary, Wright's court testimony—in particular his pointing to Milam and saying "dar he" when asked to identify one of the murderers—is considered to be the genesis of the modern civil rights movement.

There will be laurel wreaths
For heroes of the sea,
As rightly it should be,
Bestowing honor on their daring feats.

But Moses, not for you.

There will be medals placed
On proudly heaving chests
For bravery that met the tests
The others had not faced.

But Moses, not for you.

Red carpets will be rolled,
A governor will coo
A pleasing word or two
Appearing in the aura of the bold.

But Moses, not with you,
Not with you.

You dared too much for laurel wreaths.
You stood up in the lion's den
And dared accuse the lion's teeth.

Moses of the cotton counties.

Your hard-earned pride
No trophy can attend,
Nor medal can bestride.

Moses of the blood-red fields.

Your boldness was too bold for praise.
You sent a shudder thru the government
That questions its indifferent ways.

Moses of the outraged mourners.

You called a lyncher by his name.
The South will never be the same.

Moses, clap of thunder behind mountains.

Promotional Flyer for "A Good Place to Raise a Boy"
Wade Dente (1956?)

Many creative works about the murder of Emmett Till have been lost.
Richard Davidson's aforementioned play *Mississippi* is one such work. Another is Wade Dente's *A Good Place to Raise a Boy*. The exact contents of the
play are unknown, and it is not mentioned in any previous studies or bibli-
ographies. Nor is anything known about the playwright. The only evidence
remaining that such a play existed is the following flyer, found in the Papers

of the NAACP in the Library of Congress. While the typeface of the original has not been recreated, the flyer is reprinted here without emendation.

EMMETT TILL IS NOT DEAD !!!!

The Daily Journal have long since filed away the stories of the case of Emmett Till. The Weekly Journals carry only a flyer on the murder that shocked the world, when some character once associated with the tragic case becomes involved in an incident of minor news-importance. Newsworthily, EMMETT TILL IS DEAD.

There are more Emmett Tills in mississippi. Not being subjected to brutal murder as was the young Chicago-born boy, but murdered nevertheless. The awakening of the Negro in Mississippi, the Poor Whites becoming aware of their plight as equal to the Negro; this is the story the author unfolds, in making a literary epic of the EMMETT TILL STORY. The whole story was never told in the newspapers. Unless this story is told, the valiant efforts of the few Negroes and Poor whites struggling in the South will be useless. That's why everyone who hates despots, who has ever felt the boot of Racial Suppression and Extinction MUST SEE "A GOOD PLCE TO RAISE A BOY."

Some Critics didn't like it. Truth is usually more brutal than fiction, less furbished with imaginative happy endings. The story of the "CRUCIFIXION" or of the "WARSAW MASSACRES" or the extinction of the Jews in Germany is not a pretty picture, but these stories must be told, so that, "THE WORLD" will not become less vigilant while the "Vandals" of democracy steal away our very foundations.

We have enjoyed your confidence in the past in recommending to you certain plays Off-Broadway. " A LAND BEYOND THE RIVER " , SIMPLY HEAVENLY " , TWISTING ROAD " , AFRICANA " are but few of the plays enjoyed by our friends, who visited Off-Broadway shows.

Believe us this time too !!!!

For sheer dramatic impact, *YOU MUST SEE,* "A GOOD PLACE TO RAISE A BOY"

Place: Hotel Theresa (125th St. at 7th Ave.)
N.Y.C.

Time: Tues. thru Sat. Eves. at 8:30 P.M. (incl. Sat. mat.)
3:30 P.M.
Price: Contribution-$2.00 (club rates at reduced price available)
Info: For information (New Jersey—call—Pilgrim 4.6779)
New York—call—Riverside 9-8300

S.S. Auerbach— Producer   Wade Dente—Autthor
George Greenleaf— Publicity

A Bronzeville Mother Loiters in Mississippi. Meanwhile, a Mississippi Mother Burns Bacon
Gwendolyn Brooks (1960)

Gwendolyn Brooks was the first African American to receive the Pulitzer Prize (for *Annie Allen,* 1949), and in her long and distinguished career she garnered numerous honors. Recipient of the American Academy of Arts and Letters Award (1946), a National Endowment for the Arts Senior Fellowship for Literature (1989), and the National Book Foundation's medal for Distinguished Contribution to American Letters (1994), Brooks was the poet laureate of the state of Illinois and the author of more than twenty books of poetry, one novel, a children's book, and an autobiography. In the following poem, first published in *The Bean Eaters* (1960), Brooks imagines the murder from the perspective of Carolyn Bryant. It remains, more than forty years later, one of her most anthologized works. Brooks died in 2001.

From the first it had been like a
Ballad. It had the beat inevitable. It had the blood.
A wildness cut up, and tied in little bunches,
Like the four-line stanzas of the ballads she had never quite
Understood—the ballads they had set her to, in school.

Herself: the milk-white maid, the "maid mild"
Of the ballad. Pursued
By the Dark Villain. Rescued by the Fine Prince.
The Happiness-Ever-After.
That was worth anything.
It was good to be a "maid mild."
That made the breath go fast.

Her bacon burned. She
Hastened to hide it in the step-on can, and
Drew more strips from the meat case. The eggs and sour-milk biscuits
Did well. She set out a jar
Of her new quince preserve.

. . . But there was a something about the matter of the Dark Villain.
He should have been older, perhaps.
The hacking down of a villain was more fun to think about
When his menace possessed undisputed breadth, undisputed height,
And a harsh kind of vice.
And best of all, when his history was cluttered
With the bones of many eaten knights and princesses.

The fun was disturbed, then all but nullified
When the Dark Villain was a blackish child
Of fourteen, with eyes still too young to be dirty,
And a mouth too young to have lost every reminder
Of its infant softness.
That boy must have been surprised! For
These were grown-ups. Grown-ups were supposed to be wise.
And the Fine Prince—and that other—so tall, so broad, so
Grown! Perhaps the boy had never guessed
That the trouble with grown-ups was that under the magnificent shell of adult-
    hood, just under,
Waited the baby full of tantrums.
It occurred to her that there may have been something
Ridiculous in the picture of the Fine Prince
Rushing (rich with the breadth and height and
Mature solidness whose lack, in the Dark Villain, was impressing her,
Confronting her more and more as this first day after the trial
And acquittal wore on) rushing
With his heavy companion to hack down (unhorsed)
That little foe.
So much had happened, she could not remember now what that foe had done
Against her, or if anything had been done.
The one thing in the world that she did know and knew
With terrifying clarity was that her composition
Had disintegrated. That, although the pattern prevailed,

The breaks were everywhere. That she could think
Of no thread capable of the necessary
Sew-work.

She made the babies sit in their places at the table.
Then, before calling Him, she hurried
To the mirror with her comb and lipstick. It was necessary
To be more beautiful than ever.
The beautiful wife.
For sometimes she fancied he looked at her as though
Measuring her. As if he considered, Had she been worth It?
Had *she* been worth the blood, the cramped cries, the little stuttering bravado,
The gradual dulling of those Negro eyes,
The sudden, overwhelming *little-boyness* in that barn?
Whatever she might feel or half-feel, the lipstick necessity was something apart.
   He must never conclude
That she had not been worth It.

He sat down, the Fine Prince, and
Began buttering a biscuit. He looked at his hands.
He twisted in his chair, he scratched his nose.
He glanced again, almost secretly, at his hands.
More papers were in from the North, he mumbled. More meddling headlines.
With their pepper-words, "bestiality," and "barbarism," and
"Shocking."
The half-sneers he had mastered for the trial worked across
His sweet and pretty face.

What he'd like to do, he explained, was kill them all.
The time lost. The unwanted fame.
Still, it had been fun to show those intruders
A thing or two. To show that snappy-eyed mother,
That sassy, Northern, brown-black——

Nothing could stop Mississippi.
He knew that. Big Fella
Knew that.
And, what was so good, Mississippi knew that.
Nothing and nothing could stop Mississippi.

They could send in their petitions, and scar
Their newspapers with bleeding headlines. Their governors
Could appeal to Washington. . . .

"What I want," the older baby said, "is 'lasses on my jam."
Whereupon the younger baby
Picked up the molasses pitcher and threw
The molasses in his brother's face. Instantly
The Fine Prince leaned across the table and slapped
The small and smiling criminal.

She did not speak. When the Hand
Came down and away, and she could look at her child,
At her baby-child,
She could think only of blood.
Surely her baby's cheek
Had disappeared, and in its place, surely,
Hung a heaviness, a lengthening red, a red that had no end.
She shook her head. It was not true, of course.
It was not true at all. The
Child's face was as always, the
Color of the paste in her paste-jar.

She left the table, to the tune of the children's lamentations, which were shriller
Than ever. She
Looked out of a window. She said not a word. *That*
Was one of the new Somethings—
The fear,
Tying her as with iron.

Suddenly she felt his hands upon her. He had followed her
To the window. The children were whimpering now.
Such bits of tots. And she, their mother,
Could not protect them. She looked at her shoulders, still
Gripped in the claim of his hands. She tried, but could not resist the idea
That a red ooze was seeping, spreading darkly, thickly, slowly,
Over her white shoulders, her own shoulders,
And over all of Earth and Mars.

He whispered something to her, did the Fine Prince, something
About love, something about love and night and intention.

She heard no hoof-beat of the horse and saw no flash of the shining steel.
He pulled her face around to meet
His, and there it was, close close,
For the first time in all those days and nights.
His mouth, wet and red,
So very, very, very red,
Closed over hers.

Then a sickness heaved within her. The courtroom Coca-Cola,
The courtroom beer and hate and sweat and drone,
Pushed like a wall against her. She wanted to bear it.
But his mouth would not go away and neither would the
Decapitated exclamation points in that Other Woman's eyes.

She did not scream.
She stood there.
But a hatred for him burst into glorious flower,
And its perfume enclasped them—big,
Bigger than all magnolias.

The last bleak news of the ballad.
The rest of the rugged music.
The last quatrain.

The Last Quatrain of the Ballad of Emmett Till
Gwendolyn Brooks (1960)

A companion piece to "A Bronzeville Mother," this poem was also first published in *The Bean Eaters* (1960). In it, Brooks explores further the idea that
the Till murder violates all narrative conventions and expectations, possessing as it does a kind of surreal quality that moves toward ambiguity rather
than understanding.

> after the murder,
> after the burial

Emmett's mother is a pretty-faced thing;
    the tint of pulled taffy.
She sits in a red room,
    drinking black coffee.
She kisses her killed boy.
    And she is sorry.
Chaos in windy grays
    through a red prairie.

The Death of Emmett Till
Bob Dylan (1962)

Bob Dylan has been called the poet of the American sixties, and his songs of social protest and youthful self-reflection inspired and defined a generation. "The Death of Emmett Till" was one of Dylan's earliest protest songs, and he appears to have become quickly disillusioned by it. In a 1964 interview he admitted, "I used to write songs, like I'd say, 'Yeah, what's bad, pick something bad, like segregation, OK, here we'd go,' and I'd pick one of a thousand million little points I can pick and explode it, some of them which I didn't know anything about. I wrote a song about Emmett Till [in this way]. . . . I realize now that my reasons and motives behind it were phony. I didn't have to write it." It must also be noted that, as with many of Dylan's songs, "The Death of Emmett Till" exists in several versions. The following lyrics are taken from Dylan's *Writings and Drawings* (Knopf, 1973).

'Twas down in Mississippi not so long ago.
When a young boy from Chicago town stepped through a Southern door.
This boy's dreadful tragedy I can still remember well,
The color of his skin was black and his name was Emmett Till.

Some men they dragged him to a barn and there they beat him up.
They said they had a reason, but I can't remember what.
They tortured him and did some things too evil to repeat.
There were screaming sounds inside the barn, there was laughing sounds out on
    the street.

Then they rolled his body down a gulf amidst a bloody red rain
And they threw him in the waters wide to cease his screaming pain.

The reason that they killed him there, and I'm sure it ain't no lie,
Was just for the fun of killin' him and to watch him slowly die.

And then to stop the United States of yelling for a trial,
Two brothers they confessed that they had killed poor Emmett Till.
But on the jury there were men who helped the brothers commit this awful crime,
And so this trial was a mockery, but nobody seemed to mind.

I saw the morning papers but I could not bear to see
The smiling brothers walkin' down the courthouse stairs.
For the jury found them innocent and the brothers they went free,
While Emmett's body floats the foam of a Jim Crow southern sea.

If you can't speak out against this kind of thing, a crime that's so unjust,
Your eyes are filled with dead men's dirt, your mind is filled with dust.
Your arms and legs they must be in shackles and chains, and your blood it must
    refuse to flow,
For you let this human race fall down so God-awful low!

This song is just a reminder to remind your fellow man
That this kind of thing still lives today in that ghost-robed Ku Klux Klan.
But if all us folks that thinks alike, if we gave all we could give,
We could make this great land of ours a greater place to live.

Note for *Blues* (Preface to *Blues for Mister Charlie*)
James Baldwin (1964)

James Baldwin's *Blues for Mister Charlie* was performed to mixed reviews on Broadway in 1964. For many, the character of Richard Henry, the play's Emmett Till figure, was too brash, confrontational, and sexualized. Because Baldwin only loosely based his work on the Till murder, he felt free to play with the "facts" of the case, but these changes—no matter how dramatic— never fully erased Till's presence from the play. Accused of promoting sexualized stereotypes of black men, Baldwin nonetheless stood by his decisions to increase the age of his victim, add a deeper sexual element to his "crime," and put the language of black militancy into his mouth. In the following preface, Baldwin, who at the time had been dubbed the leading literary spokesman for African Americans on matters of civil rights, explains both the genesis of the play and his purpose for writing it. An influential essayist and novelist, Baldwin died in 1987.

This play has been on my mind—has been bugging me for several years. It is unlike anything else I've ever attempted in that I remember vividly the first time it occurred to me; for in fact, it did not occur to me, but to Elia Kazan. Kazan asked me at the end of 1958 if I would be interested in working in the Theatre. It was a generous offer, but I did not react with great enthusiasm because I did not then, and don't now, have much respect for what goes on in the American Theatre. I am not convinced that it is a Theatre; it seems to me a series, merely, of commercial speculations, stale, repetitious, and timid. I certainly didn't see much future for me in that frame-work, and I was profoundly unwilling to risk my morale and my talent—my life—in endeavors which could only increase a level of frustration already dangerously high.

Nevertheless, the germ of the play persisted. It is based, very distantly indeed, on the case of Emmett Till—the Negro youth who was murdered in Mississippi in 1955. The murderer in this case was acquitted. (His brother, who helped him do the deed, is now a deputy sheriff in Ruleville, Mississippi). After his acquittal, he recounted the fact of the murder—for one cannot refer to his performance as a confession—to William Bradford Huie, who wrote it all down in an article called "Wolf Whistle." I do not know why the case pressed on my mind so hard— but it would not let me go. I absolutely dreaded committing myself to writing a play—there were enough people around already telling me that I couldn't write novels—but I began to see that my fear of the form masked a much deeper fear. That fear was that I would never be able to draw a valid portrait of the murderer. In life, obviously, such people baffle and terrify me and, with one part of my mind at least, I hate them and would be willing to kill them. Yet, with another part of my mind, I am aware that no man is a villain in his own eyes. Something in the man knows—*must know*—that what he is doing is evil; but in order to accept the knowledge the man would have to change. What is ghastly and really almost hopeless in our racial situation now is that the crimes we have committed are so great and so unspeakable that the acceptance of this knowledge would lead, literally, to madness. The human being, then, in order to protect himself, closes his eyes, compulsively repeats his crimes, and enters a spiritual darkness which no one can describe.

But if it is true, and I believe it is, that all men are brothers, then we have the duty to try to understand this wretched man; and while we probably cannot hope to liberate him, begin working toward the liberation of his children. For we, the American people, have created him, he is our servant; it is we who put the cattle-prodder in his hands, and we are responsible for the crimes that he commits. It is we who have locked him in the prison of color. It is we who have persuaded him that Negroes are worthless human beings, and that it is his sacred duty, as a white man, to protect the honor and purity of his tribe. It is we who have forbidden him, on pain of exclusion from the tribe, to accept his beginnings, when he and black people loved each other, and rejoice in them, and use them; it is we who have made it mandatory—honorable—that white father should deny black son. These are grave crimes indeed, and we have committed them and continue to commit them in order to make money.

The play then, for me, takes place in Plaguetown, U.S.A., now. The plague is race, the plague is our concept of Christianity: and this raging plague has the power to destroy every human relationship. I once took a short trip with Medgar Evers to the back-woods of Mississippi. He was investigating the murder of a Negro man by a white storekeeper which had taken place months before. Many people talked to Medgar that night, in dark cabins, with their lights out, in whispers; and we had been followed for many miles out of Jackson, Mississippi, not by a lunatic with a gun, but by state troopers. I will never forget that night, as I will never forget Medgar—who took me to the plane the next day. We promised to see each other soon. When he died, something entered into me which I cannot describe, but it was then that I resolved that nothing under heaven would prevent me from getting this play done. We are walking in terrible darkness here, and this is one man's attempt to bear witness to the reality and power of light.

Till
Julius E. Thompson (1977)

Julius E. Thompson's mournful interrogation first appeared in *Blues Said, Walk On* (1977) and was later collected in *Black Southern Voices,* the influential 1992 anthology edited by John Oliver Killens and Jerry W. Ward. A native of Mississippi and a Fulbright scholar, Thompson is the author of nine books of poetry and history, the most recent of which is *Black Life in Mississippi: Essays on Political, Social and Cultural Studies in a Deep South State.* He currently directs the Black Studies Program at the University of Missouri–Columbia.

have you seen a black son, walking
down a mississippi highway headed
home?
have you seen his eyes all red
with hope, not more than thirteen
years?
can you understand, can you understand,
can you,
can you feel four hundred years,
can you? can you awake to see
yourself
dead like he died? can you?
can you see him, one black son,
one?
one that god didn't save, or
his people? can you spread,
can you spread
one,
just one
lie?
can you spread, can you spread out
death
in no man's
land?
she said
he touched her,
or was it that he had whistled—
does it matter?
pure christians don't
lie
or die.
her good men said
he would never
see chicago again
except in a box nailed
in.
can you, can you spread, spread
out death?
his mother
looking on,

down on their knees,
they were giving prayers
for the son who wasn't saved,
and throughout the world his picture
was seen
in
jet magazine.
some people even cried too soon,
before the preacher
said,
"amen."
then there came
a telegram from the president,
he was so sorry
that
you can't change people with
laws.
justice
had a dream
falling
from the second window
of the whi
te house.
can you spread? can you,
can you spread
out death
on her
head?
can you?
can you, can you,
can you save one black son
who god didn't?

Afterimages
Audre Lorde (1981)

A self-proclaimed "black, lesbian, mother, warrior, poet," Audre Lorde always sought to express in her poetry a profound sense of resistance and individuality. Author of more than a dozen collections of poetry—one of which, *From a Land Where Other People Live,* was nominated for the National Book Award in 1974—Lorde was the recipient of many honors, including being named poet laureate of New York in 1991. As with Gwendolyn Brooks's "Bronzeville Mother," Lorde's poem takes as its point of interest Carolyn Bryant (although neither poem mentions her by name). However, whereas both Brooks and Lorde explore the psychic cost of Till's lynching to the "dishonored" white woman, Lorde goes further and probes the burden of imagery carried by all blacks in the aftermath of Till's murder. Lorde died of cancer in 1992.

I

However the image enters
its force remains within
my eyes
rockstrewn caves where dragonfish evolve
wild for life, relentless and acquisitive
learning to survive
where there is no food
my eyes are always hungry
and remembering
however the image enters
its force remains.
A white woman stands bereft and empty
a black boy hacked into a murderous lesson
recalled in me forever
like a lurch of earth on the edge of sleep
etched into my visions
food for dragonfish that learn
to live upon whatever they must eat
fused images beneath my pain.

II

The Pearl River floods through the streets of Jackson
A Mississippi summer televised.
Trapped houses kneel like sinners in the rain
a white woman climbs from her roof to a passing boat
her fingers tarry for a moment on the chimney
now awash
tearless and no longer young, she holds
a tattered baby's blanket in her arms.

In a flickering afterimage of the nightmare rain
a microphone
thrust up against her flat bewildered words
    "we jest come from the bank yestiddy
    borrowing money to pay the income tax
    now everything's gone. I never knew
    it could be so hard."
Despair weighs down her voice like Pearl River mud
caked around the edges
her pale eyes scanning the camera for help or explanation
unanswered
she shifts her search across the watered street, dry-eyed
    "hard, but not this hard."
Two tow-headed children hurl themselves against her
hanging upon her coat like mirrors
until a man with ham-like hands pulls her aside
snarling "She ain't got nothing more to say!"
and that lie hangs in his mouth
like a shred of rotting meat.

III

I inherited Jackson, Mississippi.
For my majority it gave me Emmett Till
his 15 years puffed out like bruises
on plump boy-cheeks
his only Mississippi summer
whistling a 21 gun salute to Dixie
as a white girl passed him in the street
and he was baptized my son forever
in the midnight waters of the Pearl.

His broken body is the afterimage of my 21st year
when I walked through a northern summer
my eyes averted
from each corner's photographies
newspapers protest posters magazines
Police Story, Confidential, True
the avid insistence of detail
pretending insight or information

the length of gash across the dead boy's loins
his grieving mother's lamentation
the severed lips, how many burns
his gouged out eyes
sewed shut upon the screaming covers
louder than life
all over
the veiled warning, the secret relish
of a black child's mutilated body
fingered by street-corner eyes
bruise upon livid bruise
and wherever I looked that summer
I learned to be at home with children's blood
with savored violence
with pictures of black broken flesh
used, crumpled, and discarded
lying amid the sidewalk refuse
like a raped woman's face.

A black boy from Chicago
whistled on the streets of Jackson, Mississippi
testing what he'd been taught was a manly thing to do
his teachers
ripped his eyes out his sex his tongue
and flung him to the Pearl weighted with stone
in the name of white womanhood
they took their aroused honor
back to Jackson
and celebrated in a whorehouse
the double ritual of white manhood
confirmed.

IV
"If earth and air and water do not judge them who are we to refuse a crust of bread?"

Emmett Till rides the crest of the Pearl, whistling
24 years his ghost lay like the shade of a raped woman
and a white girl has grown older in costly honor
(what did she pay to never know its price?)

now the Pearl River speaks its muddy judgment
and I can withhold my pity and my bread.

    "Hard, but not this hard."
Her face is flat with resignation and despair
with ancient and familiar sorrows
a woman surveying her crumpled future
as the white girl besmirched by Emmett's whistle
never allowed her own tongue
without power or conclusion
unvoiced
she stands adrift in the ruins of her honor
and a man with an executioner's face
pulls her away.

With my eyes
the flickering afterimages of a nightmare rain
a woman wrings her hands
beneath the weight of agonies remembered
I wade through summer ghosts
betrayed by vision
hers and my own
becoming dragonfish to survive
the horrors we are living
with tortured lungs
adapting to breathe blood.

A woman measures her life's damage
my eyes are caves, chunks of etched rock
tied to the ghost of a black boy
whistling
crying and frightened
her tow-headed children cluster
like little mirrors of despair
their father's hands upon them
and soundlessly
a woman begins to weep.

Emmett Till
Wanda Coleman (1986)

From its opening reference to the "river jordan" to its concluding image of a "third day" resurrection, Wanda Coleman's poem conceives of Emmett Till as a sacrificial lamb whose Christlike death contains the promise of redemption. A Guggenheim fellow and a member of the Academy of American Poets, Coleman won the prestigious Lenore Marshall Poetry Prize in 1999 for *Bathwater Wine*. She is the author of eight collections of poetry (most recently *Mercurochrome*, 2001) and one novel. "Emmett Till" was first published in *Callaloo* (spring 1986).

1

river jordan run red

rainfall panes the bottom acreage—rain
black earth blacker still

blackness seeps in seeps down
the mortal gravity of hate-inspired poverty
Jim Crow nidus

the alabama the apalachicola the arkansas the arroostook
the altamaha

killing of 14-year-old
stirs nation. there will be a public wake

works its way underground
scarred landscape veined by rage
sanctified waters flow
go forth

the bighorn the brazos

along roan valley walls blue rapids
wear away rock
flesh current quickly courses thru

the front page news amber fields purple mountains
muddies

*the chattahoochee the cheyenne the chippewa the cimarron
the colorado the columbia the connecticut the cumberland*

waftage

spirit uplifted eyes head heart
imitation of breath chest aheave
the grotesque swim up the styx
level as rainwater into its floodplain

the des moines

blood river born

2

ebony robe aflow
swathed hair of the black madonna
bereft of babe

the flint

that hazel eye sees
the woman
she fine mighty fine
she set the sun arising in his thighs

the hudson the humboldt the illinois

and he let go a whistle
a smooth long all-american hallelujah whistle
appreciation. a boy

the james the klamath

but she be a white woman. but he be
a black boy

*the maumee the minnesota the mississippi the missouri
the mohican*

raping her with that hazel eye

the ohio

make some peckerwood pass water mad
make a whole tributary of intolerance

*the pearl the pecos the pee dee the penobscot
the north platte the south platte the potomac*

vital fluid streaming forth in holy torrents

think about it. go mad go blind
go back to africa go civil rights go go

the red the white and the blue

run wine

3

silt shallows the slow sojourn seaward

they awakened him from sleep
that early fall morning
they made him dress
they hurried Emmett down to the water's edge

the roanoke

after the deed
they weighted him down

tossed him in
for his violation

the sacramento the salt the san juan the savannah
the smoke

from the deep dank murk of consciousness a birth
oh say do you see the men off
the bank dredging in that
strange jetsam

the tennessee the trinity

a lesson
he had to be taught—crucified (all a nigger
got on his mind) for rape by eye that
wafer-round hazel offender plucked out
they crown him

the wabash

cuz she was white woman virtue and he
be a black boy lust

the yazoo the yellowstone

oh say Emmett Till can you see Emmett Till
crossed over into campground

spill tears
nimbus threatening downpour
sweetwater culls into its soulplain

come forth to carry the dead child home

4

at my mouth forking

autumn 1955, lord!
kidnapped from his family visit
lord!
money road shanty
lord!
his face smashed in
lord! lord!
His body beaten beyond cognition

river mother carries him

laid in state
sovereign at last

that all may witness true majesty
cast eyes upon

murder

the youth's body too light
was weighted down in barbed wire & steel

dumped into the river agape a ripple a wave
(once it was human)

aweigh. awade in water. bloated
baptized

and on that third day awaft
from the mulky arm of the tallahatchie
stretched cross cotton-rich flats
of delta

on that third day
he rose

and was carried forth to that promised land

From *1935: A Memoir*
Sam Cornish (1990)

No poet has written more extensively about Emmett Till than Sam Cornish. A native of Baltimore and the author of thirteen collections of poetry—most recently *Cross a Parted Sea: Poems* (Zoland Books, 1996)—Cornish has published more than a dozen works that either directly address or make reference to the Till case. The following sequence is lifted from "Southern Interlude," a chapter in Cornish's innovative memoir *1935*. The six pieces included here are interspersed throughout the chapter as Cornish weaves Till's story into the story of African Americans throughout the South in the 1950s. Cornish currently lives in Boston, where he teaches literature and writing at Emerson College.

In Memoriam
In the schoolyard he was a bad dresser, a snappy fellow in good clothes who liked the schoolgirls too much, and his books not enough. He was five feet eight, one hundred and sixty pounds, muscular and, if he lived long enough, would have gone fat in his late twenties from beer, liquor, soul food and lack of exercise.

Calls Me From Thunder
He was born in 1941, his father a soldier, dead since '45, and divorced from his mother. His father was born in Missouri, his mother in Tallahatchie County, now living in Chicago, the city Southern Mississippi migrated to, and was now taking a vacation from her son. His mother had remarried and divorced again, thought her son to be a trickster, a prankster to be away from her because she needed a rest, as mothers do, from growing boys known as "manchild," more child than man, the boy who called attention to himself, and carried pictures of white boy and girl classmates in his wallet, the boy from the North where the police sometimes scared you to death, in the South the deep and darker America which saw the Negro attempting to climb the pedestal where his white woman stood.

Tough in the Streets
Dead in Mississippi

He was staying with an uncle; having a downhome vacation. . . . He put his hands in his back pocket, this boy from the North, and took out the wallet with pictures of white girls he called girlfriends, he was made tough on the streets of Chicago, the high schools of street gangs, and the false promises of urban cities since the days of the migrations.

He knew the dark children of Southern blacks had the tan that only black skin turns under the sun. They chop, plant and bag cotton for a dollar an acre. Their words are so measured they melt in the mouth, this Southern language of school-children taught by black teachers about Claude McKay and Sterling Brown, blind men picking guitars and singing, "I would have picked his body, but it wasn't fit to eat."

The song goes on, "The boy is home/home again/blues . . ." This is the South, and no matter how hard the North with its Detroit riots and Jim Crow, its ghettos and niggertowns and Burma Road, this is Memphis, New Orleans, this is Mississippi, and you are a smart-assed little black boy. He was not an Uncle Tom, faced white cops for assault, stood before the judge, faced off the bullies, smoked a reefer in the bathroom . . . to the Southern boys, afraid to walk into a store and buy a Coke, waiting in line to say, "Suh." He said he knew white girls and called them "baby." He kept his hat firm upon his head, opened his wallet. Two white men leaned forward, muscles in their necks throbbed, muscles in their arms gleamed with sweat. In spite of the pleas of his uncle that his nephew be spared—"The boy didn't know what he was doing"—he was forced facedown in the truck and later was found in the river, weighed down with a heavy fan.

During the school desegregation crisis, a white man pointed at the river and said, "Emmett Till is a river . . ."

The Good Men

    pistol-whipped a Northern boy
    for fine clothes

    pistol whipped a Northern boy
    too much money in his pocket

with rifles have stalked the woods
these are lessons that are never taught in
school
& white hotels
with   gin
and cocaine

of Moses a ghost in the woods seeking the
promises

of the North the words of the good
Northern book
made whole and possible
and
Frederick Douglass and Nat Turner mulattoes
blood of the master skins of their mothers

slave and thinking
free

The Heart That Breaks

Dwight D. Eisenhower
does not wish to legislate the heart
but it is the heart that ties the fan to the
body

of Emmett Till plunges it deep
into the river it is the heart that cries
out
Never
Never
Never
to the law
that rides
the Southern night
the heart that breaks
in the breast of good men
of Tallahatchie

the heart
that writes
the letters
the thousands
sitting
in the meetings
of the white
citizen's councils
the great
heart
for many ears
sweet
as an unspoken
word
whispered
in the dark

The Floating Line

The black nation awakes to the bus boycott. Three months later in Memphis, people will walk and the buses will ride empty through the city. The people walk, Emmett Till in their memory. In the buses of Memphis, you pay at the front door and walk around to the back to board. A floating line is drawn between the knees of a Negro man and a white man, Till's death says every Negro man is a marked man.

Emmett Till and the Men Who Killed Him

June Akers Seese (1994)

Although it deals with a white woman's memory of her racist uncle and only briefly mentions the Till case, this story by June Akers Seese—by its very indirection—manifests the way in which Till's murder came to represent for an entire generation the worst excesses of racism. Recipient of a 2002 Yaddo Writer's Fellowship, Seese is the author of two novels, *What Waiting Really Means* (1990) and *Is This What Other Women Feel Too?* (1991), and the 1994 short story collection *James Mason and the Walk-in Closet,* from which the following work is drawn. She currently lives in Atlanta, Georgia, where she teaches at Callanwolde Fine Arts Center.

I never really knew my uncle. He lived somewhere apart from the places he went and the things he touched. Eventually I saw some of those places and a few of those things. I even learned some facts about his life before I was born, but in the beginning, he was twenty dollars at Christmas and a laugh that scared me every Saturday morning. There wasn't room for me and my uncle in the house I grew up in.

It was a one-bedroom frame built on a slab and paid for as it went up. At first, there were no walls separating us, then came drywall, plaster, and finally paint and baseboards. I slept on the studio couch next to the oil stove, and my uncle had the davenport across the room on his weekend visits. He snored and slept in his undershirt.

On Saturday afternoons in the summer my father's friends drank beer in the backyard and traded stories. The cut grass was damp, and flecks of it stuck to their shoes. My mother made lemonade in a pitcher she won at the movies. It was wartime, and sugar and gas were hoarded. Not by us. By the Jews. My father knew what was going on outside our fenced yard.

"The niggers are taking over the factories," he said.

The Japs were, however, far away. I saw them nosedive in tiny planes at crowded movie theaters where my mother was one of the faithful—a fat woman in a print housedress and warped brown shoes.

"You have nice feet," she said, and she bought me Buster Browns because her mother had forced her feet into shoes she had already outgrown. My mother took me to the dentist for the same reason. She hated the sight of her crooked teeth in the mirror. When the bills came, my father said, "You find out who your friends are when you need money."

I tried to put their maxims and sacrifices together to make something to live by, but there were too many missing parts—told in whispers and not to me.

My uncle seemed like a man of the world. He lived in the city. Twenty miles from our subdivision. A bachelor who chain-smoked in his rented room piled high with newspapers. One or two tall beer bottles lay on the floor next to his gray work pants. The air was undeniably his.

We picked him up outside the National Biscuit Company when the night shift changed on Friday and drove to a steak house where we ordered for three and asked for an extra plate. He paid for it. I was glad to be included, and I kept my mouth shut. My father did most of the talking. He told stories I didn't understand about the past—in Arkansas, Louisiana, and southern Illinois. We took the early edition of the *Detroit News* home with us, and sometimes my father carried me on his shoulders.

My uncle had a college degree. He was the first grown-up I knew who had finished high school, but all he read was the paper and Mickey Spillane. In 1930, liberal arts at Centenary College included French and world history and physics. My uncle made *A*s in all of them. I saw for myself a cardboard box with his school records and a snapshot of his family the year before his parents and four sisters died. The flu epidemic of 1918. My uncle was twelve. My father was a baby.

My father said my uncle had been jilted. My mother said: "He makes me nervous." After their fights, they insisted I call my uncle "Sir."

When I was twelve, I saw two movies that made me think I understood more than I did. *Gentleman's Agreement* and *Home of the Brave.* Message movies, they were called. All about injustice and victims and pain and being left out. The villains in those movies couldn't hold a candle to my uncle. He said: "Niggers should be shot." The set of his mouth and the look in his eyes made me feel he might shoot one. My father was a hunter, and guns were everywhere.

"Give 'em an inch, and they'll take a mile!" My mother told me a hundred times there was one colored boy in her high school, and everybody l-o-v-e-d him.

My father said, "I took up boxing till they put a nigger in the ring. Then I quit. Their heads are harder."

At the National Biscuit Company, my uncle was a foreman. He checked the saltines for thirty years to make sure they were neither burned nor doughy.

"Niggers are everywhere," he told me.

I saw them once. The room was hot, and my uncle wore a white apron. It was a private tour. The niggers laughed—their white collars limp, looking at the flour on their shoes. My uncle's neck stiffened, and he dropped a tray of Ritz crackers on me.

I decided then my father's guns were safe. My uncle was alone. Unmatched in his hate. He seemed to be laughing at me and my parents, who had been fooled by desire and marriage and the scraps of pleasure we rubbed up against, that he paid for. Finally, Republic Aircraft shut down, after the Japs had been subdued, we had sugar for our lemonade. The Jews bought up the scrap metal, and my father was out of work.

"A livink, ve got to mik it!" My father did his best to imitate a Yiddish accent. He was the only one who ever thought it was funny.

I imagined I understood them all by the time I entered college and made my own *A*s in psychology and American history. Certainly, when I fell in love and was left flat by the urbane man who was miles away from our meager Christmases and muddy subdivision. Scholarships. Fellowships. Summer jobs. Independence.

The National Biscuit Company closed its Detroit plant, and my uncle moved back to Arkansas and became a recluse. The newspapers blew the sixties through our brains, and I made my voice known in the picket lines outside Woolworth's and read about Viola Liuzzo's journey south. My father crossed a picket line too, and goons from the Teamster's gave him a six-inch scar and a story to tell for the rest of his life. Unemployment. Hard rock. Fire. The 101st Airborne came to town to quell the riots, and a cop told my husband in the emergency room at Receiving Hospital: "I'm goin' out to shoot another nigger." The Algiers Motel was not a "incident." Boundaries were gone, and anything was happening.

Emmett Till left Chicago to visit relatives in Mississippi. He whistled at a white woman standing on the hot sidewalk and before the sun went down he was buried in concrete.

I knew my uncle could have done it if he had been in Mississippi with the mob. He could have done worse if he had been in the right place with the others. He was outnumbered at National Biscuit. Instead, he played solitaire and grew old and died on six acres of scrub pine. After the sixties died down.

What happened to him?

I don't think losing his mother or being jilted explains it. Or raising my father. Or money. Had a scholarship too. Neither the Depression, the war, nor the South gets at the horror. Who ever knows why? But I have long since stopped feeling superior to him. I, after all, took his money, and that is nothing to be proud of.

I travel in circles where his words are never spoken, and bitterness is disguised as wisdom. So much is private in life! Like the moment when Emmett Till realized his whistle was a death rattle, and the moment those men went home and ate their suppers in the heat with wet concrete on their pants, bragging, in my uncle's voice.

The Lovesong of Emmett Till
Anthony Walton (1996)

> Anthony Walton is best known for his 1996 memoir *Mississippi: An American Journey,* in which he recounts his journey from the North into the heart of the Deep South in search of racism. "The Lovesong of Emmett Till," which was included in this memoir, picks up on a detail that few other writers have chosen to explore: the picture of the young Chicago white girl that Till allegedly had in his wallet and was showing to his Delta cousins on the day he was challenged to go into the Bryant grocery. In his poem, Walton

emphasizes Till's innocence and reimagines the boy's meeting with Carolyn
Bryant in those terms. Walton is currently professor of English at Bowdoin
College in Maine.

More than likely she was Irish
or Italian, a sweet child who knew him
only as a shy clown.
Colleen, Jenny or Marie, she
probably didn't even know
he had her picture,
that he had traded her cousin
for baseball cards or a pocketknife,
that her routine visage
sat smoldering in his wallet
beyond any price.
He carried his love
like a burden, and devotion
always has to tell.
Hell, he was just flirting
with that lady in the store,
he already had his white
woman back up in Chicago.
He wasn't greedy, just showing
off, showing the rustics
how it was done. He had an eye,
all right, and he was free
with it, he knew they loved it.
Hey baby, was all he said,
and he meant it as a compliment,
when he said it in Chicago
the white girls laughed.
So when they came to get
him, he thought it was
a joke, he proclaimed himself guilty
of love, he showed them
the picture and paid the price of
not innocence, but affection, affection
for a little black-haired, blue-eyed
girl who must by now be an older
woman in Chicago, a woman
who will never know

she was to die for, that he died
refusing to take back her name,
his right to claim he loved her.

Emmett Till
Bryan Johnson (1999)

In this work, Bryan Johnson, whose poems have appeared in *New American Writing, Denver Quarterly,* and *Paris Review,* is writing out of the surrealist tradition. As in June Akers Seese's story "Emmett Till and the Men Who Killed Him," this work is not a specific exploration of the events surrounding, or the figures involved in, Till's murder. Instead, in Johnson's prose-poem Till emerges as a subtle but controlling metaphor, an innocent who, by tenuous association with the unnamed Mississippi woman and with Jesus, expresses the transformative possibilities of suffering. Johnson is currently an assistant professor of English at Samford University in Birmingham, Alabama.

Sheet forced down her throat for a morning of prayer. She admires the bird's blue egg gone too far, sticking her tongue through the spokes she clings to a jawbone spending time on her childish knee. Her little red cabbage squeezed through a fist at the chamber's ladder.

In the heat of the wire's rotations one might think of the body sustained by filth, the eroding sky sucking wooden shoes against warm weather. Here in Sunflower County, one might think of Jesus who calmed the vagrants by boiling a pork bone, like any child hanging in branches his luminosity faltering in the century's dark.

In Sunflower County she appears at the morning table, her oily scalp washed in vinegar. When it is over she is clean as a whistle, her hair glowing like a tongue on the broth. For a time she transcends the Devil's lack of beauty, giggling suggestively, her husband sobbing on her burning buttocks.

Here in Sunflower County one might think of ripping out a man's liver. One might think of the emaciated body, the stuffed skull dropped in a well. Of Jesus floating through air, his private honey cut from the object of sacrifice. Or Jesus poaching walnuts, his near-nakedness glistening, unfriendly head nested and glutting.

She twitches in her unbridled cage. On the batture the twins near insane with her voice like old bells. Clamor spilling over the onions, she cherishes her sleep. She spits on the plums. She smells the scissors. Her nipples raising out of the grass, fluttering like a diseased wolf her suckled doll papered and raved.

Here one moves like a small animal, a finished sentence on the small culture's hand. Here one might say nothing or repeat the abetted story or say who is a bird who is the silent alter. One might think of Jesus, his foot turning blossom at the very moment, his awkward summer, his words bundled to the air and burning. Or yellow flowers, the blameless.

Can I Write of Flowers?
Jeanne Miller (2001)

A Chicago native, Jeanne Thompson Miller received her undergraduate degree from the University of Illinois and her law degree from Washington University in St. Louis. In "Can I Write of Flowers?," her first published poem, she wrestles with the reach of Till's legacy and the elusive demands it continues to make upon the African American literary imagination. Miller currently lives just outside of Chicago and has recently completed her first novel.

Must I write
Of Emmett Till

problems plaguing
Black Folks

Still

Apartheid
Lynchings
Reparations
Political elections
Race Relations

Issues
make my heart implode

hoist responsibility
ten-fold

on shoulders
tiny——
naive perhaps
tossing knowledge
onto laps
where men come
to rest their heads
bury sadness
inside beds
float rose petals
across blank pages
lick my lips
while trouble rages——
    continents away
children shot down
while they play

but I write poetry
not real life
I'm a poet
and
that man's wife

So   can I write of flowers
please
ducklings
swans and
honey bees

Understand this
I hide from you

Poets
Writers
Historians, too

who may suggest
my hand
examine time
face feared
annihilation
by mankind

with covered ears I run away
shield my eyes
in hopes to stay
in this
velvet box
where love
resides
between four
walls where cowards
hide

Octavia Butler
wrote of me
penned hyper
sensi
tivity

So   can I write of
flowers   please
sing this song
in sweet release
forsake war
choose inner peace

Emmett Till sleeps
in my bed
haunts me
with his swollen
head
missing eyes
I can't forget

my pen bleeds tears
of silence   yet

Someone else
must capture pain
spin the words
that often rain
truth across this continent
where evil breeds
our discontent

Flowers
boldly call my name
echo beauty with the same
fervor mixed in violent rage
that I can't capture

on my page

Afterword

At 9:30 P.M. on June 16, 2000, the body of Raynard Johnson, a seventeen-year-old black man, was found hanging from a tree in Kokomo, Mississippi. Although the coroner's report cited no evidence of foul play, and county officials later ruled the hanging a suicide, local blacks were convinced that Johnson had been lynched because of his open relationship with two white girls. According to Johnson's brother, relatives of the two girls were angry about the relationship, and during the two nights preceding Raynard's death the Johnsons had been awakened by the frantic barking of their usually quiet hunting dogs. Moreover, on the night of his death Raynard had been watching a basketball game with his brother and showed no signs of depression. During the game, he told his brother he was going outside to clean out his car. Less than a half hour later, Raynard's father found him hanging from a small pecan tree in the front yard, and looped around his neck was a braided leather belt that no one in the family recognized. According to witnesses, Raynard Johnson's feet were still on the ground, his legs bent slightly at the knees. For the family, these did not look like the signs of suicide.

Frustrated by a lack of official response to their concerns, Maria Johnson, the boy's mother, contacted Jesse Jackson, who promised to lead a "Mississippi March Against Racism and Bigotry" in order to secure national media attention for the case. While having many reasons for wanting to take up the cause, the civil rights leader was particularly struck by the death's historical resonance. According to Jackson, the alleged lynching "had the smell of Emmett Till all around it." And Jackson was not alone in believing this. At a press conference devoted to hate crimes legislation just a month after the killing, Congressman John Conyers (D-Michigan) observed, "In that part of Mississippi, that particular image of a young black man sends a specific message to a community. While the local coroner has ruled the death a suicide, events surrounding Johnson's death have raised the specter of a racial hate crime reminiscent of Emmett Till." When Jackson led his march from the Marion County courthouse to "the hanging tree" in the Johnsons' front yard, he walked much of the way side by side with Mamie Till Mobley. Standing before a crowd of microphones much as she had done nearly fifty years before, Mrs. Mobley told the more than one thousand marchers that "there has not been one week free of pain" since the death of her own son in the summer of 1955. Lending her support to those in search of justice, Mrs. Mobley proclaimed, "I am here because I need to be here."

In the summer of 2000, the citizens of Kokomo, Mississippi, were standing in the long shadow of Emmett Till. So too were Jesse Jackson and John Conyers. And so too, of course, was Mamie Till Mobley. In many ways, we are all standing there, and this is due in large part to the narratives we have encountered in this anthology. When Jesse Jackson senses the "smell of Emmett Till," when John Conyers feels the young boy's "specter" rising from the waters of remembrance, when the citizens of Kokomo hear the echoes of Till's abductors in the barking dogs outside Raynard Johnson's house, this is possible only because of the many stories that were told about the tragic lynching. It would not be possible to see in Raynard Johnson's hanged body the presence of Emmett Till unless there had been a long narrative tradition that kept alive that presence. Without that tradition, there would be no memory of Emmett Till; his story would have met the fate for which his corpse was intended: oblivion. When Till's body emerged from the depths of the Tallahatchie River after three days in its watery grave, officials in Sumner County, Mississippi, wanted to bury it right away. Mamie Till Bradley wouldn't let them. Instead, she wanted the whole world to see what they had done to her boy. By not allowing her son to be buried immediately beneath the Mississippi soil, and then requesting that his casket be opened for a three-day viewing in Chicago, she forced a nation to make sense of an apparently senseless crime, to pull meaning from the swollen and broken face of a fourteen-year-old boy. This was done primarily through narrative. Not all of these narratives look alike, and certainly not all of them agree on the meaning of Till's murder. But whether we read a news column by Murray Kempton, a magazine article by William Bradford Huie, a poem by Gwendolyn Brooks, an essay by John Edgar Wideman, or a story by June Akers Seese, we are witnessing the power of narrative at work, a power that allows us to give shape to the unshapen and through this find the forms that give all stories their meaning. If an unnarrated event is one that can never be understood (or known, for that matter), then this anthology gives us a glimpse into that process of understanding. Emmett Till is known to us today because we have never stopped telling his story, and this is why so many people saw his "specter" hanging from a pecan tree in Kokomo nearly fifty years after Till himself had met his tragic end.

Which leads to one last point. When Emmett Till was lynched, we used all of our narrative abilities to make sense of it. We put our stories to work so as to give his death (and thus his life) some definable meaning. But if the case of Raynard Johnson teaches us one last thing, it is this: the narratives we have told about Emmett Till have begun to shape us as much as we have shaped them. The stories we have told about the lynching have become a lens through which we view race in America. Not every image of racial violence makes sense within the field of that lens. The Los Angeles riots of 1991, for instance, do not recall memories of Emmett Till. Nor do the "million men" who marched on Washington at the end of that decade. But the hanging body of a black boy in Mississippi who had been dating white girls? This does. So too does the violated corpse of an older black man who has been dragged through the streets of a small town in Texas while chained to a pickup truck. So too does the closing argument of an African American attorney who stands before a carefully selected jury in the most infamous race trial of his day and tells them, in words less racially coded but no less racially motivated than the ones used in Sumner, Mississippi, to think not in terms of justice but in terms of heritage and pass a verdict of not guilty in order to "send a message." In fact, what happened on August 28, 1955, in Money, Mississippi has become a template for injustice on an even larger scale. How else would it be possible to say, as one commentator did in the wake of the terrible events of October 1998, that Matthew Shepard had become "the Emmett Till of the hate-crimes movement"?

Because so much narrative energy has gone into understanding Till's death, that narrative has become part of our collective memory. In turn, we have begun to use that narrative to read the present. The event that made so little sense in 1955 has now become a means by which, where possible, we seek to make sense of the present; we can see then how the narratives we form come full circle and begin to form us. The work of memory not only becomes part of our history but it also influences the way we try to understand our history yet to come. In the end, then, Emmett Till is not "there" in the past. He is here in the present. Here because we both need him to be and cannot prevent him from being. When J. W. Milam and Roy Bryant went looking for the "boy who had done the talking," they were hoping to shut him up. Whether they intended to kill him that night is not clear, but if we are to believe Milam's "confession" to William Bradford Huie, young Till wouldn't shut up, and thus he had to be silenced in the most extreme way. But Milam and Bryant couldn't silence James L. Hicks, Langston Hughes, Richard Davidson, James Baldwin, Anne Moody, Julius Thompson, Sam Cornish, Lewis Nordan, John Edgar Wideman, and Bryan Johnson. In their stories, Emmett Till will not be silent, and because of this we now can say for certain that he did not die in vain. How so? Because the boy who had once "done the talking" now shapes the way we talk about ourselves. It may not be the justice that many people wanted in 1955, but it is justice nonetheless.

Index

Note: page numbers in italics refer to a complete selection, where the indexed term is its author, title, or source.

The American South Series

Anne Goodwyn Jones and Susan V. Donaldson, editors
Haunted Bodies: Gender and Southern Texts

M. M. Manring
Slave in a Box: The Strange Career of Aunt Jemima

Stephen Cushman
Bloody Promenade: Reflections on a Civil War Battle

John C. Willis
Forgotten Time: The Yazoo-Mississippi Delta after the Civil War

Charlene M. Boyer Lewis
Ladies and Gentlemen on Display: Planter Society at the Virginia Springs, 1790–1860

Christopher Metress, editor
The Lynching of Emmett Till: A Documentary Narrative